Apartheid in Transition

'South Africa is a country where you
hope on Mondays and despair on
Tuesdays.'

Alan Paton, 1985

ANTHONY LEMON

Fellow of Mansfield College and Lecturer
at the University of Oxford

Gower

Published by
Gower Publishing Company Limited
Gower House
Croft Road
Aldershot
Hants GU11 3HR
England

Gower Publishing Company
Old Post Road
Brookfield
Vermont 05036
USA

British Library Cataloguing in Publication Data

Lemon, Anthony
    Apartheid in transition.
    1. Apartheid
    I. Title
    323.1'68   DT763

ISBN 0-566-00635-9

Printed and bound in Great Britain by
Billing and Sons Limited, Worcester.

APARTHEID IN TRANSITION

Contents

List of Figures

Preface

Few societies remain so consistently in the public eye as South Africa. Essentially this is so because the issues raised by apartheid are among the foremost shared concerns of the world's nations. Political domination by a white minority is a glaring anomaly in the late twentieth century. Insistence on ethnicity as the major organising principle of society is offensive to liberals and radicals alike. Furthermore, South African economic and geographical realities mirror global north-south relationships of wealth and poverty. Association of these with a broadly capitalist system in which the West has a longstanding involvement also gives the situation an east-west dimension, which is strengthened by the economic and strategic importance of South Africa.

There is no lack of literature on South Africa. Much of it consists, however, either of specialist works written within the confines of particular disciplines, or works for the general reader which are often crudely simplified and in many cases polemical. This book attempts to fill the gap for serious students, teachers, church people and others who wish to go beyond the necessary superficialities of the media, but who have not the time to search out a wide range of literature and make their own synthesis. Not least I hope that many South Africans will find it a useful work of reference which helps them better to understand their own society. The aim of the book is above all to inform: to provide a detailed explanation of the historical context in which apartheid has developed and the way in which it has been implemented, together with the nature, extent and direction of recent changes.

Apartheid is arguably 'the most ambitious contemporary exercise in applied geography' (Smith 1982a, 1), attempting as it does to restructure the spatial character of society, economy and polity on local, regional and national scales. But to confine this work within the bounds of my own geographical discipline would have been too limiting. In the course of many extended visits to South Africa, I have become increasingly grateful for the absence of disciplinary barriers between academics in that country, concerned to promote peaceful change. As a glance at the references will readily reveal, I have drawn freely on the work of political scientists, historians, sociologists, economists, anthropologists, theologians and philosophers as well as that of my fellow geographers. Personal contact with many of them has been indispensable, and my debts in this direction are too many to mention. I do, however, want to give special thanks to my typist, Diana Steer, and to Angela Newman who drew most of the maps. Figures 2.1 and 2.2 were drawn by Bruno Martin.

No one can write about South Africa with complete objectivity. Interpretation and assessment are inevitable, and of course inherent in the selection of information presented. My central concern however, has been to inform rather than to argue, and I have tried to leave the reader free to form his or her own judgements. My perspective is one of commitment to rapid but peaceful change, in the belief that full-scale revolution, with the almost unimaginable violence, suffering and destruction it would entail, would provide a grim starting point for democracy in South Africa. Revolution is not yet inevitable, despite the turbulent state of so much of the country since 1984. If greater understanding on all sides can promote peaceful change, I hope that this work may contribute in some small measure to that end.

Since the manuscript reached the publishers early in 1986, the succession of events has been rapid. The localised state of emergency was lifted in March, only to be followed by a nationwide one in June. The Commonwealth Eminent Persons Group paid two visits to South Africa in February/March and May, but failed to persuade the South African government to accept its negotiating framework. Sir Geoffrey Howe's visit in July was predictably no more successful. In the face of these failures increasing but still limited economic sanctions are being applied by the USA and the EEC, whilst the Commonwealth has (apart from Britain) agreed a package of sanctions which appears to have been only patchily applied thus far. But the screw is tightening, and Pretoria is evidently preparing to adapt to a siege economy. Disinvestment is growing apace, with IBM, General Motors and Barclays Bank among the most notable firms to leave.

As such measures take effect, a gradual turning of the screw by South Africa on her neighbours is all too likely. Her decision in October 1986 to repatriate Mozambiquan migrant workers can only add to that country's desperation in the face of escalating guerrilla warfare. The death of President Machel has added a further element of instability to the regional situation.

In South Africa itself white emigration began to exceed immigration in the early months of 1986, heightening concern at the drain of skilled manpower. Incremental reform has continued, most notably in the publication in April 1986 of a White Paper making a formal commitment to the ending of influx control. The President's Council Report on the Group Areas Act has, however, been delayed, perhaps because the government wishes to hold a general election in 1987 before embarking upon reforms in this highly sensitive area. But two events confirm, if confirmation were needed, that white attitudes are changing. In October 1986 the Nederduits Gereformeerde Kerk opened membership to all races. The following month agreement was reached at the Natal-KwaZulu *indaba*: with Pretoria's consent, this would lead to a multi-racial parliament in the region, albeit with safeguards for minorities in a second chamber. Notwithstanding its undoubted shortcomings, a negotiated constitutional agreement between whites and other races in any part of South Africa is a sign of hope which should not be lightly disregarded, least of all by Pretoria. The latter's initial rejection of the agreement will, if confirmed, inevitably be seen as signalling that Pretoria is not interested in genuine power-sharing, and that can only strengthen the voice of those who believe that revolution is inevitable.

Anthony Lemon
1st December 1986

Part 1
HISTORICAL
BACKGROUND

1
The peopling of South Africa

In 1904, the year of South Africa's first official census, the inhabitants numbered 5,175,000, and all the major elements of today's ethnically complex society had been assembled. This figure had trebled by 1960 (15,994,000), and it has doubled again since then, exceeding 32 million in 1984. Of this figure some 22.9 million (73 per cent) were black (African); remarkably, this group was larger in 1984 than the total South African population just thirteen years earlier. The 4.8 million whites constituted the second largest group (14.8 per cent), followed by 2.8 million people officially classified as coloured, or mixed-race (8.7 per cent), and 890,000 Asians (2.7 per cent).

The social, economic and political problems which confront South Africa cannot be understood without reference to the past. It is necessary to know something of the origins, movements, characteristics and early development of the various population groups which are the subject of the present chapter. The contacts and conflicts which have occurred between these groups and sub-groups in the past three centuries have had a direct bearing on the attitudes and policies which prevail today. Chapter 2 examines these cultural contacts in the context of evolving spatial patterns of economy and political organisation, to which they are closely related.

A word of caution is necessary. It was only towards the end of the fifteenth century, when Columbus was discovering America, that Portuguese sailors rounded the southern tip of Africa and found a new trade route to the East. The absence of written records prior to this time explains much of the confusion which prevails concerning the origins and extent of the various peoples already present within the borders of what is now South Africa. The picture has only gradually become clearer using archaeological evidence and anthropological research based on the oral traditions of present-day inhabitants and genealogies, where these

3

survive. This short introductory account of the peopling of South Africa can therefore only outline the present state of knowledge, without attempting to present the detailed evidence on which these conclusions are based.

The earliest inhabitants: Bushmen and Hottentots

Much confusion surrounds the use of the terms 'Bushmen' and 'Hottentot', owing to the mistaken assumption that physical type, language and economy are necessarily correlated (Wilson and Thompson 1969, ix). It is by no means the case that all Bushmen were small in stature, hunters, and spoke a distinct language (San), nor that all Hottentots were taller people, pastoralists, and speakers of a different language (Khoikhoi). Physical anthropologists argue as to how to differentiate Hottentot from Bushman, and there was considerable overlap between the two economies (Elphick 1985).

Equally mistaken is the assumption that Hottentots, Bushmen, Bantu and Europeans each occupied, at least in the seventeenth and eighteenth centuries, a specific area, where they remained isolated from the others. Such territorial separation was equally uncharacteristic of physical, cultural and linguistic groups. The assumption that it once existed appears to reflect present-day preoccupations with race and the existing social structure rather than historical reality.

The first people to inhabit South Africa were almost certainly ancestors of the Bushmen and Hottentots. The latter were both yellow-skinned and physically much alike; early European accounts do not distinguish between them on physical grounds, though it is likely that the herders were taller than the hunters, for whom shortness of stature was a physical asset. There is a marked similarity in the techniques and material culture of all the hunters and herders, and some similarity in their religious ideas, which argues long interaction. Khoikhoi speakers did not, however, share with San speakers a proclivity for painting.

The nomadic hunters and gatherers had no collective name for themselves, but were called *Bosjesmannen* (Bushmen) by the Dutch. Their social organisation consisted only of hunting parties, numbering between 50 and 100 people in most cases. Only the rudiments of tribal organisation and chieftainship existed. Amongst the herders, on the other hand, the number acknowledging one chief might reach 2500. The long-haired cattle and fat-tailed sheep of the herders must have been introduced, since there were no potentially wild ancestors in southern Africa. This has been one of the major reasons for the widely held

4

traditional belief that the herders migrated from east Africa, but there is little anthropological or archaeological evidence to support such a hypothetical pastoral migration (Inskeep 1969, 23–9).

Linguistic and other evidence indicates that contact between Khoikhoi speakers and the Nguni group of Bantu peoples began before the seventeenth century. There is also ample written evidence of continual interaction between cattle-owning Xhosa and one Khoikhoi group, the Gona, in the country between the Kei and Gamtoos rivers (Wilson 1969, 103). Interaction between Xhosa and Khoikhoi further west appears to have been more restricted, to judge from the difference between their respective breeds of cattle.

There is likewise evidence to show that Nguni and San long occupied the same territories, living side by side in some sort of symbiotic relationship. Periodic conflicts between the two groups may have reflected population pressure leading to competition for grazing and hunting grounds. The San generally occupied the more arid areas and the high mountain grasslands where buck abounded; whereas the Nguni sought better watered and less frost-bitten grass and forest land suitable for cultivation as well as grazing. They were clearly conscious of the ecological boundary to the west, since they settled neither beyond the hills marking the eastern boundary of the dry Karroo, nor on the very sour veld west of the Gamtoos. It was the transition between these different habitats which was disputed between Xhosa, Khoikhoi, San and Dutch settlers in the late eighteenth century.

Neither Khoikhoi nor San are significant elements in the present South African population. The hunting groups were forced by the combined pressures of Khoikhoi and Nguni herders and, somewhat later, Europeans to retreat north and west into semi-desert regions from the beginning of the seventeenth century. Today most surviving Bushmen are found in the central and northern Kalahari, largely in Botswana, and in southern Angola and northern Namibia. In the latter territory Bushmen numbered 30,000 in 1981.

Two major epidemics of smallpox during the seventeenth century killed a large proportion of the 'Hottentot' herders. The remainder were largely absorbed by racial admixture with incoming Europeans and East Indian slaves, and have contributed not only to the Cape coloured population but also to smaller groups known as Griquas (who still live in South Africa and are classified as coloured) and Rehoboth Basters (a group of about 28,000 people in 1981, mainly concentrated in the Rehoboth Gebiet around the settement of the Rehoboth in Namibia).

Africans: the southern Bantu

Africans known as Bantu occupy the southern two-thirds of sub-Saharan Africa. They are defined primarily on linguistic criteria, most simply as those Africans who use the root 'ntu' for human being. With the plural prefix this becomes 'ba-ntu' (Bantu) meaning simply 'men' or 'people'. It is because the term has such a general meaning that its official use – abandoned in the 1970s – was disliked by the people concerned, who have preferred to call themselves Africans or blacks. Bantu peoples in South Africa fall into two main language groups, Nguni and Sotho, and two much smaller ones, Venda and Tsonga.

The Nguni are a people who can understand one another's speech. Two of the more distinct dialects were written down by missionaries in the nineteenth century – Xhosa, as spoken on the Eastern Cape frontier; and Zulu, as spoken north of the Tugela river – and these have stabilised into the two main forms of Nguni speech. In 1980 Nguni speakers in the Republic numbered some 11.8 million; others were living in Swaziland and Zimbabwe.

The Nguni are herders and cultivators with a deep attachment to cattle, which were shifted from one pasture to another so long as land was plentiful; the new growth on sour mountain grassland was burnt in winter and used for spring grazing. They also kept dogs, goats and sheep, whilst other animals were introduced by Europeans. At least until the early nineteenth century the Nguni also depended for food and clothing on hunting and collecting, but avoidance of fish is an important characteristic. Sorghum was the major crop until the nineteenth century, by which time maize, today the staple crop, began to displace it.

Scattered homesteads are a distinguishing feature of Nguni peoples. Among commoners each homestead was composed of 2 to 40 huts. Those of chiefs were larger, and with the development of Zulu military power a population of 2000 may have been reached in exceptional cases by military concentration at royal homesteads.

The precise distribution of the Nguni in space and time has long been debated. It now seems clear that the Nguni speakers reached their present wide distribution in southern Africa within historical time, spreading northwards from the area which lies between the Drakensberg and the sea, from the Fish river in the south-west to Swaziland in the north-east. Monica Wilson cites detailed evidence to disprove the long-held theory of a relatively recent migration of Nguni peoples (in association with other Bantu) southward from Central Africa (Wilson 1969, 78–102). A much more ancient migration to the country south of the Drakensberg now seems more likely.

The widespread scattering of Nguni peoples in the first half of the nineteenth century resulted from internecine strife associated with the consolidation of Zulu power under Dingiswayo and Shaka. Increased population pressure to the south-west of Natal was a direct result of this dispersal, and undoubtedly accentuated conflict with Europeans along the 'Eastern Frontier' of the Cape (Chapter 2).

Sotho peoples include those who speak 'southern Sotho', 'northern Sotho' or Pedi, and Tswana languages. In 1980 there were some 6.1 million Sotho speakers in South Africa, and nearly 2 million more in Botswana and Lesotho. In the early nineteenth century the Sotho were hunters, herders and cultivators much as the Nguni were. Some of them eat fish, but many avoid it, as do the Nguni. The main distinction between the economy of the Sotho and that of their neighbours was the skill of the Sotho as craftsmen. They mined and smelted iron, copper and tin, and traded extensively in metal goods. They were also skilled in leatherwork and in carving wood and ivory.

The remains of stone buildings are widely distributed over the areas the Sotho occupy. It seems that all or most of these were built by the Sotho, and in Lesotho at least they continue to build in stone. Most of the Sotho lived in large settlements of several thousand people, each of which was a capital in which an independent chief lived with his followers. Concentration of settlement has continued to some extent in Botswana, where it is explicitly linked with the authority of chiefs. Beyond the larger settlements there were cattle posts, whilst the more distant areas were occupied by small groups of hunters who owned no cattle and became clients of those who did (a relationship characteristic of many Bushmen in Botswana today).

Traditions point to the well-watered and well-wooded Magaliesberg and to the watershed between the Limpopo, Malopo and Harts rivers as the area of earliest Sotho occupation and as the centre of dispersion. Successive waves of Sotho immigrants from the north crossed the Limpopo, the first possibly in the thirteenth century or even earlier. Each group in turn either absorbed the earlier inhabitants or forced them to move westwards into the desert. By the early nineteenth century the Sotho were concentrated between the Limpopo and Orange rivers, north and west of the Drakensberg, and across the upper reaches of the Limpopo.

The Venda are a small but linguistically distinct people, whose speech shows close affinity with Shona (the majority language in Zimbabwe) as well as clear connections with Sotho. They are a fusion between a lineage of incoming chiefs which did not cross the Limpopo until about the end of the seventeenth century and the Ngona and other earlier inhabitants. Like the Sotho, the Venda built in stone; their villages were sited in inaccessible places for protection, and were similar in size to the smaller Sotho settlements. The economy was based on cultivation, hunting and metal-working, including the mining and working of gold. In 1980 the Venda numbered only 500,000, many of whom continue to occupy the wooded Soutpansberg range which runs east–west to the south of the Limpopo.

Several dialects are spoken by the Tsonga people, who are known by several names. The most common in South Africa is Shangaan, which was derived from one of Shaka's warriors, Sashangane, who conquered the Tsonga in 1820–21. Oral tradition confirms that the Tsonga have long lived on the coast between the Save river and Kosi lake, and at one time they stretched considerably further south, beyond Lake St Lucia, until they were driven out. The Tsonga were deeply influenced by their Zulu conquerors, but remained culturally and linguistically distinct. One effect of the nineteenth-century wars was to drive many Tsonga westward, so that they came into much closer contact with the Sotho and Venda, with whom they already traded. Their economy differs radically from that of the other peoples discussed, as fishing in coastal lagoons and rivers is an important activity. The rural Tsonga live in small, scattered homesteads like the Zulu. In 1980 they numbered 889,000, but more than twice that number were living in Mozambique.

Whilst Nguni, Sotho, Venda and Tsonga are real and significant subdivisions of the Bantu peoples of South Africa, none of them should be thought of as a homogeneous group. Nguni and Sotho are further subdivided by the government, which recognises ten black 'nations', as listed below:

Each of these peoples shows great internal variation. Historically, fragmentation of political power into many chiefdoms has been the norm. Strong tribes frequently subordinated and incorporated weak ones, but consolidation into larger units (as with the Zulu under Shaka) was exceptional and generally temporary. Today, after much consolidation, there are still over 600 tribes organised as tribal authorities, although there are constellations farming large blocks of territory, notably the 138 Transkeian tribes (Moolman 1974).

It is equally important, however, to stress the common ground between the four main peoples. Whilst they must have lived in relative

Language group	People	Homeland
Nguni	Zulu	KwaZulu
	Swazi	KaNgwane
	South Ndebele	KwaNdebele
	Xhosa	Ciskei
	Xhosa	Transkei
Sotho	North Sotho	Lebowa
	South Sotho	QwaQwa
	Tswana	Bophuthatswana
Venda	Venda	Venda
Tsonga	Shangaan	Gazankulu

isolation to grow so different in language and custom, there was certainly movement between them, each absorbing remnants of others. The chiefdom was always made up of peoples of diverse descent; strangers, even those who spoke another language, were accepted. There are marked similarities between the four groups in terms of symbolism, ritual and law. All thought in terms of kinship, and assumed the dependence of the living on their dead ancestors. The existence of the chief was assumed by all; his health was seen as related to the general well-being, and his function was primarily to settle disputes.

To this traditional common ground must now be added a common and growing experience of urban, industrial life (Chapter 10).

The white population

The European contribution to the peopling of South Africa consists of two distinct elements, Dutch and British, which have largely absorbed other European groups. Each element has its historic 'core area' of settlement, which is reflected in present-day patterns: the Dutch in Cape Town and the south-west Cape, the British in the eastern Cape, including Grahamstown and Port Elizabeth.

The Dutch East India Company first sent Jan van Riebeeck to establish a refreshment station for its ships at the Cape in 1652. It was never regarded by the company as anything more than this, although attempts to contain the areal extent of the settlement and to avoid trouble with the Khoikhoi and San inhabitants were quickly frustrated (Chapter 2). The first few non-official Europeans came to settle as 'free burghers' in 1657, and their numbers increased slowly but steadily. Soon cattle farmers began to move across the Hottentots Holland mountains to become semi-nomadic *trekboere*.

The company made only one significant effort to encourage immigration to the Cape. About 200 French Huguenots who had fled from France to the Netherlands subsequently emigrated to South Africa between 1688 and 1700. As they were interspersed with Dutch farmers and Dutch was the only medium of instruction in public schools, the French language soon began to disappear. The Huguenots intermarried with Dutch burghers, helping in the process to stabilise the 'free' white population. Huguenot surnames survive today as a reminder of this early group of immigrants.

During the eighteenth century more Germans than Dutchmen entered the Cape, but the pressure towards cultural uniformity continued to be strong. Burchell, writing of the 'Dutch part of the community' in 1810, described them as 'Africaanders, whether of Dutch, German or French origin' (Schapera 1953, vol. 1, 21). By 1806 the Cape colony consisted of four districts with a total population of 76,865 – 26,568 whites, 29,861 slaves and 20,436 Hottentots (Christopher 1976a, 52). Only in the Cape district did the European population density exceed two per square mile (0.77 per square kilometre; Figure 1.1). It was inhabited by the company's officials and a non-official population that lived by keeping lodging-houses, fishing, brickmaking and market gardening. At Stellenbosch there were well-to-do farmers who cultivated vines and corn, kept sheep and cattle, and built splendid 'Cape Dutch' houses. In more distant Swellendam and Graaff Reinet lived the stock farmers, occupying 2500 hectares or more per farmer and trekking on when the need arose.

When the French revolutionary armies invaded Holland in 1795, Britain occupied the Cape by arrangement with the Dutch king. By the Treaty of Amiens (1802) the Cape was restored not to the company, which was now bankrupt, but to the (Dutch) Batavian Republic. The latter ruled the Cape for only three years before Britain realised that it would endanger her trade with the East if the Cape were to remain in the hands of an ally of France. She therefore occupied the Cape and retained it until the Act of Union in 1910.

The British government's initial attitude to emigration appeared apathetic, if not antagonistic. Its change of heart in 1820 is partly attributable to the high unemployment prevailing in Britain during the depression following the end of the Napoleonic Wars. The catalyst, however, was provided by the Cape Governor, Lord Somerset, who was

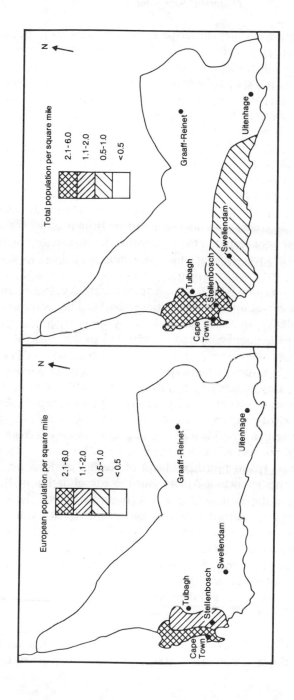

Fig. 1.1 Population densities in the Cape Colony in 1806 (after A.J. Christopher)

concerned to protect the very dispersed Dutch settlements in the east of the Colony. Although growing rapidly, the European population in the districts of Graaff Reinet and Uitenhage was only 11,650 in 1815, approximately one person per 10 square kilometres (Christopher 1976a, 63). Somerset proposed the plantation of a densely settled British population in the Albany district west of the Fish river as an inexpensive way of securing the eastern frontier of the Cape against the Xhosa (Edwards 1934; Hockly 1949).

The 1820 settlers quickly discovered that much of their land was incapable of cultivation. Wheat, the intended mainstay of the settlement, was attacked by rust, whilst climatic extremes of drought and flood also contributed to crop failure. Most settlers migrated to the towns, where many resumed the trades they had followed in Britain as artisans and mechanics. Those remaining on the land were able to develop extensive mixed farming and sheep-raising which were more suited to the physical environment.

The 5000 settlers of 1820–21 thus laid the base for the economic growth of the eastern Cape, despite initial setbacks. They increased the European population of the Cape Colony by only 10 per cent, but doubled the British population and thereby led to the British–Dutch dualism which has characterised South Africa ever since. Because the settlers were English-speaking and had friends and relatives in Britain, the British government was compelled to pay greater attention to the Cape, and to institute a whole series of reforms. Later, when the Dutch frontiersmen trekked northwards (Chapter 2), men of British stock found themselves engaged in frontier wars: 'it was as if the old garrison had moved and a new one was left to man the frontier' (Marquard 1955, 108).

Similar motives explain a further scheme of planned colonisation. This time it was not the defence of Albany but the consolidation of British Kaffraria, between the Fish and Kei rivers (Figure 2.1), that the British government desired, following annexation of the territory in 1847. Members of a German legion which had fought with the British army in the Crimea were granted land in the present Stutterheim–King William's Town area between 1857 and 1859. Nearly 3000 settlers arrived, although more than 600 legionaries amongst them subsequently failed to return from the suppression of the Indian mutiny. In the interests of social stability, 1600 German peasants were also settled as small farmers in the same area.

The Germans' willingness to accept relatively low living standards helped to make the settlement of Kaffraria probably the most successful example of systematic colonisation in South Africa (Christopher 1976a, 75). The settlers were dispersed among a predominantly English-speaking population, but in small nuclei rather than on isolated farms. Like the Huguenots they gradually lost their cultural distinctiveness: the British authorities saw the importance of language as a means of preserving the identity of a cultural group, and in various steps compelled the public use of English in schools and courts. The legion itself was disbanded in 1861, and German place names like Berlin, Potsdam and Hamburg mark the site of military posts from which the legionaries dispersed.

A series of privately promoted settlement schemes brought 5000 British colonists to Natal in the years 1848–51, most of them to the ten settlements established by Joseph Byrne. Almost three-quarters of the colonists were located on what was essentially grazing land in the interior, where farms of 7.5 hectares for a single man and 15 hectares for a married couple, with 2 hectares extra per child, proved utterly inadequate. Markets were distant, communications poor, and cotton proved unsuccessful as a cash crop. Thus the scheme was in most respects a failure (Christopher 1976a, 72–5; Pollock 1980). Nevertheless, most of the Byrne settlers stayed in Natal, whose European population increased from about 3000 in the 1840s to 7500 in 1852; thus the foundation of Natal's predominantly 'British' character was laid.

The low numbers involved in these settlement schemes reflect the generally small volume of migration to South Africa in the nineteenth century and subsequently. In the period 1820–60, when over a million people emigrated from Britain to Canada, Australia, New Zealand and the USA, only 40,000 emigrants of all nationalities went to South Africa. Likewise between 1860 and 1945 South Africa was relatively unaffected by the waves of non-British migrants who went to the other Dominions and the USA. Environmental conditions alone are insufficient to explain these differences. The real reason was the existence of a large indigenous population. More than half the people who emigrated from Britain were crofters and agricultural labourers, but in South Africa agricultural labour was performed by slaves, Hottentots, coloureds and Africans at rates of pay too low to attract labourers from Europe. South Africa, unlike the other Dominions, had room only for those who could immediately become members of the employing class.

Slaves and coloured people

In the first ten years of European settlement at the Cape, a few hundred slaves from the west coast of Africa were brought in. After 1662 slaves were imported from Mozambique and Madagascar and from the Dutch East India Company's sphere of influence in the East. Many of these eastern slaves were Mohammedans, and some were highly skilled in various arts and crafts. Some of the Malays still form distinctive communities in the Cape Peninsula, Paarl, Stellenbosch and one or two other towns. The African slaves were a grade lower, working on the settlers' farms. Shiploads of African slaves continued to arrive throughout the eighteenth century, especially from Madagascar. The eastern supply of slaves, which was never large, ceased in 1767. In the period 1807–21 the import of slaves gradually ended, and with the arrival of the 1820 settlers slaves ceased to be a majority of the non-indigenous population. There were 39,000 slaves at the time of emancipation (1839), the vast majority of them in Cape Town and its agricultural hinterland.

The fact that 'white South Africa' started its career as a slave-owning society is historically important. The Dutch, even had they wished to work in urban trades, were effectively denied such opportunities by the presence of skilled slaves. Consequently, farmers' sons shunned the town, and the tradition grew up that, except in one of the learned professions (to which hardly any rural colonist could aspire in the seventeenth and eighteenth centuries), there was no occupation worthy of an Afrikaner but that of landholder. Thus the white farmers spread rapidly inland and away from civilisation, whilst slaves and their freed descendants contined to do all the unskilled work as well as some of the skilled work in the western towns.

The coloured population owes its origin to the seventeenth-century slave population. During the first 20 years of settlement, 75 per cent of children born of slave mothers had European fathers. Intercourse and marriage with slave women were prohibited after 1685, but miscegenation continued owing to the predominance of European males over females. Intercourse between slaves and colonists became rarer as the Dutch farmers developed pride of race, but soldiers and sailors still had intercourse across the colour line. Children of these mixed unions could not hope to join Dutch society, and by the second half of the eighteenth century they were becoming a people apart. They tended increasingly to marry amongst themselves and also to have larger families than the Europeans.

Numerically, the most important type of miscegenation in the history of the coloureds is that of slave and Khoikhoi. In 1708 the proportion of adult male slaves to adult females was 6:1, and even in the 1830s men still outnumbered women considerably. Since many farmers had both slaves and Khoikhoi on their farms, it is not surprising that miscegenation took place. San peoples also made a minor contribution to the coloured population, as some of them, especially the children, were captured in skirmishes and apprenticed by white farmers. Later, San were hired as herdsmen by Boer pastoralists on the northern frontier, where they again contributed to the coloured population.

The infusion of European blood continued, on a small scale, long after that of Khoikhoi and San had ceased and was still occurring in the 1930s (Marais 1939). In the present coloured population of South Africa the slave strain is most important, particularly in the western Cape. It is less prominent in the Cape Midlands and northern districts, where Khoikhoi and Bantu labour was much more important than slave labour. The Hottentot–Dutch 'bastards', who were fewer in number, tended to concentrate along the Orange river, where their descendants can still be found.

Of South Africa's coloureds, 85 per cent still live in the Cape Province, and nearly 40 per cent of Cape coloureds live in the Cape Peninsula. Most of those in other provinces, or their ancestors, came originally from the Cape, either in the early days of the *Voortrekkers* or subsequently.

Indians in Natal
In Natal coloured labour was lacking, and the coastal planters who were trying to create sugar and cotton industries required workers with skills and interests which were remote from the experience of African men, who left most of the field work to their womenfolk. At first the planters sought a break-up of the locations (Chapter 2) in order to force more Zulus to work for them, but when the chances of this faded they eventually turned to India, following the precedent set by sugar planters in Mauritius and the Caribbean. The indenture system was duly extended to Natal in 1860. After five years' service the Indian worker became free to make a private arrangement with an employer, or to branch out on his own; many were offered land as an inducement to reindenture. After another five years they became entitled to a free return passage to India, but there was nothing to prevent their staying in Natal. This, combined with the requirement that at least 25 women were shipped with every 100 men, encouraged the establishment of a permanent Indian population in Natal, although this was not foreseen at the time. Between 1860 and 1866 over 6000 Indians arrived, mostly low-caste Hindus drawn from areas of poverty and unemployment in

India's south and central provinces. A major element was thus added to the Natal population, which included only 7000 Europeans in 1860. Altogether 140,000 Indians came between 1860 and 1911, some of the later immigrants working on the railways, in the coalmines and in domestic service. About 10 per cent were 'passenger' immigrants who entered South Africa at their own expense to trade and serve in commerce until the restriction of such immigration in 1896.

The Indians were the final element of South Africa's multi-ethnic society to enter the country, and for a long time their permanence was questioned by whites. Prohibition of further immigration and strict controls on movement have ensured that they remain numerically the smallest and geographically the least dispersed of the major population groups: more than 80 per cent still live in Natal.

2
Spatial patterns of political and economic development, 1652–1948

The contradictions of Company rule

The Dutch East India Company instructed van Riebeeck to build a fort and lay out a vegetable garden, and to obtain sheep and cattle from the natives by barter, but to retain good relations with them. These orders soon led him to pursue contradictory policies. To produce supplies of meat as economically as possible he wanted the Khoikhoi to drive cattle to market at Cape Town, but when they did so thieving and quarrelling occurred. The company's servants, discontented with an arduous life in a desolate spot, were inefficient workers. They saw in the presence of the Khoikhoi an opportunity for private trade, which led to more quarrelling and dissatisfaction with the company for prohibiting such trade. Settlers were allowed to barter stock with Khoikhoi only in 1657–58 (and later in 1700–2 and 1705–27), but the company could not prevent widespread illegal trading at other times (Katzen 1969, 208–9). When supplies from Khoikhoi proved insufficient, van Riebeeck began to establish his own herds and, from 1657, to encourage 'free burghers' to farm. The latter occupied grazing lands which the Khoikhoi regarded as their own; after a brief war in 1658, they were compelled to accept the loss of these lands.

Above all, the company wanted to limit its occupation at the Cape to what was strictly economic, but the very establishment of a class of free burghers and the introduction of slaves were bound to lead to the expansion of settlement. Partly to contain it and partly to guard against Hottentot thieving, van Riebeeck planted a bitter almond hedge enclosing an area of 2400 hectares. The hedge failed in its purpose because the economic demands which van Riebeeck tried to serve broke all boundaries. There is an obvious symbolism in this early example of economic realities breaking down attempted spatial segregation between races. Subsequent *placaats* (edicts) in 1727, 1739 and 1770, which tried to prevent the frontiers of African and European settlement from meeting, recognised past expansion of the latter but failed to prevent further expansion (de Kiewiet 1957, 25).

The first free burghers were given holdings of only 11.3 hectares on which they bound themselves to live for 20 years. Their freedom was very limited: they retained certain military duties, and were not allowed to grow tobacco (a company monopoly). They suffered from lack of capital and labour, and when in 1664 South African farming endured its first depression, the burghers 'cried aloud at the poverty of their opportunities' (de Kiewiet 1957, 6). This was to be a familiar cry for many generations faced with environmental difficulties. The monopoly and restrictions of the company were exasperating to a population still experimenting with its natural environment. The real failure of the company in these early decades, however, was in its attempt to insist on a type of settlement more suited to the climatic conditions of Europe, one which faced the sea and carried out an intensive agriculture which could be easily supervised from the castle (ibid., 8, 10). The task of the eighteenth century at the Cape would be to find a level of economic activity appropriate to the colony's environment and geographical position in the world, and to produce a community adapted to its environment.

The size of the settlement grew slowly. The first permanent European settlement beyond the sandy Cape Flats was founded in 1672, with the establishment of a post at Hottentots Holland. Simon van der Stel, van Riebeeck's successor, sanctioned further expansion, although he attempted to control it. By 1685 there were about 125 settler families on the land and the company began actively to encourage immigration to the Cape as a means of holding on to what had become a strongly fortified strategic post guarding the Dutch trade routes to the East. The immigration of some 200 Huguenot refugees, who were mainly settled at Franschhoek (French corner), was part of this policy (Christopher, 1976a, 40). Van der Stel established South Africa's first village at Stellenbosch in 1679, granting freehold farms of about 50 hectares there and to the north-east at Drakenstein and Paarl in the Berg river valley. This policy of close settlement was seen as a means of checking illegal cattle barter and obtaining an easily mobilised militia, as well as guaranteeing cheap provisions. In 1699 the European population totalled 1265, but there was no further Huguenot immigration, and in 1707 free passages to the Cape were cancelled. In 1717, influenced by the strong opinions of the Cape government against further white immigration to provide farm labour, the company's directors decided instead to continue importing slaves. This decision may be regarded as a turning-point in South African history, confirming the role of whites as an occupational élite in relation to other races.

The end of the seventeenth century found the colony unable either to pay its own way or to satisfy the needs of the 40-odd ships which called annually. Yet the company's limited economic aims in promoting free agriculture were in sight of success: the Cape was becoming self-sufficient in cereals, as the first export of wheat in 1684 showed, and gradually viticulture was combined with cereal growing on many farms. At the same time the colonists' flocks and herds increased rapidly, partly as a result of continued illegal barter, and trekking well beyond the settled area. In 1700 the government was successfully petitioned to allow grazing outside the existing settlement, and the separation of pastoralism and agriculture was confirmed (Katzen 1969, 197, 209).

The Trekboers
Small as the population was in 1700, it successfully challenged the personal monopoly which Simon van der Stel's son, Willem Adriaan, was building up for himself during his governorship. A new period of colonisation was opened by the outcry of the colonists which finally led to Willem Adriaan's dismissal in 1707. The independence of the Afrikaners, as they were soon to be known, was foreshadowed by this incident: they regarded the function of government as 'protection', in the sense of ensuring that farmers had sufficient labour and that farm prices were high (Marquard 1969, 4).

The eighteenth century was the century of the *Trekboers* (trekking farmers) who were large-scale cattle ranchers. The increasing demands of the Cape market for meat encouraged cattle farming, but more fundamentally the *Trekboers* were people who turned their backs on the difficulties and frustrations of life under company rule. On a slowly widening frontier they developed an economy in which self-sufficiency was more important than profit. Three or four generations of unhindered movement with little effective government encouraged the *Trekboers* to regard all government as interference with personal liberty. They also came to believe that the possession of at least 2570 hectares of land – a roughly circular farm measured by walking a horse for half-an-hour in all directions from the homestead – was an inborn right of all free men (Christopher 1976b).

The company was unwilling to spend money on extensive land surveys, and in 1717 halted the issue of freehold land. Three years earlier, the leasing system had been regularised. Grazing rights were leased on a yearly basis, and *leeningsplaats* ('loanplaces') could be obtained for 12 rix dollars (£2.50) per annum, which was doubled in 1732 (Katzen 1969, 210). The need to renew licences annually spelt no lack of security in practice; renewal was usually a formality, and although loanplaces could not be bequeathed, they were often held in families for generations.

It was an ideal system for the stock farmer. He could occupy land without any capital outlay, at a very low rent, and move away at will without loss. This stimulated the rapid dispersal of farmers, encouraging them to overgraze and then move on to still more distant pastures. Theoretically they could not do so without the sanction of the administration, but the *Trekboers* soon availed themselves of land without heed to anyone, those on the farthest frontier not always registering their farms or paying their dues. The precise doctrine of Crown Lands, which was so important in the history of settlement in Australia, New Zealand and Canada, was thus utterly lacking in South Africa.

Prior to 1745 most grazing took place within 200 miles of Cape Town, but thereafter a more general movement eastwards and northwards occurred (Botha 1923). The physical environment has a dual importance in understanding the rapidly widening frontier of the eighteenth century. On the one hand, it was permissive: the terrain was relatively easy to cross, without great mountain ranges, wide rivers or dense forests, and the climate posed none of the formidable obstacles which faced pioneers in Australia and Canada. In addition, the very mildness of the climate rendered intensive effort unnecessary: adequate homes were easily built. Yet on the other hand the environment was also limiting – much more so, indeed, than settlers initially realised (Christopher 1973). Over half the total area of the present Cape Province receives an annual rainfall of 250mm or less, and as this falls in the summer months, the rate of evaporation is much higher than in the narrow belt of winter rainfall around Cape Town. Such a regime precludes arable farming and severely limits stocking densities, as those trekking northwards quickly discovered. Eastwards, however, South Africa's rainfall increases, and when Boers and Africans finally met in the last third of the eighteenth century, the latter had already penetrated beyond the area of comparatively high rainfall which lay behind them, further east. This circumstance alone, according to de Kiewiet (1957, 24–5), was enough to force the Boers to take the offensive.

Isolation from the forces of civilisation, emphasised by distance, poor communications and the lack of further immigration in the eighteenth century, was as important a formative influence as the physical environment. Tenacity, endurance and self-respect were qualities developed by the Boers, but in the face of isolation these qualities could all too easily degenerate into obstinacy, resistance to innovation, suspicion of foreigners and contempt for those regarded as inferior. Lichtenstein (1812), travelling in South Africa between 1803 and 1806, comments on the 'joyless existence' of the lives of the Boers, which is mirrored all too vividly 80 years later by Olive Schreiner (1883). They were isolated even from one another, coming together only in time of crisis or danger. In the absence of formal education and sufficient pastors, the Boers found justification for their beliefs and way of life in the Old Testament, particularly in the experiences of the Children of Israel in their search for the Promised Land. Such attitudes have not entirely disappeared today, especially in the rural *platteland*.

The Eastern Frontier
By 1770 the Boers had reached the Gamtoos and Sundays rivers and the Bruintjeshoogte (Figure 2.1). Five years later they had reached a line stretching from Bushmans river to the upper Fish river. By the end of the century they had crossed into the Zuurveld (sour grassland) and were facing Nguni tribes across the lower Fish river. The Eastern Frontier, so named in relation to the Cape Colony, was the scene of the so-called 'Kaffir Wars' which began in 1779. Each had its storm centre a little further east than the one before, beginning near the Gamtoos river, moving through the Zuurveld and the Fish river bush to the Keiskama, the Amatolas, beyond the Kei, and finally, in the rebellion of 1878 which ranks as the last war, to the Bashee river country. A detailed geographical interpretation of events on the Eastern Frontier has been made elsewhere (Pollock and Agnew 1963), whilst the work of Macmillan (1963) is outstanding amongst studies which attempt to explain the historical complexities. Only the broad environmental circumstances and men's responses to them need be noted here.

Within the border region, as it is known today, there is a threefold territorial division which clearly reflects past struggles. West of the Great Fish river and its tributary the Kat lies the land which was occupied by Boer farmers before 1780. To the east, between the Great Fish and Kei rivers, largely hemmed in by the Katberg and Amatola escarpment, lies the Ciskei. It is clear that Nguni tribes were in effective occupation of this area long before Europeans, and were forced to withdraw spasmodically before the pressure of better armed white peoples. Part of

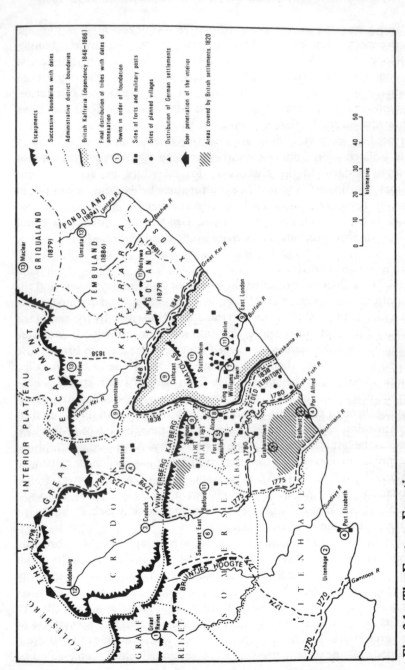

Fig. 2.1 The Eastern Frontier

Source: N.C. Pollack and S. Agnew, *An Historical Geography of South Africa*

this territory was variously known during the 'Hundred Years War' as the Ceded Territory (from 1819), Queen Adelaide Province (1836–37) and British Kaffraria (from 1847). This belt remains today an area of heavily populated African reserves and large, virtually empty white farms. East of the Great Kei and its tributary the White Kei is the third division, Transkei. This almost wholly African territory is amongst the most densely populated and closely settled rural areas in South Africa.

Differing attitudes to land were a fundamental source of conflict. In the subsistence economy of the Nguni tribes, it was to no one's advantage to claim exclusive rights to *property* in land. Colonial farmers, on the other hand, regarded tribal areas as wastefully used for intermittent grazing, and readily planted themselves on unoccupied sites where there seemed to be room, without asking about grazing or hunting rights. But the wide dispersal of the colonists themselves made their cattle an easy target for tribesmen who felt they were being dispossessed and had the advantage of being grouped more closely together in the bush country which afforded ample cover. Both the colonists and their rulers in Cape Town failed to see how the increasing disorders arose directly from the devastating effects of the colonial advance on the social and economic life of the dispossessed tribes. Meanwhile the expansion of the colony merely intensified Boer disposition to trekking and superficial agricultural methods.

For the Nguni tribes the problem was essentially one of *lebensraum*. This was partly an internal problem: the territorial expansion natural to pastoralists, and indeed necessary in the face of population growth, had reached its environmental limits. The highveld was uncongenially cold, whilst the Karroo, which lay ahead, was so dry as to make the normal Bantu way of life impossible. The resulting struggles may well have contributed to the Shaka wars in Natal, which resulted in successive waves of displaced people pouring into Xhosa territory. The coincidence in time of this internecine strife in Zululand and their own eastward advance was unknown to the Boers at the time, but put the Xhosa in an impossible position. All through the 1820s they had to come to terms with organised hordes or broken tribes such as the Fingos and Tembu killing, stealing and seeking new homes. Yet in the same decade the Xhosa were faced with the problem of accommodating other groups from the west, displaced by the Boers. The clearing of the Zuurveld in 1812 had involved driving 20,000 Ndhlambi and Gqunukwebe tribesmen across the Fish river. After an attack on Grahamstown in 1819, the same people were pushed into the hands of hostile kinsmen further east beyond the Keiskama, and out of the Ceded Territory. The latter was not returned until 1836 ('on loan' during good behaviour), only to suffer military occupation in 1844. Meanwhile the position of the Xhosa and other claimants to territory became increasingly desperate. Violence against the colonists was their inevitable response to droughts which hit the border country in 1834 and 1846.

Despite these pressures, peaceful intercourse was by no means absent on the frontier. New slave laws in the 1820s made the labour shortage acute, and Ordinance 49 of 1828 provided for the granting of passes to tribesmen who wished to enter the service of colonial farmers. Trade across the frontiers increased in the same decade; the attractions of the Grahamstown fairs which had been established in 1817 proved so great that they were moved to Fort Wiltshire, a frontier post on the Keiskama. In 1830 this method of controlling trade was judged to be no longer necessary, and colonists were allowed to trade freely in tribal territory. This relaxation of restrictions and the 1828 Ordinance suggest that peaceful coexistence on the frontier was by no means impossible, given an equitable apportionment of land between rival claimants. Unfortunately, despite growing tension in the years after 1829, there was no hint of measures calculated to meet the essential problems of the frontier. Dr John Philip of the London Missionary Society was almost alone in arguing the need to establish the authority of law and ordinary civil government on the frontier (Macmillan 1963). Instead, the colonists continued to resort to patrols and commando raids, whilst the government attempted a series of solutions involving a neutral belt (the Ceded Territory), the shortlived Queen Adelaide Province, and a collection of unsatisfactory treaties in the late 1830s.

Drought and war had already done much to ruin the tribal system when 'British Kaffraria' was annexed in 1847. Two years later tribesmen were forced to choose between assigned 'locations' and service on colonial farms, thus initiating the modern search for work caused by shortage of land. At the time no one could foresee the cumulative ecological effects of the continuous application of extensive agricultural methods to increasingly restricted locations. The best of the Ceded Territory and the Amatolas was lost for ever in the peace of 1853 which followed yet another war. Many of the forfeited districts were allocated to Europeans, an act described by Macmillan (1963, 339) as 'the first deliberate exploitation of the plan of making South Africa a chess-board of black and white'.

In 1856 the Xhosas were induced by prophets among them to kill their

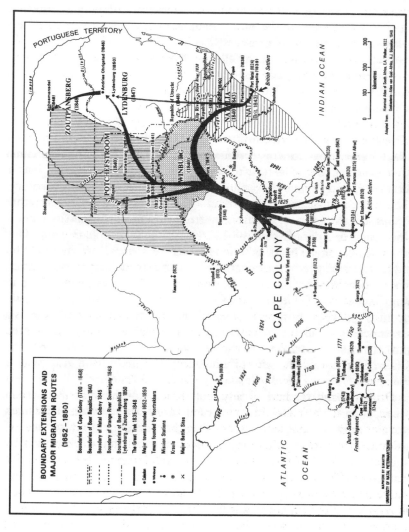

Fig. 2.2 Boundary extensions and major migration routes 1652–1850

own cattle and destroy their crops, in the belief that their dead ancestors would rise and drive the white men into the sea. At least 150,000 cattle were slaughtered, and by February 1857 the whole countryside was starving. The government chose to regard the cattle-killing as rebellion. It confiscated much of the land remaining in the hands of the chiefs and planted it with Europeans, especially Germans (Chapter 1). The spontaneous dispersal which followed the cattle-killing itself was thus confirmed, and the reunion of fragments of Xhosa territory finally prevented. Only in the late 1970s, prior to accepting 'independence', has Ciskei once more become a single territory.

The Northern Frontier and the Great Trek
The human barrier to further coastal movement was extremely disappointing to the Boers, who were forced to turn northward instead of eastward, away from the well-watered grassland of the Transkei and beyond. Small-scale northward movement occurred well before the 1830s, but the volume of movement from 1836 onwards was such that in the course of a decade between 12,000 and 14,000 people trekked out of the Cape Colony. The distribution of these *Voortrekkers* by the end of the 1840s foreshadowed the extent of South Africa today. Amongst the many consequences of the Great Trek, two are absolutely fundamental to an understanding of the country's subsequent development. First, the frontier between European farmers and Bantu-speaking peoples was extended from about 320 to more than 1600 kilometres in a great horseshoe-shaped curve. From the middle of the nineteenth century onwards, these tribes were progressively confined to the arid western periphery of the highveld or the malarial northern and eastern subtropical and tropical plateau slopes and lowlands. This successful occupation of the highveld is the second great consequence of the Trek, for not only was Afrikaner nationalism bred there, but the region also proved to be 'the richest parcel of real estate in the world' (Ransford 1972, xii) and as such became the economic, demographic and political core area of South Africa.

The Great Trek has been the subject of extensive historical study, notably by Nathan (1937) and Walker (1965), and its causes have been intensively scrutinised. Tactically, it represented a decision to give up the frontal attack and to undertake an outflanking movement, with Natal as the ultimate objective. Politically, the Great Trek was an essentially conservative movement, an attempt to preserve a way of life and the manner and thought of an age which elsewhere was quickly passing.

More specifically, the Boers were retreating from a government which interfered with the relationship between master and servant, and was responsible for the freeing of the Hottentots in 1828 and the slaves in 1833. Environmentally, the underlying cause of the Great Trek was land hunger: this was inevitable in a colonial economy characterised by a lack of agricultural markets and poor communications, and therefore dominated by subsistence pastoralism despite the dry climate and lack of winter feeding. By perpetuating and accentuating the dispersal of population (see below) the movement made Boer isolation more extreme than ever.

The first people encountered by the Trekkers were the Griquas, weakly organised groups of mixed-breed refugees from the Cape, who had with the aid of missionaries built up small, unstable states north of the Orange river. Conflicts arose from the fact that the Griquas had settled upon the most desirable land in the region, where crumbled layers of shale and jaspers beneath the soil held moisture, thus enabling the survival of permanent pasture (de Kiewiet 1957, 63). The government refused to extend the colonial boundary beyond the Orange, but made ineffective efforts to protect the Griquas which engendered Boer antagonism. By obstructing the way northwards at a critical period these weak states attained disproportionate importance. They forced the Boers further afield into the better watered country of the upper Vaal river, true highveld, where grass replaced scrub. Ultimately, however, these weak Griqua states succumbed to the onslaught of the trekkers; in return for wagons, oxen and possibly brandy, the Griquas gave the Boers extensive rights to lease or occupy the land, until they themselves were forced to make a 'Great Trek' across the Drakensberg with their leader Adam Kok in 1862–63 (Macmillan 1963; Ross 1976).

The horseshoe-shaped curve of dense Bantu population extended from Kaffraria, through Basutoland, Natal and Zululand, and Swaziland, to the northern Transvaal and its western border. Within this curve the wide open spaces of the highveld were unquestionably capable of supporting many more inhabitants. Their exposure to cold winter winds, the want of shelter for cattle, and the difficulty of hiding from human enemies made them unattractive to Bantu tribes except for summer grazing. In addition the regiments of the Zulu king, Shaka, had crossed the Drakensberg and left a trail of destruction in the Transvaal, whilst one of Shaka's former lieutenants, Mzilikazi, who had broken away and established his own following (the Ndebele), had laid waste vast areas in the eastern Transvaal. Tribes such as the Hlubi and the Mantatees, which

27

moved north, exterminated other tribes or drove them further northwards. The charred remains of huts and villages understandably reinforced the Boer impression of an empty highveld, which became firmly entrenched in the Afrikaner interpretation of history (Cornevin 1980, 101–5).

The truth was more complex: from the beginning Boer and Bantu were intermingled. The open plains of the highveld are frequently broken by low ridges, shallow depressions (*leegtes*) and clefts (*kloofs*) which, particularly when they have a northerly exposure, have patches of bush and often permanent water. Refugees sought security in these spots, which were precisely those likely to attract Boer farmers, and emerged when the latter had broken the power of their enemies. These scattered fragments of Bantu tribes were powerless against the Boers, and were in time reduced by trekker 'protection' to a large landless proletariat of farm 'natives'.

President Kruger of the South African Republic (Transvaal), anxious to defend himself against British accusations of ill-treatment of the natives, claimed in a letter of 1884 to the Aborigines Protection Society that 'The natives who were placed under the protection of the Trekkers when the latter arrived in the Transvaal, some 30,000, had grown to some 700,000 by 1884' (van Jaarsveld 1964, 18). Such population growth, even allowing for considerable migration, strains credulity. Rather it seems that after Mzilikazi's departure for what is now Matabeleland (western Zimbabwe) in 1837, the Sotho returned in great numbers to the lands from which they had been driven by the Ndebele, only to face the *Voortrekkers* shortly afterwards.

The Transvaalers faced encroachment on the Zulu border, but managed to escape a Zulu war. Further north, in the direction of the Swazis, the Pedi and the tribes of the Soutpansberg, fever and broken country aided the Bantu in opposing European settlement, which helps to explain the extent of homeland territory in the northern Transvaal today. On the western border of the Transvaal the struggle was less for land than for the springs and water courses without which the land was useless. The Bantu in these areas found their access to water, and hence the area of land in which they could live, severely limited. It was only at British insistence that formal rural locations were finally established in the Transvaal in 1907.

The Orange Free State came to regard Basutoland as the 'location' for its Bantu population, although two other small areas were set aside for groups who found favour with the government (Christopher 1972, 24).

These survive as the only homeland territory in the Free State today, amounting to 0.4 per cent of the area of the province. The Free Staters struggled for many years to clear the east of tribes professing allegiance to the great Basuto chief Moshesh, who was strongly ensconced in the foothills of the Drakensberg. In 1866 the Basuto were finally forced to yield well over half of this arable land, notably the fertile Caledon Valley cornlands. Many Basuto became squatters on the new Boer farms, whilst this nineteenth-century Boer victory has left the Lesotho of today overpopulated and impoverished, with much of its population crowded into the narrow lowlands bordering the Orange Free State.

Britain's attitude to the Boers was ambivalent. The importance of the Cape sea route to India underlay Britain's concern that southern Africa should be a British sphere of influence, but she was reluctant for economic reasons to assume greater colonial responsibilities (Schreuder 1980). Independence was thrust on the Transvaal Boers in 1852 despite their reluctance to shoulder responsibility for defence against Bantu tribes. The independence of the Orange Free State followed in 1854, thus destroying Britain's land bridge between the Cape and Natal. Political isolation reinforced the aloofness of the Boers, whose fundamentally different view of the status of dependent peoples became a great unifying bond. Political unification was more difficult to achieve in the Transvaal than in the Free State, owing to its extent (250,000 square kilometres), sparse white population, and poor communications, but its four constituent republics did merge in 1864.

The underlying assumption remained that Britain could resume full sovereignty if necessary, which she did over the Transvaal in 1877. Britain's pretexts for this action arose from long-standing missionary charges that the Transvaal practised slavery, concern over British investments, and (exaggerated) reports of a Pedi victory over Transvaal commandos which reached London in September 1876. In practice, the annexation was intended to facilitate the plans of the Earl of Carnarvon, the then Colonial Secretary, for a South African federation (Thompson 1971, 295–6). British annexation did little to alleviate black–white conflict and the distress of tribes on the various borders. The Boers themselves successfully rebelled in 1880, inflicting a military defeat on the British at Majuba in what has become known in Afrikaner historiography as the First Anglo-Boer War, or 'First War of Freedom' (van Jaarsveld 1975). The South African Republic regained its independence under the Pretoria Convention of 1881, which also defined the Bechuana frontier to Boer advantage. The Transvaalers, having found themselves masters of more Bantu than at first they realised, had begun to insist on their right to manage these people in their own way, thus contributing to the mounting strain between Britain and themselves which ultimately led to the War of 1899–1902.

Meanwhile Britain remained watchful of her interests, especially the Cape sea route. Fear of the Orange Free State gaining access to the coast was a major motive in the annexation of Basutoland in 1868, in addition to protecting the Basuto against further displacement. Similar anxieties in relation to the Transvaal encouraged the insertion of a guarantee of the independence of Swaziland in the Pretoria Convention, and the proclamation of Bechuanaland as a British protectorate in 1885. Together these moves prevented the Transvaal from gaining access to the coast either eastwards through Portuguese East Africa or westwards through the newly proclaimed German protectorate over Damaraland and Namaqualand.

Natal and Zululand
The Voortrekkers hoped that, after the devastation of the Shaka wars and despite the presence of the Zulus, there would be room for many of them in the more genial climate of Natal. By 1840, less than three years after crossing the Drakensberg, the Trekkers had broken the military power of the Zulus under Dingaan. But they soon found the country far from empty. Away from the great stretches of highveld seen by early travellers there are many secluded, inaccessible bush valleys such as the Umkomaas and the rugged upper valleys of the Mooi and Tugela rivers. Dingaan's overthrow allowed the weaker tribes who had found refuge in these valleys to move freely once more, but the Boers mistakenly assumed that these natives – reputedly 50,000–80,000 in number – were 'filtering' from Zululand into Natal. Although they were glad of a labour supply, it was found necessary to restrict the number of squatters on any one farm to five families in 1840.

British annexation of Natal in 1843 was both a strategic move and a humanitarian gesture. The Colonial Office was uneasy over reports that Boers were capturing and apprenticing native children, but it was seriously alarmed when the Trekkers found their way to the coast at Port Natal, a small British trading settlement established a few years earlier. Annexation turned whatever republics the Trekkers might erect into landlocked states, economically dependent on British ports.

Britain's first problem was to provide for 'surplus' natives created by the usual Boer claims to farms of at least 2500 hectares. A Land

Commission appointed in 1846 to delimit reserves included farms claimed by Boers in native areas. Many Trekkers withdrew rather than abate their full claims, thus giving way to the anglicisation of most of Natal, which was confirmed shortly afterwards by the Byrne settlers (Chapter 1). The demarcation of reserves made no provision for population growth. At first this mattered little, as extensive Crown Lands were only gradually swallowed up by new white settlers (Christopher 1984a, Chapter 4), whilst white farmers welcomed labourers or share-paying squatters. In later years, however, as commercial agriculture prospered in Natal, the days of unrestricted squatting gradually ended: the coastal belt was thickly planted with sugar-cane, subtropical fruit and vegetables, whilst mixed farming spread over the highveld districts. Thus a growing population of physically insecure Africans existed in 1893 when Natal became a self-governing colony.

Meanwhile the Zulu kingdom east of the Tugela remained intact, and was by far the most powerful African state south of the Limpopo in the 1870s. As such it appeared increasingly anachronistic, and a major obstacle to Carnarvon's federation policy which Sir Bartle Frere had been sent to South Africa to carry out. Encouraged by Theophilus Shepstone, the Secretary for Native Affairs, Frere presented the Zulu ruler Cetshwayo with an ultimatum with which compliance was impossible (Thompson 1971, 262–4). The Zulu war which followed began with a disastrous defeat for the British at Isandhlwana in January 1879. But such a devastating Zulu victory actually made vindication of the British army's reputation and the eventual defeat of Cetshwayo all the more certain (Brookes and Webb 1965, 140). The last Zulu army was defeated on 4 July 1879 at the royal kraal of Ulundi, today resurrected as the new capital of the KwaZulu homeland.

Zululand was not annexed initially but divided into 13 separate territories under 13 different chiefs, each undertaking not to create an army and to accept the arbitration of the British resident. This policy of 'divide and refrain from rule' consummated military victory without further cost or responsibility on Britain's part. In 1897, however, despite previous promises to the contrary, Britain incorporated Zululand in Natal. This led to the confinement of the Zulus to reserves within their own territory east of the Tugela, and to the opening of the rest of Zululand to white settlement in the years 1902–4. This process of alienation, together with the much earlier loss of land to the Boers in Natal proper, explains why KwaZulu is today the most fragmented of the ten officially recognised homelands.

Land and population on the nineteenth-century frontier
Interpretation of the nature of frontier societies and their environments
has produced a number of recent comparative studies involving South
Africa (Frederickson 1981; Lamar and Thompson 1981; Thompson
1981). Comparisons with the American frontier have predominated, no
doubt reflecting the tradition of frontier studies in the USA since Turner
(1894) sought to explain the unique qualities of American character and
development in terms of frontier influence. The South African frontier
suffered two major constraints relative to that of America: the
comparatively poor physical environment and resultant lack of large-
scale immigration, and the large indigenous population which supplied
much of the labour needed to develop settler agriculture (Christopher
1984b, 56). Another major contrast, related to environmental differences,
concerns the dominance of the pastoral frontier in South Africa
(Christopher 1983a). Whereas in the American Great Plains the
pastoralists were but transient squatters who were rapidly replaced by
crop farmers, in South Africa 'it was the pastoralist who determined the
pattern of settlement into which later occupants had to fit' (Christopher
1984b, 59). The arable frontier was largely a later development in areas
physically capable of closer settlement after initial pastoral occupation.

The main advances of European rural settlement had already occurred
by 1860, leaving the processes of filling in and enclosing the farm frontier
to take place between 1860 and 1911. The area of European farms
doubled during the latter period, reaching 80 million hectares, two-thirds
of South Africa's total area in 1911. The white population in rural areas
increased from 90,000 in 1855 to 600,000 in 1911, but even in the latter
year only 46.9 per cent of South Africa had a European population
density of more than one per square mile (0.4 per square kilometre). The
frontier consisted of a corridor of land extending from the eastern Cape
to the southern Transvaal. The original core of settlement in the western
Cape remained essentially peripheral to this axis, as did Natal, which
became a third point of entry for British immigrants after British
annexation (Christopher 1982a). Frontier movement to the west of this
eastern Cape–southern Transvaal axis resulted in low-density occupation
of the Cape interior between 1880 and 1911. In 1829 the Cape
government had recognised that in these semi-arid regions, 2500 hectares
were insufficient for commercial pastoralism, and introduced a flexible
system of survey and assessment which allowed farm sizes on the frontier
to reach 20,000 hectares. To the east of the frontier axis, land alienation
was severely restricted by compact blocks of African settlement, and

until 1880 by restrictive land laws in Natal. The northern Transvaal remained largely beyond the settlement frontier, divided into farms on paper but attracting few permanent settlers: the farm-owners made their living from rents, leaving an essentially African landscape upon their holdings (Christopher 1976a, 127).

The growth of rural population after 1860 led to pressures to expand, and thus to conflict with neighbouring African states. Small groups of trekkers entered south-west Africa and Angola, and others established the Kalahari Desert state, which for a brief period in the late 1880s offered 12,500-hectare farms in a tract of semi-sand dune country (Christopher 1982b, 80). The main areas of settlement expansion in the 1880s included the ephemeral republics of Stellaland and Goshen (1882) and the New Republic in north-west Zululand (1884). These states adopted the standard 2500-hectare farms (by then measured as a square with sides equal to the distance of one hour's ride on a horse), but the New Republic had to reduce farms to 1400 hectares to satisfy all applicants for land. In 1885 much of Stellaland and Goshen were annexed by Britain to form the Crown Colony of British Bechuanaland, thus reopening the road to the north for settlers in the Cape with expansionary aims, notably Cecil Rhodes. British Bechuanaland was later annexed to the Cape Colony (1895). Part of the New Republic was also included in British territory, in 1886, and the rest incorporated into the Transvaal in the following year.

The gradual closing of the settlement frontier led to increasing pressure of rural population, and to processes not unlike those which occurred in overcrowded African areas. Fragmentation of holdings and multiple ownership of farms reached extreme levels in some areas (Christopher 1976a, 149), and a landless population of squatters (*bywoners*) became more numerous and increasingly insecure. In times of crisis they were the first to be ejected, and were forced to migrate to the towns in search of work. Thus were the seeds of the 'poor white' problem sown. Early responses included church-run labour colonies from 1895 and the government's closer settlements between 1902 and 1906 in the southern Transvaal. As the problem magnified in the 1920s, a much more fundamental government response was forthcoming (see below).

Kimberley, the Witwatersrand and the Anglo-Boer War

It was not until the mid-nineteenth century that South Africa's white population reached 200,000. By that time the country's first large export commodity, wool, was beginning to introduce a commercial element into

Boer pastoralism. The semi-self-sufficiency of the rural areas began to break down, first in the coastal colonies and later in the interior states. Wool exports increased in value from £178,000 in 1846 to £2,082,000 in 1866 (Schumann 1938, 47). Hopeful though this was to a struggling colony, sheep-farming was hardly likely to attract capital investment from abroad or a large number of immigrants. However the discovery of diamonds in 1867 in Griqualand West (annexed by Britain in 1871), followed by the discovery of the world's greatest goldbearing reef on the Witwatersrand in 1886, drew South Africa's patriarchal subsistence economy into the full stream of world economic development with dramatic suddenness. Investment and white immigrants poured into the country, much internal migration of both blacks and whites occurred, and South Africa faced modern problems of capital and labour for the first time.

The diamond fields were South Africa's first industrial community. The major fields around Kimberley were in Griqualand West, but the Orange Free State benefited considerably both from its proximity to Kimberley and from its own small diamond mines at Koffiefontein and Jagersfontein. By 1871 Kimberley had about 50,000 inhabitants, and the number of whites exceeded that which had taken part in the Great Trek. Some 10,000 Africans worked in the mines each year, although the numbers decreased somewhat as diggers formed partnerships, partnerships gave way to companies, and companies were swallowed up by Rhodes' De Beers Consolidated Mines. Experience gained on the diamond fields paved the way for even more rapid growth on the Witwatersrand goldfields, which were proclaimed public diggings at the end of 1886. Johannesburg had a population of 102,000, half of them Africans, whilst nearly 100,000 Africans were employed altogether in the goldmines on the eve of the Anglo-Boer War. In South Africa as a whole, 53 per cent of whites (676,000) were urbanised by 1911.

The distinctive characteristics of South African labour economics also derive from the circumstances in which these early mining operations took place. Labour was from the beginning divided into two classes: a large body of African labour earning very low wages, and a much smaller group of whites earning high wages. This enduring division was not in the first instance simply the result of colour prejudice, although this certainly existed, as was shown by opposition to the attempted application of the more liberal labour laws of the Cape Colony. African labourers were unskilled, and left their kraals only for the duration of their contracts, whereas whites who came formed a permanent population, bound by many ties to their place of work. They were also a compact, self-conscious community in a way that the Africans, drawn from every tribe south of the Zambezi and many farther north, could not be. The special position of skilled labour was further strengthened because it was, of necessity, imported labour: except for wagon-builders South Africa had no skilled workers on whom the mines could draw. An important consequence of this emphatic separation of black and white in the mines was, and largely remains today, the elimination of an area of semi-skilled occupations which in most industrial economies offer the possibility of upward mobility based on effort and experience.

The cheapness of black labour was crucial to the development of the Rand. Whilst its goldbearing deposits are the most extensive in the world, they are also the poorest of those commercially exploited in gold content per ton. The major problem has always been one of payability, and it is most unlikely that the goldmines would have been developed so extensively if only white labour had been available. In this sense the black contribution in laying the foundations of South Africa's present economic strength was crucial.

At the same time white farms were demanding much more black labour than hitherto, as industrial and urban demand created the base for a major extension of commercial agriculture. This development also affected the reserves, many parts of which appear to have experienced a period of relative prosperity in the 1870s which contrasts markedly with the subsistence, or more accurately sub-subsistence, agriculture prevailing in the homelands today (van der Horst 1942, 103–5; Wilson 1971, 55). Missionaries were closely involved in gearing blacks to commercial agricultural production (Atmore and Marks 1974; Pirie 1985, 27). Colin Bundy (1972, 1979) argues that the period 1870–90 witnessed a virtual explosion of peasant economic activity. He quotes detailed evidence of peasant production from the observations of magistrates in the 1870s and early 1880s, as well as impressive recorded statistics of African production. Even in the Transvaal and Orange Free State, despite the minimal land allocation made to Africans, they found means of entering the market economy. The tenuous rule of the republics was insufficient to prevent blacks tilling and grazing nominally white lands. In areas of the Transvaal where land appropriation had been made effective, African peasants even succeeded in using the money acquired from the sale of agricultural surpluses to buy back land. Closely related to this emergence of a peasantry, Bundy argues, was the growing degree of differentiation and social stratification occurring within it.

Bundy's interpretation has recently been challenged by Lewis (1984), who regards increased agricultural production of blacks in the eastern Cape as less a response to market conditions than to favourable political and demographic circumstances, in particular those related to the migration of 30,000 Mfengu people from Ciskei into the Butterworth area of Transkei. Increased agricultural production was, Lewis argues, based not so much on increasing *productivity* (the more intensive exploitation of limited land resources) but on increased agricultural activity over a greater area by a reduced population. When favourable circumstances were reversed, both by drought and the 1879 rebellion which led to increased densities in Ciskeian locations, agricultural production began to fall, and the long-term contraction of living standards which occurred for the majority of households 'from the moment that effective conquest was achieved' (Lewis 1984, 24) continued.

More research on areas outside the eastern Cape is needed before the relative merits of Bundy's and Lewis's arguments can be assessed. What is certain is that the African's participation in the cash economy on his own terms threatened to reduce the availability of labour on mines and farms, particularly given the failure to raise wages. The whites used various methods to ensure a sufficient supply of cheap labour. Land under black occupation was reduced, and accepted systems through which blacks farmed white-owned land (labour tenancy, share-farming, renting of land) came under attack, as for instance in the Location Acts of 1876 and later in the Cape. Likewise it was one of the goals of the Native Land Act of 1913 to increase the supply of black labour (van der Horst 1942, 291–3). The introduction of taxes was also designed to force peasants to enter the labour market.

Amongst various less calculated factors which adversely affected African commercial agriculture the most important was the relative ease of access by white and black farmers to markets. This was essentially a consequence of the development of the railway network associated with mineral discoveries, urban growth and greater commercialisation of European agriculture. Although the railway network grew from 101 kilometres in 1870 to 4067 kilometres in 1891 and 11,095 kilometres in 1909, most reserves were circumvented or entirely missed even by the many branch lines built during the latter period (Macmillan 1930, 212; Pirie 1982).

Thus the distance between the races in terms of economic development was actually widened by capitalist development initiated by mineral discoveries. With less land in the face of an increasing population, and a greater need for cash income, Africans inevitably became increasingly involved in migrant labour. This in turn depleted the intensity of economic activity in the reserves (Chapter 6), thereby reproducing the necessity for more migrant labour. The first steps had been taken towards creating the detribalised and landless proletariat which is characteristic of South African towns today, and which has represented the most obvious geographical contradiction of apartheid since the inception of the latter in 1948.

Meanwhile the great influx of whites to the Rand caused more immediate political problems. Resentment at British annexation, triumph over the subsequent regaining of independence, and justifiable anger at the selfish refusal of Natal and the Cape to share import dues had stimulated Transvaal patriotism. The Boers inevitably felt their rural lifestyle and homogeneous society to be threatened by the arrival of cosmopolitan, aggressive immigrants (*uitlanders*) in such numbers that by 1985 they outnumbered the Boers themselves by 7 to 3. President Kruger responded with measures which made it virtually impossible for *uitlanders* to obtain the franchise, and also imposed other disabilities upon them. The Transvaal, no longer struggling financially, was also able to punish Natal and the Cape for their previous selfishness by imposing its own tariffs, constructing a railway to Delagoa Bay in Portuguese East Africa, and forcing the railway line of Rhodes' imperial vision to skirt the Transvaal through the unproductive scrub of Bechuanaland. Rhodes in turn sought to foment dissident elements in the Transvaal, and planned the disastrous and ill-conceived Jameson Raid from Bechuanaland, after which war seemed inevitable.

The Jameson Raid and the attitudes it revealed were an irrevocable reverse for Rhodes' carefully nurtured alliance with Hofmeyr and his Afrikaner Bond in the Cape (Davenport 1966, Chapter 8). Likewise it led to a change of course in the Orange Free State, which until President Brand's death in 1888 had managed to champion republican independence yet remain within the orbit of the Cape Colony, but which in 1897 concluded a firm alliance with the Transvaal. Thus the war of 1899–1902 became essentially one between British power and Afrikaner republicanism, and one which destroyed Britain's long-cherished hopes of achieving federation in South Africa by peaceful means (an objective which is being discussed in a new context today: see Chapter 16). The prolonged duration of the war and the memories it left inevitably cemented the unity of the Afrikaner people, which was to make its political comeback in 1948, and – in the eyes of some – to win the last battle of the Anglo-Boer War when South Africa became a Republic in 1961 and subsequently left the Commonwealth.

Liberal historians have emphasised humanitarian considerations in seeking to explain the course of Britain's policies in South Africa. Leonard Thompson reflects such views in judging Britain to have achieved its primary goal, the unification of the territories of southern Africa occupied by white people in a British Dominion, at the expense of the secondary goal of justice and freedom: 'The price of unity and conciliation was the institution of white supremacy' (Thompson 1971, vol. 2, 363–4).

A very different interpretation is advanced by Atmore and Marks (1974) who regard Britain's prime motivation as the protection of her economic interests in South Africa, whether by formal or, preferably, informal means. The latter involved the use of 'collaborative élites', beginning with the Dutch merchant class at the Cape in the early years of British rule and later embracing both African politics and the Boer republics on which independence was conferred in the early 1850s. The 'free flow of labour' was the predominant colonial interest, crucial in both 1877 (the annexation of the Transvaal) and 1899: 'The Transvaal in the 1870s was as much an obstacle to the achievement of the kind of southern Africa demanded by imperial interests as Cetshwayo's Zulu kingdom' (Atmore and Marks 1974, 126). In 1899 the Transvaal Afrikaners failed to meet the demands of the mining magnates. Atmore and Marks argue that an important reason why Britain went to war was to establish a modern polity in South Africa which would provide the necessary infrastructure for the maintenance and development of British economic interests. Judged on these criteria Britain succeeded: 'at least until 1948 and probably even after that (notwithstanding the flutter in Whitehall because of the Nationalist victory in that year's election) Britain has found in South Africa's white governments entirely satisfactory collaborators in safeguarding imperial interests, whether one regards these as strategic or economic' (ibid., 132).

Such views epitomise the radical historiography which has increasingly challenged traditionally dominant liberal analyses of South African history (Wright 1977). This liberal–radical controversy has increasingly pervaded contemporary South African studies too, in geography as in the other social sciences (Beavon and Rogerson 1981; McCarthy 1982; Wellings and McCarthy 1983).

Agricultural problems after Union

Soon after the Act of Union in 1910 an attempt was made to bring some order into the African land situation. With the passing of the Native Land Act of 1913 practically all existing reserves and locations were registered as 'scheduled Native areas' which might not be disposed of to non-Africans. Such areas amounted to 7.3 per cent of South African land, at a time when Africans constituted 67 per cent of the population (according to the censuses of 1904 and 1921). The Act also made it illegal for any African to be on European land unless he was a hired servant. This caused an immense upheaval in African life, forcing thousands of tenants into the reserves. In doing so, it naturally improved the 'free flow of labour' from the reserves to white farms and to the mines.

The 1913 Act was regarded as a temporary measure until the position could be reconsidered. The Beaumont Commission, set up to do this, recommended in 1916 that a further 6 per cent (6.7 million hectares) should be added as 'released areas'. The Commission's map suggested a considerable degree of consolidation, and included much white land within the proposed released areas. The denunciation of its recommendations by white public opinion and their rejection by Parliament were significant pointers to white attitudes.

The distribution and extent of the reserves remained more or less stable for 20 years. In 1936 rural population densities per square kilometre were 30.7 in the Transkei, 36.8 in the Ciskei and 16.1 in Zululand (Lord Hailey 1957, 761). Under such pressures the carrying capacity of the land was thought to be decreasing. The Report of the Native Economic Commission warned that:

> Unless precautionary measures are taken against overstocking, the conditions in the Transkei and Native areas in the rest of the Union will be tomorrow what that of the Ciskei is today. The same causes are at work there, and they will inevitably produce the same effects in the near future – denudation, donga-erosion, deleterious plant succession, destruction of woods, drying up of springs, robbing the soil of its reproductive properties, in short the creation of desert conditions. (South Africa 1932, para. 73)

The government responded by passing the Native Trust and Land Act 1936, which earmarked a further 6.1 million hectares, a little less than had been recommended by the Beaumont Commission, for transference to the Native Reserves over a period of ten years. In practice, the purchase of these additional areas was slow, especially with the rise in land prices after 1945, but until recently it was to the letter of the 1936

Act that the government adhered in its homeland consolidation policies.

Meanwhile the reserves continued to deteriorate. In 1946 the Social and Economic Planning Council produced a report on the position of the reserves which observed that:

> Not only is the deterioration of the Reserves affecting the European areas through the drying up of watersheds, the spreading of soil erosion and so forth, but the general debility of the Reserve population means that the major portion of the Union's labour force is attaining only a very low degree of efficiency. (South Africa 1946, para. 98)

It even appeared that the reserves were producing less food than a generation before. The Council stressed the need for improved farming practice, but urged that this should go hand in hand with diversification of the economy of the reserves.

A sharp decline in agricultural (as opposed to pastoral) production did indeed occur in the mid-1930s, and has generally been viewed as the onset of a substantial decline in the production of the reserves (Wilson 1971, 55–6; Wolpe 1972, 440–1). However Simkins (1981) regards it as only a short-term deviation. He characterises the period 1918–54 as one of 'fragile productivity maintenance' in the reserves, assisted by a high rate of emigration and small additions of land. Owing to emigration, the overall population density of the reserves increased only from about 19.3 per square kilometre in 1918 to 23.2 per square kilometre in 1955. Because the homelands constituted part of a wider 'open system', population pressure on resources was insufficient to produce the innovation and intensification of agricultural practices described in other situations by Boserup (1965). Instead, Africans responded by large-scale migration to industrial centres and remittance of part of their earnings to families in the reserves.

European agriculture in South Africa was also beset with problems at this time. The instability of agricultural prices in the 1920s and the low level to which they fell during the Great Depression, together with very imperfect knowledge of sound husbandry under South African conditions, combined to produce a critical situation. White farms as well as the reserves were badly eroded as the result of overstocking, burning the veld, and insufficient care for maintaining the humus and water content of the soil. Farming had degenerated into *Räuberwirtschaft* (a 'robber economy') in the 1930s, and South Africa was probably the most eroded country in the world.

Such conditions were partly responsible for the plight of between

200,000 and 300,000 'poor whites' in the 1920s and 1930s. The legacy of the Anglo-Boer War and the reconstruction of agriculture as it sought to produce for urban markets and export were also important factors. Drifting into the towns, this largely Afrikaner population lacked experience of urban life, possessed no industrial skills, and found mining and industry largely controlled by English interests and conducted in what to them was a foreign language. They were forced to compete with blacks and coloured people whose wages were too low to support a 'civilised' way of life.

Such degradation of their fellows was unacceptable to whites generally. The seriousness with which they viewed the problem is reflected in the fact that the Carnegie Commission Report of 1932 runs to five volumes (Carnegie Commission 1932). The government embarked upon a policy of encouraging manufacturing industries to provide a new field of employment for poor whites, and introduced labour legislation designed to protect white workers. The Industrial Conciliation Act 1924, the Wages Act 1925 and the Mines and Works Amendment Act 1926 laid the foundation upon which subsequent apartheid policies have been built, just as the Native Land Act had done in the rural areas.

Industrialisation
The South African gold mines, unlike those in other countries, lasted long enough and were sufficiently large to sustain regional economic growth. The geological conditions were such that much machinery and equipment was needed and many 'backward' linkages developed to supply the industry's needs, particularly during the First World War when South Africa suffered from shipping difficulties and the inflated costs of European suppliers. With coal nearby, the Witwatersrand was the natural location for the development of heavy industry, whilst its growing population provided a large consumer market. The Transvaal overtook the Cape as the leading industrial area of the Union during the war, and continued to increase its share of industrial output until 1934–35, when it reached 46.6 per cent; since then it has remained approximately stable. The ports gradually became the 'servants' of this virile industrial interior (McCrystal 1969, 53).

Tariff barriers, first erected in 1914, were strengthened after 1925, whilst the establishment of the South African Iron and Steel Corporation (ISCOR) in 1928 and a higher gold price further contributed to rapid expansion of manufacturing in the latter half of the 1920s and in the post-Depression 1930s. The powerful anti-cyclical effect of the goldmining industry (the demand for gold increasing in time of world recession) helped South Africa to weather the Great Depression more easily than almost any other country. The number of workers of all races in manufacturing increased from 115,000 in 1924–25 to 245,000 in 1939–40, by which time secondary industry provided 18 per cent of the national income (Bell 1973b, 27).

The 1933–45 period is seen by Hobart Houghton as one of take-off into self-sustained growth (Houghton 1973, 16–17). The general boom attracted foreign capital, and domestic capital formation also increased markedly. Employment of whites in industry rose rapidly after the Depression, and employment of other groups still more rapidly. The movement of Africans out of low-productivity subsistence farming into the modern sector of the economy was accelerated. During the Second World War, the manufacturing sector exceeded the share of mining in the national income. Manufacturing employment reached 361,000 in 1945, by which time the functioning of the South African economy was irrevocably dependent on the economic integration of all races.

Part 2
APARTHEID IDEOLOGY AND WHITE VOTERS

3
Apartheid in theory and practice

Finding political expression for Afrikaner unity after 1910
After Union, three major themes dominated South African politics for at least the next 40 years: South Africa's relationship with Britain, relations between Afrikaners and English-speakers, and policies to be pursued towards Africans ('the native problem') and 'non-whites' generally ('the colour question'). The original South African Party of Botha and Smuts was committed to reconciliation of Afrikaners and English speakers through the fostering of South African unity on the one hand and cooperation with Britain and the Empire on the other. Such healing of wounds so soon after the Anglo-Boer War was not surprisingly unacceptable to some on both sides. The more extreme English speakers formed a Unionist Party, whilst their Afrikaans counterparts formed the National Party under General Hertzog in 1914. The latter, a forerunner of today's governing National Party, was committed to gaining equality for Afrikaners in white South African society, and to asserting the primacy of South African interests *vis-à-vis* Britain and the Empire.

Ironically, it was the largely English-speaking white mine-workers who indirectly gave the Nationalists their first taste of power. To protect their privileged position the miners staged a virtual civil war in 1922, and briefly controlled the greater part of the Witwatersrand (Houghton 1971, 27). Smuts' harsh repression of the Rand rebellion, using infantry, artillery and even aircraft, strengthened support for the small Labour Party and encouraged it to enter an alliance with Hertzog's Nationalists, based essentially on their common attitudes to the 'colour question'. This pact was bolstered by the frustrations of white farmers and the mounting 'poor white' population, and was able to win 81 of the 135 seats in the 1924 General Election. A battery of protective labour legislation quickly followed, beginning with the Industrial Conciliation Act of 1924.

Even since the formation of the 'Pact' government in 1924, it is fair to say that race has been the major preoccupation of South African politics. For a brief period in the early 1930s during the acute financial crisis facing the country (largely owing to its obstinacy in remaining on the gold standard), economic issues headed the political agenda. The crisis led to the merging of the South African and National Parties to form the United Party and the 'Fusion' government of 1933, with Hertzog as Prime Minister. The latter's segregationalist policies were reflected in the Representation of Natives Act 1936, which removed black voters from the common roll in the Cape (the only province where they enjoyed this position) and substituted instead a minimal form of separate representation. In the same year, the Native Trust and Land Act (Chapter 2) in effect laid the foundations for the Bantustan policies of the 1950s.

The 'Fusion' government had broken the political unity of Afrikaner-dom. Those who regarded Smuts as an arch-imperialist formed the 'Purified' National Party, later the Herenigde (reunited) Nasionale Party (HNP) under Dr Malan. The outbreak of the Second World War at once fatally divided the United Party, when Hertzog's advocacy of South African neutrality was defeated in Parliament by 13 votes. For a few years longer, the imperial connection was to remain ascendant. The Governor-General refused Hertzog a dissolution of Parliament and he resigned from the government, which was reformed under Smuts. This created the opportunity to re-establish Afrikaner political unity, but the gap between Hertzog and the increasingly narrow and militant Afrikaner nationalism of Dr Malan's HNP proved too great to bridge. Hertzog retired altogether from politics, leaving his supporters to form the new Afrikaner Party. The latter was, however, effectively submerged by the HNP, which won 35.7 per cent of the total votes cast in the 1943 General Election, compared with a mere 1.6 per cent for the Afrikaner Party. This success established the HNP as the body which provided political expression for the fundamental unity which most Afrikaners sought, at least subconsciously. It was a unity which, given the numerical preponderance of Afrikaners in the white population, would inevitably bring electoral success.

That success came unexpectedly early in 1948, on a minority vote. The HNP and Afrikaner Party together won 41.2 per cent of all votes cast. If allowance is made for votes which would have been cast in uncontested seats, all except one of which fell to the other parties (collectively known in 1948 as the United Front), this figure falls to 39.4 per cent (Heard 1974, 40–2). None the less the HNP won 70 seats and the Afrikaner Party

9, out of a total of 150 seats. The two parties finally merged in 1951 to form the National Party, which proved to be the old HNP in all but name (Carter 1958, Chapter 9). The political unity of Afrikanerdom was complete, and the stage set for the implementation of apartheid.

The nature of apartheid

The word 'apartheid' appears to have been first used in the columns of the Nationalist newspaper *Die Burger* in 1943 (Louw 1965). Its first parliamentary use was followed on 25 January 1944 when Dr Malan, in supporting a republican motion, described the nature of the republic which he envisaged *inter alia* as follows: 'To ensure the safety of the white race and of Christian civilisation by the honest maintenance of the principles of apartheid and guardianship' (Louw 1965, translated from Afrikaans and quoted by Brookes 1968, p. 1).

Once in power, the Nationalists faced demands from the new Opposition for apartheid to be defined. A notable response came from Dr H.F. Verwoerd, then a Senator, in a Senate speech on 3 September 1948. It is appropriate to quote this source at some length given Dr Verwoerd's widespread subsequent characterisation as the prime architect of apartheid in his roles as Minister of Native Affairs in the 1950s and Prime Minister from 1958 until his assassination in 1966 (Liebenberg 1975, 428). In this early speech he claimed that

> Nobody has ever contended that the policy of apartheid should be identified with 'total segregation'. The apartheid policy has been described as what one can do in the direction of what you regard as ideal. Nobody will deny that for the Natives as well as for the European complete separation would have been the ideal if it had developed that way historically.
> (Verwoerd 1948, 234)

In practice, advocates of total segregation have never been totally absent. Certain Nationalist theorists including elements of the South African Bureau of Racial Affairs (SABRA) and some Dutch Reformed Church *predikants* (clergy), have insisted that only a complete separation of races into distinct areas can provide a lasting solution on apartheid lines. But Nationalist governments have always held this to be unrealisable, and envisaged a less tidy and more fragmented solution: separate areas for blacks, and perhaps for coloureds and Indians, where these groups would enjoy opportunities for advancement, but priority for whites in other areas, where blacks would be restricted to certain fields of employment, largely on a migrant labour basis. Social and residential segregation would be enforced everywhere, to minimise contact, but the economic dependence of South Africa on non-white labour would not be abandoned.

With regard to the last point, Dr Verwoerd emphasised that 'the non-European worker will be there to assist in the economic progress of the country'. He quoted with approval a 1942 statement by J.G. Strydom, who was to succeed Dr Malan as Prime Minister in 1954:

> [total segregation] would have been the ideal solution, but in practice it is incapable of being carried out, because quite apart from all the other differences, our own people, our farmers and thousands and tens of thousands of others, who use the services of the Natives and coloured people as labour, would never agree to it. (p. 235)

What could be effected, Dr Verwoerd explained, was territorial segregation of blacks and 'naturally, political segregation as well'. Towards the end of his speech he foresaw developments in black local government which did not actually occur until the late 1970s (Chapter 14):

> Natives will not be able to go any further within the European area than the obtaining of local government. If they have ambitions in the direction of full citizenship, then they have to go back to the areas that are theirs; but if for their own selfish interests and their own economic gain they want to stay in the Native residential areas within the European areas, then the greatest share in government which they can achieve will be local government. (p. 246)

These brief extracts from a long speech point clearly to the central and enduring contradiction of apartheid: the need for blacks to 'assist in the economic progress of the country', yet the denial of political rights outside rural 'homelands' to those same blacks who 'for their own selfish interests and their own economic gain' lived in the 'white' areas. Thus whilst the labour of blacks was admitted to be necessary for the country's development, that country could never be theirs. It is this same contradiction which for the first time became constitutionally entrenched in the new constitution of 1983, which excludes 73 per cent of South Africa's population which is black from participation in national politics, and which has been a major source of rising black frustration since then (Chapter 13).

Whilst the roots of apartheid have been shown to go back long before 1948, South African political development up to that year was not unique. The policies applied were not without parallels in white settler colonies elsewhere in Africa (Christopher 1984c, Chapter 6), allowing for the specific circumstances of each territory. The year 1948 does represent a real parting of the ways, given the emphasis on the ideal of separation. The 'partnership' policy of the Central African Federation (1953–63) envisaged cooperation between races in all economic and political fields, even if it was interpreted in practice to imply the existence of senior and junior partners (Brookfield 1957, 225; Welensky 1964). Just as the first gentle breezes of the 'wind of change' were blowing over Africa, especially west Africa, in the early post-war years, South Africa had elected a government intent upon confirming, rigidifying and regularising the segregationist policies of three centuries of white settlement. Although it was not obvious at the time, the rest of Africa was set to move in one direction and South Africa in another. After a period of relative internationalism, exemplified above all by Smuts' role in drafting the Covenant of the League of Nations, South Africa was beginning a trek into isolation reminiscent of that of the *Voortrekkers* a century before.

The implementation of apartheid

What followed the change of government in 1948 has been described by Leo Kuper (1971, 459) as 'counter-revolution'. It involved an attempt to reverse, by legislation and penal sanctions, those processes which were gradually drawing the peoples of South Africa away from plural division towards a common society. Social change was to be controlled in the interests of white domination, by a monopoly of the constitutional means of change. This included not only control of relationships between whites and other groups, but also the fragmentation of Africans by policies designed to strengthen tribal organisation and solidarity and the raising of barriers to association between blacks, coloureds and Indians.

One of the first legislative actions of the Nationalist government was the Asiatic Laws Amendment Act 1948. Smuts' attempts to resolve political conflicts centring upon Indians had proved both unpopular and unsuccessful (Chapter 11). In particular, those clauses of the Asiatic Land Tenure and Indian Representation Act 1946 extending a limited degree of representation to Indians in Natal and the Transvaal had strengthened the Nationalist cause in the 1948 election campaign. Accordingly, repeal of this franchise (which had never come into operation owing to the opposition of Indians themselves to the package contained in the 1946 Act) was enacted at the earliest possible moment by the new government.

Retrospectively this action may be viewed as the beginning of a systematic removal of non-white affairs from politics to administration. The government began to tackle both coloured and black representation in 1951, but the former proved unexpectedly difficult. The Separate Representation of Voters Bill 1951 provided for the removal of Cape coloured voters (then some 47,000 in a total electorate of 1.5 million) to a separate roll, through which they might elect four white members of the House of Assembly and two white or coloured members of the Cape Provincial Council. The validity of this legislation, passed only by the two Houses of Parliament sitting separately by simple majorities, was successfully challenged in the courts. It was only after a protracted struggle culminating in legislation to recast the Senate that the government was able to obtain the necessary two-thirds majority in a joint sitting of both Houses; the Cape coloured voters were finally removed from the common roll in 1956. The history of this measure illustrates the determination of the government to overcome all obstacles to the implementation of an apartheid plan which it regarded as a coherent and logical whole, no part of which could be sacrificed.

Meanwhile the Bantu Authorities Act 1951 had abolished the Natives Representative Council and given new powers to headmen and chiefs. This Act allowed for mergers between different tribes and provided for Bantu authorities which would be responsible for larger regions and ultimately whole territories administered under Bantu laws and customs. It was thus a forerunner of the Promotion of Self-Government Act of 1959 which reduced the many reserves to eight larger units (in the political, not geographical, sense), and appointed a commissioner to head each one and ultimately to guide his region towards self-government. Such granting of black political rights was held to render the black parliamentary representation granted in 1936[1] unnecessary, and it was abolished in the 1959 Act.

Two measures of 1950 were fundamental to the whole apartheid design. Given the artificiality of the 'coloured' population category, which in reality represents part of a continuum from the darkest to the lightest skin colour, many other measures would have been unenforceable without the passage of the Population Registration Act, which provided for the compilation of a racially classified national register. This is particularly true of the Prohibition of Mixed Marriages Act 1949 and the Immorality Amendment Act 1950. The former made only marriages between whites and non-whites illegal: there had never been more than 100 per year anyway. Section 16 of the Immorality Act, as it is usually known, prohibited extramarital sexual relations between whites and non-whites. Relations between blacks, coloureds and Indians were unaffected by these measures, which were clearly concerned primarily to preserve what was popularly but misleadingly regarded as the 'purity of the white race'.

The second major measure of 1950 was the Group Areas Act, variously described as 'the kernel of apartheid policy' (Dr Malan) and 'the cornerstone of positive apartheid' (Dr T.E. Dönges, a member of Dr Malan's first Cabinet).[2] The Act provided for the extension to the whole of South Africa and to all races of the land apportionment principle long existing in the African reserves. In practice it affected urban areas (Chapter 10), as the countryside was already largely divided. Closely related pieces of legislation were the Resettlement of Natives Act 1954, which resulted in 100,000 blacks being removed from squatter camps in the western suburbs of Johannesburg and resettled in Meadowlands, and the Natives Urban Areas Amendment Act 1955, which became known as the 'Locations in the Sky Act' because it ended the large-scale accommodation of non-white servants on the top floors of buildings (Selby 1973, 246).

As well as controlling the location of blacks within the cities, the government was anxious to control black urbanisation more tightly: the Smuts government had been much criticised for failing to do so in its final years of office. The Abolition of Passes and Coordination of Documents Act 1952 streamlined the existing 'pass laws' and provided for a new reference book to be carried by all African men.

To minimise racial contact (and thereby, it was argued, minimise friction), all races were compelled by the Reservation of Separate Amenities Act 1953 to use separate public amenities in every sphere of life including eating and drinking, transport, entertainment, recreation and personal hygiene. The Act ensured, necessarily given the minimal facilities available to blacks, that it would henceforth be no defence to plead inequality in the provision of such amenities.

Mention must also be made of two educational measures in the 1950s. The Bantu Education Act 1953 placed all African education, which had formerly been mainly in the hands of subsidised churches and mission societies, under the control of the state. This produced an education system geared to the perpetuation of tribalism and the pre-industrial way of life, on the grounds that 'There is no place for the Native in the European community above the level of certain forms of labour' (Dr Verwoerd, quoted by Brookes 1968, p. 57). Edgar Brookes, a veteran liberal opponent of apartheid, describes Bantu education as:

51

the only education system in the world designed to restrict the productivity of its pupils in the national economy to lowly and subservient tasks, to render them non-competitive in that economy, to fix them mentally in a tribal world. (Brookes 1968, 57)

The Orwellianly titled Extension of University Education Act 1959 was to apartheid planners 'a logical development of the principle of ethnic self-sufficiency' (de Klerk 1975, 243), but to its many opponents a denial of academic freedom. The Act closed the 'white' universities, except for individually permitted exceptions, to all Africans, coloureds and Indians. These groups would henceforth attend their own institutions for which rules are prescribed in the Act.

This growing volume of apartheid legislation ran directly counter to the aspirations and demands of blacks, coloureds and Indians, who found themselves supported by an increasingly sympathetic world opinion. The government armed itself with a powerful battery of legislation to suppress the political activities of these population groups, and to prevent political cooperation between whites and non-whites. Its main legislative instruments were the Suppression of Communism Act 1950, the Public Safety Act 1953, the Criminal Law Amendment Act 1953, and the Unlawful Organisations Act 1960. These measures created a wide range of offences punishable with severe penalties. The administration was given a discretion in the application of many of their provisions which was both extremely broad and beyond the reach of the courts. The Suppression of Communism Act defined communism in terms wide enough to enable action to be taken against almost anyone of radical inclinations. The Criminal Law Amendment Act was used to break the passive resistance campaign of 1952–53 against unjust laws. The trade union movement was intimidated by the process of 'naming' individuals who were thereafter not allowed to pursue their occupations or professions. The Public Safety Act gave the government power to declare a state of emergency, which it did after the Sharpeville massacre in 1960, and again in 1985 in the face of prolonged violence in the east Rand and the eastern Cape (Chapter 17). The Unlawful Organisations Act made it possible to proscribe organisations deemed to prejudice the safety of the state even if they were not communist. In 1960, again after Sharpeville, the government banned both the African National Congress and the Pan-Africanist Congress, both of which have remained unlawful organisations since then.

Such legislation inevitably had the effect of driving most non-white and inter-racial political activity underground. The new leadership which emerged was more radical and less amenable to cooperation than its predecessors such as Chief Albert Luthuli, sometime President-General of the ANC and a winner of the Nobel peace prize. After it was banned from peaceful protest and resistance, the ANC resorted to violence. By the mid-1960s the government had virtually ended African political activity and almost all recognised leaders of the previous decade were either in gaol or refugees (de Villiers 1971, 413). Such methods could hardly be expected, however, to bring lasting peace or stability (Chapter 17).

Social restructuring and applied geography

By 1960, if not earlier, the government's opponents were no longer in any doubt about the nature of apartheid. The legislative energy and sense of purpose of successive Nationalist governments carried through what amounted to a radical restructuring of South African society in the course of less than one generation. 'Never in history', claims de Klerk (1975, 241), 'have so few legislated so programmatically, thoroughly and religiously, in such a short time, for so many divergent groups, cultures and traditions, than the nationalist Afrikaners of the second half of the twentieth century.' To most people outside South Africa, Nationalist motives have been simply perceived as the perpetuation of white power and privilege, together with the preservation of the Afrikaner nation and culture. Neither perception is inaccurate, but nor is it sufficient: strange as it may seem, it is undoubtedly true that the political, religious, cultural and intellectual leaders of Afrikanerdom for the most part viewed the implementation of apartheid with a high sense of purpose, vocation and idealism. Hence de Klerk (1975, 241), in commenting on the massive volume of criticism the world has directed against the 'tyranny of apartheid', says that

> It was ineffective because it did not understand that the manifest harshness, the patent injustices, were all the oblique but necessary results of a most rational, most passionate, most radical will to restructure the world according to a vision of justice; all with a view to lasting peace, progress and prosperity.

Such a vision was deeply rooted in what Moodie (1975) has rightly called 'Afrikaner civil religion'. It is a vision which has strayed far from the theology of Calvin to whom Afrikaners have traditionally appealed (Chapter 4), but which has none the less fuelled the fundamental restructuring of South African society.

A major element of that restructuring has been a state-directed reorganisation of the spatial structure of society, economy and policy which David Smith (1982a, 1) has described as 'the most ambitious contemporary exercise in applied geography'. The results of this exercise may be viewed in terms of three spatial scales of segregation. The *microscale*, commonly termed 'petty apartheid' in South Africa itself, involves segregation in the use of amenities. It is at this scale that the earliest changes occurred, such as the desegregation of post offices and the opening of some parks and theatres to all races in the 1970s, but such changes have been uneven over the country as a whole, as many of them fall within the powers of municipal or provincial authorities rather than central government; others may, depending upon the legislative framework, depend on the policy decisions of private entrepreneurs. Such reforms have been widely labelled 'cosmetic', and it is indeed true that 'petty apartheid' is not essential to the apartheid design. Its rationale is supposedly the avoidance of friction between culturally incompatible groups, but ideally such friction would anyway be reduced as other parts of the overall plan reduced black population numbers in 'white' areas, thus lessening the perceived need for micro-scale segregation.

More fundamental to apartheid planning is *meso-scale segregation*, which is achieved primarily through the Group Areas Act and related measures (Chapter 10). If it is true, as social geographers have suggested, that 'the greater the degree of difference between the spatial distributions of groups within an urban area, the greater their social distance from each other' (Peach 1975, 1), then South Africa's enforced urban social segregation does indeed provide an effective instrument for maintaining group divisions. It is not difficult to see why this should be so. In the first place, much voluntary association takes place at the level of neighbourhood or suburban community, through sports and social clubs, churches and other organisations. Even where, as in some at least of South Africa's churches there is a desire for more inter-racial contact, this is made more difficult in practice by transport and other problems in the 'apartheid city'; as a result, joint worship or social events require careful planning and are unlikely to occur often. When they do, the very character of apartheid society may tend to render them contrived or self-conscious.

Secondly, urban social segregation is vital to apartheid planning because it provides a territorial basis for segregated schools and hospitals. The former are particularly crucial to the maintenance of divisions in a plural society, as the Northern Ireland experience has shown, and both are regarded as an important element of their way of life by most whites.

54

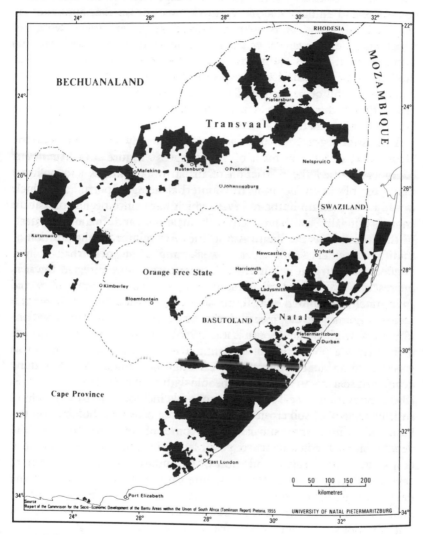

Fig. 3.1   Bantu areas, 1955

The third role of meso-scale segregation is political, in that it provides a territorial basis for local government (Chapter 13). In this way blacks, coloureds and Indians may be granted some measure of autonomy at least at local levels, whilst whites continue to govern their own areas which include the central business district and major industrial and commercial districts. The financial corollary of this is the expectation that each local authority, irrespective of the income levels of its inhabitants, will be basically self-financing, thus perpetuating inequality rather than reducing it by some form of redistributive mechanism at local, regional or national level.

A basis for segregation at the *macro-scale* already existed in 1948, for blacks at least, in the form of the reserves (Figure 3.1). Apartheid planners justified the restriction of urban opportunities and political rights for blacks by pointing to counterbalancing opportunities which would be opened up in the reserves, which have since been successively known officially as 'Bantustans', 'homelands' and 'national states'. Within these areas the Bantu Authorities Act reinforced the position of traditional chiefs and elders, weakening that of urban-trained intellectuals. African cultural development was to be directed towards the reserves and around tribal tradition. In terms of economic policy, the government appointed the Tomlinson Commission to report on the socio-economic development of the reserves. The Commission put forward a detailed plan (South Africa 1955) whereby the reserves, which then carried a population of 3.6 million Africans mostly dependent at least to some degree on outside earnings or remittances, would be developed so as to carry 8 million people with only partial dependence on labour migration. The Tomlinson proposals included land-use planning and the control of soil erosion; the creation of economic holdings on the basis of a minimum subsistence income of £60 per annum; the development of irrigation where possible; the introduction of commercial crops, especially sugar and fibres, in suitable areas; afforestation, especially in north-east Zululand; intensive mineral surveys and the development of mining where feasible; and the establishment of manufacturing industry within the reserves, employing outside capital initially, but with progressive 'Africanisation'. Tomlinson also proposed the creation of towns both in the heart of the reserves and on their fringes, where Africans could commute to jobs in 'white' areas.

By no means all these proposals were accepted by the government, not least because of the expense involved. This is hardly surprising: given that the reserves had been intended as subsistence areas for those blacks

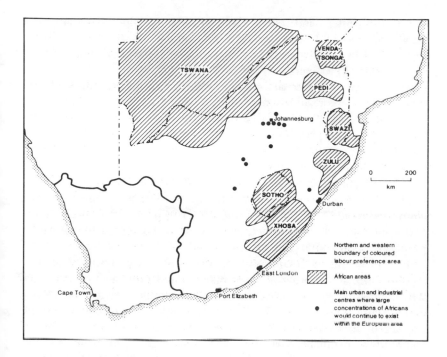

Fig. 3.2   Consolidation proposals of the Tomlinson Commission

not involved in the modern economy, they were inevitably amongst the least accessible areas of South Africa, and their existing infrastructure was negligible. To implement the Tomlinson proposals so as to create significant economic development and employment opportunities at all levels for blacks would have been prohibitively expensive. Yet not to do so was to undermine the moral basis of the whole apartheid design, and to leave the reserves as mere labour reservoirs, increasingly over-populated areas which offered negligible opportunities, economic or political, for meaningful black advance. This is a dilemma which has remained with successive Nationalist governments up to the present day (Chapter 9), and is in no way resolved by the granting of 'independence' to some of these territories.

The Commission further proposed major changes in South Africa's political geography. Ultimately, it proposed that all Africans should be removed from west of a line known as the 'Eiselen line' (after the administrator who devised it in 1955) in the Cape Province, leaving an area in the western and central Cape where only coloureds, whites and small numbers of Indians would reside and work. At the time some 180,000 blacks, mostly temporary migrants, lived west of this line. Such a policy did begin to operate in 1962 (Chapter 12).

Much more fundamental, however, was Tomlinson's recommendation concerning the consolidation of the existing fragmented reserves into seven blocks or 'heartlands' around 'historico-logical' (sic) centres (Figure 3.2). This proposal was rejected outright by the government. It would in any case have required the incorporation of the British High Commission territories of Bechuanaland, Basutoland and Swaziland into the Union, which the political course followed by South Africa after 1948 rendered it impossible for Britain to accept. The government instead continued to add land to the reserves in terms of the 1936 Native Trust and Land Act, which became the basis for its homeland consolidation proposals in the 1970s (Chapter 14).

The problems and contradictions presented by macro-scale segregation of blacks were clearly formidable, and remain so in a country with increasing spatial concentration of economic activity and clearly defined core areas (Chapter 7). This same geography of economic activity presented an even greater problem for macro-scale segregation of coloureds and Indians, both of whom were already highly urbanised and occupationally integrated into the 'white' economy. Successive governments temporised over this problem, creating 'parallel' representative institutions of a largely consultative nature for these groups (Rhoodie 1973). Only in 1983 was it conceded that the reality of coloured and Indian spatial and economic integration with whites made political integration inevitable (Chapter 13).

4
Afrikaners and Englishmen: language, religion and *volk*

Language is one of the most formative influences in the growth of nationalism across the globe. As such it has been both a unifying and a dividing force in different states, depending upon the linguistic composition and spatial distribution of their populations. Religion is less obviously associated with nationalism, but examples are not hard to find, including the recent resurgence of strongly Islamic régimes. Examples of religion as a divisive force are legion: the Indian sub-continent, Lebanon, Northern Ireland and Sudan are some of the more prominent instances. Elsewhere religion often plays a secondary role, reinforcing linguistic differences, as in Canada, Belgium and Yugoslavia. Both language and religion may be instruments of state policies aimed at creating or reinforcing national unity, which may involve attempts to suppress minority cultures as in the Soviet Union. Alternatively, political advantage may be perceived in the strengthening of divisions, as in South Africa itself where the promotion of tribal languages and culture amongst blacks has been part of the philosophy of 'separate development'.

Although no similar emphasis is placed upon separate development of Afrikaans- and English-speaking South Africans, the cohesion of the former has led to their being dubbed 'the white tribe of Africa' (Harrison 1981). Language and religion have been exceptionally vital forces both fostering Afrikaner nationalism and giving it expression. To these influences have been added institutional forces which have fostered the cultural, economic and political unity of Afrikanerdom. For South Africa's English speakers, language and religion have played a different role, emphasising links outside South Africa to Britain, the Commonwealth and with western culture generally. Whilst it may be argued that English-speaking whites have developed ethnic consciousness in opposition to Afrikaners, in-group identification among English speakers is tempered by a broader South African identity, by recognition of a community of political interests with Afrikaners as fellow whites in a largely black population, and by differences within the English-speaking population in terms of socio-economic status, religion and lifestyle (Schlemmer 1976, 96, 130). Language in particular has given to South Africa's English speakers a greater internationalism than is possessed by Afrikaners, whose relative isolation has led to the stereotype of a '*laager* mentality'.[1]

The Afrikaans language

The Afrikaners are descendants of the only white emigrant group from the Old World to evolve a language of their own in Africa. This underlines the fact that they are, as they regard themselves, ''*n Afrika-horende volk*' (a people belonging to Africa). Today Afrikaans is accepted by linguists as the latest independent offshoot of the family of Indo-Germanic languages. Dutch is the main source of its 300,000-word vocabulary, but there are many words and expressions of English, German, French and to a lesser extent Portuguese, Malay, Hottentot and Bushman origin. Afrikaans is today the home language of 57 per cent of white South Africans and 86 per cent of coloureds; the latter are almost as numerous as the Afrikaners themselves, and are likely to become more so given their higher birth rates (Tables 4.1 and 4.2). The political significance of Afrikaans is, however, primarily related to its close association with Afrikaner nationalism.

Afrikaans was the home language of the Dutch burghers and the normal language of intercourse at the Cape well before the end of the eighteenth century. Dutch was regarded as the cultural language, and Afrikaans was seen as inferior, partly because it had become the language of the coloureds. It was first used consciously in written form about 1795. English superseded Dutch after Holland finally ceded the Cape to Britain in 1814, but Afrikaans began to appear regularly in print after the attainment of press freedom in 1828. Dutch remained the official language of the northern republics, but there too Afrikaans was the everyday language. Remarkably, given the distances involved and poor communications, Afrikaans as it developed at the Cape did not differ materially from Afrikaans on the frontier (de Klerk 1975, 16).

The formation in the Cape of *Die Genootskap van Regte Afrikaanders* (the Association of True Afrikaners) in 1875 has been officially regarded as the beginning of the language, and its centenary was accordingly celebrated in 1975. The society strove for the full recognition of Afrikaans and the unity of Afrikaners in all parts of South Africa. The

Table 4.1: Home languages of white South Africans, 1951–80

	1951 %	1960 %	1970 %	1980 %
Afrikaans	57.0	58.0	56.9	57.0
English	39.3	37.3	37.2	38.9
Afrikaans and				
English	1.4	1.4	1.0	–
German	0.7	1.1	1.4	0.9
Portuguese			1.1	1.3
	1.6	2.2		
Others			1.8	1.9

Source: Based on sample census tabulations.

Table 4.2: Afrikaans and English as home languages amongst whites, coloureds and Indians, 1980

	Afrikaans	%	English	%
Whites	2,581,080	53.2	1,763,320	63.3
Coloureds	2,251,860	46.4	324,360	11.6
Indians	15,500	0.3	698,940	25.1
Total	4,848,440	100.0	2,786,520	100.0

Source: Based on sample census tabulations.

issue shortly afterwards of a periodical, *Die Afrikaanse Patriot*, was followed by the publication of books and pamphlets. This literary movement petered out but was succeeded by a much stronger language movement and literary revival in the early twentieth century which produced several notable poets. In 1914 Afrikaans was adopted instead of Dutch in Cape schools (Fisher 1969, 266), and an Afrikaans dictionary and approved style of spelling was adopted in 1917. In 1925, a year after its election, the 'Pact' government of Hertzog secured a unanimous vote in the House of Assembly to replace Dutch with Afrikaans for official purposes. Since then Afrikaans and English have remained the only official languages of South Africa. The Hertzog government applied a language policy which provided greater opportunities for the advancement of Afrikaans than Dutch had ever enjoyed. It was promoted as a technical and scientific medium, and the requirement of bilingualism in the civil service – a dead-letter since its inception in 1912 – was now applied, giving Afrikaners a considerable advantage as more of them than of English-speaking whites were bilingual. The 1930s also witnessed a new Afrikaans literary awareness, associated with the emergence of major poets including N.P. van Wyk Louw. The first translation of the Bible into Afrikaans appeared only in 1933, owing to opposition from the Dutch Reformed Church until about 1920.

Afrikaans was essentially associated with a rural way of life in the early twentieth century. As late as 1923, Dr Malan was urging that urban Afrikaners be resettled in the *platteland* (Moodie 1975, 49), but a small group of Afrikaners on the Witwatersrand had by then discovered the positive potential of urbanisation. In 1919 they had founded the Afrikaner Broederbond, the early activities of which were principally aimed at securing Afrikaners as equal to English speakers in the social and economic life of the city. Their progress was necessarily slow, and for urban Afrikaners in the 1920s and 1930s 'towns were pre-eminently the places of the oppressor', many attributing their rural poverty to the financial power of the English and Jewish groups (Welsh 1971, 202). The contempt shown by many English-speaking urban-dwellers for Afrikaans language and culture was bitterly resented and contributed to the growth of nationalism. English dominated even the former Trekker capitals of Pietermaritzburg, Pretoria and Bloemfontein. Continuing Afrikaner urbanisation and occupational mobility have changed this situation dramatically since the 1930s, although Afrikaners are still under-represented in the towns. No urban–rural breakdown on a language basis is available, but church membership (Table 4.3) is a guide. In 1980 some 43 per cent of urban whites were members of one of the Dutch Reformed churches; this probably understates the percentage of Afrikaans speakers, a minority of whom belong to other churches or none at all. Afrikaners remain dominant in the rural areas, where 63.2 per cent of whites belonged to the Dutch Reformed churches in 1980.

Today Afrikaans has an assured position. It is established throughout the state school system as a first or second language, and is the language used in five white universities and a major medium of instruction in a sixth. Afrikaans is increasingly the language of politics and government as well as of Afrikaner nationalism. Within the National Party itself hardly a word of English is heard in a congress or branch meeting: the atmosphere is that of a 'family', reflecting traditional Afrikaner ways, though this may change as the party comes to rely increasingly on English votes (Chapter 5). In commercial and industrial life, the use of

Table 4.3: White church adherents, 1980

Church	Urban	%	Rural	%	Total	%
Nederduits Gereformeerde Kerk	1,414,920	35.4	278,720	53.0	1,693,640	39.8
Gereformeerde Kerk	104,940	2.6	23,420	4.5	128,360	3.0
Nederduitsch Hervormde Kerk	200,320	5.0	46,020	8.7	246,340	5.8
Anglican	424,940	10.6	31,080	5.9	456,020	10.7
Methodist	386,040	9.6	28,040	5.3	414,080	9.7
Presbyterian	120,820	3.0	8,100	1.5	128,920	3.0
Roman Catholic	375,380	9.4	18,260	3.5	393,640	9.2
Apostolic Faith Mission	109,900	2.7	16,020	3.0	125,920	3.0
Other Christians	514,340	12.9	52,300	9.9	566,640	13.3
Jewish/Hebrew	118,380	3.0	840	0.2	119,220	2.8
Other non-Christians	25,460	0.6	1,580	0.3	27,040	0.6
No religion/objection to stating religion	206,560	5.2	21,720	4.1	228,280	5.4
Total	4,002,000	100.0	526,100	100.0	4,528,100	100.0

Source: Based on a 5 per cent sample of 1980 census results.

Afrikaans has grown considerably with the rise of Afrikaner capitalism, but remains clearly in second place.

In the minds of the Afrikaners themselves, the language is closely associated with their wider historic struggle against the British, and what they see as their present struggle to survive as a distinct nation or *volk*. Thus Afrikaans continues consciously to assert itself against English, a major international language with which it has to coexist in the same country. This is clearly shown by the government's attitude to black education. For some time it insisted on the use of Afrikaans as well as English as a medium of instruction in all black schools. When homeland governments were allowed to choose their own language of instruction, all chose English. The government none the less persisted with its dual-medium approach in black township schools outside the homelands, and it was this insistence on the use of Afrikaans – a third language to most blacks – which was the immediate catalyst of the 1976 Soweto riots. Eventually the government was forced to concede on this issue, but its persistence reflected the relative insecurity of Afrikaners. Their language reinforces both isolation and nationhood; it is used both defensively against the inherent strength of English, and yet as an instrument and symbol of political domination. Both elements were apparent in 1976.

The community institutions of Afrikaner nationalism

The National Party has long benefited from *verzuiling* – the insulated nature of Afrikaans sub-culture, in which every institution of the Afrikaner community reinforced its nationalism (Nolutshungu 1972, 452): the schools, the Dutch Reformed churches, local officials, storekeepers, voluntary societies and cultural organisations all worked consciously or unconsciously towards building a remarkable degree of cohesion and single-mindedness. The political expression of this has been an effective ethnic mobilisation at the ballot box (Adam and Giliomee 1979) which has guaranteed Nationalist rule since 1948. There are strong signs that this may be breaking up in the 1980s (Chapter 5), but it is important to examine the nature of the major institutions of Afrikanerdom in order to understand what has supported the National Party hitherto and what is now at stake.

The spearhead of ethnic mobilisation was the *Afrikaner Broederbond* whose influence grew rapidly from the early 1930s. The Broederbond became a secret society in 1922, only three years after its foundation (see above), but is paradoxically one of the best-known Afrikaner institutions. It had some 12,000 members in 1977, organised in 800 local cells across the country (Pirie, Rogerson and Beavon 1980). Owing to the secret nature of the Broederbond it has never been possible accurately to determine its influence on, and precise role in, Afrikaner nationalism. The Broederbond itself claims to be a national rather than a political organisation, and a one-man government commission of enquiry into secret organisations appointed in 1964 accepted this, describing the Broederbond as 'a service organisation intended to serve the Afrikaner, and its field of operations is the sphere of work of the Afrikaner people as a separate, historical, Protestant-Christian language and cultural community' (South Africa 1965). It is viewed very differently by its opponents, who have included Hertzog and Smuts. The latter regarded the Broederbond as a dangerous political organisation which was operating in secret in order, *inter alia*, to promote the interests of one section of the population at the expense of the other (i.e. English speakers), and which was attempting to capture key positions in the country with a view to influencing national policy.[2]

Smuts' view is supported by two recent exposés of the Broederbond (Wilkins and Strydom 1979; Serfontein 1979), in which it is apparent that the Broederbond seeks to dominate all other Afrikaans organisations and is effectively their governing agency. It is particularly active in politics and education: its membership includes most Nationalist MPs and cabinet ministers, and numerous university lecturers, professors and principals, headmasters and schoolmasters (membership is limited to male Afrikaans-speaking Protestants). According to Serfontein (1979, 162), 'the three Afrikaans churches are completely in the hands of the Broederbond' and almost 1000 *predikants* belong either to it or to the *Ruiterwag*. The latter is a fully-fledged junior secret organisation functioning separately but with a similar organisational structure under tight Broederbond control.

Contrary to its self-proclaimed image, Wilkins and Strydom (1979, 443) claim from documentary evidence that the Broederbond spends remarkably little time on purely cultural affairs. Few major Afrikaans authors today belong to the organisation. The reason, perhaps, is that another organisation, the *Federasie van Afrikaanse Kultuurverenigings* (FAK), the Federation of Afrikaans Cultural Organisations, was founded on Broederbond initiative in 1929 to look after Afrikaner cultural interests. By 1937 the FAK had over 300 affiliated organisations, one-third of them language and cultural organisations and the rest made up of church councils and other church organisations, charitable groups, student and youth groups, scientific study circles and educational organisations (de Villiers 1971, 398). The FAK stimulated interest and pride in Afrikaans literature and art, and had important influence on education. It also encouraged parallel movements to existing English organisations; thus the Voortrekkers were a counterpart of the scout and guide movement. This contributed to Afrikaner separateness in fields where united endeavour could have contributed to a wider South Africanism.

In the 1920s, between 30 and 50 per cent of all Afrikaners were in or close to the 'poor white' category (Chapter 3). To support Afrikaans language and culture the FAK had almost inevitably to attempt to reinforce the economic position of the Afrikaners. In any case 'culture' to the Afrikaner has a far broader, more sociological connotation than its normal English usage, embracing the ideology of a nation as expressed in every sphere of national life. Thus the FAK became involved on a wide front, creating agencies in all aspects of Afrikaner life. Its economic role was most important in the years immediately before and after the Second World War when it helped Afrikaners to enter more fully than previously into the industrial and business life of South Africa, and launched two further organisations with fundamentally economic aims, the *Reddingsdaadbond* and the *Economic Institute*, in 1939, at the Afrikaans Economic Congress in Bloemfontein.

The Reddingsdaadbond (Rescue Action League) was founded to save Afrikaners from penury and train them to take their place in industrial society. Much of its early success was inspired by another FAK project, the centenary celebrations of the Great Trek, and the task of the Reddingsdaadbond was indeed to aid and direct the second great trek of Afrikaners, to the cities. During the Second World War in particular the Reddingsdaadbond acted as an employment agency which found places for young Afrikaners to work and gain experience. At the same time it sought to keep the Afrikaner within his own cultural tradition of church, language and *volk* amidst alien elements. The Reddingsdaadbond also sought, together with the Economic Institute, to mobilise the capital resources and purchasing power of Afrikaners, giving loans and advice to those starting businesses and persuading people to pool their capital and underwrite Afrikaner businesses. The greatest success of the Reddingsdaadbond was in the *dorps* (country towns), where almost all business enterprise was in English or Jewish hands in 1939, but most of it had been transferred to Afrikaners by 1950.

A third organisation, the *Institute for Christian-National Education*, was born at a FAK-organised conference in 1939. The Institute insisted on mother-tongue instruction, encouraging the establishment of single-medium as opposed to dual- or parallel-medium schools wherever the National Party came to power, thus separating children of the two language groups. The educational philosophy of the Institute emphasised amongst other things a view of life 'based on Holy Scripture and formulated in the Articles of Faith in our three Afrikaans churches' and 'love for everything that is our own, with special reference to our country, our language, our history and our culture' (Carter 1958, 262).

The FAK itself had become less influential by the late 1950s. This was partly a reflection of its own success: although still economically inferior to English speakers, Afrikaners had greatly strengthened their economic position by 1945, helped by wartime expansion as well as the organisations founded to help them. Even more important, perhaps, was the victory of the National Party in 1948, when political power began to reinforce economic progress (Bunting 1969, Chapter 14). A 'great leap forward' took place as Nationalist governments encouraged Afrikaner penetration of commerce, mining and manufacturing, to the extent that by 1970 Afrikaners controlled 40 per cent of total invested capital in manufacturing industry, 37 per cent of uranium, 32 per cent of asbestos and 20 per cent of coal production, although still only 9 per cent of gold production (Holzner 1970, 485). As Moodie (1975, 207) comments, 'Despite its rural origins, the Afrikaner civil religion adapted surprisingly easily to urban industrial life.'

The Dutch Reformed Churches and Apartheid

Probably no Protestant Church in any country has a stronger and more pervasive contemporary influence than that of the Dutch Reformed Church (DRC) of South Africa on the Afrikaner people. In the time of the *Voortrekkers*, Boer families journeyed for days to the *nachtmaal* (communion service) which brought together isolated and scattered settlers for a week or more, perhaps two or three times a year. Today Sunday observance in a South African *dorp* remains an important unifying influence as farm families and townspeople converge on the open square in front of the Dutch Reformed Church. For many Afrikaners the church is a focal point in their culture and the religious expression of their nationalism, just as the National Party is the political expression. The DRC has always been closely linked with the distinctive spirit of the Afrikaners. Its *predikants* shared their hardships during the Anglo-Boer War and the reconstruction which followed. They participated actively in the growth of Afrikaner nationalism, and its intensification in the 1930s and 1940s led the Afrikaner churches to withdraw from cooperation with English-language churches. Such was the opposition of DRC *predikants* to South African participation in the Second World War that there were not nearly enough of them to minister to the Afrikaner troops. Since the National Party came to power there has been a close relationship between church and state which is in marked contrast to the opposition of most English-language churches to apartheid.

There are not one but three Dutch Reformed churches in South Africa, with over 2 million white members or adherents (Table 4.3). Over 80 per cent of these belong to the Nederduits Gereformeerde Kerk (NGK) which has eleven regional synods and over 1100 white congregations. It also has daughter churches for other race groups: the NG Sendingkerk (mission church) in Suid-Afrika with 678,000 coloured members or adherents in 1980, and the NGK in Afrika which claimed the allegiance of 1.1 million blacks in 1980. The Nederduitsch Hervormde Kerk (NHK) was originally established in the Transvaal in 1853 to care for the trekkers with whom the parent church had lost touch.

It became the state church of the South African Republic and retained this status in the Transvaal until 1910. It did not arise out of theological differences and remains broadly similar in approach to the NGK. The smallest of the three, the Gereformeerde Kerk (GK), is also the most fundamentalist. It was formed in 1859 as a conscious breakaway from the parent church in the Cape, and is centred at Potchefstroom in the Transvaal. Although small in numbers, it has been disproportionately influential, partly because a high proportion of its members go into education and the ministry. The GK has traditionally been more truly Calvinist than the NGK, and its attitudes have sometimes been confused with those of the NGK. Hexham (1974) argues that it was the GK rather than the NGK that really provided the theological basis for Afrikaner nationalism.

Separate development within the NGK has a long history. Several synods from 1829 onwards refused to allow race to determine church practice, but social pressures eventually proved stronger than synodical resolutions (de Gruchy 1979, 8). In 1857 the synod considered it desirable that 'our members from the Heathen be received and absorbed into our existing congregations wherever possible' but permitted exceptions to accommodate 'the weakness of some' (i.e. whites not prepared for joint worship). Although mixed congregations continued to exist, what was meant in 1857 to be an exception became the rule. The resolution also committed the church to the practice of separate ministry which subsequently led to the establishment of the Sendingkerk in 1881, and later the NGK in Afrika and the tiny Indian Reformed Church, as well as mission churches elsewhere in southern Africa.

Since 1948 the Dutch Reformed churches have enjoyed close access to the policy-makers of the state. Their members include a majority of members of the House of Assembly and the provincial councils, and they virtually control many town councils. The majority of white government employees, including the police and the military, also belong to the Afrikaans churches. The NGK has also traditionally had considerable influence over the black and coloured members of its daughter churches, which are heavily subsidised by the parent body. Such an assured position, and the access it brings to the corridors of power, have made the NGK an important factor in South Africa's political development. In the 1950s all three Dutch Reformed churches 'were almost constantly busy trying to justify, reconcile and pronounce on the matter of apartheid and the scriptures' (de Klerk 1975, 252). In a series of conferences, reports and statements various church bodies concluded, though not without anguish at times, that the policy of separate development could be accepted as a healthy basis for coexistence, and one with scriptural justification.

An early indication of the nature of church–state relationships came in 1952. The Federal Mission Council of the three Afrikaans churches had met at Bloemfontein in 1950, and sought to develop a comprehensive African policy. Amongst other things, it had agreed that Africans must be gradually eliminated from European industrial life, and integrated into a new industrial system in their own territories, where they should gradually become self-governing. The latter was ahead of official policy at the time, whilst the revolution in white lifestyles implied by withdrawal of black labour from the modern economy was certainly not contemplated. Government pressure on churches to modify their stance succeeded in 1952, when it was made clear that any withdrawal of black labour would be a very long-term process, taking perhaps 50 or 100 years.

A decade of such scriptural and moral support was briefly but dramatically ended at the Cottesloe Conference in Johannesburg in December 1960. This discussion between the World Council of Churches and its eight South African member churches, including the NGK of the Cape and the Transvaal, came to conclusions which seemed to be a complete rejection of what the Afrikaans churches had previously sanctioned as being in accordance with scripture. The Cottesloe resolutions stated, *inter alia*, that urban blacks should not be denied home-ownership and participation in the government, that migrant labour had a disintegrating effect on African family life, which Christianity was inherently concerned to safeguard; that coloureds could not be denied direct representation in Parliament; that no biblical grounds existed for the prohibition of mixed marriages, and that no one should be excluded from any church on grounds of race or colour.

All this came as a considerable shock to the Prime Minister, Dr Verwoerd. He responded 'magisterially' (de Klerk 1975, 284), calling the Dutch Reformed theologians to order and reminding them of the high purpose of apartheid. For the most part they obediently recanted, explaining as best they could how it had all happened, laying much emphasis on the shadow of the Sharpeville tragedy only months before Cottesloe.

The subsequent position of the NGK on race and related issues has been set forth fully in two major synodical documents (Dutch Reformed Church 1966, 1975). From these it is clear that the NGK rejects racial injustice and discrimination in principle, but accepts the policy of separate development. A distinction is drawn between 'the blatant racism of apartheid and the anticipated blessings of separate development' (de Gruchy 1979, 73). This has led to misunderstanding and false hopes internationally, for whenever the NGK has spoken out against racism, many have presumed it to be an attack on government policy, which is not necessarily the case. The NGK believes that the policy of separate development is not inherently contradicted by scripture, and that the idea of diversity in the Bible (as for example in Genesis 11, 6 and 9: the Tower of Babel) lends some credence to the policy. But the NGK is equally emphatic that separate development must be pursued according to the biblical norms of justice and love. It has tended, however, to shy away from the practical implications of this; thus de Gruchy (1979, 74–5) notes that the original draft of the 1974 report presented to the synod was 'far bolder in its prophetic stance and more consistent in its application of scriptural norms to socio-political realities', but political pragmatism apparently triumphed and the final report 'lost its teeth and cutting edge'.

There have been several signs of a theological shift in recent years. As long ago as 1966 a report to the NGK General Synod described migrant labour as: 'an evil which rages thus in life of the Bantu population must necessarily affect the whole social and religious life of all the races in our fatherland' (Dutch Reformed Church 1966). Such wording is characteristic in its Afrikaner terms of reference and its implied condemnation of the operation rather than the inherent evils of apartheid policies. More fundamental was the publication in 1982 of an open letter in *Die Kerkbode*, the official journal of the NGK, condemning apartheid as unscriptural, and signed by 123 Dutch Reformed clerics and theologians, including at least 40 ministers of conservative rural congregations. The letter demanded the union of the NGK and its daughter churches. It stated that the migrant labour system, low black wages, poor housing and inferior education, and the laws concerning mixed marriages, race classification and group areas could not be reconciled with biblical demands for justice and human dignity.

The Western Cape Synod gave some official sanction to such views the following year. It resolved that the Mixed Marriages Act and section 16 of the Immorality Act (which forbids intercourse between white and non-white) were unscriptural and harmful to human dignity. According to press reports in October 1983, the synod also accepted that apartheid did not have a biblical foundation and that any attempt to present separate development as if it were laid down by the Bible should be disowned by the NGK (SAIRR 1984, 628).

Such tentative signs of change have been insufficient to prevent increasing isolation of the Afrikaans churches within both South African and world Christianity. The NHK withdrew from the World Council of Churches in March 1961, having dissociated itself from the Cottesloe resolutions. The GK and NGK soon followed. In 1978 the NGK approved an earlier tentative decision to break with the Reformed churches in the Netherlands. None of the Afrikaans churches belongs to the South African Council of Churches (SACC) although the growing rift between the NGK and its daughter churches was reflected by the admission to the SACC in 1975 of the NGK in Afrika, after its General Synod had decided for the first time to reject apartheid. It was followed in October 1982 by the NG Sendingkerk, which declared the NGK guilty of 'heresy and idolatry' in its support for apartheid, and voted to abandon all reference to the NGK as the 'mother church'.

This break between 'mother' and 'daughter' churches was dramatically symbolised by the actions of the World Alliance of Reformed Churches (WARC) at its 1982 meeting in Ottawa. A minister of the NG Sendingkerk, Dr Allan Boesak, was elected President of the WARC for five years, whereas the NGK and NHK were suspended from membership for the 'heresy' of apartheid. Three conditions were imposed for their readmission:

(i) Black Christians should no longer be excluded, especially from Holy Communion;
(ii) the adoption of a formal, 'unequivocal' statement rejecting apartheid;
(iii) the provision of 'concrete support, in word and deed [for] those who suffer under the system of apartheid'.

The open-ended nature of the third condition made the churches suspect that readmission to the WARC was impossible whatever (within the possibilities realistically open to them) they were willing to do.[3]

Later the same year, the NHK withdrew from the WARC rather than renounce racial segregation, whilst the NGK responded by declaring that unless its membership were restored unconditionally within the next four years, the NGK synod would terminate its membership. The isolation of the Afrikaans churches even within Reformed Christianity was complete when the Reformed Ecumenical Synod, meeting at Chicago in 1984, censured the NGK for its support of apartheid, albeit in milder terms than had the WARC (Bosch 1985, 73). This resulted in provisional suspension of NGK membership of the Reformed Ecumenical Synod in January 1985.

Whilst the NGK has therefore suffered isolation as the price for its continuing support of apartheid, its political influence appears to have declined in recent years; it is now largely negative, as a brake on reform, rather than as an innovating force. Even as a force for conservatism the influence of the churches may be weakening: whereas the NGK synod voted overwhelmingly in favour of retaining the Mixed Marriages and Immorality Acts in 1982, both the former and section 16 of the latter were abolished in 1985 (Chapter 17). The trend is towards the state assuming an increasingly independent role in the moral sphere (Adam and Giliomee 1979, 241-2). This reflects both the strong tendency of the church leadership to avoid confrontation with the National Party, and an ongoing process of secularisation amongst laymen.

Much has been made of the Afrikaner's Calvinist heritage, but De Klerk (1975, 340) points out that Calvin regarded religious nationalism as a destructive force in society. He recognised the need for civil authority, but stressed that human society was always a *société provisoire* (provisional society), never an absolute order or authority. The civil order is therefore enjoined never to exceed its bounds: 'no temporary authority can pretend to be the architect and engineer of its own fundamentals' (de Klerk 1975, 339). De Klerk's words, based on 1 Corinthians 3, 11,[4] may have a prophetic ring for those who are tentatively beginning to dismantle the apartheid edifice.

The English language in South Africa

The number of white English speakers (Table 4.2) grew faster (25.5 per cent) than that of white Afrikaans speakers (20.2 per cent) in the 1970s. This reflects in part the effects of intermarriage, and also the high proportion of English-speaking immigrants (Table 4.4). The United Kingdom continued to account for 40 per cent of all net immigration to South Africa in the years 1974-84, although the annual figure in this period was only two-thirds of the average for the years 1961-73. Net immigration from the Netherlands, probably the only source of immigrants likely to be absorbed into the Afrikaans-speaking population, decreased from 3.1 per cent in 1961-73 to less than 2 per cent in 1974-84, a change which reflects the increasing cultural and political isolation of Afrikanerdom from the birthplace of its forbears.

The roots of South African English go back to the British occupation of the Cape and the 1820 settlers, but a far greater volume of British

Table 4.4: Immigration to and emigration from South Africa, 1961–84

Immigration	Total	UK	% UK
1961–73	457,519	168,847	36.9
1974–84	369,941	149,136	40.3
Emigration			
1961–73	120,063	37,303	31.1
1974–84	135,676	54,768	40.4
Net immigration			
1961–73	337,456	131,544	39.0
1974–84	152,834	64,067	41.9

immigration followed the diamond and gold discoveries of the late nineteenth century (Chapter 2). Most white English-speaking immigrants then and since have come to South Africa as urbanites with skills and abilities to develop an urban industrial economy. English speakers remain a majority amongst whites in the cities, and as a group they come from the most culturally advantaged home backgrounds of any ethnic or sub-cultural group in South Africa, although the gap between English speakers and Afrikaners is narrowing in both respects (Watts 1976, 87).

As a relatively minor group amongst the English-speaking peoples of the world, it is hardly surprising that English has not been the focus of a nationalism comparable with Afrikaans. Indeed Lanham (1976, 296) comments that English has often been valued and maintained 'more assiduously by those having it as a second language than by those having it as their birthright'. The potential influence of English-speaking whites in spreading ideas and values is increased by virtue of the fact that the use of English as a home language is rapidly spreading to other ethnic groups, whilst its dominance of the homeland school system is increasingly paralleled in black schools in the rest of South Africa. The use of English in Asian homes increased from 28.5 per cent in 1970 to a remarkable 85.1 per cent in 1980,[5] reflecting the high degree of Asian urbanisation and more particularly the concentration of Asians in the predominantly English-speaking cities of Durban and Pietermaritzburg in Natal. The growth of English-speaking amongst coloureds is somewhat different. Whereas the vast majority have grown up speaking Afrikaans, relatively few speak it well. Many use the patois known as

Gam taal and find it easier to read English-language newspapers. Afrikaans is seen as the language of the *dominee* (Dutch Reformed minister) and of the oppressor, or when spoken badly as the language of the street. For the better educated and ambitious coloureds (and blacks) English is regarded as the universal language which enables one to learn about the world as it really is, rather than through the limited perspective of the Afrikaner. The census figures for 1970 and 1980 are somewhat unhelpful, owing to the exclusion of an 'Afrikaans and English' category in 1980, at a time when this would be the most accurate answer for large numbers of coloureds (perhaps even a slight majority). As it is, the percentage stating their dominant home language as English rose from 6.0 in 1970 to 12.4 (324,360 people) in 1980.

The English-speaking churches

The somewhat awkward designation 'English-speaking churches' is used *faute de mieux*, to refer to those churches of British origin which have grown closer as a result of the ecumenical movement and their common attitude to apartheid. Together they make up the largest segment of the South African Council of Churches, given the absence from that body of the Afrikaans churches. Each of the denominations concerned – principally Anglicans, Methodists, Presbyterians and Congregationalists – has a different tradition and ethos. Although English is the common language of communication above the local level, the membership of these churches is predominantly black (Table 4.5), and the mother-tongue of most worshippers is not English. Nor does 'English-speaking' mean 'anti-Afrikaans': in recent years these churches have consciously tried to prevent their attacks on the ideology of apartheid from becoming anti-Afrikaans or anti-DRC (de Gruchy 1979, 87).

Table 4.5: Adherence to Anglican, Methodist, Roman Catholic and Lutheran churches, 1980

	Black	White	Coloured	Asian
Anglican	797,040	456,020	351,480	8,900
Methodist	1,554,280	414,080	140,120	3,700
Roman Catholic	1,676,680	393,640	264,820	21,160
Lutheran	698,400	37,000a	95,640	1,140

Note: a. A 1984 estimate including the German Evangelical Lutheran Church in Namibia.

The synods, conferences and assemblies of the English-speaking churches have protested against every piece of legislation they have considered unjust since 1948, and also against state actions such as the removal of squatters or the banning, detention and imprisonment of individuals. Innumerable resolutions have been passed, pastoral letters written, deputations sent to the Prime Minister and government ministers, and programmes initiated to combat racism at the local level. As de Gruchy (1979, 88-9) comments, 'There must be few comparable instances in the history of the Christian church where such a sustained protest and battle has been waged over such a long period against state legislation and action.' Whereas the DRC and government have tended to see the prophetic role of the church in terms of its 'own' spiritual sphere, and political responsibility as something for Christians as individuals, the English-speaking churches see themselves as having a political responsibility as institutions. They oppose not only the implementation of apartheid, but the ideology itself which is fundamentally opposed to their belief in the reconciliation of groups and the implementation of social equality as part of the churches' task.

The English-speaking churches have been relatively free to speak out, and have enjoyed reasonable access to authority, but their critique is disregarded, and sometimes leads to conflict and confrontation. Tension between church and state has been increased in recent years by deportations of missionaries and the banning, detention and imprisonment of South African Christians involved in Christian agencies and projects of various kinds, or in wider political organisations such as the United Democratic Front. Such behaviour by the state is made easier by the divisions of the church: not those of denomination, but the gap between synods and church leaders on the one hand and many white congregations on the other. Whilst the black and coloured members of the English-speaking churches fully support their churches' political involvement (and would often like to see it go further), many whites are politically conservative and would prefer their churches to 'keep out of politics'. The churches themselves have not been without discriminatory practices, and many of their white members have tended to practise their faith essentially within a white 'moral community', almost unconsciously limiting their Christian social responsibility. The authority of Dutch Reformed clergy over their Afrikaans congregations is not generally found amongst whites in the English-speaking churches, whose clergy find it difficult to change the attitudes of their congregations.

In part this reflects the wider situation of white English speakers in

South African society. As Guy Butler (1976, 11) points out, they are a group 'split among many religious denominations, secular by temperament, with very few cultural organisations; without a political party which makes it its business to look after [their] interests ... a socially mobile group sprinkled over a large country'. English-speaking whites are the most affluent and the best educated population group in South Africa, yet since 1948 they have effectively had no share in central government and little public responsibility in provincial councils, or in government boards, commissions and agencies. They are substantially under-represented in the army, civil service and teaching profession. The successful ethnic mobilisation of Afrikaners at the polls since 1948 makes English-speaking white South Africans politically impotent, and many have tended to take refuge in this, laying vague claim to a liberalism which has not been put to the test. Where English-speakers do wield enormous influence in finance, mining and industry it is by no means clear that apartheid legislation has been the major obstacle to liberalisation of employment practices, although it has often been made the scapegoat. The old jibe that in South Africa the Englishman 'talks Progressive, votes United Party and thanks God for the Nationalists' was not devoid of truth, and mirrors the equivocal position of English speakers in South African society as does the behaviour of many conservative churchgoers.

Lutherans and Roman Catholics

Until recently, neither Roman Catholics nor Lutherans have been prominent in the church struggle against apartheid. Although Lutheran membership is mainly black (Table 4.5), much of the struggle of black Lutherans has centred on the unity of the Lutheran Church itself. Historically, black Lutheran synods grew out of American missionary activity in Natal and the Transvaal, and were independent of one another and largely isolated from the white synods. In 1966, the various synods throughout South Africa and Namibia joined to form the Federation of Evangelical Lutheran Churches in Southern Africa. This brought Lutheran communities closer together (and closer to other churches), but an attempt in the early 1970s to unite all Lutherans in one church failed due to the conservatism of most German-speaking Lutheran congregations. The four black synods subsequently united to form the Evangelical Lutheran Church of South Africa in 1975. Resentment of white conservatism grew, leading to a resolution of African Lutheran churches meeting in Harare in December 1983 calling for suspension of the white Lutheran churches from the Lutheran World Federation (LWF). The latter, at its Budapest assembly in 1984, duly suspended the Evangelical Lutheran Church of Southern Africa (Cape) and the German Evangelical Lutheran Church in South West Africa, whilst a third white Lutheran church, from Natal and the Transvaal, withdrew its application for membership of the LWF. White South African Lutherans thus face an isolation comparable with that of the Afrikaans churches, although one resulting from conservatism in church matters and relative silence on political matters rather than explicit support for apartheid.

The Roman Catholic Church has been affected by the strong position of Protestant and especially Dutch Reformed churches in South Africa. There has been a clearly acknowledged anti-Catholic bias in Nationalist policies, particularly with regard to immigration, although this has changed in recent years with increasing numbers of migrants from Catholic countries including Portuguese from Mozambique and Angola. Anti-Catholic sentiment remains strong amongst Afrikaners, and has led the Roman Catholic hierarchy to be more diplomatic in relation to the state than their counterparts in the 'English-speaking' churches (de Gruchy 1979, 97). Catholic bishops have none the less spoken out boldly, especially since the Second Vatican Council, after which Roman Catholics began to develop clear relationships with other churches. Archbishop Dennis Hurley of Durban has been and remains one of the most outspoken Christian critics of apartheid, and called for a boycott of the Indian and coloured elections in 1984 (Chapter 13). Roman Catholics have led the way in certain respects, including integration of their church schools. As in Namibia and Rhodesia/Zimbabwe, the Catholic Church has produced political analyses of South Africa which have examined labour and other economic issues from a radical standpoint.[6] But at grassroots level the Roman Catholic Church suffers like Anglicans from the reluctance of whites to follow the lead of their bishops. Black priests have been highly critical of this, leading to tension and even confrontation within the church. The strongly centralised character of Roman Catholicism as a universal church has, however, safeguarded it against the kind of black–white break suffered by the Lutherans with their loose federal structure.

Dr Beyers Naudé and the Christian Institute

Not all Dutch Reformed participants at Cottesloe could accept their churches' subsequent rejection of what had been agreed there. Dr Beyers Naudé, who at the time of Cottesloe was acting moderator of the NGK in the Transvaal, sought a new way forward in personal cooperation between Christians of different churches in a non-denominational body, the Christian Institute (CI), of which he became director at its foundation in 1963. Initially, its emphasis was on changing the awareness and understanding of white Christians of the political implications of the Gospel. This was unacceptable to the NGK and Naudé's acceptance of the directorship cost him his position as a minister. The CI, and Naudé in particular, were regarded as 'driving a wedge down the middle of Afrikaner society' (de Gruchy 1979, 105). Subsequently, Naudé turned first to white English-speaking Christians for support but, finding that they too were reluctant to support fundamental change, he attempted to become more directly involved with blacks.

Aided largely by overseas financial support, the CI embarked on ambitious programmes. It was instrumental in bringing many of the multitude of African independent churches (with a combined membership of 5 million) into relationship with each other and the wider church. The CI also played a central role in the Study Project on Christianity in an Apartheid Society (SPRO-CAS), which began by trying to work out alternatives to apartheid, but after 1972 became more directly involved with blacks, and in particular the black consciousness movement, and began to offer a radical critique of South African economy and society (de Gruchy 1979, 108–9). This led to the CI being declared an 'affected organisation' in 1975, which meant that it was no longer able to receive overseas financial aid. Its continued support for black leaders and publicising of allegations of police torture and brutality eventually led to the CI being declared illegal and its senior white staff including Beyers Naudé banned on 19 October 1977. The identification of the CI with black protest was underlined by the simultaneous banning of the black newspaper *The World* and the arrest of its editor, Percy Qoboza, the declaration of many black organisations working for social change as illegal and the arrest of their leaders.

The CI had been weakened by its dependence on overseas financial support until 1975, but its impact was nevertheless quite disproportionate to its relatively small membership. For fifteen years it had provided by far the most radical Christian witness in South Africa. Its radicalism was regarded with unease by the churches, but it none the less challenged them to witness more effectively against apartheid. For individuals already doing so, the CI had provided a supportive community. Its banning left the task of prophetic leadership to the churches themselves, and to the South African Council of Churches.

The South African Council of Churches (SACC)

The SACC exists only because the churches have created it, but it is much more than a bureaucratic ecclesiastical organisation. Its work includes many community and development projects throughout the country, emergency aid, a scholarship programme for black students, care for the dependants of political prisoners, and more obvious ecumenical tasks. Inevitably, however, it is mainly known both within and outside South Africa for its opposition to apartheid. The SACC was much influenced by the World Council of Churches (WCC) Geneva Conference on Church and Society in 1966, which considered the question of Christian participation in revolutionary struggle. It also paved the way for the introduction in 1970 – traumatically for South African members of the WCC – of the Programme to Combat Racism which gives aid to liberation movements, including the African National Congress.

Following the Geneva Conference, the SACC established a theological commission to consider the implications of Christian witness in South Africa. Its conclusions were published in 1968 in a six-page *Message to the People of South Africa* which attempted to show, very forthrightly, how apartheid and separate development are contrary to the Gospel. It aroused great controversy amongst whites and made dialogue between the English-speaking and Afrikaans churches difficult by, in effect, condemning those who were prepared to justify separate development on theological grounds. The *Message,* together with the stand taken by the SACC on conscientious objection to military service in 1974, reflected the beginning of a new phase in the existence of the SACC, in which it changed during the 1970s from being a white-dominated institution to one much more widely representative of the black Christian community. The appointment in 1978 of Desmond Tutu, previously Bishop of Lesotho, as General Secretary of the SACC confirmed this process, which has led to the SACC being regarded as too radical by most whites. The latter cannot easily share the first-hand experience of white church leaders who have, through their black counterparts, come to a deeper knowledge and understanding of the feelings of blacks.

A government commission of inquiry into the SACC (the Eloff Commission) reported in 1983 (South Africa 1983c). Although expressing reluctance to involve itself in theological debate, the commission nevertheless promotes an overtly apolitical theology. An academic critique accuses it of 'selective use of sources, virtually devoid of any serious grappling with the classic texts or the topics under investigation',

79

non sequiturs and substantial contradictions (Villa-Vicencio 1985, 115); in particular, the same rejection of politicised theology was not applied to the commission's treatment of Afrikaner civil religion. Its report was critical of the SACC for its alleged support of the overseas disinvestment campaign against South Africa, and recommended that a new offence of economic sabotage be written into the Internal Security Act. The government undertook to consider this. The commission also noted a significant gap between the SACC and its member churches, from which it had failed to gain grassroots support for its political activities. These included 'psychological warfare' to persuade foreign governments to bring pressure to bear on South Africa, and 'ceaseless prognostication of imminent violence' unless apartheid was rapidly abandoned. The report expressed concern at the SACC's support for conscientious objection to military service, and questioned the implications of its attitude to the ANC. It was highly critical of Bishop Tutu and approved official decisions to refuse him a passport. Despite these strong criticisms the commission recommended against declaring the SACC an 'affected organisation', which would have debarred it from receiving overseas financial support. The government accepted this, at least for the time being, but also decided on the commission's advice to impose statutory control over the SACC's finances by bringing it within the ambit of the Fund-Raising Act.

In December 1984, after Bishop Tutu had been appointed Bishop of Johannesburg, Dr Beyers Naudé became the new General Secretary of the SACC, an Afrikaner at the head of a body to which the Afrikaans churches were largely opposed. His appointment symbolised both the political and religious divisions of Afrikaans- and English-speaking Christians, and the attempt of the SACC to assume the mantle of the Christian Institute in giving prophetic leadership to all races.

The articulation of basic Christian values

As part of its wider research on inter-group relations (Chapter 17), the government-funded Human Sciences Research Council (HSRC) recently published a report on religion in South Africa (Oosthuizen *et al.* 1985). It found that 77 per cent of all South Africans claim to be Christians, and sought to explore the implications and potential this held for inter-group relations and social change. Many churches were found not to be represented in the socio-political arena, especially the rapidly growing black indigenous churches which represented 39 per cent of all black Christians. The report stressed the destructive consequences of polarisation within religious communities, noting that 'The fact that most South Africans are Christians and therefore ought to draw on essentially the same pool of symbols and teachings has not been enough to overcome the tendency of religion to serve particular group interests' (p. 105). It noted, however, 'a surprising consensus within the most important church-groupings in South Africa as to what constitute basic human rights' which figured more prominently than hitherto in the Afrikaans churches (p. 107). Problems arose when specific content was given to abstract concepts and dialogue was needed to give substance to the common ground which existed. The report found most whites 'extraordinarily insensitive to the suffering which existing social structures inflict on those who are not White' (p. 107), which implied failure on the part of the churches to develop and maintain such sensitivity. The preponderance of Christians in the population placed a heavy responsibility on the churches to build bridges in a deeply segmented society and to provide the context where 'conflicting perspectives can be confronted with one another without necessarily erupting' (p.110).

One such attempt to articulate shared Christian values took the form of a 'National Initiative for Reconciliation' in Pietermaritzburg in September 1985, attended by nearly 400 Christian leaders from 47 denominations including both the NGK and black indigenous churches. Remarkably all except four of those present, including some 40 NGK representatives, voted for the concluding 'Statement of Affirmation' which included a call for a day of 'repentance, mourning and prayer for those sinful aspects of our national life which have led us to the present crisis' and the decision to send a delegation to the State President urging, *inter alia*, the ending of the state of emergency and removal of army and emergency police forces from the townships (Chapter 17), the release of all detainees and political prisoners, and the commencement of talks with 'authentic leadership of the various population groups with a view towards equitable power sharing in South Africa'.[7] Such church involvement in politics is worrying white South Africans, whose response was divided. None the less this degree of common purpose and specific agreement in the socio-political arena, at least among many elements of the church leadership, breaks new ground and offers tentative hope for the articulation and mobilisation of shared values amongst South Africa's Christian majority.

5
White voting behaviour

Introduction: the National Party ascendant

The previous chapter examined some important aspects of Afrikaans and English culture, giving some insight into the perceptions, attitudes and organisations of the white minority which rules South Africa. Voting behaviour may be viewed as the political expression of such attitudes; it is a measure of the whites' reaction to the social, economic and political circumstances in which they find themselves. It is easy to dismiss the electoral process in South Africa as part of the status quo, and as such incapable of contributing to fundamental change. The continuing dominance of the National Party (NP) has seemed inevitable, given the successful political mobilisation of Afrikaners as an ethnic group (Peel and Morse 1974; Adam and Giliomee 1979). Nevertheless, if there is to be peaceful change in South Africa it will have to be brought about by whites and their elected representatives (Lemon 1984a, 14). This has long seemed a very slender hope, and is only marginally less so today, but the early 1980s have witnessed both a new volatility in the political scene and the approval by whites of a constitution which enfranchises coloureds and Indians (but not blacks), albeit in a carefully structured manner (Chapter 13). Such developments, and the reform process embarked upon by the Botha government (Chapter 17), lend to the analysis of white voting behaviour a new relevance.

The NP has traditionally benefited from the over-representation of rural areas, where its supporters predominate. Electoral delimitation commissions are permitted to 'unload' rural seats so that they have up to 15 per cent fewer electors than the electoral quota, or average electorate,[1] whilst urban areas may be positively 'loaded' by up to 15 per cent. Since 1965 an 'unload' of up to 30 per cent has been permitted in constituencies with an area of 10,000 square miles (25,900 square kilometres) or more. In a detailed submission to the Tenth Delimitation Commission in 1953,

A. Suzman argued that such over-representation of rural areas was equivalent to a Nationalist advantage of six seats (Carter 1958, 152). Successive delimitation commissions have none the less continued to 'unload' sparsely populated areas and the six-seat advantage remained in 1981 (Lemon 1984a, 12).

In the early years of Nationalist rule, several measures were passed which, whatever their primary objectives, served to reinforce the ascendancy of the NP. Thus in 1949 the small white population of South West Africa was given six seats (producing an electoral quota less than half that in South Africa) despite the fact that it was not part of the Union. These seats were represented continuously by Nationalist MPs until 1977 when they ceased to exist. The three seats for 'Natives' Representatives' were abolished in 1959, and coloured representation was removed from the common roll in 1956 (Chapter 3), the latter measure significantly reducing the anti-government vote in several western Cape seats. In 1968 coloured parliamentary representation ceased to exist altogether.

Consolidating victory: the General Elections of 1948–58

The NP increased its proportion of seats from just over a quarter in 1943 to just over a half in 1948, winning this overall majority (with the help of its Afrikaner Party partner) on a minority vote. The NP share of parliamentary seats has increased steadily since then, with minor setbacks in 1970 and 1981 (Table 5.1). The same is true of its share of votes, if allowance is made for uncontested seats, particularly in 1961.

A number of events conspired to aid the NP in its dramatic breakthrough in 1948. The inheritance of wartime austerity was resented, whilst the admission of newly independent Asian nations into the Commonwealth transformed it into a multi-racial body with even less appeal for Afrikaners. Within South Africa the government's attempts to resolve political conflicts centring upon the Indians were both unpopular and unsuccessful, whilst attention was also focused on racial issues by the strike of the African Mineworkers Union in 1946 (Heard 1974, 31–2). The election of a Nationalist government could thus be portrayed as a defensive action by a white minority alarmed by events at home and abroad – words which could be re-echoed in the 1970s and 1980s – but it was neither expected nor inevitable, and it rested on a distinct minority of votes cast.

Undeterred by its narrow and apparently tenuous majority, the first NP government showed an uncompromising determination to add to and

Table 5.1: Electoral performance of the National Party, 1943–81[a]

General Election	% of seats	% of votes cast	% of votes cast + estimated votes[b]	Uncontested seats (NP)
1943[c]	28.7	35.7	33.4	18 (1)
1948[c]	52.7	41.2	39.4	12 (1)
1953	59.1	49.0	44.5	20 (2)
1958	64.7	55.1	48.5	24 (0)
1961	66.0	45.9	53.5	67 (47)
1966	75.0	57.7	59.2	19 (17)
1970	69.8	54.3	53.5	9 (3)
1974	70.9	55.3	56.6	43 (30)
1977	81.8	65.2	68.2	44 (42)
1981	79.4	57.0	56.7	16 (14)

Notes: a. Representation of blacks and coloureds, and of the whites of South West Africa, which existed for various parts of the period 1943–81, is excluded from this table.

b. Estimated votes relate to uncontested seats. The estimates for 1943–70 are those of Heard (1974); for 1974 and 1977 those of Lemon (1981); and for 1981, a previously unpublished estimate by the author.

c. Figures for 1943 refer to the Herenigde Nasionale Party (HNP) and for 1948 to the HNP and its coalition partner, the Afrikaner Party; the two parties merged in 1951 to form the National Party.

Sources: Heard (1974); Lemon (1981); and the Government Gazette vol. 191, no. 7587, 15 May 1981.

transform the existing segregationist structures according to its apartheid ideology (Chapter 3). It perhaps calculated that, given the efficiency of NP organisation and the numerical strength of the Afrikaner vote, it would not have to pay the price of defeat at the next election. The 1953 campaign was a particularly tumultuous one with strenuous efforts on the part of opposition forces which believed (perhaps for the last time) that victory was possible. In this sense the 1953 election was arguably the most critical in the post-war period. The NP stressed not only the race issue but also what it claimed to be the dangers of communism, against which the United Party (UP) could offer no protection. The NP was assisted by the clearcut nature of its purpose, whereas the UP suffered in

1953 (and in all subsequent elections until its demise in 1977) from the inherent difficulties of a white party appealing to the interests of white electors, but attempting to do so in more liberal and usually less tangible and more ambivalent ways than its principal opponent. In 1953, however, the UP was strengthened by alliance with the Labour Party and the Torch Commando, a war veterans' organisation brought into being to oppose the government's handling of the Separate Representation of Voters Act (Chapter 3) because of its constitutional implications. This alliance, known as the United Front, won a bare majority of votes (50.2 per cent), plus 18 uncontested seats, yet the distorting effect of the electoral system reduced its tally of seats from 71 to 61, leaving the NP with a comfortable majority of 27 seats.

The Nationalists' main objective in the 1958 General Election was to consolidate the political cohesion of Afrikanerdom. Thus the NP campaign was an appeal not to the wider nation, which it could afford to disregard, but to the *volk*, calling for united defence against the *swart gevaar* (black menace). It also promised that South Africa would become a republic as soon as a majority of white voters clearly favoured this course. The essential argument of the NP campaign was that only apartheid could preserve 'white civilisation' in South Africa, and do so with fairness and justice towards other races. Dr Verwoerd promised to reverse the migration of Africans from the 'homelands' to 'white' towns, claiming that he would be able to restrict the number of non-whites in 'white' areas to only 6 million by the year 2000. (In 1983 the actual number exceeded 14 million, and was increasing.)

Most potential Nationalist voters lacked the genuine if misguided idealism of Dr Verwoerd, and were anxious above all to maintain white political and economic dominance. There was little in the UP campaign to attract them. The party was beset with internal divisions, and forced onto the defensive in relation to controversial racial issues, where its stance was popularly described as 'me too, only not so loud' (Heard 1974, 75). It was blamed for African unrest and even linked in the public mind with the African National Congress. The UP manifesto concentrated on relatively safe economic issues, and 'lacked the evocative appeal of the "tribal drum"' (Heard 1974, 77). In such circumstances its defeat was no surprise. The NP for the first time achieved a majority of votes, and an unassailable 97 seats out of 150 in the House of Assembly.

Triumph in isolation: the referendum and the Republic

The long-cherished hope of committed Afrikaner nationalists for the establishment of a republic was achieved on 31 May 1961, after a referendum in October 1960. Voting took place against the background of several dramatic events. The election as Prime Minister after the death of J.G. Strydom in 1958 of Dr Verwoerd, the 'man of granite', gave South Africa the most inflexible and undeviating of all its post-war leaders. His recovery from an attempted assassination in April 1960 was greeted by the Afrikaans press as miraculous: to attack Dr Verwoerd became almost heretical (Heard 1974, 98). Meanwhile, the British Prime Minister Harold Macmillan, in his famous 'wind of change' speech in Cape Town, warned that the direction of apartheid policies made it difficult for Britain to give continued support and encouragement to South Africa as a fellow member of the Commonwealth. Only weeks afterwards the Sharpeville tragedy, and the demonstrations and riots which occurred in Langa (Cape Town), Durban and elsewhere between 21 March and 9 April 1960 costing more lives, led to increased repression at home and widespread shock overseas. It was a singularly unpropitious time for South Africa to seek continued membership of the Commonwealth when she became a republic.

Unlike his predecessors who had considered that a republic could only be established on the broad basis of the national will, Dr Verwoerd declared that a nationwide majority of a single vote in the referendum would be sufficient, and even hinted that if this was not secured, a majority in Parliament itself might be sufficient in certain circumstances. The chances of republican victory were enhanced by the lowering of the voting age for whites from 21 to 18 after the 1958 election, as Afrikaners had a more youthful age profile than English speakers: for younger Afrikaners in 1960 whose political awareness did not extend further back than 1948 the republic seemed a natural course. The inclusion of South West African whites and the exclusion of coloured voters from the referendum further strengthened the republican cause.

Dr Verwoerd assured the electorate that 'there will be no radical changes in our parliamentary institutions or constitutional practices' (Pelzer 1966, 332). The opposition nevertheless made much of an earlier, markedly authoritarian, draft Republican Constitution of 1924 which had relegated the English language to a subordinate role, as evidence of the nature of the republic which the Nationalists would seek to create. Even more central to the opposition campaign was the threat to the Commonwealth connection posed by the establishment of a republic. The postponement of a decision on South Africa's conditional request for continued membership of the Commonwealth Conference in May 1960 did nothing to allay the threat, despite the government's outward expression of confidence in a positive outcome.

The NP, in contrast to its markedly sectional appeal to Afrikanerdom in 1958, sought to stress the necessity of the republic for 'national' (i.e. Afrikaans–English) unity, arguing that the monarchy was inevitably a source of division. This cut little ice with English speakers, who rightly perceived the republic as an Afrikaner ideal, and who associated it with a governing party they had come to equate with the erosion of civil liberties, a disregard for constitutional propriety, and insensitivity to the opinions of all except Afrikaners.

The outcome of the referendum was a Nationalist victory of 74,580 votes, only 4.5 per cent of the total votes cast in an exceptionally high poll of 90.8 per cent. The result might have gone the other way had coloureds but not South West African whites been allowed to vote, and had the voting age remained at 21 (Heard 1974, 116–17). Predictably the Orange Free State and rural areas of the Transvaal proved to be the strongest areas of republican support, with Pretoria and rural areas of the Cape not far behind. The Durban and Pietermaritzburg seats registered the strongest opposition, and Natal as a whole voted against the republic by a margin of three to one. The predominantly English-speaking Border areas of the eastern Cape produced a similar result, whilst both Johannesburg and Cape Town also voted strongly against a republic. Only in Port Elizabeth and the Witwatersrand, urban industrial areas with relatively large Afrikaans populations, and rural Natal which has fewer English speakers than Durban and Pietermaritzburg, was there a relatively close result.

It was on this slender base that South Africa became a Republic on 31 May 1961, notwithstanding secessionist noises from Natal. By that time hostility from the Afro-Asian nations at the Commonwealth Prime Ministers' Conference in March had induced Dr Verwoerd to withdraw South Africa's application for continued Commonwealth membership. This underlined the irrevocable nature of the step South Africa had taken: Afrikaners who had trekked first into the highveld, then into the cities, were now firmly engaged in their third 'Great Trek', a trek into isolation.

Nationalism ascendant: the General Elections of 1961 and 1966
The government used the advent of the republic to call an early General Election in 1961. The central issue, as in all subsequent elections, was the country's race policies, and on this occasion the electorate was presented

with clearly articulated alternatives. Dr Verwoerd elaborated the 'bantustan' policy, recognising that the logic of separate development demanded eventual political independence for each bantustan and insisting that all blacks in white areas were temporary sojourners who would exercise political rights in their own territories. Challenged by the Afrikaans press about the future of coloureds, Dr Verwoerd firmly resisted proposals for political integration, outlining instead an apartheid structure of separate political institutions for coloureds, albeit without a territorial base. The UP, on the other hand, proposed direct coloured representation in Parliament and the abolition of job discrimination against coloureds. In an uncharacteristically clear programme, the UP also proposed that Asians be accepted as a permanent part of South Africa's population, that negotiation should begin on their political status, and that attention be given to the economic effects on Asians of the Group Areas Act (Chapter 11). With regard to Africans, the UP proposed that workers in white areas should be accepted as permanently domiciled there, and that an African middle class should be fostered and represented in Parliament, policies reminiscent of the 'partnership' approach of the then Central African Federation (Keatley 1963). The fledgling Progressive Party, founded as a breakaway from the UP in 1959, advocated a multi-racial democracy with a system of checks and balances to prevent discrimination or group tyranny.

An unprecedented number of uncontested seats (Table 5.1) reflected the increasingly clear geographical polarisation of the electorate. There seemed little possibility of a Nationalist defeat, and the turnout was low by comparison with 1953 and 1958 (77.6 per cent). Whilst the NP secured less than half the votes actually cast, allowance for its 47 uncontested seats makes 1961 the first General Election at which more than 50 per cent of the projected vote should be credited to the NP (Table 5.1). Its overall majority of seats increased to 48. The Progressive Party, which contested only 21 seats, lost all but one of the seats held by those who had crossed the floor in 1959; it did however establish itself as a significant force in Johannesburg (where it has retained the Houghton seat in the northern suburbs ever since), Durban and Pietermaritzburg.

The ensuing five years were eventful ones in the continent of Africa, with the independence of Algeria and mass return of French settlers, the *pieds noirs*, to France, the independence of Kenya, Uganda and Tanganyika, and the dissolution in 1963 of the Central African Federation leading to independence for Zambia and Malawi, and to Rhodesia's Unilateral Declaration of Independence in 1965. The independence of Basutoland (Lesotho) and Bechuanaland (Botswana) was imminent. A spate of military *coups*, including those in Ghana and Nigeria, underlined the violence and instability of the new Africa. Macmillan's 'wind of change' had blown with a force that took white South Africa, and especially its English-speaking, Commonwealth-oriented minority by surprise. The effect of these events was to increase unity among white South Africans who felt themselves to be an increasingly beleaguered minority.

Violence within South Africa added to the perceived need for white unity. Much of it was perpetrated by two militant black political organisations, Poqo ('pure') and Umkonto we Sizwe ('spear of the nation'), which were underground movements of the PAC and ANC respectively. Acts of sabotage became frequent in 1962-63, many of them committed by Umkonto we Sizwe. Many political trials took place including the Rivonia trial at which Nelson Mandela and seven others were sentenced to life imprisonment. A series of legislative measures were enacted to tighten state security still further.

In contrast to 1961, the election campaign of 1966 was largely negative, consisting of attacks by the NP and UP on each other's policies portrayed in very general terms (Heard 1974, 158). The UP castigated the government for its neutrality towards (instead of support for) the Smith regime in Rhodesia, and for its policy of leading the bantustans to independence, to which the Transkei Constitution Act of 1963 was a pointer. The UP thus chose to attack the NP from the political right, posing as the champion of continued white leadership over the whole of South Africa, and doing little to articulate its concept of 'race federation'. The NP for its part stressed that both UP and Progressive Party (PP) policy could only lead to political integration and an eventual black majority; only the NP could give South Africa the strong and determined government it needed to face both external and internal threats. Assured of overall victory, the NP turned its attention to the task of capturing English-speaking support, and made Natal a particular target. In the event the NP won four rural seats out of six in Natal compared with two out of five in 1961, but lost a Pietermaritzburg seat to the UP, which was thus reasonably successful in defending Natal. Overall, however, the UP won only 39 seats, its lowest total ever. The PP held Houghton, leaving the NP with 120 seats and an impregnable 30-seat overall majority.

Divisions in Afrikanerdom: the 1970 General Election
The assassination of Dr Verwoerd in September 1966 was the signal for

latent Nationalist divisions over his policies to surface. The election of Mr J.B. Vorster as his successor was itself controversial (Heard 1974, 182). Conservative Afrikaners, first christened *verkramptes* in 1966,[2] challenged several elements of Verwoerdian policy including eventual independence for the bantustans, cooperation with English speakers, the promotion of large-scale immigration, and a foreign policy which sought to look outwards, especially to black Africa. An increasing battle between *verligte* ('positive', 'enlightened' or reformist) and *verkrampte* factions affected all sectors of Afrikanerdom, and led eventually to the formation of the Herstigte ('reconstituted') Nasionale Party (HNP) in October 1969, under the leadership of Dr Albert Hertzog.

It was widely assumed that Mr Vorster called an early election in April 1970 in order to rout the HNP and reunite Afrikanerdom. Certainly the election campaign focused more on the struggle within Afrikanerdom than that between NP and UP. Mr Vorster's own leadership was also at stake, an unusual phenomenon in post-war Nationalist politics which had hitherto been characterised by strong loyalty to party leaders. The NP again emphasised the need for unity between Afrikaners and English speakers in the building of a 'white nation', a policy which was unacceptable to *verkramptes*. It stressed the communist threat – the *rooi gevaar* (red menace) – to South Africa, possibly to counterbalance the 'liberalism' of its foreign policy. Racial policies were less prominent in the NP campaign than usual, perhaps because the message was essentially unchanged. Separate development was credited with the relative internal peace and stability of the country, and it was claimed (misleadingly) that the tide of black movement to 'white' areas had been reversed.

The HNP revealed itself as rigid and sectarian in its appeal, attacking the NP as cosmopolitan and liberal. It advocated, *inter alia*, stricter application of apartheid, the combining of the offices of Head of State and Head of Government (a change which the NP itself brought about in the 1983 constitution), and stricter Sunday observance. Immigration would be restricted to those who could speak and read Afrikaans, and foreign capital inflows would be reduced: economic growth would be subordinated to ideological ends. Afrikaans would become the sole official language, with English recognised only as a second language.

The UP for the first time attacked the government strongly for economic mismanagement, blaming the fact that South Africa was beginning to experience high inflation on labour policies such as job reservation and the controls of the Physical Planning Act (Chapter 8).

Stress was also laid on Nationalist abuse of civil rights. As in 1961, a relatively detailed picture of the UP's own race policy was presented.

The 1970 election was the first since 1948 in which the Nationalists lost ground, and to this extent challenged the seeming inevitability of increasing political rigidity among white South Africans. The UP won eight seats, reducing the NP majority to 63, although its share of the votes (37.4 per cent) remained virtually unchanged. The swing to the UP was markedly concentrated in Johannesburg, the Witwatersrand and the major urban areas of Natal (Vosloo 1970, 4–5). The seats lost by the Nationalists were without exception among those gained by them in 1966, and ones where English-speaking votes played a major part. A degree of Afrikaans support for the UP, probably of a protest variety, was indicated by reduced Nationalist majorities in some Orange Free State and northern Cape *platteland* constituencies where English speakers were few in number. Elsewhere, the conservative line taken by a NP fearful of losing support to the HNP may explain the return of English-speaking Nationalist voters of 1966 to their normal allegiances, as well as the loss of small numbers of *verligte* Afrikaner and immigrant votes. In addition, many English-speaking voters may well have regarded sentiments voiced by the HNP as confirmation of their worst fears about the true nature of the Nationalists themselves.

The Nationalist losses were a significant setback to the party's aim of increasing white unity, but its more crucial concern to crush the HNP and minimise divisions in Afrikanerdom was essentially satisfied. All four MPs who had crossed the floor to the HNP lost their seats, and the party's 77 candidates gained a mere 53,000 votes. This figure decreased still further in the 1974 and 1977 General Elections, yet the significance of the HNP cannot be measured only in terms of votes. Lever (1972) suggests that the turnout of 74.7 per cent, although continuing a decline that began in 1960, conceals significant differences between English-speaking and Afrikaans voting behaviour which arose essentially from different perceptions of the Afrikaner split engendered by the HNP. Afrikaner divisions gave English speakers renewed electoral optimism, especially in urban areas, and encouraged relatively high levels of political activity amongst young and middle-aged UP supporters, and a relatively high percentage poll. These same divisions had the opposite effect on Nationalist voters:

> When there is unity within the party, political interest and activity on the part of the Nationalists is high. But interest and enthusiasm decline with

dissension. Abstentions on the part of the Nationalists seem to have been of far greater importance in determining the outcome of the election than shifts of allegiance from party to party. (Lever 1972, 242)

These words were to have renewed significance in relation to by-elections in 1979 (see below). In the meantime, 1970 had been very much 'a Herstigte election': this small party had not only precipitated the election but also dominated the campaign and significantly influenced the outcome.

An alternative Afrikaner party has always posed the threat of a wider Nationalist split which would, given Afrikaans *volkseenheid*, or togetherness of the people (Chapter 4), cause a split in church, education and culture too. The prospect of such a *volkskeuring* has been a major deterrent to a Nationalist political split, but the price of preventing this has been the need to take disproportionate notice of right-wing views within the party. The maintenance of Afrikaans political unity has thus been 'a fundamental obstacle to reform in South Africa' (du Toit 1980), and successive Nationalist governments since 1969 have seemed to outside observers excessively preoccupied with an apparently un-important threat from the right.

Opposition divisions and Progressive breakthrough: the General Election 1974

The General Election of April 1974 was announced on the grounds that 'the next 3–5 years ... would be decisive for the continued existence of South Africa and her people',[3] and that in these circumstances the government must be assured of its people's confidence. Once again Parliament had failed to run its full term, and most observers saw the government as taking advantage of the divisions which were racking the UP. After the 1970 election it had seemed that the UP could, if it pursued a consistently reformist line, hold its new voters and, with improved organisation, add to them (Kleynhans and Labuschagne 1970, 8). In the event it failed to follow such a line, with the reformist or 'Young Turks' arousing fierce and unconcealed opposition, which led to unseemly struggles over the nomination of candidates in 1974. By-election results and opinion polls none the less gave the UP some grounds for optimism.

Although all parties professed to view the election as crucial to the country's future, few major issues emerged in a campaign which was unremarkable, even sterile. The NP stressed the need for white unity in the face of uncertainty, demanding 'a clear and unequivocal mandate to carry on protecting South Africa from within and without':[4] in other words, a blank cheque. *Swaart gevaar* tactics were used by both sides, the Nationalists concentrating on the dangers of the UP's federal policy, and the UP stressing the issue of white land needed for the government's proposed homeland consolidation (Chapter 14). It thus failed to provide truly *verligte* opposition, despite the abundance of ammunition available: South Africa's increasing international isolation; the impracticability of apartheid as evinced by increasing numbers of urban blacks, the negligible economic advance of the homelands, and the paralysis of government policy in relation to coloureds and Indians; growing internal divisions and deteriorating race relations; the often inhuman application of apartheid ideology; the violation and diminution of democratic rights; and widespread administrative incompetence (Lemon 1981, 423).

A return to high numbers of uncontested seats was a feature of both the 1974 and 1977 General Elections, with the NP the main beneficiary in 1974 and almost the only one in 1977 (Table 5.1). It also made a net gain of three seats from the UP in 1974, increasing its overall majority to 69. It was the PP which provided the major surprise, however, winning five seats from the UP (two in Cape Town and three in Johannesburg) and a further Cape Town seat in a subsequent by-election. The HNP, despite having had four years to organise, won no seats and suffered a decline in its total vote, but this was seen by the English-language press as 'a measure of the reactionary extremists who prefer to influence the National Party's direction from within'.[5]

The Progressive success deserves closer scrutiny. After a poor showing in 1966 which had threatened the party's continued existence, the PP had made a relatively strong comeback in the major urban areas in 1970, winning over 35 per cent of the popular vote in the Johannesburg and Cape Town seats which it fought. In 1974 the PP mounted a strong attack on the UP for its participation in the Schlebusch Commission, a parliamentary commission appointed to inquire into aspects of national security, portraying the UP's 'Old Guard' as junior partners in alliance with the NP. The selective nature of the PP attack was evidenced by its decision to refrain from contesting seats in which the UP was represented by reformist candidates (Stadler 1975, 210). The Progressive victories were conspicuously concentrated in areas of high socio-economic status (Lemon 1981, 423), whose electoral behaviour may be interpreted as reflecting either the enlightenment of the better educated or, more cynically, the remoteness of the better-off from any threat to their jobs and lifestyle.

The distribution of Progressive support confirmed the popular image of the PP as a party of capital. Harry Oppenheimer, then Chairman of the Anglo-American Corporation, was its only major backer in the mid-1960s, although he was joined by a wider group of industrialists in the 1970s. Their support is viewed by Hackland (1980, 10) as an attempt to find an alternative vehicle to ensure protection of their interests in the event of the NP being unable to resolve the conflicts threatening capitalism in South Africa. The economic difficulties of the 1970s prompted these elements of capital to turn to the PP not instead of, but as well as, the NP, in what amounts to an insurance policy. The PP itself was committed to bringing about a free enterprise economy untrammelled by apartheid restrictions, especially those relating to the movement and use of black labour. It believed that a free enterprise economy could be a prime instrument of peaceful political change, because 'rapid economic development of South Africa would in the long run prove incompatible with the government's racial policies' (Oppenheimer 1974, 402).

For the UP the 1974 General Election represented a clear warning. Unless it could overcome its divisions and present a more coherent reformist message, it was in danger of losing further support to both right and left. The percentage poll in 1974 declined still further to 69.1, and it is probable that most of the additional abstentions represented potential UP voters discouraged by the party's lack of clear purpose (Lemon 1981, 426–7). The UP position was not altogether hopeless in 1974. NP support at the polls represented only 38.7 per cent of the total electorate compared with 22.4 per cent for the UP, and, given improved organisation and clearer direction, there was considerable untapped voting potential which could do much to close the gap. The UP did, however, suffer one built-in handicap as a result of immigrants, some of long standing, who had chosen not to become South African citizens and were thus ineligible to vote. They numbered well over 300,000 in 1974, a figure approximately equal to the gap between Nationalist and UP votes in 1974 (Lemon 1981, 427). Few of these immigrants were Afrikaans-speaking and they represented potentially fertile ground for the UP in the 1970s which it could not usefully cultivate.

The General Election of 1977: towards a one-party state?
The announcement of a General Election to be held on 30 November 1977, 18 months before one was due, surprised almost everyone. Even the voters' rolls were in disorder because the Department of the Interior

was in the process of switching to a computerised system. Mr Vorster gave three reasons for calling the election:[6] first, to allow the electorate 'to add its voice to government protests against international "meddling" in South African affairs'; secondly, to obtain a verdict on the government's proposed constitutional changes, which involved the creation of coloured and Indian parliaments and an executive presidency (Vosloo 1979); and thirdly, because of the 'unreal' situation created by the disintegration of the UP.

To most observers it appeared that the Prime Minister had once more chosen the moment of maximum disarray for the opposition. The UP had collapsed in two main stages. Its reformists had first departed to form the Reform Party, which soon merged with the Progressives to become the Progressive Reform Party (PRP). More recently the UP had formally dissolved itself, splitting into three fragments. The 'hardliners' formed the South African Party (SAP), whilst the remainder of the UP absorbed the minuscule Democratic Party and reconstituted itself as the New Republic Party (NRP). Subsequently, six former UP MPs who had refused to join the NRP joined the PRP to form the Progressive Federal Party (PFP). Whilst these developments might be viewed as healthy for the long-term growth of white opposition, the new parties were in no position to face an election in 1977; the PFP was a mere 16 days old when the election was announced.

It was further suggested that Mr Vorster wanted his 'mandate' for constitutional change quickly, before the electorate properly understood the new proposals. Retrospectively, it also seems likely that he was anxious to hold the election in favourable circumstances before the full extent of the 'information scandal' was revealed.[7]

In other respects electoral circumstances were hardly propitious for the government. A year after the Soweto riots policy for urban blacks appeared unclear. The black education system had partially collapsed, with many schools closed, boycotts of classes, and resignation of teachers. The Coloured Labour Party and Coloured Representative Council, and even the moderate South African Indian Council, had all rejected the new constitutional proposals. More important perhaps for white voters, South Africa had followed Western Europe into prolonged recession: just when some signs of recovery appeared, the clampdown on the black newspaper, *The World*, on two editors and 18 organisations including the Christian Institute (Chapter 4) had provoked an intensely adverse overseas reaction. So too had the death in detention, under suspicious circumstances, of the founder of the black consciousness movement,

Steve Biko, and the subsequent insensitivity displayed by the Minister of Justice, Police and Prisons, Mr Kruger. Meanwhile the short-lived African détente policy had collapsed entirely, and relations with the West were the worst ever, as the absence of a veto against the UN Security Council mandatory arms embargo against South Africa had demonstrated. The head of the South African Defence Force had warned that South Africa must go over to 'an economy of survival' in the face of deepening domestic problems and isolation abroad.

Paradoxically, the very seriousness of the situation created by government policies rebounded to the advantage of the NP. In the words of the *Rand Daily Mail*: 'Spectacular all-round failure has created a national crisis – and the resultant public anxiety is causing some people to respond to the Government's emotional appeal to patriotism.'[8] The parallel with Rhodesia is striking: the critical situation there led whites to close ranks in the July 1977 election behind the government of Mr Ian Smith, which had itself led Rhodesia into crisis (Lemon 1978, 527–9). The 1977 General Election in South Africa was to demonstrate that white South Africans had either not realised the dangers of such a syndrome, or had failed to perceive those dangers as applicable to themselves.

The PFP started the campaign with real expectation of ousting the NRP as the official opposition, and the NP was not unhappy that this should happen, believing that it would encourage more conservative English speakers to vote Nationalist in greater numbers. Claiming to be the only real opposition to the NP, the PFP attacked the latter strongly on civil rights issues in the wake of Steve Biko's death and the October bannings. It was however forced onto the defensive on several key issues (Midlane 1979, 379). In blaming the government for international isolation and the arms embargo, the PFP could not afford to appear unpatriotic. Likewise the war psychosis and the need to support 'the boys on the border' prevented the PFP from exploiting the increasingly costly campaign on the Namibian border. It was also defensive over its proposals for a qualified franchise, making a distinction between majority rule (a non-racial concept) and black majority rule which must have been lost on most voters. There had been no time to work out the PFP's own policy in detail, but it stressed that a future constitutional dispensation must be the subject of negotiation by the authentic leaders of all sections of the South African society.

The NRP stressed the cultural and ethnic pluralism of South African society, advocating a form of federation with substantial decentralisation of power to local communities. It made little impression on the election campaign outside Natal, the former stronghold of the UP. The NRP suffered from the same ambivalence as had the UP, but could not depend on the tradition and loyalty which had sustained the latter beyond the days of credible opposition. Much the same applied to the SAP which tried to present itself as a true successor to the UP of Smuts. The SAP also advocated a federal solution, but pledged itself in somewhat anachronistic language to continued white leadership. It accepted the permanence of urban blacks and argued for the consolidation of a home-owning black middle class, but its similarity in other respects to the NP was such that Mr Vorster described it as a 'responsible' opposition party. Its appeal was mainly to conservative English-speaking voters who wished to retain the status quo.

For the first time since 1948, no opposition party contested sufficient seats to win (Table 5.2). The NP was unopposed in 42 seats and faced only HNP opposition in 49 more. The NRP virtually abandoned the rural areas and fought less than half the urban seats, fewer than the PFP which was actually unopposed in two Johannesburg constituencies. The inevitability of NP victory almost certainly contributed to a further decline in the turnout to 64.4 per cent. Other factors included the

Table 5.2: Seats and votes, 1977

Party	Contested seats urban	Contested seats rural[a]	Seats won[b]		Votes	%
NP	58	47	135[c]	(42)	690,384	65.3
PFP	48	9	17	(2)	181,049	17.1
NRP	35	11	10		127,335	12.0
SAP	4	3	3		19,308	1.8
HNP	23	33	0		34,161	3.2
Others	3	2	0		6,271	0.6
Total	171	105	165		1,058,508	100.0

Notes: a. 'Rural' includes towns outside the major cities; 'urban' covers Johannesburg, Pretoria, the Witwatersrand, Cape Town, Port Elizabeth, East London, Durban and Pietermaritzburg.

b. Figures in parenthesis indicate numbers of uncontested seats.

c. Includes Springs, a Witwatersrand seat where the contest was postponed until April 1978 owing to the murder of the NP candidate after nomination day.

'homelessness' of many former UP supporters and the lack of enthusiasm of the NP rank and file for the proposed constitutional changes.

Total opposition strength declined from 48 to 30 seats, and the PFP become the official opposition with 17 seats. Its new seats included several high-income constituencies where Progressive support had been rising in 1974, but also others of more mixed socio-economic composition including Groote Schuur and Wynberg in Cape Town. It seemed as if PFP support was beginning to diffuse geographically from the concentrated pockets of high-income population to which it was largely confined in 1974 (Lemon 1981, 433). SAP victories were limited to three of the seven seats held at the end of the old Parliament, all of them uncontested by the NP. The HNP vote declined by a further 10,000 votes, despite the fielding of eleven more candidates than in 1974.

The Nationalists increased their share of the vote by 10 per cent to a record level. Their seats included all 66 of those won by majorities of over 5000, 54 of them in the Transvaal and Orange Free State, whereas most opposition seats were held with considerably smaller majorities. Such Nationalist dominance was only made possible by an unprecedented level of English support. From an estimated trough of just over 10 per cent in 1972, English-speaking support for the NP rose, according to opinion polls, to 13–15 per cent in 1973 and over 20 per cent by 1975; by late 1976 it verged on 30 per cent, a level maintained in the 1977 General Election (Schlemmer 1978, 77). The election produced four English-speaking Nationalist MPs, and the NP emerged ahead of the NRP in several PFP seats with largely English-speaking electorates. This erosion of traditional voting along lines of ethnic identification appeared very much a one-way process: a survey carried out by the Afrikaans newspaper *Rapport* shortly before the election showed that more than 86 per cent of Afrikaans-speaking voters backed the NP.

The geographical distribution of seats and votes underlined the new Nationalist ascendancy (Lemon 1981, 435–8; Figure 5.1). The NP grasp on rural areas and small towns was virtually complete: of 74 seats, the NRP won only three (in Natal) and the PFP none. The NP won a majority of votes even in rural Natal and the eastern Cape. With the halving of its support to 11.7 per cent in the northern Transvaal, the HNP was left without strong rural support anywhere. In urban areas its support was negligible outside Pretoria, and even there it mustered a mere 8027 votes (6.2 per cent) for 13 candidates. The NP won all 23 Witwatersrand seats for the first time, together with three more in Johannesburg, where it gained equality with the PFP. The Nationalists

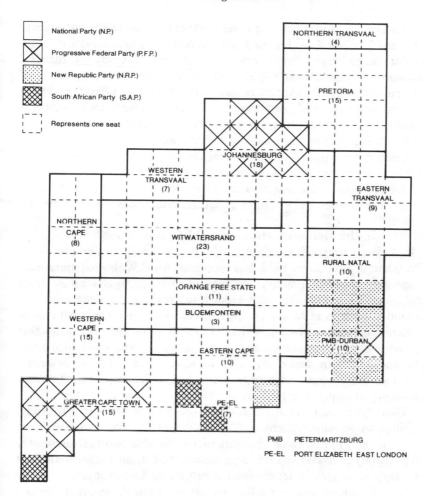

Fig. 5.1   1977 General Election results by seats won

also threatened the NRP in its only stronghold, Durban–Pieter-maritzburg, winning three more seats, and made gains in Cape Town, Port Elizabeth and East London. In terms of votes, the PFP became the leading party in both Cape Town and Port Elizabeth–East London. It also won over one-third of all Johannesburg votes and a quarter of those in Durban–Pietermaritzburg, and seemed poised for further growth in these cities.

99

In such circumstances of overwhelming Nationalist dominance, Midlane (1979, 385-7) points out that a *de facto* one-party state potentially endangers democracy and threatens excessively bureaucratic government which is more open to corruption. At the same time it now seemed that the only hope of peaceful change in South Africa rested in the National Party itself, but despite the undoubted presence of reformist elements in the government there was little sign that major reforms were forthcoming. The main task of the PFP seemed not to offer itself as an alternative government – a clearly unattainable goal, the pursuit of which might result in compromise of principle to gain more votes – but to use its parliamentary platform as a sounding board for ideas which might contribute to a new dispensation in South Africa.

Cracks in the monolith: the General Election of 1981
Mr Vorster resigned as Prime Minister in order to become State President in September 1978. His successor, Mr P.W. Botha, inherited a huge parliamentary majority and seemed prepared to effect significant policy changes. His approach tended to combine or relate measures intended both to relax and to impose constraints on the behaviour of different non-white groups, which has been interpreted as evidence that his government was simultaneously mobilising for political change along the lines of reform and revolution (Woodward 1981). It was, however, the reformist trend in government policy which received the most publicity and led to renewed divisions in Afrikanerdom.

The first setback occurred in the by-election of October 1979. The HNP won an unprecedented 40 per cent of the votes cast in three contests, all in 'blue-collar' constituencies (Koedoespoort, Rustenburg, Germiston) characterised by large numbers of mining and/or railway workers. This clearly represented a protest against proposed liberalisation of labour legislation following the Wiehahn Report (Chapter 7). Three of the four by-elections produced unprecedentedly low polls of 23-32 per cent, which could only be interpreted in terms of deliberate large-scale abstention by Nationalist supporters unhappy about Mr Botha's projected reforms. Unlike many supporters of opposition parties, they seemed unable to bring themselves actually to vote for another party.

When Mr Botha chose to go to the polls 18 months early in January 1981 it was widely assumed that he wanted not only a clear personal mandate, but also a vote of confidence in his policies in the face of strong and continued infighting within the NP itself between *verligte* and *verkrampte* forces, the latter led by the Transvaal NP leader Dr Andries Treurnicht. In addition, the large number of by-elections pending, mainly because of the transfer of Nationalist MPs to the new President's Council,[9] raised the spectre of HNP gains, whereas a General Election seemed more likely to unite the NP behind Mr Botha (Lemon 1982a, 512).

In the event it was far from plain sailing. Early evidence of dissension within the NP included disputed nominations, especially in Mr Botha's own Cape NP, right-wing rebellions and resignations in protest against nominated candidates in some constituencies. In the Transvaal, *verkrampte* candidates swept the board in winning nominations in vacant and new constituencies, defeating sitting MPs in Losberg and Springs. The Nationalist campaign was also compromised by the appearance of groups like Aksie Eie Toekoms (Action Own Future), a right-wing group started by academics and joined by Dr Verwoerd's widow. In addition, Dr Connie Mulder, the disgraced former Information Minister, had formed a new party in November 1979, the National Conservative Party (NCP).

With only twelve uncontested Nationalist seats, the NP was forced to fight in many places where the party machinery was rusty. Doubts over the direction of government policies lowered the enthusiasm of party workers and made recruitment of sufficient canvassing assistance impossible in many areas, whilst party organisation was probably further weakened by the loss of traditionally loyal and active supporters to the HNP (Olivier 1981, 26).

The central Nationalist campaign theme was that of 'total onslaught', with almost every ministerial speech containing an appeal for South Africans to unite in the face of the supposed 'Marxist threat' building up around the country's borders. The NP manifesto represented the struggle as one 'between the forces of chaos, violence and suppression on the one hand, and a Christian civilisation of law, order and justice on the other' (National Party 1981). The NP responded to a strong HNP challenge by portraying itself as a party of moderation, claiming the 'middle ground' and trying to increase its English-speaking support. The HNP was portrayed as evil and beyond the bounds of decency, whereas the PFP was seen merely as misguided and naive, notably for its advocacy of a negotiated constitution which could lead to what were portrayed as the disastrous results of black rule in Zimbabwe. The NRP was attacked as irrelevant on the national scene, whilst its policies in Natal were condemned as leading to Zulu domination.

In some respects the Nationalist campaign was weakened by the need to fight on two fronts. The party was accused of presenting two faces according to whether it faced HNP opposition as in most of the Transvaal, Orange Free State, rural areas of the Cape and northern Natal, or PFP/NRP opposition in Johannesburg, Cape Town, the eastern Cape and most of Natal. Its manifesto largely reiterated established policies, but it was the changed emphases and areas of vagueness which attracted attention (Lemon 1982a, 515–18). These included the future of Indians and coloureds (the issue which was to split the NP the following year), labour legislation, homeland consolidation and urban blacks. The latter were to be given some say over their own local affairs in a new confederal dispensation or 'constellation of states', but the PFP questioned how the wider political aspirations of urban blacks, who were likely to number 21 million by the year 2000, could be met in the homelands. It was proved right four years later by widespread violence in black townships (Chapter 17).

The HNP entered the campaign full of optimism, with a larger membership and improved organisation. It fielded 86 candidates, but did not oppose Dr Mulder's nine NCP candidates. The HNP contested many rural seats outside the Transvaal for the first time, hoping to gain the support of farmers worried about homeland consolidation in Natal and the eastern Cape. It also benefited from white reaction to the government of Mr Robert Mugabe, fed by stories of whites who had recently left Zimbabwe for South Africa. The HNP leader, Mr Jaap Marais, attacked the government for supplying food, fuel and railway services to neighbouring states harbouring anti-South African guerrillas. He also criticised changes in 'petty apartheid', arguing that they would promote integration and the ultimate removal of racial divisions in schools, hospitals and residential areas. Black trade unions, recently legalised, were seen as a threat to white workers, and the President's Council was viewed as a step towards a multi-racial constitution. Finally, government policies were attacked for excessive transfer of wealth from whites to blacks. Other economic issues – opposition to big business, inflation, salaries of teachers, police, nurses and civil servants – played only a secondary role in the HNP campaign. The major stress was the unity of white South Africa 'in a solid front to protect what we have and what we are and to be a beacon of light and faith for the White Christian civilisation'.[10]

The PFP entered the campaign far better organised than in 1977 and with a new leader, Dr F. van Zyl Slabbert, who conducted an extremely energetic campaign. The party's constitutional message stressed the need to negotiate with leaders of all race groups 'while there is still time', i.e. time to avoid violent confrontation. A new constitution would, if the PFP model were accepted at a national convention, be based on proportional representation and consensus government, with a system of checks and balances, including a minority veto. People could choose allegiances under such a system: the Population Registration Act would go, and there would be freedom of association. Dr Slabbert argued that most blacks preferred negotiation to confrontation, and blamed apartheid for making Marxism attractive to those who were angry and frustrated; it was, he said, 'futile to defend security on the borders while we threaten it ourselves'.[11]

A second major thrust of the PFP campaign concerned the 'failure' of apartheid (Lemon 1984a, 10). Findings of the government's own research organisation showed meaningful homeland consolidation and economic viability to be impracticable; they also underlined the impossibility of voluntary movement by urban blacks to homelands with which most had few ties. With considerable political courage, Dr Slabbert stressed that the only solution to mass rural poverty was to settle people in urban areas, in order 'to get the balance right between people and land, so that you can restore the natural resources'.[12] In the urban areas, the informal sector[13] in both housing and employment must provide part of the solution.

'Bread and butter' issues also provided the PFP campaign with major impetus. White incomes were lagging behind inflation which by April 1981 had reached 15.8 per cent p.a. This was attributed to the costs of defending apartheid (R 2400 million in 1981), and of implementing aspects of apartheid such as influx control, residential segregation, separate amenities and resettlement. More generally, the NP was portrayed as arrogant, overbearing and out of touch, the image of Nationalist 'fat cats' taking firm hold in the English-language press.

The NRP fielded only 38 candidates, seven fewer than in 1977. It nevertheless sought to replace the PFP as the official opposition, claiming that 1977 was a 'phoney' election because it took place so soon after the dissolution of the UP. The NRP campaign was a largely negative one. It attacked the government on homeland consolidation, inflation and food prices, but directed its main energies against the PFP, whose policies were attacked as leading to black domination nationally and enforced integration at local level. The NRP offered instead rather complex compromises which were difficult for most electors to grasp. It advocated a federal state in the 'common area' involving whites, coloureds, Indians and 'certain non-homeland blacks who have no ties with their homelands',[14] together with a looser confederation between this and the 'independent homelands'. At local level the NRP advocated self-identified, not necessarily racially homogeneous communities, with control of their own affairs, and certain areas where those who wished to integrate could do so.

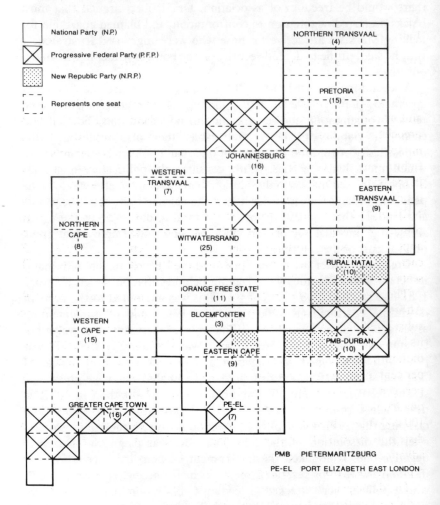

Fig. 5.2   1981 General Election results by seats won

Table 5.3: Seats and votes, 1981

Party	Seats contested Urban	Rural	Seats[a] won	Votes	% of votes
NP	75	66	131 (12)	777,558	57.0
PFP	59	17	26 (2)	265,297	19.4
NRP	27	11	8	106,754	7.8
HNP	31	55	0	192,304	14.1
NCP	5	4	0	19,149	1.4
AET	0	2	0	3,325	0.2
Ind.	1	0	0	570	0.04

Note: a. Figures in parentheses indicate number of uncontested seats.

Mr Vause Raw, the NRP leader, lacked the charisma of Dr Slabbert and attracted a bad press. Coverage of his speeches implied excessive preoccupation with electoral strategy rather than substantive issues, notably in his castigation of the PFP for dividing the opposition by fighting in every constituency contested by the NRP. This was true, but in the Natal provincial elections the PFP fought only the four seats which it believed the NP to have no chance of winning, leaving the rest to the NRP and thus ensuring that the NP would not win control of the provincial council. In the western Cape, on the other hand, there appeared to be an electoral understanding between the NP and NRP, each party staying out of contests where the other was trying to win PFP seats (Lemon 1984a, 111).

The election results represented a serious setback for the NP. Although retaining 131 seats, only four less than it had won in 1977 and substantially more than the 114 it held prior to the dissolution of the UP, its loss of votes, especially to the HNP, raised the spectre of cracks in the monolith of Afrikaner unity. The NP share of the poll decreased by 8.3 per cent, despite the party's absorption of the SAP which had polled 1.8 per cent of the votes in 1977 (Table 5.3). The HNP more than quadrupled its share of the poll to 14.1 per cent, winning nearly twice the 100,000 votes which it had itself predicted. Owing to the widely scattered distribution of HNP support, the party still failed to win a seat, but its advance overshadowed that of the PFP which increased its representation from 17 to 26 seats.

The damage inflicted upon the NP was largely in terms of dramatically reduced majorities. Comparisons can be made for 86 seats won by the NP in 1977 and contested again in 1981; the NP had majorities of under

4000 in only 20 of these seats in 1977, whereas in 1981 it had majorities of *over* 4000 in only 16 of them (Lemon 1984a, 20–2). The number of Nationalist seats held with majorities of over 5000 decreased from 60 in 1977 to only 6 in 1981. Most of this damage was inflicted by HNP candidates in the Transvaal and Orange Free State who dramatically increased their votes.

The PFP benefited from the relative geographical concentration of its support. The results confirmed the party's ability to build on its high-income strongholds and encourage diffusion of support into geographically contiguous areas (Figure 5.3). Its retention of Edenvale (won in a 1979 by-election) and increased majority in Bezuidenhout, in both cases adversely redelimited for the PFP, clearly depended on support from many lower-income voters. So too did the PFP retention of the Cape Town seat of Green Point with an increased majority despite an adverse delimitation which even included the bizarre addition to the constituency of the electors of Walvis Bay, South Africa's Namibian enclave. Such victories led the PFP National Director to speak of a 'breakthrough among "working-class" urbanised people'.[15] The PFP gains included two seats in Port Elizabeth, two in Durban and both Pietermaritzburg seats, thus establishing three new urban bases. The party also won its first two rural seats, Albany and Greytown, in the mainly English-speaking areas of the eastern Cape and southern Natal respectively.

The NRP also benefited from geographical concentration of support which enabled it to retain seven seats in Natal, although its overall share of Natal votes dropped from 40.5 per cent in 1977 to 32 per cent, reflecting Nationalist advances in the more Afrikaans northern areas and the lead taken by the PFP in Durban and Pietermaritzburg. The NRP lost its only non-Natal seat, East London North, exchanging it for King William's Town, where NRP victory owed much to suspicion of government intentions to transfer the town to the Ciskei homeland. The 1981 election thus confirmed the tentative verdict of 1977 by relegating the NRP to the status of a regional rather than truly national party. It had also become a party with a dual character: the NRP parliamentary caucus was largely rural, conservative and increasingly close to the NP, whereas the predominant urban bloc in the NRP provincial caucus was relatively liberal and closer to the PFP (Charney 1982, 532).

The long-term significance of the 1981 General Election
Both the PFP and HNP made significant advances in 1981. The former

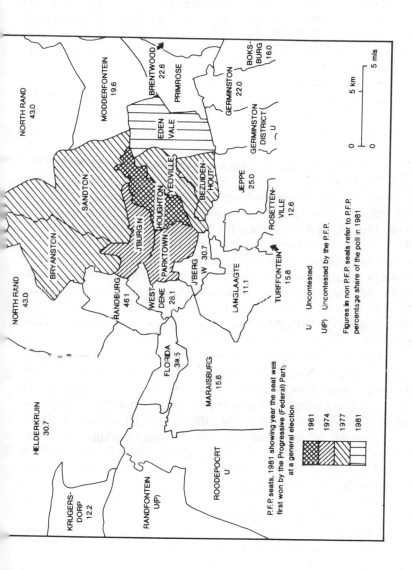

Fig. 5.3 The diffusion of Progressive support in Johannesburg, 1961–1981

clearly consolidated its position as the official opposition; it succeeded in establishing a clear alternative to government policies, and a considerably more radical one than has been presented to South Africa's white electorate since the demise of the tiny, multi-racial Liberal Party in 1968.[16] Electorally, its major advance was probably to win over many former UP supporters who identified for the first time with the PFP as successor to the UP as the real opposition. Given the conservatism of many such voters, this was a considerable achievement, and one which reduced the NP share of the English-speaking vote from its 1977 peak of 30 per cent to only about 20 per cent (Schlemmer 1983a, 27). The PFP also fielded notably more Afrikaans candidates than hitherto, and made greater use of Afrikaans in its propaganda in an attempt to broaden its appeal. There were some signs of success in this respect, mainly among middle-class Afrikaners, as evidenced by the PFP's strong performance in the affluent, mainly Afrikaans constituency of Waterkloof (Pretoria).[17] Overall, the PFP probably gained 5–6 per cent of Afrikaans votes (Olivier 1981, 33). It remained true, however, that all the seats won by the PFP and almost all those which it came close to winning were in areas of traditional UP allegiance. The combined 27.2 per cent of the poll won by PFP and NRP together was below the UP's record low of 32.3 per cent in 1974.

The problem of the PFP lies in its limited geographical and social base. Geographical concentration of support was initially an advantage enabling it to gain parliamentary representation despite a low level of support nationally, but the party has now reached a stage of development where this concentration poses problems for future growth of parliamentary representation, except perhaps in a few Nationalist seats adjoining PFP strongholds and a few NRP seats in Natal (Lemon 1984a, 22). As long as the party remains one of mainly middle-class urban English-speakers and to a lesser extent affluent Afrikaners, the 40–50 seats held by the UP in its declining years appear to be its ceiling (Charney 1982, 542). Unless the PFP can substantially broaden its social appeal, it will be unable to go beyond what Woodward (1980, 123) aptly terms 'Platonic heights of political analysis'.

The HNP, by winning the support of one voter in seven, for the first time established itself as a respectable option. It also won the vote of approximately one in five Afrikaners, a significant erosion of the *verzuiling* of Afrikanerdom (Chapter 4). That it did so without significant media support may encourage the PFP, which has tended to assume that a significant breakthrough is virtually impossible to effect in the absence of Afrikaans newspaper support (Olivier 1981, 28). The HNP capitalised on causes of white discontent which seem unlikely to disappear: the costs of maintaining and defending apartheid can only increase, thus eroding white living standards, whilst further reform will be difficult to resist given the pressures of a normally dynamic economy (Chapter 7). The HNP thus appeared far better placed than the PFP to benefit from further major swings in voting behaviour. Lemon (1984a, 23–4) calculates that whilst a swing of 5–10 per cent from the NP would give the HNP only 2–8 seats, swings of 15 and 20 per cent would give it 19 and 37 seats, respectively. Given that a loss of 49 seats would deprive the NP of its overall parliamentary majority, the significance of the new threat from the right is only too clear.

Underlying these comments on party prospects is the suggestion, supported by survey data from a Johannesburg *Star* election poll (Charney 1982), that class and status tensions are beginning to cut across ethnic allegiances, with a strong pull on blue-collar and farming communities in a conservative direction, and leftward movement among upper-status English and Afrikaans voters. The NP, dependent for its ascendancy on ethnic political mobilisation, is highly vulnerable to such changes, which reinforce the observation of Brotz (1977) that there is no historical inevitability about Afrikaner political unity. The Nationalist split which finally occurred in February 1982 was widely perceived as the long awaited *volkskeuring* in Afrikanerdom.

The Conservative Party: *volkskeuring* at last?
Growing Afrikaans discontent with government policies was signalled by a wave of resignations from the Broederbond during 1981. In September, in an attempt to contain the situation, the Broederbond took the dramatic step of reversing the decision made in 1972 to expel members who belonged to the HNP. The following month an alliance was announced between Dr Mulder's NCP, Aksie Eie Toekoms, the Afrikaans Weerstandsbeweging (Afrikaner Resistance Movement), an extreme white supremacist organisation led by the symbolically surnamed Eugene Terre Blanche ('white ground'), and the Kappie Kommando, an organisation of Afrikaner women who appeared in traditional dress to convey their commitment to the old ways of the *volk*.

When the NP itself finally split, it did so over the issue of power-sharing with coloureds and Indians. The *verkrampte* wing of the NP declared that it was not prepared to accept anything more than the 1977 proposals envisaging three separate racial Parliaments linked through a multi-racial, but white-dominated, 'council of cabinets'. But in February 1982 Mr Botha publicly backed a statement in *Nat 80s*, the NP newspaper, which said that there could be only one government in the part of South Africa left for occupation by whites, coloureds and Indians; he thus effectively supported a qualified form of power-*sharing*, rather than a *division* of power. At a NP parliamentary caucus meeting on 24 February, 22 MPs refused to support a motion of confidence in Mr Botha. Six subsequently remained in the NP, but the other 16 were expelled; all except two represented Transvaal constituencies.

Subsequently Dr Andries Treurnicht, who resigned as Minister of State Administration and Statistics on 2 March, announced the formation of the Conservative Party (CP), which brought together the NP rebels, the NCP, Aksie Eie Toekoms, and a little-known English-speaking group, the South Africa First Campaign. Two further Nationalist MPs subsequently joined the CP, giving it 18 MPs. Of its guiding principles, the most important was that 'every people should have their own political structure and authority'.[18]

Dr Treurnicht's personal charm and effectiveness as a public speaker, together with the key position he had occupied as leader of the Transvaal NP, made the CP a greater threat to the NP than the HNP, despite the latter's recent strength. Dr Treurnicht is acceptable to a far wider range of voters than Mr Marais, and seemed likely to detach more middle-class support from the NP. The CP seemed well placed to secure the 15–20 per cent swing from the NP which was needed for right-wing parties to gain significant parliamentary representation. Despite its initial organisational weakness and lack of media support, the CP enjoyed significant assets from the start: the leadership of the Broederbond and much of the Transvaal Afrikaans establishment inclined towards it, as did much of the Dutch Reformed Church hierarchy and important elements in the civil service, universities, cultural bodies and broadcasting (Charney 1982, 544). The *volkskeuring* quickly affected a wide spectrum of Afrikaans organisations. In July 1983 Professor Carel Boshoff resigned as chairman of the Broederbond because of its support for the government's constitutional proposals, which were opposed by the South African Bureau of Racial Affairs, the right-wing 'think-tank', of which Professor Boshoff was also chairman. In May 1984 he became interim leader of the newly-formed Afrikaner Wolkswag (People's Guard), which professed like the Broederbond to be a cultural rather than a political organisation but was supported by the CP, HNP and Afrikaanse Weerstandsbeweging.

The CP rapidly developed its organisation, especially in the Transvaal where many of its members were able to retain control of former Nationalist constituency organisations. By-elections have been watched closely since the formation of the CP to test the extent of the *volkskeuring*. The first one, a provincial by-election in August 1982 in a division with no previous record of HNP support (Germiston District), confirmed the worst fears of the NP, whose narrow victory depended on a split right-wing vote. The evidence of subsequent by-elections has been more uncertain. Notable CP triumphs have included Dr Treurnicht's retention of his Waterberg seat with a 1894-vote majority over combined NP and HNP opposition in May 1983, and a narrow victory over the NP in the northern Transvaal seat of Soutpansberg in February 1984. Nationalist majorities were further reduced in most contests, most dramatically in the Johannesburg constituency of Primrose where a 4399-vote majority was cut to 748 in November 1984. But the CP performance varied considerably, whilst the outcome of the November 1983 referendum on the proposed new constitution (Chapter 13) was regarded as a resounding success for Mr Botha. Only 20 or 30 constituencies seemed likely to offer the CP such fertile ground as Waterberg and Soutpansberg, and even in these seats victory could not be assured if right-wing support was split between CP and HNP. Differences of style and personality continued to hinder electoral agreement between the two parties, whilst the CP's adherence to the 1977 constitutional proposals remained a stumbling block for the HNP.

The 'mini-election' of 30 October 1985 took place after the collapse of the rand at a time of serious economic recession and widespread black and coloured unrest. It produced a further swing to the right, to the extent that the NP no longer appeared to control a substantial majority of Afrikaans votes and was increasingly dependent on English-speaking voters, many of whom were deserting the PFP. Although the NP held on to four seats out of five, it polled only 27,060 votes to the 21,911 of its right-wing opponents. A pact with the CP enabled the HNP to win its first-ever seat at Sasolburg, the only Free State town to fall under the state of emergency. NP majorities, already much reduced in 1981, fell still further, making three seats marginal. In Springs, a depressed industrial town with high unemployment, the Nationalist majority dropped from 2481 to 749, whilst in the two predominantly rural constituencies of Bethlehem and Vryburg, once Nationalist strongholds, both majorities fell to 1188. Nor did the by-elections offer any comfort to the PFP: its vote was almost halved in Springs, and in Port Natal, which it did not contest in 1981, it only just beat the CP into second place. The collapse of the NRP vote in Port Natal to a mere 550 was widely interpreted as signalling the demise of the NRP as a parliamentary force.

There seems little doubt that an irrevocable *volkskeuring* has occurred in the political forces of Afrikanerdom, but its extent remains debatable. The fact that it is now a *fait accompli* might theoretically enable Mr Botha to pursue a reformist path uninhibited by the fears of a split which constrained his predecessors (to the extent that they were reform-minded). Such a strategy would imply increased NP reliance on English -speaking votes[19] and even conceivably a future partnership with the PFP (Charney 1982, 542) in order to implement more far-reaching changes than have so far been publicly contemplated. For the moment, however, it seems likely that Nationalist policy will continue to be constrained by the fear of further disaffection from its parliamentary caucus and further loss of support to right-wing parties in the country as a whole.

Part 3
THE SOUTH AFRICAN
SPACE ECONOMY

6
Commercial and subsistence agriculture

Nowhere is the dual nature of the South African economy more apparent than in agriculture. No boundary signs are needed when one leaves the landscape of commercial agriculture for that of subsistence farming in the homelands: 'it is almost like stepping through a time warp' (Nattrass 1981, 99). The bulk of agricultural employment is in the black areas, but white-owned commercial farms are responsible for about 90 per cent of agricultural production by value. South Africa is normally a food exporter, and some 30 per cent of non-gold exports derive from the sale of agricultural products, including those which are processed. A wide variety of food crops as well as fibres (wool, cotton, phormium tenax) and meat (especially beef) are produced. Output has roughly kept pace with population growth over the post-war period, but as the rest of the economy has grown the contribution of agriculture to the GDP has declined from 20 per cent 50 years ago to 15 per cent in 1955 and just under 7 per cent today. In the homelands, however, agriculture was still responsible for 28 per cent of the GDP in 1977 (South Africa 1983a, 235). Since then there has been a rapid development of commercial agriculture in the homelands, much of it in the form of 'agribusiness' financed externally (Keenan 1984). Elsewhere, commercial farming is largely in the hands of individual white farmers, whose numbers have decreased from 117,000 in 1950 to 90,000 in 1969 and 70,000 in 1985. Although it is generally assumed that white farming is far more efficient and productive than black farming, this has not always been so and even today the debate over the extent of and reasons for the disparity between the two sectors continues (Lipton 1977, 1979; Tomlinson 1979, 1980; Bisschop 1979, 1980).

White farming and state intervention
The traditional problems of white farming stem mainly from its origins

115

in subsistence pastoralism (Chapter 2) and an imperfect understanding of a difficult physical environment. Much of South Africa is highly susceptible to erosion, because of steep slopes in the Cape mountains and near the plateau edge, high-intensity rainfall both in the latter areas and over the plateau, and an incomplete vegetative cover in the Karroo and semi-desert areas. Pioneer stock farmers unwittingly developed practices which led to the impoverishment of the vegetation, soil deterioration and soil erosion. Indiscriminate burning in the dry season aimed at stimulating young growth for winter and spring grazing, a practice which whites learnt from the Hottentots, was relatively harmless when population was sparse, but with closer settlement and increased stocking densities the rest period was progressively shortened. The effects were accentuated by the practice of kraaling livestock at night – collecting them inside a fence to protect them from wild animals – which means that their dung was not spread over the veld. There was little alternative to such practices in pioneer conditions when no fodder crops were grown and cheap fencing materials were not available (Cole 1961, 249–50), but their persistence over a long period, together with widespread overgrazing, threw back the vegetation succession. The effects were most dramatically seen in the eastward spread of Karroo scrub at the expense of grassland: in some places it reached the longitude of Durban in the mid-1950s (Cole 1956, 119–20).

Arable farming was also responsible for environmental degradation, especially in the inter-war period. The ploughing of steep slopes in the wheat areas of the south-west Cape and continuous monoculture, non-use of fertilisers and the exposure of bare ground after harvest in both the south-west Cape and the extensive maize-growing areas of the highveld caused sheet and gully erosion (Talbot 1947).

The government responded by passing conservation legislation which was advanced for its time. The Forest and Veld Conservation Act 1941 ensured control in the worst affected areas by empowering the government to proclaim them Conservation Areas in the national interest. The 1946 Soil Conservation Act led to the establishment of a National Soil Conservation Board charged with improving farming methods in coopera-tion with the farmers themselves, and provided for the voluntary proclamation of soil conservation areas (in which land consistently abused by its owner could actually be appropriated, subject to the payment of compensation). The response of white farmers was encouraging, and by 1958 some 666 districts representing 90 per cent of the land had been proclaimed under the Act (Houghton 1973, 63).

Progress in conservation after 1946 was made possible by virtue of research work on pastures, veld management and soil conservation undertaken at agricultural research stations and universities. General agricultural research and development in South Africa today are the most advanced in Africa. There are eleven specialist research institutes, a division of agricultural engineering, and eight regional agro-ecological organisations. Specific achievements have included the development of new livestock breeds, the cultivation of drought-resistant fodder crops, hybrid maize and disease-resistant, high-yielding varieties of wheat. The last-mentioned have contributed to considerable increases in wheat production, which has been extended to new areas in the Orange Free State and Transvaal.

The white farming sector has traditionally been protected and given access to cheap credit through the Land Bank, a statutory organisation established in 1912. As long ago as 1941 the Van Eck Commission argued that special assistance to agriculture 'often merely keeps inefficient farmers on the land and perpetuates or even accentuates unhealthy farming practices' (South Africa 1941, 32–4). More recently the Du Plessis Commission found that the bottom third of white farmers produced only 3 per cent of total output, and concluded that these farmers were uneconomic producers who should be encouraged to leave the land (South Africa 1970, 168). The government's acceptance of this recommendation marked the first public departure from the traditional policy of keeping white farmers on the land at all costs (Lemon 1976, 49).

State assistance to white farmers remains widespread, but since 1981 changes in emphasis have exposed farmers more to free market forces, whilst three successive years of drought conditions in the early 1980s further weakened the commercial agricultural sector. In addition, farmers have faced high interest rates and big increases in the cost of farm inputs, including fertilisers, fuel and vehicles, in part because of government import controls to protect home producers of inputs and equipment.[1] This combination of factors has led to a profound disturbance of the traditional bonds between Nationalist governments and white farmers, with the latter looking increasingly to the Conservative Party and the Herstigte Nasionale Party to represent their interests. The government, faced in the mid-1980s with the need to avoid the overspending of recent years and to reduce levels of inflation and interest rates, appears to be exerting tighter control on levels of aid to white farmers, such that the R300 million budgeted for the 1985–86 fiscal year was scarcely one-third of what the farming community demanded.

117

Relative stabilisation of prices is achieved by extensive state intervention in agricultural marketing. The prices of most agricultural products are either directly controlled or regulated in some way, and the distribution and marketing of agricultural products is mainly handled by cooperatives and/or government marketing boards. In 1982 71 per cent of all agricultural produce was controlled by such marketing boards. The operation of these boards has led to criticism of over-bureaucratisation in agriculture, whilst the unfavourable circumstances faced by farmers in the mid-1980s have led to demands on the part of organisations like NAMPO (the National Maize Producers Organisation) for dramatic rises in producer prices.

The state has also been prominently involved in the development of irrigated farming in South Africa, which is very largely in the white farming sector. Over 200 irrigation boards have been established throughout the country, but mainly in the Cape and Transvaal. The area under irrigation on government or irrigation board schemes totals 430,000 hectares, or just under half the total irrigated area, most of which is in the sub-humid or semi-arid areas of the country. Crops grown largely or wholly under irrigation include citrus fruit and lucerne, whilst about 10 per cent of the sugar cane crop is also irrigated in the lowveld of Natal and the eastern Transvaal. Surface irrigation methods, especially flooding, and water losses caused by over-irrigation and faults in the distribution systems have caused progressive soil deterioration on some irrigation projects.

Of many water development projects, the Orange River Project is by far the largest. Its objectives include the safeguarding and stabilisation of existing irrigation and provision for further irrigation in the lower Orange valley, and the transfer of water from the Orange to the Fish and Sundays river basins in the eastern Cape. Further expansion of irrigation elsewhere in South Africa would undoubtedly be beneficial, but water supplies pose major problems. By 1922 irrigation used 78 per cent of all available surface water, compared with 46 per cent in the USA (South Africa 1983a, 610). Cooperation with Lesotho to allow South Africa to use the relatively abundant surface water of the Drakensberg has been discussed intermittently for many years. Following a feasibility study, work on the R2200 million Lesotho Highlands water project is now scheduled to begin in 1987. The first water from the project is scheduled to flow in 1995 and it could be fully operational in the year 2019 if political factors do not intervene.[2]

Where irrigation is absent, drought causes dramatic fluctuations in the production of certain crops. In the 1970s the output of maize, the staple food of most Africans and the most important single agricultural commodity, varied from only 4.2 million tons in 1972 to a record 11 million tons in 1974. Whereas maize was South Africa's leading agricultural export in 1975 and 1976, there may be no surplus at all in drought years, when commercial production is needed to feed the overpopulated homelands. The general trend of maize production is upward, with the application of hybrid seed, more effective fertilisation, weed, pest and disease control, and more effective moisture conservation in the soil. Thus in the peak year of 1980–81 production reached a record 14.2 million tons, or twice South Africa's domestic needs.

Labour and capital in white agriculture

Black and coloured labourers on white farms have always been amongst the most exploited of South Africa's workers. Legislative measures have helped farmers to secure the labour they need without competing in an open market with urban employers. Cecil Rhodes, when introducing the Glen Grey Act in 1894, described taxes as a 'gentle stimulant' to Africans to work. The Native Land Act of 1913 (Chapter 2) swelled the flow of black labour to white farms. The Native Laws Amendment Act of 1952 reinforced existing controls on the movement of farm labour, such that black workers must obtain permission to leave the district from the Labour Control Board, on which local white farmers and officials sit. Once familiar with these restrictive conditions, black migrant labourers often return to the homelands, whence they can go more easily to 'white' urban areas to seek work; this tendency increased in the 1970s (Smit 1976, p. 56). Within the homelands, however, the labour supply in many areas has traditionally been reserved for and monopolised by members of the South African Agricultural Union, thus removing alternative job opportunities and perpetuating low agricultural wages.

The political leverage of white farmers even enabled them to prevent the establishment of job reservation in agriculture. They replaced white *bywoners* (squatters) driven off the land in the 1920s and 1930s with cheaper black and coloured workers. Thus apart from farm managers, whose numbers have increased in recent years, the labour force is almost entirely black and coloured. Hendrie and Kooy (1976) estimate that approximately 1.5 million people were employed in capitalist agriculture in 1973, of whom 84 per cent were black: in the western Cape, coloureds accounted for half the farm labour force, but the percentage of blacks was 90 in the eastern Cape, 97 in Natal, 98 in the Orange Free State and 99 in the Transvaal. Both blacks and coloureds perform many skilled and managerial jobs on white farms, but often earn little more than labourers.

Agricultural workers were excluded from the limited protection afforded by the Wages Act 1925 and the Bantu Labour (Settlement of Disputes) Act of 1953. Their wages remain well below those of all other sectors of the economy apart from domestic service. Lipton (1977, 81) even suggests that blacks on white farms are materially worse off than those in the homelands. However, whereas data on black wages are readily available for most occupations, only piecemeal and often conflicting figures exist for agriculture, and difficulties arise in the evaluation of figures claimed for payment in kind. A government survey[3] of monthly wages for farm labourers in 1979–80 gave figures varying from R26 per month in the Transvaal highveld (1980–81) and Eastern Free State, to R53 in Swartland and R79 in Ruens, both areas of the southwest Cape employing more coloured labour; payment in kind roughly doubled these figures according to the survey. Unofficial research has, however, suggested even lower figures.[4] Comparable figures for average monthly incomes of blacks in mining and manufacturing in 1981 were R201 and R255, respectively (South Africa 1982a, 244). The Chamber of Mines policy of increasing the domestic proportion of its labour force (Chapter 7) has at least exposed agricultural wages to market forces more than hitherto in certain areas. In terms of a 1975 agreement between the Chamber and the South African Agricultural Union (SAAU), the former obtained selective rights of recruitment in areas of labour supply previously reserved for SAAU recruitment. The resultant pressure on agricultural wages is illustrated by the Natal sugar industry, where the basic wage of a cane cutter, excluding bonuses and payment in kind, rose from 34 cents a day in 1969–70 to R 1.75 per day in 1975–76, to compete with mine wages (Knight 1977, 50).

Radical analysts see white farming as being in competition with the urban, industrial economy for available supplies of labour (Legassick 1974; Kaplan 1974), but Nattrass (1977; 1981, 108–9) argues that as capitalism has developed white agriculture has become a net supplier of labour to other sectors of the economy. In the period 1951–71, Nattrass estimates that 400,000 non-agricultural jobs were filled by the permanent movement of blacks from the white farms to urban areas. Altogether over 1.5 million blacks left the capitalist agricultural sector in this period, of whom about 1 million went to urban areas (legally or otherwise) and 500,000 to the homelands. Despite this apparent labour surplus, white farmers continue to complain of labour shortages, and remain dependent on institutional controls to keep labour on their farms (Maree 1977). This reflects the unattractiveness of farm wages and conditions, including harsh discipline and the fear of being tied to the farm. The difficulty farmers experience in getting labour varies locally according to wages, conditions and the farmer's reputation as an employer, whilst regional variations reflect the alternative opportunities available, including homeland agriculture. Thus in the eastern Transvaal, where much higher wages are available quite close at hand on the Phalaborwa mines and in ESCOM (Electricity Supply Commission) projects, farmers complain of a chronic shortage of male labour. Whilst white farms may indeed be a net supplier of black labour to other sectors, they continue to rely on what Leys (1975, 201) has called 'a totalitarian system designed for the total direction of black labour', albeit in somewhat modified form, to retain the labour they need.

Despite movement of labour from white farms to other sectors, natural increase in the black population resident on white farms enabled the overall number of labourers to increase substantially until the late 1960s. This occurred notwithstanding large-scale mechanisation and the decrease in the number of white farm units. Whilst capital stock in commercial agriculture rose by an average of 3 per cent p.a. between 1946 and 1977, in real terms, the labour force grew by an average of 2 per cent p.a. (Nattrass 1981, 105). Prior to 1970 mechanisation served to increase production and yields rather than to replace labour (Lipton 1975, 45-7). Since 1970, total employment in white agriculture has fallen, and continued increase in output is attributable to capital accumulation and the increase in labour productivity generated through the introduction of labour-replacing technology.

The period since the 1950s has also been marked by government intervention to end the labour tenancy system whereby blacks would work part-time for a white farmer and be allowed to live on the farm with their dependants and cultivate a piece of land, or even work in the town for part of the year. Black squatters on white farms were similarly to be eliminated; if their breadwinners were amongst those who had migrated to jobs in urban areas, their families would be moved to the homelands and the land they occupied freed for white farming. The government encountered some resistance from farmers in northern Transvaal and Natal who favoured the tenancy system (Lemon 1984b, 78), but the policy of eradicating squatters and abolishing labour tenancy went ahead in the 1960s, when 340,000 labour tenants and 656,000 squatters were removed, together with 97,000 people from 'black spots' – areas of

African settlement surrounded by white farmland – and small 'scheduled areas' set aside for Africans under the Native Land Act of 1913 (Baldwin 1975, 216). A further 305,000 labour tenants were removed in the 1970s (SAIRR 1981, 452). The tenancy system was finally abolished in August 1980, which resulted in several thousands of black families being evicted; one of the most severely affected districts was Weenen, Natal (ibid., 119).

Government intervention in the agricultural labour market may be explained in terms of either apartheid ideology (Baldwin 1975) or capitalist development (Morris 1977). Undoubtedly the declining white population and growing black population of 'white' rural areas gave rise to concern over the *verswarting* of the *platteland*. The Du Plessis Commission had recommended that 'white agriculture must accordingly be made less dependent on non-white labour and eventually be released from the need of it as far as possible' (South Africa 1970, 175). This was clearly impracticable, but the removal of squatters and labour tenants certainly reduced the black population in these areas. Although this stabilisation of farm labour 'was consummated under the ideological umbrella of Separate Development' (Morris 1977, 175), state intervention has clearly restructured the relations of production and permitted capitalist agricultural expansion in 'white' rural areas.

The effects on the ground of government intervention and mechanisation are much more diverse than might be supposed, and it is difficult to generalise about trends in the number and composition of the black labour force on white farms. In general terms, farmers now rely on a smaller, better-trained labour force of regular workers. Whereas the need for casual labour has declined, as the Du Plessis Commission anticipated (South Africa 1970, 158, 174–5), the demand for migrant workers has increased in some cases. This is particularly true in the western Cape, where coloureds are increasingly reluctant to stay in farm jobs and increasing use is made of Transkeian contract workers (Budlender 1984a, 307). In the maize-growing areas of western Transvaal, however, de Klerk (1984, 310–11) finds a transfer of jobs from annual migrants to a reduced permanent on-farm population; mechanisation on these farms appears to have taken place partly in response to an urban labour 'pull'. Both Budlender (p. 305) and de Klerk (p. 316) suggest that a farmer is often reluctant to retrench his own workers, but that when another farm is taken over and consolidated with his own, it is the workers on the new farm who lose their jobs. Budlender (pp. 306–7) also notes a shift to increased use of female labour (with lower wages); these women may be members of families resident on the farm, their husbands perhaps working in the towns, or they may be recruited from nearby homelands. Overall, there seems little doubt that the black labour force on white farms will continue to decrease, albeit more slowly than hitherto: the current Economic Development Programme predicts a loss of between 90,000 and 230,000 farm jobs between 1977 and 1987 (South Africa 1981a). By 1983 it was estimated that agriculture provided work for 1.2 million people, 300,000 fewer than in 1973.[5] Such a decrease should enable farmers to pay, house and feed their labour force better than hitherto, but whilst this appears to be happening in some areas such as the Stellenbosch district, the absolute and often the relative gap between farm wages and those in mining, manufacturing and construction continues to widen.

Black agriculture: the physical environment of the homelands
The homelands have been variously described as some of the finest well-watered lands of South Africa (Niddrie 1968, 145) and as economically marginal land which is too mountainous, too dry or too remote to be productive (Desmond 1971, 21). The truth is too complex for such generalisations to be meaningful. 68 per cent of the homelands do receive more than 500 mm of rain p.a. which is generally regarded as the minimum for successful dryland cultivation, compared with only 35 per cent of South Africa as a whole. Other significant environmental factors include the nature and reliability of rainfall, evaporation rates, steepness of slopes, and soil cover. Overall, the Tomlinson Commission equated the agricultural potential of 100 hectares in the reserves (as they were in 1955) with that of 147 hectares in white farming areas, which implied that the reserves possessed 23 per cent of South Africa's agricultural potential (South Africa 1955, 117). This takes no account of inaccessibility, a disadvantage common to most parts of the homelands given their origin as reserves for those outside the modern economy (Chapter 2).

KwaZulu and Transkei are both well watered, with several perennial rivers offering irrigation potential. The proximity of such rivers to some of the best farming land in South Africa confers on Transkei an agricultural potential which probably exceeds that of any other homeland, despite its low percentage of arable land (Table 6.1). Ciskei, further west, suffers from variable climatic conditions; the flow of perennial rivers such as the Fish and Keiskama fluctuates to such an extent that the water supply for irrigation depends on storage dams. In many areas of KwaZulu rainfall is episodic and unreliable, and high

123

temperatures in lowland areas such as the Tugela valley result in high evaporation rates and a low effective rainfall. Highly dissected topography also presents problems; in his study of the Tugela Location, Schulze (1970, 626) mapped only 8.4 per cent of the land as being soil-covered, the rest consisting of rock outcrops, land generally steeper than a gradient of 15 per cent, or stony areas with skeletal soil in small patches. Both Ciskei and Transkei also have much dissected land, and all three homelands have suffered extensively from soil erosion.

The three homelands in the northern and eastern Transvaal are also generally well watered but show considerable variations in physical conditions over relatively short distances. In Lebowa, rainfall varies from 710 mm in the north to as little as 350 mm in some western districts. Numerous rivers such as the Letaba provide irrigation potential in Lebowa and Gazankulu, whilst high rainfall (900 mm) on top of the Soutpansberg range feeds Venda's perennial rivers which include the Limpopo and Pafuri.

Table 6.1: Land use in the homelands, 1979

| | Arable | | Grazing land |
	Dryland (%)	Irrigation (%)	(%)
Bophuthatswana	10.0	0.1	88.7
Ciskei	14.1	0.1	70.1
KwaZulu	31.3	0.1	66.3
QwaQwa	9.5	0.0	79.6
Lebowa	15.2	0.4	79.8
Gazankulu	16.5	0.3	78.3
KaNgwane	20.4	0.3	59.0
KwaNdebele	31.8	0.2	63.6
Transkei	8.7	0.4	84.2
Venda	9.9	0.6	85.8

Source: South Africa 1983a, 233.

Bophuthatswana is the largest homeland in terms of area, but has an annual rainfall, which decreases westwards, of only 250–500 mm, making dryland cultivation risky if not impossible in most areas. The river beds of the Malopo and Limpopo are no more than dry ditches for much of the year, but the Harts river, a tributary of the Vaal, flows through the Taung region in south-west Bophuthatswana where 4300 hectares are irrigated.

The three smallest homelands are KaNgwane, KwaNdebele and QwaQwa. KaNgwane shares the subtropical climate of neighbouring Swaziland, and its western part is traversed by the Komati river which offers some potential for irrigation. Much of KwaNdebele has a relatively low rainfall and is marginal for dryland cultivation. QwaQwa is a mountainous territory in the Drakensberg which has experienced severe soil erosion. It has hard winters with frost and snow.

The Tomlinson agricultural strategy and 'betterment'

Government agricultural policies in the homelands since 1955 have strongly reflected the views of the Tomlinson Commission, although the granting of self-government to the homelands has brought a greater diversity of approach in recent years. The Commission believed that a sound agriculture implied relatively large holdings (an average of 44 hectares was recommended) and heavy capital investment. Such holdings would enable families to earn enough to satisfy their basic requirements, the cash constituent of which was estimated at £60 p.a. for mixed farming units (the vast majority). Economic landholdings were to be determined on the basis of existing farm practices. On this basis, Tomlinson calculated that the homelands could support 307,000 full-time farming families, or 1.8 million people (South Africa 1955, 114). A higher basic income of £120 p.a. was rejected because of the impracticability of moving 80 per cent of the population (p. 206), whereas the actual recommendation involved the creation of alternative employment for half the population. Tomlinson's predictions (p. 184) implied that over 5 million out of a total population of 9 million in 1981 would be dependent upon non-agricultural employment *within* the homelands. In practice population growth has been faster, owing to compulsory resettlement of blacks from 'white' South Africa (Chapter 9), whilst development of non-agricultural employment has lagged far behind the 50,000 p.a. envisaged by Tomlinson (Chapter 8). As a result it has proved unthinkable to reduce the rural homeland population to anything resembling 1.8 million, and some five-sixths of the 1985 homeland population of just over 12 million are officially classified as rural, although this includes substantial peri-urban squatter populations, especially in KwaZulu and the Winterveld of Bophuthatswana.

The inevitable result is that land reforms undertaken to date, although theoretically based on the Tomlinson strategy, have been unable to give most families anything resembling Tomlinson's 'economic units'. According to official calculations, the size of such units is considered to include 4.1 hectares of arable land in the Umtata district of Transkei and between 4.9 and 7.3 hectares in the King William's Town district of Ciskei, but the median size of arable plot in the Transkeian areas investigated by Maree and de Vos (1975, 13) was only 1.9 hectares, and in the Ciskeian areas 1.5 hectares. Yawitch (1981) gives many similar examples. Many families have in recent years received only one hectare and grazing for two cattle. Although attempts have been made to plan these lesser units so that they can ultimately be combined to form full economic units, only the abolition of influx control could enable enough blacks to leave the land for such units to become feasible. Thus in KwaZulu, evidence presented to the Buthelezi Commission showed that the tribal areas could support only 140,000 families or 1.26 million people, assuming an average of 2.5 economically active members per family; with optimal use of land this could generate an average family income of approximately R1600 p.a. (Buthelezi Commission 1982, 2, 174–5). Linkages between agriculture and commerce were assumed to provide occupations which would support a further 250,000 people. This implied an out-migration of 830,000 people from rural KwaZulu, together with all future natural increase in the rural population (ibid.).

It is perhaps fortunate that the Tomlinson recommendation to grant freehold title to arable holdings has not been carried out, given the uneconomic size of most plots and the likelihood of further land reforms in future years. For the present, the lack of alternative employment makes the implementation of any reforms in land tenure extremely difficult. Thus the Swart Commission report recommends both gradualism and diversity of approach in the application of its controversial land reform proposals for Ciskei, which 'may take decades' (Ciskei 1983, 14–24; Swart Commission Members 1984, 49).

It is within this unpromising framework of sub-economic holdings and increasing rural overpopulation that rehabilitation or 'betterment' policies have been pursued since 1955. Such concepts were not new: they had been applied in the reserves since the 1930s, but had met with considerable resistance. In the 1950s this resistance was in response not only to betterment *per se* but to a restructuring of existing systems of control over the rural population, notably Proclamation 116 of 1949 which made the penalties for refusing to implement or for destroying rehabilitation measures very severe, and the Bantu Authorities Act 1951 which removed the principle of accountability to the tribal council and made chiefs salaried officials of the government who could be replaced by government authorities (Yawitch 1981, 11, 20). The establishment of the

Tomlinson Commission to investigate and plan the socio-economic development of the reserves was partly related to this resistance and the lack of progress made hitherto in rehabilitating black agriculture. Tomlinson's solutions were by no means revolutionary, and were indeed foreshadowed by a 1945 document drawn up by the Secretary for Native Affairs.[6] Since the Tomlinson Report, however, the replanning of settlement and land use has been effected in more than half the total area of each homeland, in nearly four-fifths of Ciskei and Venda and almost the entire area of KaNgwane and Gazankulu.

The procedure is to divide the land into arable allotments and grazing areas, the latter camped and fenced so that rotational grazing may be practised. Huts are concentrated in villages to permit more effective use of agricultural land. Stock limitation is enforced, water supplies and dams are provided in each camp, and anti-erosion measures adopted: many miles of contour ridges have been constructed and planted with grass, and where necessary diversion banks have been built. The available land is reallocated to all the inhabitants who previously held land rights. Those 'squatters' who previously had neither land nor cattle receive nothing in the redistribution except a hut or a garden; many are forced to relocate in 'closer settlements' (Chapter 9). What this may mean in practice is illustrated by a detailed study of land betterment in a Ciskeian village, Cata (de Wet 1980). Here population increased by 49 per cent whilst the land area under cultivation was reduced by more than half in an attempt to check soil erosion; 41 per cent of families were left landless and those who retained land had less than before, leaving the population as a whole even more dependent on migrant labour than hitherto, apart from a minority who benefited from an irrigation scheme.

There is no question of the need for conservation and rehabilitation in the reserves in the 1950s, and the achievement of betterment schemes in these respects is far from negligible. The actual implementation was also not without positive features (Daniel 1970, 645-6), including the element of self-help involved and the relatively low cost which means that Africans are not burdened with debt as the result of resettlement. The thoroughness of the preliminary surveys undertaken prior to resettlement is another favourable aspect, although Yawitch (1981, 43) contrasts the careful reports of the 1950s with those of the late 1960s and 1970s – when the limitations of what could be achieved were all too clear – which she describes as 'cryptic in the extreme'.

Whatever the achievements of betterment, they leave the most fundamental problems unresolved. The reallocation of land has entrenched and intensified existing inequalities among the rural population, whilst the physical replanning of the land is not sufficient to raise agricultural productivity, as the Tomlinson Report itself emphasised (p. 77). Board (1964) has shown that there is no significant difference between replanned or stabilised areas and unrehabilitated areas with regard to agricultural practices, productivity or the retention of man on the land. As a result, agricultural incomes remain far below those obtainable in urban areas, even for the privileged few whose plots approach the sizes recommended by Tomlinson. For the majority with arable plots of only 1 or 2 hectares existing agricultural practices cannot provide for basic needs, and they, like the families who are landless, are faced with the necessity of the head of the family and any sons who are old enough migrating in search of work. This has led Yawitch (1981, 94–5) to conclude that, whatever the intentions of those who formulated the policy, betterment has become an instrument for the economic and political control of rural population. This is debatable, but there can be no doubt that the positive intentions of the policy are fatally compromised by the ideological framework of macro-scale apartheid (Chapter 3) in which it has been carried out.

Agricultural productivity and migrant labour
The designation 'subsistence agriculture' is somewhat misleading. Most black farming is certainly for subsistence purposes: the proportion of production entering the market in 1980 varied from 6 per cent in QwaQwa to 18 per cent in Ciskei and KwaZulu (SAIRR 1984, 363). As homeland population has grown, both naturally and as a result of resettlement, agricultural production has failed to expand significantly (Table 6.2), and the population has become increasingly reliant upon the importation of food produced on white farms (Simkins 1980). Thus few families grow enough to feed themselves, and total homeland food production is sufficient for only 30 per cent of the population (van Eeden 1980).

In these circumstances, many views have been advanced to explain the failure of black agriculture to modernise and expand its output. The limited size of arable plots is not a sufficient explanation; not only do yields remain very low compared with those of white farms, often by a factor of five or more, but much arable land is actually left uncultivated – as much as 20 per cent to 30 per cent in KwaZulu, for instance (Lenta 1982, 307). Traditional explanations blame the 'backwardness' of black agriculture on the limiting nature of the tribal system and communal

Table 6.2: Production of cereal crops in black rural areas (tons), 1918-75

Year	Maize	Sorghum	Wheat
1918	261,339	119,464	9,643
1925	299,643	78,214	2,857
1935	193,214	54,018	8,393
1945	181,161	52,143	3,661
1955	259,553	62,410	5,000
1965	189,784	29,670	8,317
1975	326,800	46,423	9,543

Source: Various agricultural censuses, after Nattrass (1981, 113).

land tenure. Thus Houghton (1973, 74) stresses the 'bottomless pit created by their cattle complex', whereas Lipton (1977, 77) responds to this criticism by arguing that 'it can be economically rational and profitable for the individual black farmer, with free access to communal grazing, to accumulate as much livestock as he can'. A less specific but widely held view, reiterated by South Africa's official handbook (South Africa 1983a, 236) is that blacks 'are not natural farmers' and that as traditional pastoralists they are uninterested in arable farming which they consider to be women's work. Thus Bisschop (1979, 30) argues that work in the diamond and gold mines constituted 'a God-sent alternative' to the tilling of the soil, enabling blacks to retain 'to a considerable extent an adventurous existence, similar to that of their pastoral past'. Tomlinson himself (1980, 50) gives general support to this viewpoint. Such generalisations concerning 'the mind of the Bantu' are difficult either to prove or disprove . The importance of black labour on white farms at all occupational levels casts doubt on the supposed refusal of blacks to do agricultural work, but it is true that the availability of employment outside the homelands removed the absolute connection between agricultural innovation and survival (Chapter 2).

However, numerous other reasons for the poverty of black agriculture are now well attested. Lipton (1977, 79) argues that, despite over-population and overgrazing, the homelands are seriously underfarmed, because migrant labour reduces available manpower. She also points out (p. 82) that 'the heavy loading of economic incentives against them effectively discourages many potentially viable black farmers from farming, while the availability of cheap labour and cheap capital encourages many marginal white farmers to stay in business'. Whereas white land has been upgraded by past allocation of capital, black land has deteriorated through overgrazing and capital starvation. Not only have whites received greater aid and protection, especially before 1946 when very little was spent on black agriculture, but they have benefited from research facilities geared to their needs, better education and training. In black rural areas low levels of income have prevented the formation of private capital, and credit has been largely unavailable: thus the resources were lacking to buy expensive new seeds and fertilisers recommended by extension officers (only 10 per cent of the cultivated area of the homelands receives fertiliser). The reliable water supply needed for effective use of many recommended inputs is also lacking. A hopelessly inadequate transport network in any case means that farmers lack assured access to market. In such conditions it may be perfectly rational to leave land uncultivated, given the availability of other sources of income to cover basic needs and the marginal returns available from cultivation; thus Lenta (1982, 315), finding that cereal cultivation in KwaZulu required the equivalent of three hours labour for a loaf of bread, concluded that 'under such conditions it seems more appropriate to ask why people cultivate at all, than why they do not make full use of the land'.

Some writers have suggested that with intensive agricultural development the homelands could accommodate many more people. Riekert (1970, 137) suggests that Bophuthatswana could support 6.2 million people, and Grobler (1972, 39–40) calculates that KwaZulu could support 7.5 million people, the northern homelands 10.9 million, and the western homelands 7.2 million people, all on the basis of dryland agriculture. But such theoretical calculations mean little if the human and material resources are not forthcoming. Nor should the sheer magnitude of the task in human terms be underestimated, especially when measured against the time-scale in which development is needed (Maasdorp 1974, 13). Lenta (1982, 325) concludes that, 'To produce the transformation of conditions which would permit blacks to make full and intensive use of their land would require an infusion of capital and skill on a scale which South Africa has never envisaged as being necessary, or indeed desirable'.

In raising the question of desirability, Lenta points to another explanation advanced to explain the continuing poverty of homeland agriculture, namely that it is a necessary concomitant of the creation of a supply of cheap labour, and, more broadly, a necessary component in capitalist development.[7] Whilst the underdevelopment of peasant agriculture assured a vast reservoir of migratory labour, the ability of the reserves to supply part at least of the subsistence needs of workers' families enabled employers to force wage levels below the level necessary to ensure the reproduction of the labour force (Wolpe 1972), whilst the government was able to minimise the cost of welfare facilities, education and social security (Chapter 9). That the existence of underdeveloped economies in the reserves has historically fulfilled this role is difficult to dispute, although Lipton (1977, 82–3) argues that even the alternative of a minimal level of subsistence in the reserves has traditionally given blacks at least some bargaining power in the white labour market. Whether neglect of homeland agriculture has been consciously directed to the labour needs of capitalism is much more questionable; the more obvious explanation of government unwillingness to provide the immense resources required for genuine homeland development may be nearer the truth.

Whatever the historical reasons for homeland underdevelopment, the radical thesis cannot be applied to the present situation. Since the 1960s capitalist production has moved from conditions of small-scale competitive capitalism to large-scale monopoly capitalism, a transformation which has required more skilled workers but reduced the demand for unskilled production workers. Under these conditions the reproduction of the black component of the labour force in the modern economy is no longer dependent on the homelands but now takes place primarily within the urban areas (Keenan 1984, 319–20). Other factors have in any case pushed black wage levels in mining and manufacturing up to and beyond the minimum levels needed for reproduction of the labour force (Chapter 7). The radical view of rural underdevelopment in the homelands today is expressed by Keenan (1984, 320) who sees the rural homeland population as 'largely dysfunctional for capital' and the collapse of peasant subsistence cultivation as having removed the barriers to white capital 'which has met no resistance in taking over control of the rural means of production' in the homelands.

Cash, crops, irrigation and 'agribusiness' in the homelands

Alongside betterment policies aimed at the mass of the rural population, a second strategy of increasing homeland agricultural production through project farming has become increasingly important since 1973, when the agricultural division of the Bantu Investment Corporation was formed. Until the mid-1970s commercial agriculture in the homelands was limited to a few plantation schemes run by the agricultural sections of the Department of Cooperation and Development or the homeland governments themselves. Commercial crops occupied less than 2 per cent of the arable land in the homelands in 1975, excluding timber which could be regarded as the most important commercial 'crop': forest covered 2.2 per cent of the total area of the homelands, although less than one-third of this (94,500 hectares) consisted of commercial plantations. Relatively large plantations were found in KwaZulu, Venda and Ciskei, but only in Transkei was forestry an important source of revenue. Some 18,000 hectares of resilient fibres, mainly sisal and phormium tenax, were grown on government plantations in 1975, one of the largest being that at Chloe, near Pietersburg (Lebowa). Sugar cane, the only cash crop grown on a significant scale by African farmers, accounted for 14,000 hectares, largely in KwaZulu where it is grown for the most part without irrigation. Other cash crops in the mid-1970s were grown only on a small scale, sometimes experimentally: they included cotton, coffee and citrus fruit in several homelands, tea in Transkei and Venda, coconuts in northern KwaZulu, and tobacco in Ciskei.

Irrigation schemes throughout the homelands covered only 22,000 hectares in 1973, of which schemes along the Olifants river in Lebowa accounted for one-third. Other notable schemes included those near Taung in Bophuthatswana and along the Luvuvhu, Phiphidi and Motale rivers in Venda, the Qamata scheme in western Transkei, the Gxulu scheme near Keiskammahoek (Ciskei), and the Bululwana scheme in the Nongoma district of KwaZulu. Irrigated plots varied according to climatic conditions from about 1.3 to 1.7 hectares. They were leased to settlers on various conditions relating to such matters as payment of rent, beneficial usage, and the number of cattle units which may be kept. Plot-holders were urged to rotate their pieces of land, and, in addition to maize, to grow other crops suited to the locality such as vegetables, fodder crops, wheat, lucerne, tobacco, fruit, sugar cane and groundnuts. Although yields were considerably higher than on dry lands, the progress of these schemes was disappointing in many respects, with a marked divergence between planned and actual behaviour of plot-holders (Lemon 1976, 169).

The agricultural projects described so far may be regarded as a forerunner of much greater development of 'agribusiness' since 1973, and especially since 1977 when significant amendments were made to the Promotion of Economic Development of Bantu Homelands Act of 1968. The Bantu Investment Corporation was renamed the Corporation for Economic Development (CED), and its constitution changed to allow all races to become shareholders instead of only blacks, and to enable the CED to buy undertakings from and sell to any racial group. This has led to an unprecedented flow of capital into commercial agricultural production in the homelands (Keenan 1984, 319). The policy of the Agricultural Division of the CED is to lease land from a tribal authority, identify suitable production methods and crops, and enter into a partnership with the tribal authority, which appoints members of the tribe to operate an economic unit of land around the main commercial project. Unsuccessful farmers are replaced, while successful ones acquire the use of more than one unit. During 1982–83 the Agricultural Division invested R15.6 million in homeland agriculture, making a total CED investment of R112.8 million in this sector; it was operating 77 agricultural projects involving 17,617 farmers and 14,469 other workers (SAIRR 1984, 375). Many of these projects had been transferred to the CED from the agriculture departments of homeland governments.

Homeland development corporations such as Bophuthatswana's AGRICOR are also involved in developing commercial agriculture, whilst homeland government agriculture departments may also operate schemes either directly or through the use of consultants as at Keiskammahoek in Ciskei. Capital may come from private as well as state sources, which leads to a complex permutation of operating arrangements (Keenan 1984, 320–1). State capital channelled through the CED may combine with a homeland development corporation to form an agricultural company such as Gazankulu Fruit Farming (Pty) Ltd. The CED may act as the agent for private capital or vice versa, whilst tripartite arrangements where equity is held by the private company and by the CED or development corporation both on its own behalf and on behalf of the people of the homeland are quite common, for example in KwaZulu. There is also an increasing tendency for both companies and individual white farmers to lease land directly from the homeland for their own use.

This growth of 'agribusiness' in the homelands has considerably raised the gross value of agricultural production, which increased by 55 per cent to R166 million in the 'independent' homelands between 1975–76 and 1979–80 (BENSO 1982, 119), and by 89 per cent to R181 million in the other homelands between 1976–77 and 1980–81 (BENSO 1983, 99). This apparent success has however been subject to close scrutiny and much critical comment. Butler *et al.* (1978, 186) question whether direct control of large farms and plantation-style units by white managers using hired black labour will permit the rapid transfer of skills and managerial ability, noting that the CED has made no commitment to any particular schedule or method of transfer to black management. Southall (1982, 229–30) points out that the potential impact of irrigation schemes is minimal in terms of employment, whilst commercial plantation agriculture erodes the basis of communal land tenure, and by dispossessing subsistence producers actually increases the proportion of the population dependent upon migrant labour.

Daniel (1981) provides one of the most detailed and balanced critiques to date, with reference to Ciskei. He studied three irrigation schemes: Keiskammahoek, where dairy farming is the main activity and 250 settlers are being given 4-hectare plots which should earn a net income of R2400 p.a.; Tyefu, where an arable scheme includes a tribal farm, 124-hectare plots allocated to individuals selected by the tribal authority, and 52 ¼-hectare plots; and Zweledinga, which includes stock farming and agricultural development modelled on the Tyefu experience. Whilst noting several positive features, Daniel makes three major criticisms of this kind of development. First, it widens inequalities by creating a small élite group of farmers earning far more than their neighbours, including those next door to them at Keiskammahoek and Zweledinga with no land rights at all. Secondly, given the overall scarcity of capital, concentration on less than 2 per cent of the surface area means the neglect of dryland farming against a background of deteriorating veld conditions, population growth and the need to increase food production from the 15 per cent of Ciskei which is suitable for cultivation. Daniel warns starkly:

> This neglect could well jeopardise the whole future of agricultural development in the Ciskei, including what is being done in the field of irrigation farming. Not only will the silting of the dams be accelerated but the declining quality of the vegetation cover will have an adverse effect on infiltration which is the key variable determining the amount of precipitation available for plants, for replenishing groundwater and for base flow. (Daniel 1981, 19)

Finally, Daniel criticises the construction of rural villages for those without land rights, with no indication as to how they will be integrated with the existing settlement network (Chapter 8). Large quantities of unskilled labour alone will not offer incentives for industrial development, and Daniel argues for a more integrated approach which will transform agricultural development into genuine rural development. This should make greater use of existing settlements and the generation of employment for landless families and the unemployed by encouraging small family enterprises using labour-intensive methods.

Keenan (1984) criticises private companies and management consultants both for their increasing exploitation of labour and for frequently excessive capital intensification and mechanisation on homeland agricultural projects. He points to the Mooifontein project in the Ditsobotla district of Bophuthatswana, where Roodt (1984, 332-3) shows that the total cost of inputs often exceeds the farmer's gross income, as evidence of overcapitalisation in a climatically marginal area for cultivation. Homeland 'agribusiness' has also served to reinforce the position of the tribal authorities whose cooperation is needed for new projects. This gives them considerable control over the lives of rural people which is often abused to favour themselves and their associates and supporters at the expense of known opponents, the poor and migrant workers who are amongst those most likely to be dispossessed of their land rights when 'development projects' are established (Keenan 1984, 324-5).

Agricultural development in Bophuthatswana

The experience of Bophuthatswana, which is by far the most economically 'viable' homeland (Chapter 8), illustrates the problems and pitfalls of homeland agricultural development. Its stated aim is to become self-sufficient in basic foodstuffs and to create an export market, and investment in the agricultural sector has been substantial. Between its establishment in April 1978 and December 1982 the Agricultural Development Corporation (Agricor) invested R50 million, whilst its development budget for 1983-84 was R30 million. Agricor has introduced a rural development concept known as *temisano*, which is intended as a comprehensive, coordinated planning effort to establish sound rural communities; every *temisano* project should embrace agricultural production, community development, training, and where practicable, agriculturally-based secondary industries.

Agricor has developed large-scale farming projects on state-owned land, much of it bought from white farmers in terms of the Native Trust and Land Act 1936, resulting in over 40,000 hectares of dryland summer grain production in central and eastern Bophuthatswana and 3000 hectares of winter wheat (Cowley and Lemon 1986). Much of this is based upon the Israeli Moshav cooperative system. Agricor has also developed the Taung irrigation scheme which in 1983 covered 4300 hectares and supported 530 farmers producing groundnuts, maize, wheat and cotton; this is to be further expanded to produce fruit, including grapes. Several other irrigation schemes are operated or planned, some

135

using sophisticated irrigation methods such as the computerised drip-feed irrigation used to grow vegetables since 1984 at Dinokana near Lehurutse. Agricor is also planning an extensive cattle-ranching scheme in eastern Bophuthatswana, as well as the establishment of more abattoirs, a meat-processing plant and feedlots to improve self-sufficiency in beef.

This wide-ranging agricultural development effort has already done much to improve Bophuthatswana's agricultural production and self-sufficiency in food crops; in good years it is now a net exporter of maize. At best Bophuthatswana's agricultural schemes are less paternalistic and more beneficial to the community than many homeland projects. This is particularly so where Agricor has put into practice the *temisano* concept (as at Mooifontein since Agricor took over from the Corporation for Economic Development), which embraces much of the integrated rural development approach for which Daniel (1981) pleads in Ciskei. The Dinokana scheme is perhaps symbolic of differences between Israeli and white South African approaches; it is designed to be wholly black-operated within a year or so of its initiation, leaving the Israeli manager free to initiate similar schemes elsewhere. The vegetables produced will improve the diet of people in the surrounding areas as well as being sold in Mmabatho and further afield.

Criticisms of Bophuthatswana's approach have revolved around the capital-intensive nature of the projects and the norm of R5000 p.a. thought necessary by Agricor to keep a full-time farmer on the land and discourage him from migrating to the urban areas (Roodt 1984, 327). At Mooifontein the attempt to achieve this on 15-hectare plots led to the overcapitalisation already mentioned, yet the use of larger plots in a subsequent scheme in western Ditsobotla means that even fewer farmers can be accommodated. This illustrates the constraints within which Agricor and all homeland agricultural programmes must operate. Many of their projects are not ill-conceived in themselves and succeed in terms of production objectives, but they use valuable resources of land and capital to support small numbers of people. Given the lack of alternative opportunities within the homelands and, as black unemployment has risen during the 1980s, the difficulties of finding urban employment even without legislative restrictions, homeland agricultural development needs to give high priority to the relatively unexciting objectives of conserving existing resources and raising production to subsistence level for as many people as possible.

7
Mining and industrialisation: the core areas

The economy in global and regional perspective
South Africa may be classified as a developing primary producer, whose manufacturing, commerce and services have been built up extensively on the foundations of mining and farming. The latter now accounts for only 4.7 per cent of GDP (1983), but the share of mining remains high at 15.1 per cent. Manufacturing outpaced mining in the Second World War and contributed 22.6 per cent of the GDP in 1983. In terms of exports, however, minerals remain dominant, accounting for 66.9 per cent of merchandise exports in 1980. This includes gold (which may be sold or added to the reserves) which alone accounts for about half of export earnings in recent years. Manufacturing accounted for 28.8 per cent of export earnings in 1981; consumer goods industries continue to supply mainly domestic markets, and the major contributions to export are made by non-ferrous basic metal industries (29.7 per cent), iron and steel (20.2 per cent) and processed foodstuffs (14.8 per cent).

The strengths of South Africa's economy are well known. An extraordinary wealth of scarce mineral resources and abundant cheap labour have permitted impressive economic expansion despite low individual productivity. In the decade ending 1972 the economy grew at an average rate of 5.5 per cent annually, slightly faster than the OECD average. This figure fell below 3 per cent in 1972–82, a decade in which the economy was adversely affected by the oil crisis from 1973 and by the impact of the Soweto riots and associated unrest elsewhere in the country. The normal tendency for South African business-cycles to lag behind western cycles by about 18 months was also disrupted by the exceptional volatility of gold prices. By 1979, however, record gold prices had assisted a remarkable turnround from the mid-1970s recession and South Africa had risen to twelfth position in the US Economic Business Risk Index, ahead of Britain and France for a brief period (Blumenfeld 1980, 336).

In the early 1980s South Africa experienced renewed and severe recession. As advanced capitalist economies contracted in the general world recession, they purchased less abroad and most raw material prices dropped sharply, whilst inflation in these same economies increased the prices of their exports of manufactured goods. As a primary commodity exporter who needs to import capital equipment, and one who trades internationally a high percentage of what she produces, South Africa was severely affected by such trends (Kaplan 1983a, 158). Nor was the gold price an effective cushion on this occasion. Thus in 1982, for the first time since the Second World War, GDP declined modestly (1.2 per cent) in real terms. This was followed by a decline of almost 3 per cent in 1983, equivalent to a 5.0 per cent decline in per capita GDP with clear implications for growing black unemployment. Recovery in 1984 proved short-lived, and growth of only 1 per cent was envisaged for 1985 even before the widespread and prolonged outbreak of unrest (Chapter 17) which badly damaged the confidence of overseas investors, accentuated pressure in western countries for economic sanctions against South Africa, and caused a dramatic decline in the exchange value of the rand.

Such consequences reflect the linkages of finance, trade and technology which lock South Africa into the world economy. In global dependency terms she is a semi-peripheral country in the world economy (Wallerstein 1974), acting as a secondary or regional core in relation to the southern African space economy (Rogerson 1981). Like other semi-peripheral economies, South Africa experiences a drain of repatriated profits to 'core' capitalist economies (Samoff 1978; Milkman 1979), but benefits in turn from the dependence on her of other, more peripheral states in southern Africa.

Within South Africa the contrasts explored in the previous chapter between commercial and 'subsistence' agriculture lend themselves to the 'dual economy' perspective much favoured in traditional studies of colonial and white settler economies. The wider contrast between undeveloped black rural areas and urban industrial cores of the modern economy may be similarly characterised, but this perspective is misleading because it ignores the vital interrelationships between the two, which centre upon the use of black labour in the modern economy. Core–periphery ideas provide a more useful conceptual framework, and Browett (1976) has related Friedmann's (1966) stages-of-growth model to the changing space economy of South Africa. He distinguishes a *pre-industrial period* extending up to 1870, when large-scale mineral exploitation began, followed by a *transitional period* which lasted until

1911. During the latter a new inland core, Pretoria–Witwatersrand–Vereeniging (PWV), supplanted Cape Town as the dominant centre and stimulated the growth of the major ports to which rail links were constructed. Mining and urbanisation also stimulated the demand for and production of agricultural commodities in parts of the inner and intermediate periphery: wheat in the south-west Cape, sugar cane in Natal and maize in the highveld. The outer periphery remained an area of subsistence farming and a supplier of black labour to the core areas. The spatial structure of the economy became increasingly polarised during both the transitional period and the subsequent *industrial period* from 1911 up to the present. Browett and Fair (1974, 114) see the corridor from PWV to Durban, the nearest port, as 'a corridor of accessibility' which might well 'herald the initiation of the stage whereby the national periphery is replaced by inter-metropolitan peripheries', whilst the emergence of the eastern Cape ports of Port Elizabeth and East London as secondary national cores is seen to reflect the maturing of the economy along the lines postulated in Friedmann's industrial stage of

Table 7.1: South Africa's role in the world's mineral supply, 1980

Commodity	Production		Reserves	
	Rank	%	Rank	%
Gold	1	71	1	64
Manganese (ore)	1	41	1	93
Chrome (ore)	1	54	1	65
Vanadium (metal)	1	51	1	62
Andalusite group	1	46	1	45
Diamonds	2	23	2	23
Platinum group metals	2	39	1	78
Asbestos	2	11	4	8
Vermiculite	2	32	2	29
Fluorspar	2	15	1	45
Zircon concentrate	2	19	2	12
Uranium (metal)	3	14	2	14
Titanium minerals	3	22	3	17
Coal (all grades)	4	7	3	13
Iron ore	8	5	6	6
Lead (metal)	8	3	4	5
Tin (metal)	8	1	11	<1
Copper (metal)	9	3	11	2
Nickel	10	2	5	8

Source: South Africa 1983a (Official Yearbook), p. 562.

spatial organisation. Nearly 70 per cent of South Africa's GDP is generated in PWV, the four ports and the lesser cores of Pietermaritzburg, Bloemfontein and Kimberley, and 40 per cent in PWV alone; between 1955 and 1975 the share of the latter changed little, but that of the 'inner periphery' – the rest of South Africa excluding the homelands – increased its share from 25.2 to 31.0 per cent largely at the expense of the non-PWV core areas (Fair 1982, 51–2). Where South Africa's space economy differs from the Friedmann model is in the far greater degree of downward transitional periphery, especially the homelands, which lag far behind the general level of economic activity and well-being achieved in the cores and the upward transitional periphery (Fair 1982, 55). Thus the homeland share of GDP actually decreased marginally from 2.6 per cent in 1955 to 2.4 per cent in 1970, but increased to 3.2 per cent in 1975, largely as a result of the decentralisation programme (Chapter 8).

Mineral production: gold, diamonds, platinum
South Africa extracts over 40 different minerals from mines all over the country, but concentrated in the mineral-rich belt extending from the northern Transvaal to the northern Cape. She is the world's leading producer of gold, manganese, chromium, vanadium and the andalusite group (aluminium silicates used to make high-grade refractory materials) and the second largest producer of several other minerals (Table 7.1). After 1945 new *gold* mines in the Orange Free State, Far West Rand, Klerksdorp and Evander areas (Figure 7.1) not only replaced output from worked-out mines on the old Rand but greatly increased total output. However, owing largely to increased mining of lower-grade ores as existing mines are exhausted, gold output declined from a 1970 peak of 1000 tons to 691 tons in 1978. Subsequently it has remained relatively stable and was 662 tons in 1984, when it contributed 72 per cent of export revenue from minerals; South Africa now produces some 60–65 per cent of the world's gold. Government aid kept several mines open in the late 1960s and early 1970s when they were no longer profitable, a policy which was briefly vindicated by price rises in the late 1970s. The latter encouraged a new phase of investment in mine extensions, new mines and dump reprocessing, but there is little scope for significant increases in production because many existing mines are close to being worked out. Production is at best likely to remain static until the turn of the century and to diminish thereafter.

World demand for gold as an investment has traditionally increased in times of recession, thus providing South Africa with an anti-cyclical

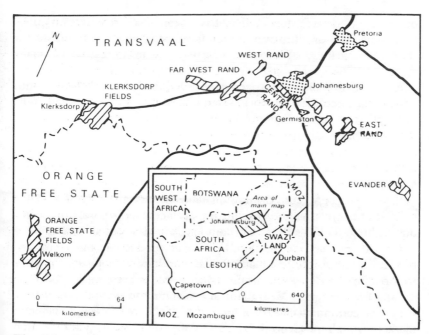

Fig. 7.1   South Africa's goldfields

shield against recession in her own economy. This worked dramatically well for her in the late 1970s and early 1980s, when financial uncertainties lifted the gold price to record levels on world markets. It reached a peak of $820 per ounce in January 1980 when uncertainty over further oil price rises, the holding of American hostages in Iran and the Soviet invasion of Afghanistan increased speculative demand for gold. Subsequently, however, the anti-cyclical effect has failed to operate; the gold price fell to $315 in June 1982 and, after some recovery in 1983, drifted towards $300 once more in 1984 and remained there in 1985. Gold mining profits have nevertheless remained high owing to the depreciation of the rand which naturally increases revenue from a commodity priced in US dollars. These profits have provided the government with an important source of additional revenue in a period of severe recession, and the 1985 budget increased the tax surcharge on gold mining companies from 20 to 25 per cent. Hitherto, capital spending on new mines could be charged against current profits of operating mines,

141

but since 1984 such tax savings have been restricted to contiguous properties. This and the overall high levels of taxation, reaching 80 per cent of taxable income for some mines, may threaten development of new mines.

After major *diamond* discoveries near Kimberley in 1869–70, South Africa soon became the world's largest producer of gem diamonds. Production from four diamond-bearing pipes near Kimberley continues. A second major discovery was made in 1902 near Pretoria, where the Premier Mine continues to operate. More recently the Finsch Mine in the northern Cape began production in 1966. South Africa remains a leading producer of both gemstones and industrial diamonds (irreplaceable in petroleum drilling bits and the cutting edges of machine tools), but her relative and absolute importance as a diamond producer is diminishing. The De Beers Corporation, which mines all diamonds in South Africa, has cut its South African production but expanded production from its Namibian alluvial workings and opened up three major mines in Botswana, whose government is pressing De Beers to expand further there. Australia is also planning to expand production. De Beers' continuing control of four-fifths of the world's rough diamond market through the Central Selling Organisation, and its determination not to cut prices, have failed to secure a sound balance between supply and demand, and De Beers' stockpile at the end of 1984 was equivalent to about two years' demand.

South Africa is the world's sole primary producer of both *platinum* and *palladium*. Canada and the Soviet Union, the other major producers, mine them as by-products of nickel. The six platinum group metals can usually be employed interchangeably by western chemical, petroleum and electronics industries, but outside the group substitutes are either unavailable or inferior in performance (Rotberg 1981, 111). World demand is growing, with prospects for further expansion as European car firms plan to follow the USA and Japan in providing platinum-based exhaust emission controllers on their cars. As a result new mining ventures are being evaluated. At least two-thirds of South Africa's current production of platinum and palladium is mined in Bophuthatswana, which has been legally independent since 1977. This endows Bophuthatswana with an economic self-sufficiency altogether lacking in other 'homelands' (Chapter 8), but could limit the strategic value of platinum to South Africa.

The strategic significance of South Africa's minerals

South Africa's possession of key minerals is one of four major arguments for her strategic importance to the West, all of them questionable (Bowman 1982). At least since the emergence in 1973–74 of OPEC as a successful oil cartel, there has been a sharp upsurge of concern in the West about access to other non-fuel minerals. South Africa is the world's fourth producer of non-fuel minerals and a significant producer of several which are critical to industrial societies. The USA imports seven of them – chromium, manganese, vanadium, the platinum group, gold, copper and coal – as well as two key alloys, ferrochromium and ferro-manganese. South African coal and copper are, however, but a small part of US and Western European consumption. Disruption of the gold supply, even if South Africa could afford it, would affect international monetary stability, but US production, government stockpiles and the holdings of other developed countries would be enough to meet western industrial needs for some time. So the argument really rests on four commodities: chromium, manganese, vanadium, the platinum group metals and their alloys. Western European dependence on South Africa for chromium, ferrochrome and manganese is higher than that of the USA, whilst Japanese dependence on South African chromium and ferrochrome is even higher. Chromium and manganese are essential to the manufacture of steel and several alloys; without them an economy such as West Germany's would be in serious difficulty within three months. Modern armaments also depend on these minerals; jet engines and armour-piercing projectiles demand supplies of specific metals for hard and heat-resistant alloys.

Concern is increased by the geographical accident that the USSR is the other major producer of most of these minerals. In terms of reserves, South Africa and the USSR together have 88 per cent of the world's manganese, 95 per cent of the vanadium, 97 per cent of the platinum and 94 per cent of the palladium. The USSR has only 3 per cent of world chromium reserves (although she is responsible for a quarter of world production), but South Africa and Zimbabwe between them have nearly all the rest. This configuration of key mineral resources has led to fears for the security of western supplies in the event of political change in South Africa. The validity of such fears depends on the answers to three questions. First, is it likely that a black (socialist?) government of South Africa would cut off strategic mineral supplies to the West? Secondly, could the West overcome the loss of South African supplies, and over what time-scale? And thirdly, could the USSR and a friendly South

143

Africa conspire to fix the price of key minerals?

The question of cutting off supplies needs a two-stage answer. Unlike Africa's other suppliers of strategic minerals, notably Niger and Gabon (uranium) and Zaire (cobalt), South Africa is *not* critically dependent on the revenues they provide: industrial metals generate only about 5 per cent of export earnings and less than 2 per cent of GDP. Even this would, if ended, increase unemployment and reduce economic growth, but it is the wider implications of cutting off supplies to the West which would be decisive. South Africa's reputation as a stable, responsible supplier would disappear, and the West would seek to reduce dependence on South Africa for all minerals, including gold, presumably seeking fundamental changes in the world monetary system. The USSR might purchase some South African minerals, given technical and economic problems in the exploitation of her own resources, but she is in no position to provide a market for most of South Africa's mineral exports and certainly not for gold, coal or iron ore. In these circumstances, an early return to the world market would be forced upon any South African government, whatever its ideological leanings. In practice this makes the initial action of cutting supplies of strategic minerals to the West inherently improbable.

If such an eventuality did occur, the situation faced by the West would be less disastrous than is suggested by the geography of strategic minerals as noted above. Such statistics ignore recycling and the exporting of scrap metal which could be used for domestic recycling: thus although the US stopped producing chromium in 1962, chromium imports as a percentage of domestic consumption actually fell from 95 per cent in 1950 to 89 per cent in 1970 (Shafer 1982, 158). Secondly, a substantial proportion of the 'strategic' minerals consumed in the West is not actually used for strategic purposes; in the USA, car emission controls and jewellery, both dispensable uses, account for over 43 per cent of platinum consumption. Substitutes are already available for some uses of strategic minerals – to the extent of 31 per cent, for instance, in the case of American chromium (Shafer 1982, 159). Finally, statistics of 'world reserves' are misleading: they refer not to what is geologically known, but to what can be profitably extracted given current legal provisions, mining and processing technology, and world prices. Price changes could encourage the mining of cobalt in Idaho, whilst changes in existing legislation prohibiting hard-rock mining at Stillwater, Montana could alone result in production of 20–25 per cent of US platinum requirements. The resources of the sea add vastly to the world's ultimate reserves of manganese, vanadium, nickel, cobalt and molybdenum.

Such possibilities clearly demand extensive further research on substitutes and on the processing and recycling of strategic minerals, as well as further exploration. The latter has moved away from the Third World in recent years, in the face of political instability and dangers of nationalisation, and great potential resources are capable of development if western governments backed investment with subsidy or guarantees of financial security. Such steps would need several years to have an impact on western supplies of strategic minerals, however, and stockpiling is the obvious short-term precaution. American stockpiles have recently been adjusted and vastly increased; their estimated total value in 1983 was $15,000 million, 50 times that of French or West German stockpiles (Gutteridge 1984, 6). They include between one and three years' consumption of major South African strategic minerals, and this period could of course be extended by reducing non-critical uses. In addition to the national American stockpile, large supplies of critical minerals, probably equal to 6 or 12 months' consumption, are held by major companies (Shafer 1982, 16). If there is a problem in the West, it is the vulnerability of Western Europe and Japan. This is underlined by Britain's decision in November 1984 to dispose of her official reserve of industrial raw materials, established less than two years before, for budgetary reasons.[1]

The possibility of the USSR conspiring with a future South African government to fix the prices of key minerals seems more likely than the cutting-off of supplies. In practice, surprising as it may seem, a degree of cooperation already occurs. The peculiar case of diamonds, with most Soviet exports channelled through De Beers, has long been taken for granted. But South African–Soviet contacts are also thought to take place on a wider front, between mining corporations, expert metallurgists with official standing, and even senior official agencies (Gutteridge 1984, 14–15). The two countries have a common interest in the gold price, as the USSR tends to sell gold to make up for shortfalls in grain harvests. There have been discussions on the price and availability of platinum, the refining of vanadium and the price of chrome. Such cooperation would be likely to increase with a change of government in South Africa, but the prudent long-term western response would appear to be not to seek to prevent political change in South Africa but to influence the course of change and to minimise ultimate dependence on South African strategic minerals in the ways already considered.

Uranium and nuclear power

South African uranium is largely a by-product of gold-mining. It is processed and marketed by the Nuclear Fuels Corporation (NUFCOR) which is controlled by eight mining finance houses including Anglo-American which has a 50 per cent share. The quintupling of uranium prices between 1974 and 1977 led to major expansion of uranium production from gold mines (helped by the high gold prices prevailing) and to the opening in 1978 of the Beisa Mine in the Orange Free State where uranium is the primary product and gold the by-product. Small quantities are also produced as a by-product of copper at Phalaborwa in the eastern Transvaal, and new discoveries have been made in the Karroo. Whereas the American uranium mining industry faced closures in the early 1980s with falling prices, the by-product character of South African production makes it cheap and reliable. Thus unless political considerations intervene, South Africa is likely to maintain her exports whilst mines elsewhere become uneconomic in the face of world over-capacity.[2] NUFCOR does not reveal the identity of its trading partners or the value of its exports, but Japan is thought to have a contract for the period 1984–93 and other customers include West Germany, who depends on South Africa for 50 per cent of her needs, as well as Taiwan and Israel (Rotberg 1981, 147). In 1983 South Africa's production of 6100 tons of uranium oxide was equivalent to 16 per cent of western production and placed her third among producing nations.

South Africa's first nuclear power station, Koeberg, was commissioned in 1976 and built at Duynefontein, between Cape Town and Saldanha Bay. It was designed by an American firm and built under licence by a French consortium. The plant was damaged by sabotage for which the ANC claimed responsibility in December 1982 but began operating in March 1984. When fully operational it will represent some 10 per cent of South Africa's electricity generating capacity. The Cape Town area is the most remote of South Africa's major population centres from the coalfields of Natal and the Transvaal, and nuclear power is more attractive than the alternative of either moving coal or transmitting electricity over distances of up to 1500 kilometres.

Uranium enrichment by a locally developed process is undertaken at the Valindaba plant near Pretoria, which should eventually be able to supply enough fuel for Koeberg to become fully operational. In the meantime this is prevented by the refusal of the USA since 1975 to supply enriched uranium to South Africa until she signs the Nuclear Non-Proliferation Treaty. Her refusal to do so, ostensibly to protect what is claimed to be the uniqueness of her enrichment process, has fuelled suspicions that she is developing nuclear weapons. There is no clear evidence of this, but alleged nuclear weapon testing facilities were discovered in 1977 in the Kalahari Desert, whilst in 1979 an American satellite detected a light flash characteristic of a low-yield nuclear explosion. In practice South Africa's refusal to sign the Treaty may reflect not the actual manufacture of nuclear weapons but the government's wish 'ostentatiously to reserve the right to develop nuclear weapons as a last defence against external pressures to accede to black rule' (Rotberg 1981, 154). By demonstrating her capacity to enrich uranium effectively and to build a bomb, irrespective of whether she actually does so, South Africa is no doubt seeking to demonstrate her determination and credibility as a regional power.

Coal, oil and natural gas

The development of South Africa's energy sector since 1970 epitomises the survival imperative of her white minority government. The oil crisis of 1973-74 exposed the potential weaknesses of South Africa's energy position. Whilst her coal reserves were more than sufficient to supply thermal power stations, South Africa had no oil and was threatened by oil boycotts; with the Iranian Revolution in 1979 she lost her major oil supplier. In addition South Africa had limited indigenous hydro-electric power capacity and no commercial nuclear reactor. Since then, not only has Koeberg been built but the oil-from-coal programme has been greatly extended to produce 40-50 per cent of liquid fuel requirements and a massive coal export industry developed.

Coal has been mined in South Africa since 1864, and on a significant scale since the development of gold mining. The country has some 51 billion tons of coal extractable under current economic conditions. Most of this is soft, bituminous coal with a low calorific value and high ash content, inferior to British and American soft coal, and South Africa produces relatively little anthracite or coking coal. Most of her coal is, however, found in thick, easily worked seams near the surface, which makes costs very low, whilst a high proportion of current production is mined in close proximity to major industrial centres in the Witwatersrand and Newcastle in northern Natal. Overall selling prices have risen faster than mining costs despite South African producers having to give a 'political' discount of around $2 per ton. Since the opening in 1976 of a new rail link and coal terminal at Richard's Bay in northern Natal coal exports have risen dramatically and by 1978 South Africa was

147

supplying a quarter of the world market for internationally traded coal and 23 per cent (second only to Poland) of EEC requirements (Rotberg 1981, 118). She also had long-term contracts with Japan and Israel. Subsequently coal exports reached 30 million tons in 1983 and 38 million tons in 1984, making coal South Africa's most valuable non-gold export. The capacity of the Richard's Bay loading facility is planned to reach 44 million tons by 1987 and over 70 million tons by the end of the century, by which time South Africa hopes to be exporting a total of 80 million tons of coal annually.

Total coal production reached 162 million tons in 1984. The Electricity Supply Commission (ESCOM) purchases some 60 million tons a year, largely from collieries supplying the line of thermal power stations strung across the Transvaal and Orange Free State coalfields. Coal provides about 90 per cent of locally generated electricity. It is also used by the parastatal corporation SASOL, founded in 1950 to produce oil from coal. The initial plant at Sasolburg in the Orange Free State pioneered new technology but was relatively small and its products highly subsidised prior to the 1973 oil crisis. The latter induced South Africa to build a second oil-from-coal plant, SASOL 2, in the eastern Transvaal where the town of Secunda has since developed. A third plant, also at Secunda, became fully operational in 1984.

Over-production of oil in relation to demand has prevented further rises in world prices in the mid-1980s, and made the SASOL programme less competitive than seemed likely a decade earlier. This was dramatically altered by the depreciation of the rand in 1985, leading to more expensive imports. SASOL's major drawback is that its output is predominantly petrol, which means that South Africa is short of diesel oil and has at times actually exported surplus petrol. One solution would be to convert coal into methanol, which can be burned in diesel engines. However in 1984 there were indications that after almost 20 years of exploration SOEKOR, the state oil exploration company, had delineated reserves of offshore gas from which diesel fuels could be produced. The largest reserves lie about 120 kilometres offshore and just inside Namibian territorial waters; the Chevron company has relinquished its claim because of uncertainty as to who has jurisdiction over the area, and development is unlikely except by the government. This field could produce at least 500 million cubic feet per day, enough to provide 30 per cent of South Africa's liquid fuel requirements, for at least 20 years.[3] The second offshore gas field is near Mossel Bay, 250 kilometres east of Cape Town. In November 1985 the government announced its decision to proceed with a R3500 million project to exploit this field and construct facilities to convert the gas into synthetic fuel. The project should provide up to 10 per cent of South Africa's liquid fuel requirements for at least 20 years. Finance will come both from the Central Energy Fund (which benefits both from a levy on fuel sales and capital repayments received from the privatisation of SASOL 2 and 3) and from private capital; over 70 per cent of the equipment will be manufactured domestically. The project, which should directly employ up to 10,000 people at the peak of the five-year construction period, should give a boost to the depressed economy of the east-central Cape.

SOEKOR has yet to find oil itself in commercial quantities. The land search has been abandoned as unfruitful, but the most promising offshore finds are also in the Mossel Bay/Plettenberg Bay area, where exploration continues. Meanwhile South Africa has built up stockpiles of oil which could probably last three years at normal consumption rates and twice as long if rationing were adopted. Since the Iranian Revolution, South Africa has purchased oil on the spot market and clandestinely from various suppliers, paying a premium over OPEC prices and probably paying inflated transport charges too. To minimise the cost of imports, several mandatory conservation measures have been applied at various times including higher petrol prices, lower speed limits and restricted opening hours of service stations. Under the Petroleum Supply and National Supplies Procurement Acts of 1977, oil companies may be required to sell to the government or the military for stockpiling and other purposes. Since 1979 it has been an offence to divulge information about South Africa's oil crisis and methods of coping with it, or otherwise to endanger supplies. In the event of serious supply problems, South Africa is in a position to hold Botswana, Lesotho and possibly Swaziland hostage, as their supplies normally come from South African refineries. Procurement is currently somewhat easier, however, given excess of supply over demand in world markets, whilst offshore developments seem likely to bring self-sufficiency nearer. Oil is therefore rapidly ceasing to be the Achilles heel of the South African economy.

Industrialisation
Mineral exploitation in an otherwise undeveloped economy often leads to little further economic development in the region, as in Namibia and the Zambian copperbelt. The South African mining industry likewise did little initially to stimulate industrialisation, preferring cheap imported goods. Ironically, it was the schism which developed between Afrikaners

and English speakers regarding their political and economic interests which paved the way for widespread economic development by separating the sources of economic and political power and enabling political means to be used to divert the surplus earned by the mining industry for investment within South Africa (Nattrass 1981, 162–3). Thus the success of South African industrialisation owes much to the rise of Afrikaner nationalism and particularly to the 'Pact' government which came to power in 1924 (Chapter 3). The latter not only sought to entrench the position of white labour and farming interests and to promote Afrikaner industrial capitalism (Magubane 1979, 163–92) but also laid the foundations for state intervention through both protective tariffs designed to encourage import substitution and direct investment in parastatal corporations which provided the foundations for future industrial growth in the private sector. ESCOM (electricity: 1923) was succeeded by ISCOR (iron and steel) in 1928, and many others followed, especially after 1948, including FOSKOR (phosphates), SASOL, ARMSCOR (military equipment), SENTRACHEM (chemicals) and NATREF (oil refining). Most important of all is the Industrial Development Corporation (IDC), which was originally established in 1940 to help small industry but soon found itself almost exclusively involved with monopoly capital, and usually in partnership with foreign corporations (Bloch 1981, 55). It assisted in the 'rationalisation' of firms and often brought the major parastatals into association with foreign companies. Sectorally, the IDC is strongly represented in the chemical, textile and clothing industries (Rogerson 1975, 44).

In the early stages of industrialisation, the goods produced were closely allied to mine needs, and subsequent development of manufacturing relied heavily on both human and capital resources built up by the mining industry. Thus foreign exchange from mineral exports financed the import of capital goods and intermediate inputs essential for a growing industrial sector. The latter was able to draw upon the pool of skilled labour and financial expertise which had developed as the mining industry expanded. Mining houses steadily diversified their activities, diverting accumulated capital into industrial expansion. Foreign capital also began to invest in South African manufacturing after 1945, when factors favouring industrial growth included the pent-up domestic demand of war years, a large foreign demand for the same reason, and the discovery of new goldfields in the western Transvaal and Orange Free State. British capital dominated inflows until the 1960s, after which American and EEC investment increased considerably (Seidman and

Makgetla 1980). Foreign investment has ceased to be synonymous with foreign funds, and Suckling (1975, 27) estimated that foreign firms in South Africa finance 70 per cent of their investment from locally generated profits. It has, however, produced a high degree of foreign ownership of local companies and Rogerson (1982a) estimated that 28 per cent of South African manufacturing employment is in foreign-controlled enterprises. The latter dominate motor cars, oil, tyres, electrical equipment, computers and pharmaceuticals, and are strongly represented in food and chemicals (Rogerson 1982b, 49).

The location of industry
South African industry displays marked spatial concentration. Half the gross manufacturing output comes from the PWV area alone; it was followed in 1976 by Durban–Pinetown (14 per cent), the Cape Peninsula (9 per cent) and Port Elizabeth–Uitenhage (6 per cent). The growing degree of concentration in the PWV area particularly has for some time concerned the government, although the absolute size of urban areas and the diseconomies arising from them remain small by international standards: the four major industrial areas, together with East London, Pietermaritzburg, Bloemfontein and Kimberley had a 1980 population of just over 8 million, little more than that of New York alone. The reasons for official concern may be broadly labelled physical and political.

To provide sufficient water supplies for the continuing growth of PWV involves expensive transfer schemes, and hopes of diverting industrial expansion to areas with adequate water supply led to the establishment of growth points in the Tugela basin of Natal. By 1974, however, demand from the area supplied by the Vaal river, including PWV, was equal to its reliable yield (South Africa 1983a, 596), and the Tugela-Vaal project was undertaken to supply the inexorably rising needs of PWV. Water from the Tugela river is pumped through a vertical lift of 506 metres into the Vaal basin, and retained in the Sterkfontein dam. The further raising of the latter will assure the requirements of the area supplied by the Vaal until 1992. Thereafter, further growth of the PWV area will depend on the R2.2 billion Lesotho Highlands water project, to which a start is needed in the mid-1980s if PWV is not to experience water supply problems in the mid-1990s.[4]

Political reasons for official concern over the spatial concentration of industry relate to the maintenance of apartheid and the ultimate security of the state. In part this relates to the strategic vulnerability of such spatially concentrated manufacturing capacity. Primarily, however, it

151

concerns the physical dislocation between capital and labour which has been apparent at least since the mining developments of the nineteenth century, and which has steadily increased ever since. As long as government policies aim to minimise the numbers of blacks living outside the homelands, the gap can only be bridged by further increases in the volume of migrant labour; but there is now some recognition in official circles that the persistence and growth of the migrant labour system, with all its attendant evils (Chapter 9), may itself pose a threat to state security. The government has sought an answer in industrial decentralisation, which is in any case essential if the homelands are to become more self-sufficient in economic and employment terms, but there are massive obstacles to its successful implementation.

Export Industries
The location of half South African industry in the southern Transvaal is also unfortunate in terms of export orientation, and may help to explain the lack of export-mindedness regarded by the Reynders Commission into exports as characteristic of South African businessmen and in-dustrialists (South Africa 1972). The South African Railways (SAR) tariff structure has also traditionally discouraged export-orientated location of manufacturing. By favouring foodstuffs and raw materials over finished goods, it has provided a locational advantage for regions with large markets, and therefore favoured the southern Transvaal. In the early 1970s SAR introduced export incentives for inland producers: reduced freight rates may be charged if it can be shown that payment at the full rate would prevent competitive export sales. This encourages exports but does nothing to alter the inland location of manufacturing industries. The recommendation of the Reynders Commission that the government should provide incentives to exporters moving to growth areas near the ports was only partially implemented (unlike most other recommendations which were accepted in full), because such incentives did not necessarily accord with the political aims of industrial decentralisation (Chapter 8): thus Cape Town and Port Elizabeth, far from attracting incentives, actually remained 'controlled areas' in terms of section 3 of the Physical Planning and Utilisation of Resources Act of 1967, whereas Durban and East London were exempted owing to their proximity to black commuter labour in KwaZulu and Ciskei, respectively. The current regional development strategy likewise pays no special attention to coastal location; of 48 proposed industrial development points (excluding the Walvis Bay enclave), only five –

Table 7.2: Growth in manufacturing output, 1945–80

Year(s)	Growth in output per annum (%)
1945–55	7.1
1955–63	6.3
1963–69	9.1
1970	6.9
1971	6.6
1972	3.9
1973	9.2
1974	6.4
1975	4.0
1976	2.4
1977	-3.7
1978	6.8
1979	9.5
1980	9.3

Source: South Africa 1983a, 491–2

Vredenburg-Saldanha on the west coast, East London, Richard's Bay-Empangeni, Isithebe (KwaZulu) and an unspecified point in KwaZulu near Richard's Bay – are coastal.

Despite these locational disadvantages, not to mention the great distance of South Africa from major western markets, the contribution of manufactures to exports has steadily increased. In the favourable conditions of the early post-war period, exports of manufactures increased from 10 per cent of total exports in 1945 to 18 per cent in 1955. Thereafter, although overall growth of the manufacturing sector continued (Table 7.2), its contribution to exports rose more slowly, reaching 28.8 per cent in 1981. In the early 1980s industrial exports rose to one-third of the total, but this partly reflected the depressed gold price. The depreciation of the rand in 1985 should, if it persists, make South African goods more competitive, although imported inputs will naturally cost more. Overall the manufacturing sector is still a net importer of goods and services, unlike mining and agriculture, but the ratio of imports to exports in manufacturing has decreased from 3:1 in 1975 to 2:1 in 1982 as exports have grown (to R5247 million in 1982) and the ability of South African industry to supply a growing home market has increased.

The major industrial sectors

During the Second World War backward and forward linkages developed between different branches of South African manufacturing to the extent that a built-in growth factor became evident. Growth became less ¯dependent on the demands of mining, agriculture and final consumption, and more on the intermediate demand of manufacturing itself. Today, most materials required by the makers of consumer goods are produced in South Africa, and in many cases intermediate material processors (making capital equipment, spares and components, semi-processed and construction materials) obtain their needs from those who process the raw materials of South African agriculture and mining. Thus, for example, the iron and steel industry supplies producers of motor vehicle parts who in turn supply assemblers of motor vehicles.

This 'maturing' of the manufacturing structure is reflected in an increasing share of basic raw materials and capital goods industries at the expense of final or consumer goods industries in total production. Thus the largest industrial sector in South Africa is metal products and engineering (Table 7.3), which includes basic metals, metal products, machinery and transport equipment. The making of *iron, steel and ferro-alloys*, South Africa's largest single industry in the late 1970s, illustrates the transformation which has taken place. It has turned a sizeable import deficit into an export surplus in 1981 of 2.7 million tons worth R216 million, and exported to more than 50 countries. South African steel is among the cheapest in the world owing to favourable locational factors, the availability of cheap raw materials and cheap labour, and an efficient scale of production. The overall ouput rose by 62.4 per cent between 1975 and 1980 but has since declined in the face of reduced domestic and world demand to only 41.4 per cent more than the 1975 level in 1983. The iron and steel industries accounted for only 6.5 per cent of total manufacturing sales in 1983 compared with 10 per cent in 1978, and exports were reduced to 1.63 million tons. ISCOR supplies some three-quarters of the Republic's steel requirements, producing 5.6 million tons of liquid steel in 1982–83 from its steelworks at Pretoria, Vanderbijlpark and Newcastle; the bulk of the raw materials comes from mines and quarries owned by ISCOR itself in the Transvaal and Natal. Six private companies produce a further 2 million tons annually.

Exports of iron ore have also become important in recent years, especially to Japan. Total reserves are estimated at 9500 million tons, of which 4000 million occur in the Postmasburg–Sishen areas of the northern Cape. The latter ores are of high quality, all over 60 per cent

154

Table 7.3: Output and employment in major industries, 1982

Industrial group	Output (Rm)	Employment
Metal products and engineering	21,357	535,000
Food, beverages and tobacco	12,084	221,600
Clothing and footwear	1,989	143,100
Textiles	2,177	118,900
Chemicals	10,385	106,400

Source: Katzen 1984.

iron content and 85 per cent of them between 66 and 70 per cent. A railway from Sishen to Saldanha Bay was completed in 1976, and handling facilities capable of exporting 30 million tons a year have been constructed at Saldanha. These facilities remained under-used in the early 1980s, when total domestic iron ore production did not exceed the 28.3 million tons achieved in 1981. Iron ore exports amounted to only 10.4 million tons worth R238 million in 1983–84. The ability of the Saldanha harbour to handle only relatively small 100,000-ton ore carriers increases transport costs of South African iron ore whilst there are indications that the ore becoming available from Brazil's new Carajas mine is of better quality. The South African government has, however, agreed to a financial restructuring of the Sishen-Saldanha railway to help exporters, who should also benefit from a weak rand.

Some of the ferro-alloy industries, especially ferro-chrome, ferro-vanadium and vanadium pentoxide, have weathered the 1980s recession far better than iron and steel. Not only has the world market improved greatly since 1983, but high-cost Japanese producers have removed capacity allowing South Africa to take a greater share of the market. She should also benefit from Finland's closure in late 1985 of plants capable of producing 11 per cent of western capacity.

Transport equipment industries employed 120,600 workers in 1982 and produced an output worth R5054 million. The first Ford assembly plant was established in Port Elizabeth as long ago as 1924, but today there are ten independent car-makers and 14 truck manufacturers. The entry of so many firms into a relatively small market (less than 400,000 vehicles a year in 1985) reflected a combination of incentives and protectionism (see below) with expectations of market potential. Car ownership among whites is approximately 500 per 1000 but among blacks it is only 22 per 1000, and with increasing black income a rapidly growing car market

155

seemed likely. Although dampened by recession in the early 1980s, such hopes may still be realised in the medium term, but comparisons with Australia and Brazil, where less than six manufacturers compete for markets currently much larger than South Africa's, indicate the overcrowded nature of the South African market.[5] Fiat and Volvo were the first to withdraw some years ago, whilst British Leyland ceased to assemble cars in South Africa, concentrating instead on trucks, buses and Landrovers. The recessionary conditions of 1985 witnessed more dramatic rationalisation including the merger of Ford and Amcar (an Anglo-American subsidiary) and the announced withdrawal of Alfa Romeo, Peugeot and Renault.

Manufacturers' costs have risen with government measures requiring increasing local content, and thus increasing costs given the relative absence of scale economies. Since 1978 for cars and 1981 for light commercial vehicles the local content required has been 66 per cent by weight, which has meant local manufacture of engine blocks and body shells. Manufacturers have requested relaxation of the local content requirement, arguing that exports of components (at present largely within southern Africa) should be offset against imports. The latter have themselves become more expensive, however, as the international value of the rand has fallen.

Local content regulations shifted the logistical advantages of proximity to a good port in favour of local sources of steel; this, together with market potential, benefited the Witwatersrand. Established manufacturers including Ford and General Motors (Port Elizabeth), Volkswagen (Uitenhage) and Mercedes Benz (East London) now face twin disadvantages of a 1000-kilometre distance from both markets and steel sources. Trade union militancy in Port Elizabeth–Uitenhage may also have encouraged a partial migration of existing firms to PWV and elsewhere. The Ford–Amcar merger is likely to add to already severe unemployment in and around Port Elizabeth.

Food and drink industries were among the first established in South Africa, and their relative importance has declined, but there has been a steady growth of production and the industry contributed 3.2 per cent of merchandise exports in 1981. Some 60 per cent of the canned fruit and vegetables produced is exported, mostly to Britain and Europe. Duties of 25–30 per cent in EEC countries put South African products at a disadvantage compared with their main competitors, including Greece, Spain and the Ivory Coast, whose products are imported free of duty. The Natal sugar industry lost its quota under the Commonwealth Sugar

Agreement when South Africa left the Commonwealth in 1961, and must now compete in a world market which was over-supplied in the mid-1980s. Other food industries include the processing of dairy products, bakeries (a major industry given the importance of bread in the diet of blacks) and meat and fish processing.

The South African *chemical* industry was established in 1900 to provide explosives for the mining industry, and the Modderfontein factory near Johannesburg is today probably the world's largest privately-owned explosives factory. SASOL plants have been the major development in the chemical industry in recent years, and a major petrochemical complex has grown up at Sasolburg alongside SASOL 1. Otherwise the chemical industry is dominated by AECI (African Explosives and Chemicals Industry), which is jointly owned by Britain's Imperial Chemical Industries and De Beers. Like SASOL, both AECI and Sentrachem have turned increasingly to coal as the feedstock of their products. The industry has made substantial strides towards making South Africa self-sufficient in plastics raw materials, but continues to require protection by import tariffs and quotas; as the government moves away from import licensing it is likely that tariffs will rise further to protect South African products from American and other producers benefiting from cheap oil and gas feedstocks. Continuing protection seems assured given South Africa's drive for industrial self-sufficiency, and several major projects have been undertaken in the early 1980s, including the world's largest polyvinyl chloride (PVC) plant close to SASOL 1 and a synthetic rubber complex at Newcastle which should replace almost all natural rubber imports. Major developments in synthetic fuel production were anticipated in the early 1980s, but government financial incentives have not been forthcoming, probably because of the ease with which it has proved possible to buy crude oil on world markets and the potential significance of the recent gas discoveries already mentioned.

The *clothing and footwear* industries were well established before 1939 and today supply 90 per cent of domestic demand. Exports are mainly to neighbouring countries. Clothing and footwear remain labour-intensive industries, as the ratio of employment to output shows (Table 7.3), and are therefore more attracted than most others by cheap labour in the homelands and other decentralisation incentives (Chapter 8).

The *textile* industry is essentially a post-war industry and now meets 60 per cent of domestic requirements as well as exporting on a substantial scale (R409 million in 1982). It is also a labour-intensive industry, although less pronouncedly so than the clothing industry.

157

The growth of monopoly capitalism and its consequences

Since 1945 the South African economy has been transformed from being based on conditions of small-scale competitive capitalism to conditions of monopoly capitalism[6] (Innes 1983, 170). In the mining sector, where considerable capital concentration had already been occurring since the late nineteenth century, a new phase of expansion occurred with the opening-up of new goldfields and the growth of base metal production. The combination of expansion and mechanisation encouraged unprecedented concentration and centralisation of capital from which the Anglo-American group emerged dominant in the mid-1950s. Capital concentration occurred more slowly in manufacturing, and much of what did take place was a product either of state or foreign capitalist investment, or investment by the mining houses. The latter produced a significant merging of mining and industrial capital which was paralleled by the first mergers of mining and bank capital (ibid., 172–4).

Monopoly relations spread rapidly through all sectors of the economy in the 1960s, a process which emphasised the industrial, commercial and financial supremacy of Johannesburg in terms of the location of head offices and the proportion of total assets controlled (Rogerson 1974a). Recession in the mid-1970s actually intensified the advance of monopoly capitalism as large corporations merged with one another to protect themselves against deteriorating trading conditions, and as they absorbed smaller, struggling concerns. Recession in the early 1980s prompted further mergers aimed to minimise competition and rationalise production and marketing so as to maximise scale economies. By April 1982 ten of South Africa's top 100 companies accounted for 45 per cent of the latter's total market capitalisation value, and 20 of them accounted for 61 per cent of the total (Innes 1983, 178). Concentration of economic power is accentuated by a growing network of interlocking corporate directorships with a spatial pattern which emphasises the dominance of Johannesburg even more than the location of head offices (Cox and Rogerson 1984).

The Anglo-American group of companies, of which the Anglo-American Corporation itself is the principal holding company and other central companies include De Beers, Charter Consolidated and MINORCO (Minerals and Resources Corporation), today holds undisputed predominance in many sectors of the South African economy. It does so to an extent which is probably unrivalled in any other developed or 'middle income' economy (Kaplan 1983b, 485). As well as producing 36 per cent of the gold, 35 per cent of the coal, 41 per cent of the uranium and most of South Africa's diamonds, the Anglo Group has a virtual monopoly over the production of explosives and many chemical products (AECI), is the largest private iron and steel producer (Highveld), the principal builder of electric locomotives and railway coaches (Union Carriage), and the largest vehicle assembler (SIGMA). It also dominates in many sectors of engineering, owns the largest forestry and sawmills operation (SAFI), and remains a dominant force in sugar (Huletts) and insurance. Much of this diversification is recent, assisted particularly by record gold prices in the 1970s and at the beginning of the 1980s. The combined assets of the Anglo-American Corporation and De Beers puts them ahead of South African Railways and Harbours which otherwise heads the league of private and public concerns in terms of total assets. The Anglo Group held 52.5 per cent of the shares listed on the Johannesburg Stock Exchange in 1982, and was in effective control of 70 listed companies with a total market value of R47 million (Innes 1983, 178). Its nearest rival, the Afrikaner-controlled Sanlam group, held only 9.4 per cent of total shares, whilst another Anglo associate, Barlow Rand, was third with 7.4 per cent. Other Afrikaner monopoly interests ranked ninth (Rembrandt) and fifteenth (Volkskas).

A consequence of growing monopoly capitalism in South Africa has been increasing foreign investment *by* South African-based concerns, above all Anglo-American which is a major investor worldwide and especially in the USA. South African foreign investment in adjacent countries, especially Zimbabwe, is long established but has declined sharply since independence for political reasons, and to some extent owing to adverse economic performance. Recent South African foreign investment is largely in advanced capitalist countries, particularly Britain and the USA. This reflects some of the major reasons for such investment, which include the protection or stimulation of exports in countries which are South Africa's major markets, the acquisition of new or assured sources of technology, and in some cases the capitalisation of the most advanced 'know-how' for which the market is in the most advanced capitalist countries (Kaplan 1983b, 475). Most South African foreign investment involves the purchase of, or partnership with, existing firms, and represents an extension of the South African concern's domestic activities. Kaplan's (1983b) investigation of Anglo-American foreign investment suggests that, by contrast with the overseas expansion of MNCs located in advanced capitalist countries, the overseas expansion of Anglo-American will not entail an international division of labour which locates many of the skilled, managerial, research and development and ancillary services within its 'home' country, South Africa; nor will overseas expansion of associated companies entail any large-scale capital repatriation to South Africa. Rather the Group's capital will continue to flow *from* South Africa towards the advanced capitalist countries, reflecting both a desire to spread risks (the more so given an increasingly unfavourable 'political climate') and South Africa's 'less developed' character.

For the workforce monopoly capitalism has both positive and negative consequences. Increasing mechanisation has undoubtedly contributed to rising black unemployment (Chapter 17), and with increasing job insecurity the bargaining power of those in work is reduced. On the other hand, mechanisation and automation have rapidly increased the semi-skilled category of workers which has traditionally been small or non-existent (Chapter 2). Black workers have increasingly filled these positions since the 1960s, which strengthens their bargaining position considerably. The concentration of increasing numbers of workers together at a single point of production facilitates greater organisation and unity of workers, a factor which Innes (1983) regards as contributing to the Durban industrial workers' strikes of 1973 which subsequently spread to engineering firms on the East Rand and at Welkom (Orange Free State) and to firms in East London and the Border area. However monopoly capitalism also gives employers greater staying power in any dispute or strike, enabling an individual firm to draw upon the financial resources of the larger group to which it belongs.

The growth and significance of black trade unions are examined in Chapter 17, but in the final section of this chapter we turn to questions of labour supply and utilisation in mining and manufacturing.

The labour market: changing perspectives of the mining companies

Both mining and manufacturing have been affected by both statutory discrimination in favour of whites and restrictions on the geographic mobility of black labour (Chapters 8 and 9), but the restrictive characteristics of the South African labour market are not wholly due to government controls (Lemon 1982b). The recruitment policies of the mining companies in particular have further constrained the operation of a free market for black labour. The 1970s witnessed notable developments in these policies which included a shift from foreign to domestic sources of supply, wage increases, attempts to stabilise the labour force improvements in working conditions, and mechanisation.

Ever since the 1880s, the mining companies had followed a policy of moving further afield in search of labour. Independence for African territories began to reduce areas of recruitment in the 1960s, when Tanzania banned recruitment in 1962 and Zambia in 1966. The effort of Malawi's suspension of recruitment in 1974 (since resumed on a smaller scale) were particularly serious. Within South Africa, the mines faced growing difficulty in attracting domestic labour supplies as manufacturing employment, offering better wages and working conditions, expanded rapidly in the 1960s, whilst mining wages had not changed in real terms since 1911 (Wilson 1972a, 46). Thus South African blacks employed in mines affiliated to the Chamber of Mines fell in number from a 1962 peak of 157,000 to only 86,500 in 1971. The mining companies were faced with a choice of ever-increasing reliance on foreign labour from fewer countries, or attempting to compete with manufacturing.

They chose the latter option, which was made more practicable by the quadrupling of the gold price between 1970 and 1974. By June 1975, the minimum wage had risen to R2.20 per shift, more than five times that of 1972. The changes continued, if less dramatically, in the later 1970s, with the overall white:black pay differential declining from 18.6:1 in 1972 to 6.72:1 in 1979, by which time the average black miner's wage was 72.6 per cent of that in manufacturing and arguably almost the same if wages in kind are added (Spandau 1980, 215). By 1983 the white:black differential had narrowed further to 5.35:1.

Recruitment of South African blacks was assisted by the relaxation in 1974 of an official requirement that workers finishing their contracts be 'repatriated' to their homelands, irrespective of where they lived before. This had naturally minimised urban recruitment, but now workers living near the mines may enter short-term contracts and continue to live in urban areas afterwards. Recruitment has also been assisted by a new agreement between the Chamber of Mines and the South African Agricultural Union (Chapter 6) which has produced a large increase in the number of Transkeian miners.

The combination of improved wages and easier recruitment conditions within the Republic has enabled mining companies to reduce the foreign component of their labour force to only 44.3 per cent by mid-1983 (Table 7.4). Lesotho alone has almost maintained the same volume of migrant mine labour, and was responsible for 41.4 per cent of the foreign supply in 1983. The skill of the Basotho miners has long been acknowledged whilst the extreme dependence of Lesotho upon this form of labour ensures her dependability as a supplier; in this respect Lesotho is more akin to a 'homeland' labour reserve than to other foreign states which supply migrant labour.

Table 7.4: Migrant and non-migrant mineworkers, 1983

Figures represent workers registered at 30 June 1983 (total 688,095)

South Africa (excluding TVBC)	125,626
Bophuthatswana	57,003
Ciskei	20,869
Transkei	181,306
Venda	5,319
TVBC total	264,497
Botswana	19,317
Lesotho	123,311
Malawi	19,465
Mozambique	53,830
Swaziland	13,628
Other[a]	68,421
Foreign total	297,972

Note: a. The Department of Cooperation and Development attributes the large number of 'others' to changes in the categories on the forms sent to the development boards.

Source: SAIRR, 1984 *Survey*, pp. 257–8.

Numbers alone, however, do not tell the whole story. The Malawian and Mozambiquan miners were the most experienced ones who took the longest contracts, often up to the legal maximum of two years for Malawians and 18 months for Mozambiquans. They were replaced with men who had far less experience, if any, and who took shorter contracts which were often broken (legally, since the repeal of Masters and Servants legislation in 1974). Training costs soared with increased turnover, and many mines faced absolute labour shortages, despite the greater flexibility permitted by short-term contracts offered to urban blacks after 1974. This period of labour supply problems coincided with a period when blacks were permitted to do certain more skilled jobs under the Artisan Aides Agreement of 1973, which represented the first breakthrough in the face of the (white) Mine Workers Union's militant defence of job reservation. Ironically, increasing use of blacks in skilled jobs with high training costs accentuated the problems of high labour turnover.

The mid-1970s were also a period of increasing conflict on South African mines, resulting in 178 deaths in 65 incidents between September 1973 and June 1976 (Horner and Kooy 1976, 17). Possible causes are many, but conditions of life in the compounds, including sexual frustration, lack of privacy and lack of workers' representation produce underlying discontent which is easily ignited. For the mine owners, such conflicts proved costly in terms of strikes, interruptions and broken contracts.

The response of the mining companies to these problems has been twofold: increased mechanisation and related research, and efforts to stabilise the workforce. Mechanisation is relatively easy in the coal mines, but less so in the gold mines because of hard abrasive rock and deep, narrow undulating seams. It also demands a higher proportion of semi-skilled and skilled workers, which has hitherto created the danger that new jobs will be closed to blacks by the Mine Workers Union. However, in the newer open-cast mines blacks drive earth-moving equipment and do the simpler parts of artisan jobs (Knight 1977, 56). Blasting certificates continue in mid-1985 to be monopolised by whites, but the government now seems ready to legislate against this major surviving piece of discrimination with or without the acquiescence of the Mine Workers Union.

Government resistance to stabilisation of miners in family housing also impedes mechanisation with its demand for more skilled black labour. Since 1952, the gold mines have been allowed to stabilise up to 3 per cent of their black labour force, but restriction of this 'concession' to South African blacks has hitherto nullified its effects since the most experienced miners were foreigners; in practice, less than 1 per cent of black miners had been stabilised by 1970. A recent agreement allows the mines to house key black workers in urban residential areas without this traditional limitation (Spandau 1980, 216–17), but only on condition that they be 'repatriated' at the end of their contracts.

The Anglo-American Corporation, more than other mining companies, has pressed for changes in government policy. It aims to provide training, a hierarchy of jobs offering opportunity for individuals to advance, and housing for 10 per cent of its 130,000 black miners on a family basis, if permitted (Oppenheimer 1973). For non-gold mines less restrictive policies are applied, especially on diamond, platinum and coal mines where several companies are building family houses. These mines are more capital-intensive, more mechanised, and already have a higher proportion of skilled labour (Lipton 1980, 125), thus incentives to stabilise are greater. High percentages of stabilised labour are noted by Lipton at the Phalaborwa copper–phosphate mine (80 per cent), the Kimberley diamond mines (62 per cent) and the Rand Mines' new eastern Transvaal coalfields (70–80 per cent). At Phalaborwa, government restrictions do not apply as the workers can be housed nearby in the Gazankulu homeland; similarly workers on coal mines belonging to Rand Mines in Natal are being helped to buy their own homes in KwaZulu. At Kimberley, abundant local labour and rising mine wages encouraged De Beers to replace migrant (largely Basotho) labour with local labour. In the major new mining developments in the north-west Cape, however, the coloured labour preference policy (Chapter 12) was rigorously applied until its abolition in 1985, to prevent blacks being stabilised at these mines which are highly mechanised and employ a high proportion of skilled workers.

For the bulk of the labour force the mining companies are fostering a more limited form of stabilisation which encourages workers to enter into, and keep, long contracts, and to return in as short a time as possible. In part this involves major programmes of upgrading hostel accommodation to reduce overcrowding and to provide more privacy and improved facilities. New hostels are typically smaller buildings, with fewer men per room, and arranged in a village-type setting (Lipton 1980, 133). Where mines have only a short lifespan, mobile homes are sometimes being used. Such developments are long overdue, and even the more progressive companies will take many years to improve all their accommodation. The situation would be eased if the government ceased to require the mining companies to house all their workers; there is a strong argument for allowing workers the choice of a higher wage and responsibility for their own housing, as at the Selebi-Phikwe mine in Botswana (Lemon 1982b, 76).

Re-engagement Guarantee Certificates (RGCs) and bonuses are other incentives being used to induce longer service and rapid return to the mine. Workers in certain categories are provided with RGCs if they have worked for at least 26 weeks on the mine; these expire within a certain period, often six months, after a contract is ended. Men who have worked 45 weeks or more also qualify for an early return bonus (ERB) if they return within six weeks. RGCs and ERBs are given mainly to skilled and semi-skilled workers. They have succeeded in lengthening the average contract and shortening the home-stay period, thus reducing turnover and recruitment. This allows greater selectivity by employers, particularly at a time when real wages were increasing.

The labour market: job reservation, skill shortages and training
At the height of the 'poor white' problem the 'civilised labour' policy which was introduced in the public service reserved even much unskilled work for whites. Private manufacturers were urged to follow suit. During and after the Second World War, however, mechanisation began to cause fragmentation of many skilled jobs into several semi-skilled operative jobs which were performed by blacks, whilst coloureds, Indians and blacks were increasingly employed as drivers of heavy vehicles, clerks, salesmen and insurance agents. White workers feared that such changes would mean lower wages or even redundancy. Such fears were exaggerated, since South Africa's industrial growth was probably sufficiently rapid for whites possessing ability to progress in skilled and managerial jobs, but for the least able whites the threat was real. As a result of these fears, job reservation was introduced in 1956. The Minister of Labour could reserve specified types of work for a given racial group, or lay down the proportion of employees of each race group who might be employed in a stated industry.

Job reservation determinations were subsequently applied in many industries. Such restrictions on the full realisation of human potential have clearly been wasteful of the country's human resources. Not only have they prevented individuals from rising to positions which reflect their abilities, but the impossibility of doing so has been a disincentive to efficiency in the jobs actually held. Conversely, artificial protection of whites also lowers efficiency by removing the incentive of healthy competition. Job reservation has also created shortages of skilled labour which have inevitably restricted economic expansion and resulted in artificially high white wages. Although cognisant of these realities, governments have been afraid of antagonising the white (mainly Afrikaans) working class. The grudging agreement of white unions to relaxation of restrictions has instead been bought by wage increases, thus further widening the racial gap. Job reservation was also circumvented by giving different names to identical jobs when performed by different races. Nevertheless the colour bar gradually shifted upwards in major industrial occupations, and by 1977 job reservation affected only 2.5 per cent of all jobs (Parsons 1977, 131). Following a recommendation of the Wiehahn Commission (see below), the Industrial Conciliation Amendment Act of 1979 repealed the job reservation provisions of the 1956

Industrial Conciliation Act, but allowed existing determinations to remain in force until cancelled. The last statutory determination, applying to the mining industry, was abolished in 1983.

The new legislation nevertheless maintains the protection of 'group rights' by introducing the concept of 'unfair labour practice' which is left to the courts to define. Meanwhile customary discrimination in the workplace remains widespread, and the removal of legal barriers can do little to erode decades of discrimination in terms of education and training. The continuance of influx control and the migrant labour system effectively prevent large numbers of blacks from occupying permanent jobs, and thus limit their opportunity to acquire skills. Realising the growing labour shortage in certain sectors, the government in 1973 relaxed its ban on the training of blacks in semi-skilled jobs outside the homelands, and decided to establish 16 training centres in the main industrial areas. They still could not become artisans, but following a recommendation of the Wiehahn Commission in 1979 this barrier too was removed and 741 blacks were indentured as apprentices in 1982, 5.1 per cent of the total; this declined to 656 (5.3 per cent) in 1983, probably as a result of economic recession.

In recent years both government and private employers have repeatedly stressed South Africa's growing shortages of skilled and managerial labour, and the need for educational reform and training programmes enabling blacks to fill the gaps as they arise and thus ensure the continuing economic growth which is essential if unemployment is to be contained in the face of population growth (Chapter 9). In support of this viewpoint it is pointed out that the white activity rate is no longer low (it increased from 37 per cent in 1975 to 43 per cent in 1983), and that between now and the year 2000 only 7 per cent of new entrants to the labour market will be whites, whereas 18 per cent of all jobs were filled by whites in 1983 (South Africa 1983a, 476). Various statistics are quoted to illustrate the need for black advancement; for instance, the number of blacks in professional and managerial categories is required to double to 370,000 or 37 per cent of all employment in these categories between 1979 and 1987; if clerical, sales and related employment is added, these figures rise to 520,000 and 42 per cent respectively compared to 21 per cent in 1969 (ibid., 476–7).

A closer examination of such figures casts doubt on the extent and nature of present and projected skill shortages and the inability of whites to fill them (Meth 1983). The supposed shortage contrasts oddly with the poor job prospects faced by black school leavers in recent years, including those leaving with matriculation qualifications who numbered 60,000 in 1982 (Chisholm and Christie 1983, 258). The bulk of the black middle class currently occupies relatively subordinate positions in the occupational hierarchy, with teachers and nurses accounting for 89 per cent of black professional, semi-professional and technical workers, compared to only 33 per cent for whites (Meth 1983, 193–4). Managerial vacancies were relatively few, even after the rapid economic growth of 1980–81. Shortages of scientific workers, engineers, technicians and artisans, whilst serious, were low in absolute terms (27,000 artisans in 1981), whilst the shortage of nurses (9000 in 1981) was mainly attributable to low wages. In other occupations shortages are far smaller, and could easily be met by upward mobility of white, coloured and Indian women, who largely work in relatively menial posts at present, although this is changing for white women particularly. It appears that official emphasis on skill shortages may be directed at the white electorate, as a means of winning its consent to reforms in education, training and labour practices which are desired for other reasons. The latter include their inherent desirability in moving towards a more just society, economic arguments for making the best use of human resources (and minimising the price to capital of skilled labour), and the political need for such reforms. The latter relates domestically to the satisfaction of black aspirations and the perceived advantages of a growing black middle class (Chapter 17), and internationally to the provision of evidence of meaningful reform.

The recommendations of the Wiehahn and De Lange Commissions may be viewed in this context. The former was appointed in 1977 to consider all aspects of labour legislation, and presented seven reports from 1979 onwards (South Africa 1979a). Its recommendations embraced discrimination at the workplace, trade union rights and industrial relations, apprenticeship and training, employment registration, social security, health and safety. Most of the Wiehahn recommendations have already been the subject of government legislation. Some have already been noted, and others concerning trade unions will be considered in Chapter 17.

The De Lange Commission of Inquiry into Education was appointed in 1980. Its report proposed a move away from traditional formal schooling patterns towards a new structure with a system of formal (academic) education running parallel with a non-formal (vocational) system (South Africa 1981b). The former would have three tiers: pre-basic and basic up to approximately age 12, which would be free and

167

compulsory, and post-basic which would be paid for by parents. The cost of vocational education would be borne primarily by private capital. A single education department was proposed to coordinate equal quality education for all race groups. These proposals were widely viewed as indicating a new reformist direction for South African education, but the main recommendations were rejected in a 1981 White Paper. Radical analysts anyway questioned the extent of change inherent in the De Lange proposals, pointing out that black children would be channelled mainly into technical education whilst those who could afford it, including most whites, would enjoy access to secondary academic education (Chisholm and Christie 1983, 256–7).

Official policies have assigned high priority to the provision of technical education for urban blacks. A programme was introduced in 1982 to transform certain existing schools into technical and commercial high schools acting as feeders to technical colleges. Departmental training centres are being established to provide technical education for pupils at schools unable to offer such courses, and technical teaching diploma courses are now being used to upgrade black teachers' qualifications. On a higher level, technikons for blacks now train technicians and black middle management. Alongside these government efforts, private industry is providing an increasing range of training at all levels, so much so that the Johannesburg *Star* described the Anglo-American Chairman's Fund as 'South Africa's other government'.[7] Whilst all these changes improve opportunities for many individual blacks, they do not amount to any fundamental dismantling of apartheid in education, and are unlikely significantly to diminish the frustrations of blacks within the system (Chapter 17).

8
Mining and industrialisation: the homeland periphery

The undeveloped state and largely peripheral location of the 'homelands' or black states constitute an unpromising setting for the development of modern economies in territories which are either deemed to be, or intended to become, independent. Government unwillingness to accept the financial implications of the Tomlinson strategy (Chapter 6) meant that economic development proceeded very slowly before 1970. Significant policy changes occurred from the late 1960s, when the need to match political autonomy with some semblance of economic viability and domestic employment creation was recognised. The establishment of the Bantu Investment Corporation (later the Corporation for Economic Development) in 1959 and the Bantu Mining Corporation (now simply the Mining Corporation) in 1969 were gradually followed by the establishment of development corporations in individual homelands. Grants from Pretoria to homeland governments were considerably increased, especially in the build-up to independence for those states which accepted it. This enabled the homeland governments to invest in the infrastructural development which is essential in territories which are competing for private enterprise investment in the same geographical region as the economic core areas of South Africa. In the early 1980s a new regional development strategy was agreed between Pretoria and the black states, and generous incentives for industrial development at homeland growth points introduced. In September 1983 the Development Bank of Southern Africa replaced the Corporation for Economic Development as the regional development agency for the homelands, with a capital target of R2000 million, of which only R200 million will be paid up by the five member 'states' (South Africa, Transkei, Bophuthatswana, Venda and Ciskei), leaving the remainder as a liability of the member governments against which loans will be raised in the capital market. Pretoria is also to make R1.5 billion available to a development fund administered by the bank in its first five years, a commitment which will be extended annually in a five-year cycle.

The limited development so far achieved is evidenced by continuing budgetary dependence on Pretoria and the dominance of public sector activities in the homeland economies. In 1979–80, government employment represented 44.8 per cent of the total in the non-independent homelands, including Ciskei: individual figures varied from 33.7 per cent in Lebowa to 56.7 per cent in Gazankulu, whilst in Transkei the equivalent figure was 39.2 per cent in 1980. The lower proportion of public sector employment in Bophuthatswana (22.7 per cent in 1981) indicates a greater degree of development which distinguishes Bophuthatswana from the other black states (Coker 1983). It resembles them, however, in terms of the contribution made to its GNP by the remittances of migrant workers and the earnings of those commuting daily to jobs outside their homelands (Table 8.1).

Table 8.1: The contribution of commuter and migrant income to 'homeland' GNP, 1980

	Commuter income (R000s)	% of GNP	Migrant income (R000s)	% of GNP	Overall %
Bophuthatswana	394,940	29.8	440,295	33.2	63.0
Ciskei	90,488	26.6	131,320	38.5	65.1
Gazankulu	19,184	10.3	108,750	58.1	68.4
KaNgwane	74,582	32.9	108,000	47.7	80.6
KwaZulu	1,003,272	50.1	608,130	30.4	80.5
Lebowa	146,405	20.0	393,750	53.9	73.9
QwaQwa	13,974	10.1	96,750	70.0	80.1
Transkei	20,520	1.6	717,640	56.4	58.0
Venda	12,208	8.1	79,975	53.3	61.4
Total	1,775,573	27.9	2,684,610	42.1	70.0

Source: SAIRR, Survey of Race Relations in South Africa 1983, p. 364.

Mineral resources and mining

In the past it appears that areas such as Phalaborwa in the eastern Transvaal have been deliberately excluded from the homelands because of their mineral resources, but the policy of homeland consolidation has proceeded too far for this to be repeated as further resources are discovered. The ability of such discoveries to attract private capital to the black states is in any case welcome to Pretoria. Five states –

Bophuthatswana, Lebowa, Gazankulu, Venda and KaNgwane – lie within the mineral-rich belt extending from the northern Transvaal to the northern Cape. Two of the 'independent' homelands, Transkei and Ciskei, have few known mineral resources, although some quarrying takes place. Coal is the only significant mineral found to date in KwaZulu. A small uranium deposit has been discovered in QwaQwa, but no mining yet occurs either there or in KwaNdebele.

The mining sector is most developed in Bophuthatswana, where it is the main basis for the state's relative fiscal independence: total mining production was valued at R543 million in 1981. The mineral-rich Bushveld Igneous Complex penetrates Bophuthatswana in Mankwe and Bafokeng districts. Within it the most important horizon is the Merensky Reef, which outcrops over a distance of 40 kilometres in Bophuthatswana and contains the world's largest deposits of platinum group metals. Bophuthatswana is, taken alone, the third largest producer of platinum, accounting for 30 per cent of world production and 60 per cent of the southern African total. The growing world market has led both companies involved in Bophuthatswana, Rustenburg and Impala, to plan substantial increases in production. Bophuthatswana also produces chrome, asbestos, manganese, limestone and norite. Alluvial diamonds are exploited in Molopo and Taung districts, a large mine having been opened near Mafikeng (Mafeking) in 1983. Despite rapid growth of mineral production, capital-intensification has steadily reduced employment in mining from 68,000 in 1975 to 48,000 in 1980 and only 35,000 in February 1984. Ironically, the reluctance of the Tswana to work in mining is such that only 1 per cent of blacks employed in the platinum mines in 1975 were of Tswana origin.[1]

Lebowa is the only other homeland with a significant mining sector. In 1983 some 5200 Africans were employed in 17 mines exploiting mainly platinum, chrome, andalusite and asbestos. Gazankulu has only two tiny gold mines operating; exploitation of other minerals depends on the development of more sophisticated metallurgical processes, improved infrastructure and market conditions. ISCOR announced the opening of an experimental coal mine in Venda in 1983, to establish the feasibility or otherwise of a full-scale mining operation. In KaNgwane plans were well advanced in 1985 for the development of one section of a 300 million-ton anthracite reserve near the Mozambique border. An asbestos mine on the Swazi border employed 1500 Africans in 1983. The mining sector in KwaZulu has hitherto been dominated by the extraction and processing of mineral-bearing sands, especially in the Richard's Bay area, but exploration of other mineral deposits has occurred in recent years. Anthracite production is likely to begin in the late-1980s in the Nongoma and Somkele districts, and other significant coal deposits exist near Newcastle and Ladysmith.

Industrial location factors in the homelands

A cheap and plentiful labour supply is the one major economic advantage most homelands have to offer industrialists in compensation for higher costs in many other directions. Homeland wage rates are inevitably influenced by those in core areas of South Africa; the easier the access of workers from the periphery to jobs in core areas, the more wage rates in the former will approach those in the latter, although there will still be a margin reflecting the cost of movement and the workers' natural preference for staying with their families. Low wage rates in the homelands thus depend partly on the continuance of influx control (Chapter 10). Real labour costs must anyway be measured in terms of wage *costs* rather than wage rates; Selwyn (1975, 61-2), in his study of Botswana, Lesotho and Swaziland, found that owing to substantially lower productivity and higher training costs both unskilled and skilled wage costs were actually higher in some cases than in the core areas of South Africa, and similar disadvantages obtain in many homeland and border areas of the Republic. In addition much skilled and most managerial work in homeland industries continues to be done by 'expatriate' whites who are normally paid inducement allowances to work there.

The homelands depend heavily on their transport links with South Africa. Railways and main roads tend to follow 'white' corridors such as Durban–Pietermaritzburg–Newcastle and East London–Queenstown (Figure 8.1). A reasonable network of connecting roads has been established, but the monopolistic position of South African Railways (SAR) poses other problems for South African industrialists (Lange 1973, 436). Road transport permits are required for any industrial products to be transported from decentralised regions to major South African markets; without such permits trans-shipment at the nearest railhead is obligatory. The SAR tariff structure also favours market orientation of industrial location (Chapter 7), but decentralisation incentives do include rail rebates.

As access to core areas of South Africa improves, the benefit of free movement of goods tends to accrue more to manufacturers in core areas for whom peripheral markets become more accessible. Even access to

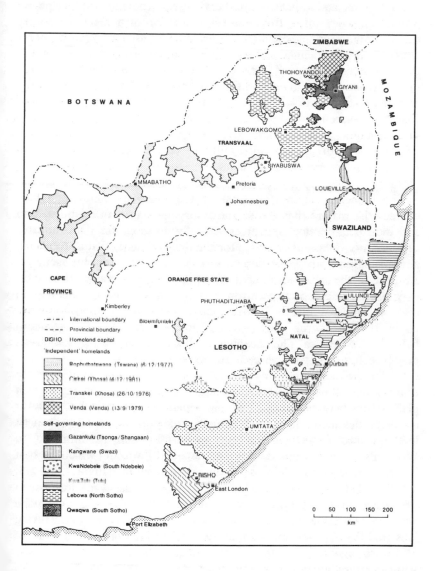

Fig. 8.1 'Independent' and self-governing homelands

limited homeland domestic markets poses problems for peripheral producers. They suffer from the fragmentation of homeland territory since communications, including information media, are usually poorer between various fragments of territory than between each fragment and the core. Even contiguous sections of homeland territory lack integrated urban systems of their own and flows of people and goods are externally oriented to South African networks, as Cook (1980a) demonstrates for Ciskei. 'Independent' homelands could theoretically counter such disadvantages by protecting their domestic markets against South African competition, but this would involve an effective transfer of resources from very poor consumers to producers of manufactured goods (Maasdorp 1974, 20).

The homelands also lack most of the external economies which characterise major urban areas. The embryonic nature of existing urban and industrial development gives virtually no scope for inter-industry linkages, nor does it offer a base for the development of legal, financial, advertising and other commercial services, and maintenance facilities. Absence of the social advantages of living in or near major urban areas may also deter prospective entrepreneurs from establishing factories in the homelands. Whilst the homelands are free from the diseconomies of large urban areas, the same is true of many decentralised locations in 'white' South Africa. The cheapness of building land in the homelands may be countered by higher construction costs.

By far the most promising industrial locations in the homelands are those which abut existing metropolitan areas and are therefore well placed to take advantage of agglomeration economies, market opportunities and perhaps inter-industry linkages. Parts of Ciskei benefit in this respect from their proximity to East London, Berlin and King William's Town, but it is Bophuthatswana and KwaZulu which are best placed in relation to core areas of the space economy (Figures 8.2, 8.3, 8.4). The Odi 1 and Moretele 1 districts of Bophuthatswana are close to Pretoria and the vast PWV market, and the Babelegi growth point alone accounted for three-quarters of Bophuthatswana's 20,000 manufacturing jobs in 1983 (Cowley and Lemon 1986). The interior growth point of Mogwase may benefit to a lesser degree from proximity to the Witwatersrand given recent infrastructural improvements. The same is true of KwaNdebele's new industrial growth point, Ekandustria. KwaZulu benefits from several points of contact with a triangle of rapid economic development with its apices at Durban, Newcastle and Richard's Bay, all of them enjoying good rail access to Johannesburg.

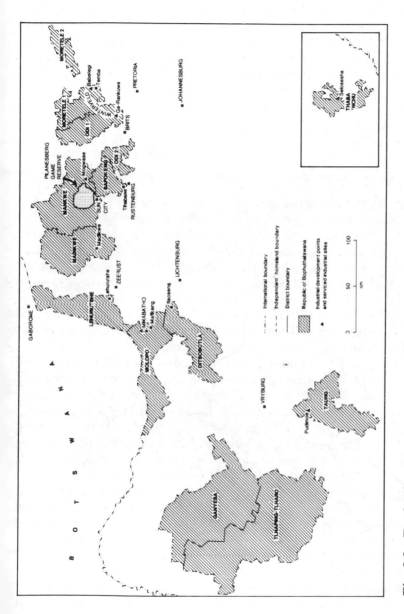

Fig. 8.2　Bophuthatswana

175

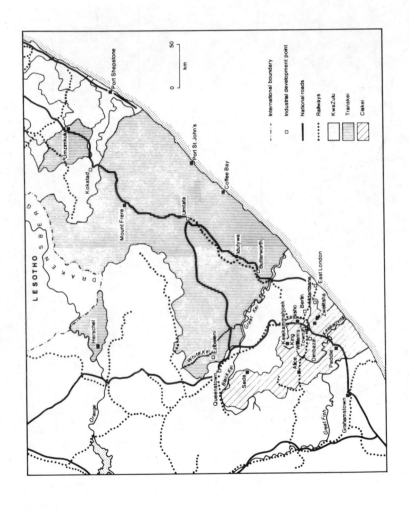

Fig. 8.3 Ciskei and Transkei

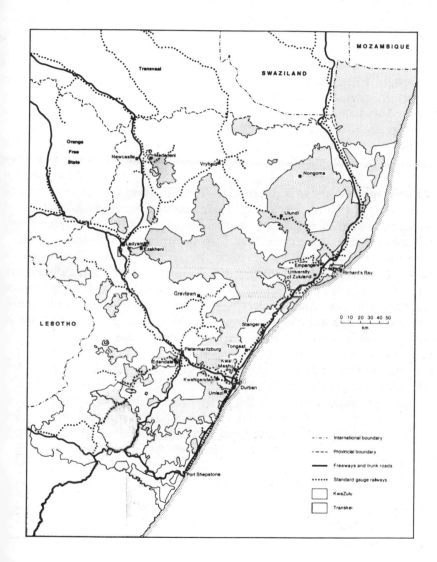

Fig. 8.4 KwaZulu

The concentration of industrial growth in such locations still leaves large parts of Bophuthatswana, KwaZulu and Ciskei distant from manufacturing employment, and has already resulted in considerable redistribution of population within these homelands: thus nearly one-third of Bophuthatswana's population of 1,630,000 lived in the Odi 1 and Moretele 1 districts in 1983, many of them in the 'informal housing' or squatter settlements of the Winterveld. Other homelands such as Lebowa and Gazankulu have only less important 'white' towns such as Pietersburg and Phalaborwa near their borders, whilst all urbanisation within the Transkei must be supported by secondary and tertiary industry within the territory itself. Venda, KaNgwane and QwaQwa are locationally least attractive for industrial development.

Early approaches to industrial decentralisation
As early as 1936 the Board of Trade and Industries considered the encouragement of industry as a means of ameliorating poverty in the reserves, but its recommendations were restricted to industries which would not compete with those elsewhere. The Tomlinson Commission recommended the establishment of industries both within the reserves and near their borders with the aid of white capital and entrepreneurial ability. The government rejected such white involvement within the reserves and concentrated instead on border areas to which Africans could commute daily or at least weekly whilst maintaining homes and families within the reserves. A new body, the Permanent Committee for the Location of Industry, later renamed the Decentralisation Board, was established to implement the plan. Initially it concentrated on the most accessible border areas including Hammarsdale (between Durban and Pietermaritzburg), Rosslyn near Pretoria, and Pietermaritzburg itself. Durban–Pinetown was excluded, as industrialists needed little inducement to establish concerns there. Progress was rapid in these areas and after 1968 attention shifted to areas further away from metropolitan complexes, notably the following (Figures 8.2–8.5):

> East London, Berlin, King William's Town, Queenstown (Ciskei)
> Newcastle, Ladysmith, Colenso, Richard's Bay, Empangeni (KwaZulu)
> Pietersburg, Potgietersrust (Lebowa)
> Tzaneen (Gazankulu)
> Brits, Rustenburg, Zeerust, Mafeking[2] (Bophuthatswana)

The remaining homelands, including Transkei, received no benefit from border industry policies; East London, the nearest border industrial area to Transkei, is 60 kilometres from the nearest part of the homeland. Even where border growth-points were accessible to homelands, they were not within commuting distance of large parts of the labour supply which they were meant to serve. The provision of high-speed rail links to major employment centres enabling blacks to travel hundreds of miles each week has been seriously suggested (Burger 1970), but Wilson (1975, 183) rightly dismissed such a vision with the remark that 'a society that cannot even afford to pay the majority of its workers a living wage is hardly in a position to turn its entire proletariat into a jet set'. Given the impracticability of such long-distance commuting, substantial migration from the interior of the homelands to townships supplying labour to border industries has taken place, and by 1970 60.9 per cent of the urban homeland population lived in eight such townships serving Durban–Pinetown, Pretoria and Rosslyn, Newcastle, East London and King William's Town (Bell 1973a, 406). Where no part of a homeland is close to such employment centres, some residents now resort in desperation to long-distance commuting by bus: the extreme case is perhaps Kwa-Ndebele, where some workers rise as early as 2.30 a.m. to commute to the Reef towns, changing buses at Pretoria.

The total increase in border area employment for blacks in the 1960s was 67,500 jobs, but of this Bell (1973a, pp. 404–5) estimates that only 11,600 were directly attributable to decentralisation policy. The latter had thus made a negligible contribution to the 20,000 jobs *per year* which the Tomlinson Commission considered necessary in relation to 1955 population levels, and employment growth in border areas slowed down considerably in the less expansionary 1970s. Bell (1973b, 217–21) seeks to explain these poor results by drawing unfavourable comparisons between the nature and value of the concessions available in border industrial areas and those available to Italian firms in the Mezzogiorno. His criticisms include the fact that too small a proportion of the benefits accrued in the first year or two after moving, when they would be most valuable, and the capital-related nature of most of the inducements. The government also reduced the effectiveness of its own policy by trying to avoid 'unfair competition' between assisted firms and others; thus it was reluctant to assist clothing firms in the early 1960s, despite the fact that the clothing industry is the most significant of the more easily divertible industries. The selective basis of assistance was another weakness, giving rise to charges of inconsistency and arbitrariness, and reducing the psychological impact of the concessions.

If the border industry policy is viewed not merely as an instrument of employment-creation but in terms of homeland development, much more fundamental criticisms must be made. Since the border areas are surrounded by more productive white farming areas, they are unlikely to provide significant markets for homeland agriculture (Bell 1973c, 32). Nor do they provide the homelands with either a corporate or an individual tax base (Maasdorp 1974, 10). Much of the money earned is spent in 'white' areas, and because of these leakages the multiplier effect on the homelands is weak, as Best (1971) showed for the border industries of Rosslyn. In short, border industries have reinforced the economic dependence of the homelands on 'white' South Africa.

Within the homelands the Bantu Investment Corporation (BIC) sought to encourage black entrepreneurs; its efforts were supplemented by those of the Xhosa Development Corporation for Transkei and Ciskei from 1966 and individual development corporations for most homelands which were created from 1975 onwards. The BIC granted loans to Africans to enable them to purchase, establish or expand trading businesses, service concerns or light industries, and to buy stock in trade. Training and 'aftercare' was undertaken by corporation officials. The BIC assisted, acquired or established a wide variety of commercial concerns, but industrial progress was minimal; between 1960 and 1966 only 35 new industries employing 945 Africans were established (Bell 1973a, 405), many of them under the control of the BIC itself. This clearly confirmed the majority view of the Tomlinson Commission concerning the necessity of white capital and entrepreneurial experience in establishing secondary industry in the homelands.

Recognising this the government modified its position. In terms of the Promotion of Economic Development of Homelands Act (1968) whites could enter the homelands as agents or contractors to the South African Bantu Trust or one of the corporations. Contracts would normally last 25 years (50 in the case of mining concerns), at the end of which the corporation had the option of buying the enterprise, selling it to a black entrepreneur, or renewing the contract. Industries thus established have been concentrated in designated homeland growth points in all homelands except Venda and KaNgwane (and KwaNdebele which was itself only established later). The concessions available in approved areas were slightly more advantageous than in border areas, but have proved insufficient to compensate for the locational disadvantages of most growth points. The total number of black employees in all agency industries was only 31,000 in 1981, excluding Transkei; this represented less than one-third of the *annual* increase in the labour force. Moreover, the distribution of new industrial jobs left most homelands with a tiny share: Bophuthatswana accounted for 47 per cent, primarily at Babelegi, and KwaZulu for 24 per cent, largely at Isithebe. The success of Babelegi clearly rests on its proximity to Pretoria, but this has drawn in many non-Tswana migrants and in the early 1970s industrial labour comprised only about 20 per cent Tswana (Rogerson 1974b).

Transkei had 23,200 industrial jobs in 1980, the vast majority of them established under the agency system. Butterworth was the major manufacturing centre, employing 57.4 per cent of the labour force (Maasdorp 1981, 12). Once again these are unimpressive figures in the context of an *annual* increase of just under 30,000 in the Transkeian labour force (Thomas 1981a, 55) and little or no possibility of daily commuting to jobs outside Transkei. Jackson (1981) and Maasdorp (1981) both stress the locational disadvantage of Transkeian growth points including distance from markets, the need to import most inputs and limited labour skills. Competition with growth points in 'white' South Africa and the other homelands as well as Botswana, Lesotho and Swaziland is a problem, whilst Maasdorp criticises the agency system itself as affording no long-term security of tenure to the investor.

Two policy developments in 1974 appeared to anticipate the 'independence' of the homelands. In July the BIC embarked on a campaign to attract British and German money to the homelands and in October the government announced that henceforth the homeland governments themselves should decide under what conditions business should operate in their areas. Neither measure in itself significantly improved prospects for homeland industrial development, but improved incentives have attracted some foreign investment. In the year ending March 1984 applications involving total capital investment of R89 million, expected to create 11,000 jobs, were approved by the Decentralisation Board; Taiwan accounted for 28 per cent of this, followed by the UK (24 per cent) and Israel (23 per cent).[3]

Most decentralisation policies employ sticks as well as carrots and South Africa's is no exception. Under section 3 of the Physical Planning and Utilisation of Resources Act 1967 industries in 'controlled areas' – PWV, the south-west Cape, Port Elizabeth–Uitenhage and Bloemfontein – require permission to increase their black labour force. This would, in terms of the Act, normally be refused for industries with a black:white labour ratio exceeding 2.5:1 if established before 1 June 1973, or 2:1 if established later. For the homelands such policies are of dubious value: first, because they merely induce the use of capital-intensive techniques

181

in metropolitan areas, thus reducing overall employment; and secondly, because decentralising industries have many non-homeland locations open to them. The Riekert Commission (South Africa 1979b, 226–33) found that section 3 was enforced so leniently that during the years 1972–77 97.9 per cent of the black workers applied for in respect of the extension of existing factories were granted, an instance of economic reality triumphing over apartheid ideology when the two conflict. Not suprisingly in view of this the controlled areas had roughly maintained their share of industrial employment; the only significant sufferer from section 3 appeared to be the PWV clothing industry. The Riekert Commission recommended the withdrawal of section 3 which was accepted by the government in principle, subject to the introduction of indirect fiscal control measures in the metropolitan areas to replace section 3. The search for such measures proved a difficult one, and the new industrial development strategy announced in 1982 referred only to 'certain indirect fiscal control measures aimed at recovering the cost of infrastructural and other government services' (South Africa 1982a, 3); some form of local tax seems probable.

A new decentralisation strategy
In November 1981 Mr Botha, addressing business and community leaders in Cape Town, announced proposals for a 'coordinated regional development strategy' for South Africa and the black states. Negotiations with the 'independent' homelands (the 'TBVC' countries') followed, leading to the publication of an agreed strategy along the lines proposed by Mr Botha in April 1982, with a revised industrial decentralisation policy as a first step in the formulation of an overall regional development strategy. Recognising the continuance of marked regional inequalities and the limited progress achieved to date in promoting economic development in less developed areas, the strategy seeks 'a rationalisation of the development process by way of close cooperation between all the states concerned' which will entail 'the elimination of duplicate structures, the harmonisation of development policies, and the mutual development and utilisation of basic infrastructure' (South Africa 1982a, 1).

The strategy divides South Africa into nine development regions which cut across homeland boundaries (Figure 8.6) and require cooperation between South Africa and the self-governing and 'independent' black states; only one development region, the Western Cape, includes no homeland territory. The development priority of each

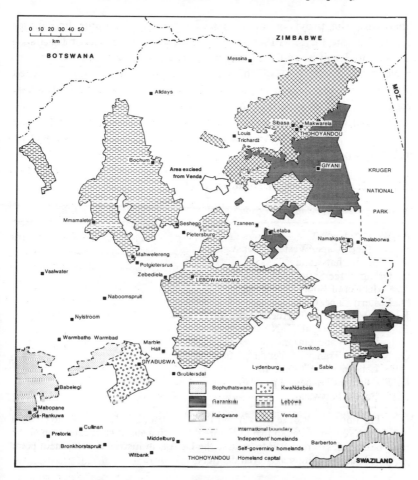

Fig. 8.5   Lebowa, Gazankulu, Venda, KaNgwane and KwaNdebele

region has been assessed according to the need for employment creation and higher living standards and the potential of each development region to satisfy its employment needs through economic growth (Table 8.2). Within these regions, three categories of area or point are recognised in terms of industrial development policy: metropolitan areas, decentralisation points and industrial development points. In the metropolitan areas (PWV, Cape Peninsula, Port Elizabeth–Uitenhage, Durban–

183

Pinetown), the provision of industrial land will be controlled under section 2 of the Physical Planning Act – a new restriction for Durban – but section 3 will be replaced by the indirect fiscal measures referred to above. The application of the latter will take into account marked differences in the degree of concentration between metropolitan areas, recognising that no severe problems of over-concentration are currently being experienced in the Cape Peninsula and Port Elizabeth; the latter is even receiving some positive incentives initially, given the severity of its problems which partly relate to those of the car industry.

Table 8.2: Development regions, 1983

Development region	Relative development need
A. Western Cape	6
B. Northern Cape/Western Transvaal/ Bophuthatswana	6
C. Orange Free State/Qwa Qwa/Thaba 'Nchu district of Bophuthatswana	6
D. Eastern Cape/Ciskei/southern Transkei	9
E. Natal/KwaZulu/northern Transkei	8
F. Eastern Transvaal/KaNgwane/parts of Lebowa and Gazankulu	6
G. Northern Transvaal/Venda/parts of Lebowa and Gazankulu	8
H. PWV/KwaNdebele/a part of Bophuthatswana	4

Note: The boundaries of regions A and B were subsequently changed to create a ninth region (J), as shown in Figure 8.6, with a southward extension of the boundaries of region B to include the De Aar industrial development point and surrounding magisterial districts.

Deconcentration points are located close to metropolitan areas and are considered well placed for growth (Figure 8.6). They include the new coloured city of Atlantis (Chapter 12); Pietermaritzburg and neighbouring black areas which either are already or are planned to become part of KwaZulu (Edendale, Imbali, Swartkops); Tongaat on the north Natal coast, an Indian growth point under an earlier strategy, and an unspecified point north of it in KwaZulu: Brits, north of Johannesburg; Babelegi and Garankuwa in eastern Bophuthatswana, north of Pretoria; and Bronkhorstspruit/Ekangala north-east of Pretoria and a nearby point in KwaNdebele. It has since been announced that Ekangala itself is to be

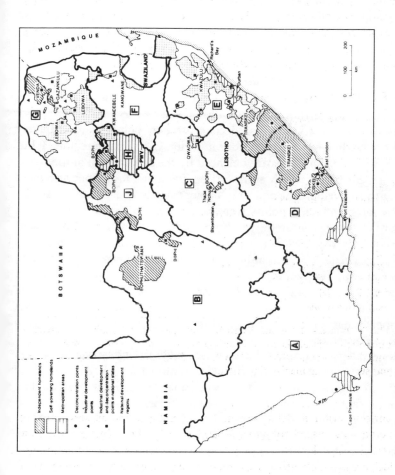

Fig. 8.6 The industrial decentralisation strategy

185

incorporated into KwaNdebele; its population of 5500 in March 1985 was reportedly planned to increase eventually to a staggering 750,000.[4] Two further deconcentration points were announced in 1985: one, Soshanguve, is a planned township 40 kilometres north of Pretoria which houses non-Tswana as its name reveals (*So*tho, *Shang*aan, *Ve*nda) whilst the second, Botshabelo, is a resettlement area 65 kilometres east of Bloemfontein with a 1985 population of 300,000 made up of non-Tswana (mainly Sotho) moved out of the Thaba 'Nchu district of Bophuthatswana and many people induced to move from Bloemfontein's black township by the offer of housing denied to them in Bloemfontein itself. Botshabelo is to be incorporated into QwaQwa, despite its distance from the existing territory of that homeland.

The uneven distribution of deconcentration points is immediately apparent, with one in region A, four in region E, and six in region H, but none elsewhere. This is partly balanced by the distribution of industrial development points which again reflects economic forces but also takes account of development and employment needs and potential. In the 1982 strategy 48 such points were named (excluding Walvis Bay), of which 28 were located in homelands. Excluding Onverwacht (subsequently renamed Botshabelo, and now a deconcentration point), Bophuthatswana has four industrial development points (Figure 8.2), QwaQwa two, Transkei four and Ciskei two (Figure 8.3), KwaZulu six (Figure 8.4), Lebowa three, and Gazankulu three (Figure 8.5), and the other homelands one each. In seven cases these points are not even specifically named in the strategy, but referred to in such terms as 'a point in KwaNdebele'.

The strategy incorporates a new schedule of industrial incentives which came into effect in April 1982. Within the 'TVBC countries', South Africa contributes half the cost of financing these incentives. The highest incentives are generally applied to the most remote points (Table 8.3); most are automatically available and not a matter for negotiation. The remarkably high percentages of the wage bill which may be subsidised underlines the employment-oriented nature of the strategy, but the maximum monthly wage to which these percentages are applicable makes equally clear the low wage levels likely to prevail at decentralised locations. In addition to the incentives mentioned in Table 8.3, electricity subsidies are available to ensure an effective end tariff equal to the ESCOM tariff appicable in the eastern Transvaal; grants are available for the housing of key personnel; and existing 50 per cent rebates on harbour dues at East London, aimed to secure better use of its

Table 8.3: Schedule: Level of industrial incentives for industrial development in the different development regions

| | Rail rebate (%) | Employment Incentives (for 7 years) | | Traning grant | Rental & interest subsidy (%) for 10 years | Housing subsidy (% of interest rate) | Relocation allowance | Price preference on tenders (%) |
		% of total wage bill	Maximum amount per worker – R per month					
	(1)	(2)	(3)	(4)	(5)	(6)	(7)	(8)
REGION A								
Industrial Development Points								
RSA – George, De Aar, Vredenburg/Saldanha, Walvis Bay, Upington	40	80	70	Yes	40	40	Yes	5
Deconcentration Points								
RSA – Atlantis	40	80	70	Yes	40	40	Yes	4
(Electricity subsidy will also apply)								
REGION B								
Industrial Development Points								
RSA – Kimberley	40	80	70	Yes	40	40	Yes	5
BOPHUTHATSWANA – Heystekrand, Mafikeng, Pudimoe	40	80	80	Yes	45	40	Yes	10
REGION C								
Industrial Development Points								
RSA – Bloemfontein, Harrismith	40	80	70	Yes	40	40	Yes	5
QWAQWA – Phuthaditjaba,	40	95	110	Yes	75	40	Yes	10
Onverwacht	40	95	100	Yes	70	40	Yes	10
A point adjoining Harrismith		Still to be determined						
BOPHUTHATSWANA – Selosesha	40	95	100	Yes	70	40	Yes	10

continued	(1)	(2)	(3)	(4)	(5)	(6)	(7)	(8)
REGION D								
Industrial Development Points								
RSA – Berlin, King William's								
Town, East London, Queenstown	60	80	100	Yes	60	60	Yes	5
TRANSKEI – Butterworth,								
Umtata, Ezibeleni	60	95	110	Yes	80	60	Yes	10
CISKEI* – Dimbaza,								
Mdantsane/Berlin South	60	95	110	Yes	80	60	Yes	10
METROPOLITAN AREA								
PORT ELIZABETH/UITEN-								
HAGE	20	No	No	Yes	No	No	No	No
(Electricity subsidy will also apply								
REGION E								
Industrial Development Points								
RSA – Ladysmith, Newcastle,								
Richard's Bay/Empangeni, A								
point in Southern Natal	50	80	80	Yes	45	50	Yes	5
TRANSKEI – A point in								
Eastern Pondoland	50	95	105	Yes	70	50	Yes	10
KWAZULU – Isithebe, Ulundi,								
Ezakeni, Madadeni/Osizweni, a								
point near Richard's Bay, a								
point in Southern KwaZulu	50	95	105	Yes	70	50	Yes	10
Deconcentration Points								
RSA – Pietermaritzburg	20	80	25	Yes	15	20	Yes	4
Tongaat	20	80	30	Yes	20	20	Yes	4
A point south of Durban			Still to be determined					
KWAZULU –								
Imbali/Swartkops/Edendale, a								
point south of Durban, a point								
north of Durban (but no further								
south than Tongaat)	20	80	35	Yes	25	20	Yes	4
REGION F								
Industrial Development Points								
RSA – Nelspruit/White River	40	80	70	Yes	40	40	Yes	5
GAZANKULU – Mkhuhlu	40	95	110	Yes	70	40	Yes	10
KANGWANE – A point in								
KaNgwane	40	95	110	Yes	70	40	Yes	10
REGION G								
Industrial Development Points								
RSA – Pietersburg, Louis								
Trichardt, Potgietersus, Tzaneen	50	80	90	Yes	50	50	Yes	5
VENDA – Thohoyandou	50	95	110	Yes	70	50	Yes	10
LEBOWA – Seshego	50	95	100	Yes	60	50	Yes	10

continued	(1)	(2)	(3)	(4)	(5)	(6)	(7)	(8)
Lebowakgomo, a point near Steelport Valley	50	95	110	Yes	70	50	Yes	10
GAZANKULU – Giyani, Nkowakowa	50	95	110	Yes	70	50	Yes	10
REGION H *Industrial Development Points* KWANDEBELE – a point in KwaNdebele			Still to be determined					
Deconcentration Points RSA – Bronkhorstpruit/Ekangala, Brits	No	80	30	Yes	20	20	Yes	4
BOPHUTHATSWANA – Babelegi, Garankuwa	No	80	35	Yes	25	20	Yes	4
KWANDEBELE – a point in KwaNdebele adjoining Bronkhorstpruit/Ekangala			Still to be determined					

*Sada will receive the same incentives as Dimbaza on an *ad hoc* basis.

harbour, apply to all goods manufactured in the eastern Cape, Ciskei and southern Transkei. Relocation costs are reimbursed where industries move from foreign countries, the PWV area or Durban–Pinetown to any decentralised area, or from Cape Town to Atlantis. Incentives may be given to supporting service industries wherever it can be proved that a lack of such industries will handicap industrial development. South Africa and the TVBC governments have agreed (undisclosed) priorities amongst the industrial development points for infrastructural improvement.

The new decentralisation strategy must be evaluated in terms of both economic and political objectives. Economically, it undoubtedly represents an improvement on earlier strategies in certain respects. The regional approach recognises the artificiality of homeland boundaries and of the previous approach which purported to treat South Africa as consisting of as many economies as there were 'independent' and self-governing states; such an approach is reflected in the development plans commissioned by the black states in recent years, which often bear little relation to economic realities. The new 'multilateral' approach is, however, marred by a complex, multi-tiered bureaucracy which consumes scarce resources and delays decisions. Regional planning *per se* cannot in any case improve the attractiveness of homeland locations. In Transkei, for instance, the designation of the East London–King

William's Town–Butterworth axis as a regional growth point (Maasdorp 1981, 12) still leaves Butterworth as the least attractive potential location of the three; employment growth elsewhere on the axis may bring work closer to Transkeians, but does not provide the fiscal advantages to Transkei as a political entity which would be generated by development within its own boundaries.

The major change in the incentive package from tax concessions to direct cash payments should assist small firms with limited cash resources, which should also benefit from recognition of the role which training and supporting industries play in decentralised industrial developments (du Toit 1982, 257). The emphasis on employment-related incentives is clearly important, but capable of abuse; it has become apparent that some firms in Ciskei took on labour to perform non-existent jobs and profited by claiming larger grants than they actually paid to the workers involved. There is also disturbing evidence that decentralising industries are highly dependent on the incentives offered, particularly short-term ones, which calls into question the prospects for self-sustaining growth of the decentralised industrial base and its stability over time (Addleson *et al.* 1985).

One partner in the new strategy, Ciskei, has already found it too expensive, and intends to abolish the existing incentives eventually. It cannot do so immediately in terms of the multilateral 'SATVBC' agreement, but has none the less unilaterally introduced an alternative scheme which became operative on 1 March 1985 (Black *et al.* 1985, 165). There will be no corporation tax apart from a 15 per cent tax on profits which are expatriated, and no income tax on personal incomes below R8000, with only 15 per cent payable on higher incomes. Firms choosing the tax holiday option are still entitled to some concessions including a 60 per cent rebate on the transport of finished goods within southern Africa, a housing subsidy scheme, electricity subsidy, and a 10 per cent price preference on government tenders. The Ciskei government hopes to draw larger, highly profitable firms which could benefit from such a regime rather than the small, labour-intensive companies it has attracted hitherto. The abolition of company tax applies to all business activities and thus offers subsidies to commercial, professional and service firms which do not qualify under the SATVBC strategy. This seems likely to benefit development of the new Ciskeian capital, Bisho, at the expense of East London–King William's Town and perhaps other towns in the eastern Cape and Transkei. Private sector response is difficult to gauge; although the tax-free option is being marketed as in perpetuity (a 75 per cent majority in the Ciskeian National Assembly is required to end it), there is no guaranteeing the actions of future governments or indeed the security of the regime itself. To allay such fears on the part of investors, Ciskei is actually attempting to secure an internationally-backed insurance package against arbitrary change in the tax system! (Davies 1985, 192). This unilateral Ciskeian action clearly threatens the multilateral character of the regional industrial decentralisation programme, and is as such unwelcome to the South African government. Whether the latter will continue to pay 50 per cent of the incentives given to Ciskeian firms choosing the package agreed multilaterally remains to be seen.

Although the 'TVBC countries' may find the new strategy expensive, the South African government's overall commitment to industrial decentralisation has increased considerably under the multilateral strategy. In the first year of its operation, South Africa budgeted for an increase in non-recoverable costs regarding industrial development from R44.7 million in 1981–82 to R93.7 million in 1982–83 (du Toit 1982, 254). However, the government sees the central financial pillar of the strategy as the new Development Bank of Southern Africa which is to make available R650 million p.a. for development and expansion projects, a sum which it is hoped to raise through debentures issued on South African and overseas capital markets (Zille 1983, 60). As the *Rand Daily Mail* pointed out, the government's own contribution is 'small change in the game that he [Mr Botha] wants to play. Anglo-American and Gencor spend that on one medium-sized new factory or a modest mine expansion.'[5] This comment neatly puts any attempt to develop industry in the homelands in true perspective against the dominance of core areas. The importance of the latter for the nurture of small industries is such that fiscal disincentives in metropolitan areas may ultimately limit industrial growth in the periphery itself. More generally, the strategy resembles its predecessors in failing to recognise the pull exerted by agglomeration economies and in the ideological constraints in terms of which homeland development has guided the identification of development regions and industrial development points. Without doubt the latter are far too numerous – almost twice the number in the previous strategy which itself attempted development in too many places (van der Kooy 1982, 214). In practice most development is likely to occur at a handful of the designated points, and the undisclosed priorities agreed in terms of infrastructural spending are likely to be influential; Maasdorp (1980, 13) actually suggests that 'South Africa should probably have no more than two or three growth points for the foreseeable future.'

The contrast between Maasdorp's prescription and the strategy adopted reflects the latter's political motivation and the policy dilemmas of apartheid planners. Economic decentralisation in South Africa 'is aimed at providing the economic base for the population distribution needed to retain ethnicity as the fundamental organising principle of the society' (Zille 1983, 65) or, as Mr Chris Heunis, Minister of Constitutional Development and Planning, succinctly put it: 'to carry the policy of separate development to its logical conclusion'.[6] Previous decentralisation strategies have failed to entrench the population distribution necessary for ethnic political partition, whether federal or confederal (Chapters 14–16), and the present one is designed to retrieve the situation. Where rural–urban migration has already undermined ethnic geographical separation, South Africa aims to promote upward class mobility to integrate urban black 'insiders' into the economy as a privileged middle class with a stake in the system. For the rest, the decentralisation strategy is intended to enable tight influx control to maintain as far as possible traditional ethnic geography, at least in broad regional terms.

Zille (1983) reveals differences amongst past and present economic advisers to the government concerning the degree of flexibility acceptable in defining this objective. Professor Jan Lombard believes that repeated attempts at industrial decentralisation to peripheral growth points are doomed to failure, whatever the incentives, and opts instead for creating 'balancing growth poles' in broad regional areas, including metropolitan areas, throughout South Africa with the prime aim of preventing further black migration to the PWV area. Lombard's successor, Professor Simon Brand, supports the far more conservative decentralisation policy actually adopted in an attempt to restrict black urbanisation in all metropolitan areas and so provide a more convincing demographic and economic basis for ethnic political partition. There seems little doubt that Lombard's view is closer to the realities of the South African space economy, and the political implications of this will have to be grasped sooner rather than later if political change is to occur by peaceful means. Mr Botha's admission in August 1985[7] that the influx control laws were 'costly and impractical' appears to herald fundamental reform on this front, although not necessarily abolition (Chapter 10). If such changes permit major increases in the black population of metropolitan areas, the political aims of industrial decentralisation policy, which might also be described as 'costly and impractical', will also become irrelevant.

Part 4
POPULATION AND URBANISATION

9
Population, migration and resettlement

Racial patterns of population growth
In such a race-conscious society as South Africa, the racial composition of the population is of great concern to government, politicians and whites generally. The country's overall population more than doubled between 1960 and 1984, when it exceeded 32 million (Table 9.1). The black proportion of the population varied little between 1904 (67.4 per cent) and 1960 (68.3 per cent), as immigration compensated for the lower natural increase of whites in these decades. White immigration has continued with a net gain of 427,000 between 1964 and 1980 (South Africa 1983a, 285), but this has proved insufficient to maintain the white share of the population. The black growth rate reached a peak of 3.3 per cent p.a. in the 1960s when death rates were declining but birth rates remained high, as in many developing countries. It has declined since and was estimated at 2.8 per cent p.a. in the years 1980–83.[1] Other population groups have proceeded further along the demographic cycle. Coloured population reached a peak of 3.31 per cent p.a. in the mid-1950s, but subsequent declines in fertility were countered by decreasing mortality, whilst the youthful age structure of the coloured population continued to produce increasing numbers of women of childbearing age (Sadie 1972, 25). The coloured growth rate is now declining, however, and was estimated at 2.1 per cent p.a. in the years 1980–83. Indians reached their maximum growth rate of 3.39 per cent p.a. as early as 1946–51, and were increasing at only 1.4 per cent p.a. in the years 1980–83, marginally below the white growth rate of 1.5 per cent p.a in these years. Almost half the latter, however, derived from immigration, leaving a natural increase of only 0.8 per cent p.a. This reflects a sharp decline in white birth rates from 23 per 1000 in 1973 to only 16 per 1000 in 1979,[2] which may be partially related to growing white insecurity and doubts about their future in South Africa. During 1981 whites accounted for only 10.02 per cent of all births in South Africa.[3]

Table 9.1: Population by race group, 1960–84

Race group	1960 ('000)	%	1970 ('000)	%	1980 ('000)	%	1984 ('000)	%
Blacks	10,928	68.3	15,340	70.4	20,886	72.5	24,103	73.8
Whites	3,080	19.3	3,773	17.3	4,528	15.7	4,818	14.7
Coloureds	1,509	9.4	2,051	9.4	2,612	9.1	2,830	8.7
Asians	477	3.0	630	2.9	805	2.8	890	2.7
Total	15,994	100.0	21,794	100.0	28,811	100.0	32,642	100.0

Sources: *Census of Population* for 1960, 1970 and 1980; 1984 mid-year estimates from the Central Statistical Service. The 1980 figures for blacks include an estimate from the Bureau of Economic Development, Cooperation and Research (BENSO) for the population of Transkei, Bophuthatswana and Venda, and are slightly inflated by the inclusion of the small non-black populations of these territories in the absence of a racial breakdown. The 1984 figures include SAIRR calculations (*Survey*, p. 185) based on information supplied by the Development Bank of Southern Africa in respect of the 'TVBC countries'; figures for non-black groups have been adjusted to allow for those living in TVBC in 1984.

Current population projections suggest that by the year 2000 South Africa will have 45 million people, of whom 34.9 million (77.5 per cent) will be black, 5.3 million (11.8 per cent) white, 3.7 million (8.2 per cent) coloured and 1.1 million (2.4 per cent) Indian.[4] Even if white immigration continues at the levels of the early 1980s (a net gain of 38,952 in 1982),[5] it would not significantly alter the projections, and a decline and even reversal of white immigration may well result from the widespread violence which erupted in 1985 (Chapter 17). Right-wing political and church bodies have at times called for government action to increase white birthrates, but this is improbable; any impact it might have would probably be outweighed by increased distrust of family planning as a 'white plot' to outnumber them on the part of blacks.

The racial composition of the population varies considerably between provinces (Table 9.2). The relatively low proportion of blacks in the Cape (excluding the homelands) reflects both their historical distribution and the operation of the Coloured Labour Preference Area policy (Chapter 12) over much of the province. Elsewhere blacks constitute an absolute majority of the population even when the homelands are excluded, although only marginally so in Natal where boundary changes have resulted in black areas of major cities being reclassified as part of KwaZulu. The exceptionally high proportion of blacks in the Orange Free State reflects the minimal provision of homeland territory in that province (only tiny QwaQwa and the Thaba 'Nchu district of Bophuthatswana), which leave relatively more blacks in 'white' areas than in other provinces. Indians live mainly in Natal (81 per cent), where their concentration was maintained after the Act of Union by continued restrictions on inter-provincial movement until 1975. Thereafter they were still excluded from the Orange Free State, but this restriction was finally lifted at the request of the National Party Congress of that province in 1985. Coloureds have faced no such restrictions, but 84 per cent continue to live in the Cape Province and about 40 per cent in the Cape Peninsula alone. Most of the rest (9.5 per cent) live in the Transvaal, as do 14.5 per cent of Indians.

Table 9.2: Provincial distribution of population, 1983 (excluding 'homelands')

Province	Population ('000)	Black %	White %	Coloured %	Asian %
Cape	5,374	31.5	24.0	43.9	0.6
Transvaal	8,950	66.7	28.9	3.0	1.4
Natal	2,842	51.1	20.6	3.4	24.9
Orange Free State	2,080	81.0	16.1	2.9	—
Total	19,246	56.1	24.9	14.4	4.5

Source: 1983 mid-year estimates, Central Statistical Service.

All groups except blacks are highly urbanised. Asians are the most urbanised group (91 per cent in 1980), followed closely by whites (88 per cent) and coloureds (77 per cent), all of them exhibiting developed world urbanisation rates. Black urbanisation has risen from 24.3 per cent in 1946 to 38 per cent in 1980, but remains more characteristic of developing world levels of urbanisation (van der Merwe 1983, 337). In absolute terms, however, blacks have outnumbered whites in the cities since the 1946 census, and it is the black component of the urban population which has shown the fastest growth since 1951. Thus the black:white ratio in urban areas increased from 1.35:1 in 1960 to 1.70:1 in

197

1980, despite all efforts to control it (Chapter 10). The 1980 census thus became the first to record an absolute majority of blacks in South African cities, a fact even more disturbing for apartheid planners than the overall rapid growth of the black population.

Official policies have been more successful in increasing the proportion of blacks living in the homelands, which rose from 39.5 per cent in 1960 to 46.5 per cent in 1970 and to an estimated 54.3 per cent in 1984 (Table 9.3). This reflects the involuntary resettlement of 'surplus people' from both urban and especially 'white' rural areas (see below); of 1.5 million Africans who left the *platteland* (white farming areas and *dorps* or small towns) between 1950 and 1980, no less than 1.4 million went to the homelands, initially at least, instead of to the metropolitan areas as they would have done in most industrialising countries (Wilson 1984, 84). Adjustments in homeland boundaries to incorporate black townships which are functionally part of adjacent 'white' towns and cities also produced apparent increases in the proportion of homeland blacks. As a result, the total homeland population increased from 7 million in 1970 to over 13 million in 1984. Despite this, only 47.8 per cent of all blacks lived in their designated homelands in 1980 (Christopher 1982c, 133). Bophuthatswana and KwaNdebele had the largest percentages of the 'wrong' ethnic groups living within their borders. At least one-third of Bophuthatswana's population consists of non-Tswana who are employed in mining or attracted to the Odi 1 and Moretele 1 districts by the proximity of employment opportunities in Pretoria. KwaNdebele, the last of the ten homelands to be officially created as such, has several substantial ethnic minorities of which the largest was the North Sotho who contributed 12.4 per cent of its population in 1980.

Migrant Labour from the Homelands

The extent and significance of migrant labour in South Africa has been extensively documented, most notably by Wilson (1972b). The number of migrant workers from the homelands grew at an average compound rate of 3.1 per cent p.a. between 1936 and 1970 (Nattrass 1976, 69). It increased by a further 36 per cent between 1970 and 1981 (Table 9.4), but this in a period when the homeland population, boosted by migration from the *platteland*, grew by well over half. Given very limited development of homeland job opportunities, this implies a major increase in underemployment and unemployment within the homelands, and migrant labourers continue to outnumber males employed within the homelands.

198

Table 9.3: Homeland blacks

Homeland	Ethnic group	% of ethnic group in 'own state' 1980	Black population of homeland 1984	% of all SA blacks
Bophuthatswana	Tswana	41.6	1,667,478	6.92
Ciskei	Xhosa	(60.5)ᵃ	903,681	3.75
Gazankulu	Shangaan	39.1	580,952	2.41
KaNgwane	Swazi	16.1	377,898	1.57
KwaNdebele	South Ndebele	32.8	176,727	0.73
KwaZulu	Zulu	56.9	3,866,273	16.04
Lebowa	North Sotho	58.1	2,046,479	8.49
QwaQwa	South Sotho	11.7	178,124	0.74
Transkei	Xhosa	(60.5)ᵃ	2,912,408	12.08
Venda	Venda	60.7	381,891	1.58
Total		47.8	13,091,911	54.31

Note: a. Refers to Ciskei and Transkei together.

Sources: SAIRR 1984 *Survey*, p. 185, based on information from the Development Bank of Southern Africa; and A.J. Christopher 1982c, p. 133.

Table 9.4: Migrant labour from homelands, 1970–81 ('000)

Homeland	1970	1977	1981	1982
Bophuthatswana	150	175	197	236
Ciskei	52	54	60	59
Gazankulu	40	43	58	64
KaNgwane	18	34	57	67
KwaNdebele	11	27	63	52
KwaZulu	270	244	280	294
Lebowa	140	155	186	180
QwaQwa	4	34	51	60
Transkei	268	301	336	346
Venda	22	28	41	37
Total	975	1095	1329	1395

Source: SAIRR, *Survey of Race Relations in South Africa*, 1984, p. 256; and D.M. Smith 1983, p. 47.

Traditional justifications for migrant labour have long since lost what relevance they may once have possessed. Oscillating migration may have eased the cultural transition from traditional subsistence society to modern urban life in the decades after the diamond and gold discoveries, but this can hardly justify the system today when a substantial proportion of the black population has considerable urban experience. The widening of the cash economy through remittances does occur, but migrant labourers are estimated to spend 80 per cent of their wages in 'white' areas; this money, and the multiplier effects it represents in terms of job opportunities, is lost to the homelands, whilst migrant workers' families struggle to support themselves on such small remittances and a diminishing or non-existent land base. The latter also invalidates the argument that migrant workers have something on which to fall back in times of unemployment; such an argument in any case seeks to relieve the state and employers of responsibility for the unemployed.

From the standpoint of the homelands and their people, the economic and social disadvantages of the migrant labour system are overwhelming. Socially, the break-up of family life and impediments to normal sexual relationships affect some of the most basic human needs: Wilson (1972b, 178–86) lists illegitimacy, bigamy, prostitution, homosexuality, drunkenness, violence and the breakdown of parental authority as direct effects of the system, whilst venereal disease, tuberculosis, malnutrition and beriberi are some of the indirect results of the lifestyle of migrant labourers. Men are degraded by a system which deprives them of a family role, whilst women are left behind feeling lonely and helpless, anxiously waiting for letters and money from their husbands.

Economically, the system forces poor rural areas to subsidise urban development. This results from the rural areas from which men come and the towns in which they work being treated as separate entities, not as belonging together or having mutual responsibility for each other. Thus migrant workers have traditionally been paid lower wages than would be needed for full family support, whilst urban municipalities and employers are saved the cost of providing family housing, social security and the greater urban infrastructure which the presence of families would demand. In short, the core areas of the economy are able to expand without having to bear the cost 'of the human being behind the labour unit' (Wilson 1972b, 188). Even these advantages to capital are being overtaken by other considerations (Chapter 7), whilst the rural areas have become so densely populated with women, children and old people that there is insufficient land for the rationalisation and improvement of agriculture (Chapter 6).

Migrant labour also drains the homelands of their best manpower, which means that homeland educational expenditure benefits the 'white' economy far more than that of the homelands themselves. Nattrass (1976, 70) found 90 per cent migration rate from the homelands at the educational level of primary school plus four years. Most migrants receive little training and acquire few skills which they might subsequently apply in the homelands.

Controls on the volume of migration which inhere in the system are both discriminatory and contrary to the free movement of labour which is a basic organising principle of capitalist economies. Such restrictions both limit the ability of individuals to find work and to develop their potential, and inhibit the development of an urban informal sector of the kind which is found in most Third World cities (Chapter 10).

Frontier commuters

The notion that the homelands should provide accommodation for those working in adjacent towns began to gain ground about 1950 when Umlazi became the first homeland town to alleviate the black housing shortage in a 'white' city, Durban (Smit 1979, 7). But it was not until the late 1960s that this new method of reducing the black population in 'white' areas was enshrined in official policies (General Circular no. 27, 1967). The circular required local authorities to obtain government approval before initiating any new black housing schemes; this would be withheld unless it could be shown that accommodation was essential and could not be provided in an adjacent homeland. From 1968 blacks were allowed only to rent houses in townships outside the homelands; in the latter they could acquire freehold and were encouraged to build their own homes. Extensions to townships in Pretoria, East London and elsewhere were subsequently suspended, and the city councils, acting as agents of the South African Bantu Trust, began large-scale construction programmes at Mabopane, Mdantsane and elsewhere in adjacent homelands (Smit and Booysen 1977, 20). These townships were used to accommodate not only the increased black population but also many blacks living in slum areas of 'white' towns such as Duncan Village (East London) and Cato Manor (Durban). Where distances are too great for daily commuting, black workers commute weekly or monthly between their families who have been rehoused in the homelands and their jobs.

An extremely rapid growth of townships just within the homelands in areas abutting 'white' urban areas and growth points has resulted. The population of these townships is attributable to five processes (Lemon 1982b, 82): resettlement from nearby 'white' urban areas, resettlement from 'white' rural areas, natural increase, migration from rural areas within homelands, and the incorporation of existing population into homelands by redrawing boundaries, as in the transfer of KwaMashu from Durban to KwaZulu in 1977.

There were 773,000 frontier commuters in 1982, an increase of 165% since 1970 (Table 9.5;). The pre-eminence of KwaZulu (51.9 per cent) and Bophuthatswana (21.9 per cent) reflects the position of parts of their territories which abut 'white' metropolitan areas and growth points (Chapter 8). Lebowa, Ciskei and KaNgwane are the only other homelands with significant numbers of commuters. Lebowa borders the mining town of Phalaborwa as well as Pietersburg and Potgietersrus. Most Ciskeians travel from Mdantsane to East London; Mdantsane was one of the first commuter towns to be built and, with a population of half a million, ranks as the second largest black settlement after Soweto, but the economic stagnation of East London (Black 1980, 65–6) explains the static number of commuters since 1970. KaNgwane's long borders in relation to its area allow more than one-third of its commuters to work on white farms.

Table 9.5: 'Frontier commuters', 1977–81 ('000)

	1977	*1978*	*1979*	*1980*	*1981*	*1982*
Bophuthatswana	148.2	151.8	155.4	161.2	162.2	173
Ciskei	34.6	36.2	37.1	38.1	38.4	38
Gazankulu	6.3	6.7	7.8	8.8	9.7	9
KaNgwane	25.2	28.2	33.1	35.6	40.0	44
KwaNdebele	1.1	1.3	3.5	5.9	8.7	12
KwaZulu	291.3	321.7	352.3	363.9	384.2	395
Lebowa	46.6	54.4	57.9	65.8	72.2	76
QwaQwa	2.1	2.0	2.5	6.8	9.5	12
Transkei	7.1	8.6	8.9	9.0	9.1	8
Venda	4.5	5.1	5.6	5.6	5.7	6
Total	567.0	616.3	664.1	700.7	739.7	773

Source: SAIRR, *Survey of Race Relations in South Africa 1983*, p. 138 and 1984, p. 416.

The building of homeland townships and, in some instances, the extension of homeland borders which were not hitherto within daily commuting distance of 'white' cities, have brought considerable proportions of the homeland population within a short distance of their borders, as rural workers move as close to 'white' urban areas as they can legally live with their families. In Ciskei, the districts of Mdantsane and Zwelitsha, serving East London and King William's Town-Berlin respectively, had 54.8 per cent of all Ciskeians according to the 1980 Ciskei census. Nearly half Bophuthatswana's population already lived within a 50-kilometre radius of Pretoria by 1970 (Smit 1979, 8). This proportion appears to have declined according to the 1980 Bophuthatswana census and subsequent official estimates, partly as a result of steps to remove non-Tswana including the excision of the non-Tswana township of Soshanguve from Bophuthatswana territory. However, official figures may well understate the large squatter population in the Winterveld, Klippan and Oskraal areas around Garankuwa, Mabopane and Temba (Figure 8.2), which represents a spatial displacement across the homeland border of a phenomenon associated with most Third World cities (Smith 1982b, 41).

Permanent migration from the remoter parts of the homelands to commuter townships could in itself prove beneficial by opening up opportunities for agricultural development which the migrant labour system and increasing population densities have long denied. Both informal housing and informal sector employment are widely viewed as logical adaptations to the Third World urban milieu, and in the right circumstances, particularly a rapidly expanding urban economy such as normally characterises most South African cities, they can be a transitional stage to something more permanent. The real problem arises when the urban economy is artificially separated from the rural–urban migration which it induces by an 'international' boundary, as the people concerned become the responsibility of a different state with minimal resources (Lemon 1982b, 86).

It has long been characteristic of many South African cities that the poorest members of the community commute long distances: the displacement of blacks from areas zoned for other groups under the Group Areas Act (Chapter 10) contributed to this situation. The housing of blacks in homeland commuter townships lengthens the average worker's journey still further. Frontier commuters travel an average of 24 kilometres per day in each direction (Mastoroudes 1983, 401), but time and cost are more important than distance. At Mdantsane, 12 kilometres from East London, the average commuter spends between two and three hours each day travelling to and from work (Matravers 1980, 40): this is partly attributable to public transport services poorly related to user needs, a common complaint in such townships, revolving around an inflexible linear system and the universal necessity of changing buses in the case of Mdantsane. Most commuters could not afford the economic cost of such journeys, and the fares are subsidised from a transport levy such that in 1982 commuters paid an average of about half the economic tariff, employers paid 13 per cent and the state 37 per cent (Voges 1983), but most black commuters still spend between 10–20 per cent of their income on transport.[6] The Welgemoed Commission of Enquiry into Bus Passenger Transportation defended the principle of subsidy (South Africa 1983b, para. 4.34), despite the fact that the total cost in 1983 was approaching R150 million p.a. (McCarthy and Swilling 1985, 239). In addition, large capital sums have been spent in new rail links, most notably that between Mabopane and the Belle Ombre station in Pretoria which was completed in 1983 at a cost of R134 million, which will eventually transport 180,000 passengers daily. Rail transport is important for commuters to Pretoria, Durban and East London but buses, which are much slower, transported 59 per cent of all frontier commuters in 1981. Dissatisfaction with the transport system is evidenced by bus boycotts centred on East London and Durban in recent years (see McCarthy and Swilling 1985, 243–7, on East London). Problems include cost, physical condition of buses and overcrowding, remoteness of termini leaving commuters open to muggings and theft, and lack of coordination with other transport modes. Increasing numbers of commuters will place heavy demands on expanded and better co-ordinated transport systems, whilst far greater volumes of cars are likely to demand much improved road links as black incomes increase.

To the inconvenience of commuting is added the need to travel to 'white' towns for most goods and services. The displacement of the labour force beyond homeland borders creates a highly artificial situation, in that what is essentially a single functional unit becomes divided into two centres competing to meet the same demand. The black townships currently have very low levels of functional complexity: thus Mdantsane and Zwelitsha, the second and third largest places in the eastern Cape, are classed by Cook (1980b, 80) only as a minor town (6th order) and local service centre (7th order), respectively. Although the population of the black towns may be sufficient to support a greater range of enterprises, the fact that adjacent centres of higher hierarchical order are already established means that local entrepreneurs cannot compete. The entry of South African national chains or retail groups might improve shopping opportunities, but provides limited benefit to the homeland concerned as money flows out to 'white' areas instead of circulating within the homeland. The lack of functional links within homelands further discourages internal flows and reinforces satellite relationships with adjacent 'white' towns.

As citizens of 'independent' or self-governing states, frontier commuters could find themselves behind blacks with 'section 10' rights to permanent residence in 'white' areas (Chapter 10). At present, however, such discrimination does not normally occur, and authority to be employed in South Africa is easily granted and renewed (Mastoroudes 1983, 402). There is also no discrimination against frontier commuters in terms of wages, union affiliation, access to health facilities in 'white' areas, and occupational mobility. Such provisions partially alleviate the fundamental inequity of locating labour supplies in distinct geographical areas, at great cost and inconvenience to those concerned, and then shedding responsibility for those areas by decreeing them to be parts of independent states. This inequity is further reduced by the channelling back of taxes collected in the Republic from frontier commuters to the 'independent' and self-governing states. Application of apartheid principles has hitherto resulted in these taxes being paid to homeland governments according to the ethnic origin of the commuter rather than his domicile, to the clear disadvantage of Bophuthatswana and KwaNdebele in particular (see above), but this is no longer the case. What remains true is that all the social costs of labour – the education of workers' children, social services, welfare benefits for the old, widowed and unemployed, housing of squatters – have effectively become the responsibility of homeland governments, whilst the benefits of the labour supply accrue to the 'white' economy.

Forced removals

Nothing has symbolised the oppressive nature of apartheid and aroused international condemnation more than the forced removals of population which have occurred since the early 1960s. Earlier works by Desmond (1971), Baldwin (1974) and Maré (1980) have all drawn attention to the massive scale of population relocation which has occurred. Removals in all parts of South Africa have now received remarkably full documentation with the publication in 1983 of the five-volume report of the Surplus People Project (SPP). This brief summary draws mainly from the general overview in volume 1 of the report and more recent data in a SPP book by Platzky and Walker (1985).

The SPP claims that over 3.5 million people have been forcibly moved between 1960 and 1983 (Table 9.6), a figure disputed by the government which regards the true figure as just under 2 million, and officially admits

205

Table 9.6: Population removals: Estimated numbers by category and region, 1960–83

	E. Cape	W. Cape	N. Cape	O.F.S.	Natal	Transvaal	Total
Farms	139,000		40,000	250,000	300,000	400,000	1,129,000
Black spots	10,000?		40,000	40,000	105,000	280,000	475,000
Consolidation	9,000				10,000	120,000	139,000
Urban	151,000?	32,000	20,000	160,000	17,000	350,000	730,000
Informal settlements	12,000	a	50,000	50,000?	b		112,000
Group Areas	—	409,000c	—	14,000	295,000	142,400	860,400
Infrastructural	30,000				18,500	5,000	53,000
Strategic	50,000	d	e	f			103,500
Total	401,000 + GA	32,000 + GA	150,000 + GA	514,000	745,500	1,297,400	3,548,900

Notes:
a. Major category of relocation affecting many thousands but difficult to quantify.
b. Some informal relocation included in above categories.
c. Cape figures to end of 1982.
d. People moving from Glen Grey/Herschel to Ciskei.
e. Already included under black spots.
f. Movement of Kromdraai people to Botshabelo included in previous figures.

Source: Platzky and Walker 1985, 10–11.

to 'encouraging', 'persuading' and 'convincing' people to move rather than forcing them to do so. The numerical discrepancy arises from the government's exclusion of removals under the Group Areas Act (Chapter 10) which account for nearly a quarter of the SPP total, and its minimisation of farm removals, claiming most of these to be voluntary. The SPP figure of 1.1 million includes all blacks who have moved from white farms, whether as a result of the abolition of labour tenancy (Chapter 6), the determination of the maximum number of black people farmers could accommodate on their land, the pursuit of policies of mechanisation and increased farm size, or simply decisions by individual workers to leave farms because they were dissatisfied with conditions, on the grounds that in all cases government policies attempt to direct dispossessed blacks to the homelands. This is, however, an attempt which frequently fails, as many of these blacks find their way to 'white' cities.

Nearly 80 per cent of the SPP totals are blacks, the remainder being mainly Indians and coloureds moved in terms of the Group Areas Act. The major categories of relocation are as follows:

(i) Relocation of black labour from white farms (see above).

(ii) Clearing of 'black spots', i.e. rural freehold land owned by blacks or missions in areas declared for white ownership and occupation only.

(iii) Removal of 'badly situated' reserves in terms of the policy developed in the 1970s of consolidating the homelands into geographically more cohesive, ethnically-based political entities.

(iv) Urban relocation involving deproclamation of and removal from black townships in 'white' areas into the homelands.

(v) Removal of informal settlements in urban and peri-urban areas.

(vi) Group Area removals.

(vii) Removals as a result of infrastructural projects (e.g. roads, dams) and conservation or agricultural projects (e.g. game reserves, forestry plantations).

(viii) Removals for strategic or military purposes including the clearing of strategically sensitive border areas in the Transvaal, northern Cape and Natal.

(ix) Avoidance of political repression: the major movements here are by people finding themselves in the 'wrong' homeland, notably the flight of people from the Herschel and Glen Grey areas to Ciskei in 1976/77, when these were ceded to Transkei, and from Thaba 'Nchu into Botshabelo.

The SPP figures exclude two important categories of movement. Removals arising from betterment planning within the homelands are usually small in terms of distance but often remove access to land (Chapter 6); in Natal alone over 1 million people may have been moved in this way since the 1950s (SPP 1, p. 5). Removals arising from the operation of influx control legislation, including Coloured Labour Preference policy in the western Cape, are also excluded, because they are difficult to quantify: of the many people arrested, only a small proportion are actually 'endorsed out' of the urban area concerned.

If 'black spot' and consolidation removals are added to the category of urban relocation as three aspects of removals which related directly to the homelands policy, these removals constitute over 40 per cent of the total relocated so far and nearly 55 per cent of those still threatened with removal in 1983 (Table 9.7). Natal, where little of the proposed consolidation planning has yet been implemented, faces the most threatened removals. All figures in Tables 9.6 and 9.7 are informed estimates rather than precise computations, and the future of those threatened depends very much on government policy, which in 1985 showed signs of responding to the particularly unfavourable international image presented by forced removals. Thus in February 1985 Pretoria decided to halt removals of blacks in 'white' areas pending an extensive review of the resettlement programme. In May 1985 the government announced a decision not to resettle some 700,000 urban blacks but to develop instead the 52 townships in which they live, of which the largest are Mamelodi (112,000) and Atteridgeville (87,000) in Pretoria, Chesterville and Lamontville (58,000)[7] in Durban, Tantyi and Fingo Village (49,000) in Grahamstown, Duncan Village (about 40,000) in East London, and the black areas of Queenstown (35,000) in the eastern Cape and Bethlehem (38,000) in the Orange Free State. Consolidation plans for Lebowa, Gazankulu and KwaNdebele announced in September 1985 will lift the threat of removal from a further 125,000 blacks. Although no assurance has been given at the time of writing that there will be no further removals, the threat does seem to be receding from most of those likely to be affected by compulsory relocation to the homelands, although

Table 9.7: Estimated number of people under threat of removal, 1983

	E. Cape	W. Cape	N. Cape	O.F.S.	Natal	Transvaal	Total
Farms	150,000	?	?	?	?	?	1,000,000
Black spots					245,000	60,000	
Consolidation	38,000						1,093,000
					300,000	450,000	
Urban	84,000+	250,000	25,000		61,000	12,000	432,000+
Informal	170,000+						170,000+
Group Areas	—	23,500a	—	150	13,000	17,500	54,150
Infrastructural and strategic	33,000					2,500	35,500
Total	475,000 + GA	250,000 + GA	25,000 + GA	150	619,000	542,000	2,784,650

Note: a. Cape figures to end of 1982.
Source: Platzky and Walker 1985, 11.

consolidation plans announced for KwaZulu in September 1985 would involve the removal of at least 42,000 people. Reduction of the black labour force on white farms is likely to continue, but relaxation of influx controls will probably make it easier for these people to go to the cities.

Whether or not removals have now ended, the scars of two decades of resettlement will long endure. Those resettled in the homelands have suffered varying degrees of material loss in terms of facilities and living conditions, especially in the early months 'when people are struggling to cope with trauma of removal, the unfamiliarity of their surroundings, the makeshift quality of everything around them and, in most cases, the demanding task of rebuilding their new houses with limited cash resources' (SPP 1, p. 20). This is particularly true of the most marginalised groups of relocated people — ex-farmworkers, former tenants on black- and white-owned land and squatters — who are most likely to end up in euphemistically described 'closer settlements' such as Glenmore (Ciskei) and Kwaggafontein (KwaNdebele). These are effectively settlements with urban densities (and therefore little land for cultivation) but no urban functions (and therefore negligible employment). The greatest material loss is perhaps suffered by those who had land before in 'black spots' but now have none (compensation is paid, though usually claimed to be inadequate) or find their new land much inferior to the old.

Physical conditions in relocation areas vary greatly, with location in relation to 'white' urban areas a crucial factor: generally, the further away from a metropolitan area a relocation site is, the poorer and more desperate facilities are likely to be. They range from formal rented housing, some of it with electricity and running water in each house, to crude, temporary shelters, pit latrines and sparse water points. Owing largely to the resilience of people accustomed to hardship, conditions do improve and relocation areas begin to resemble other homeland communities, but this very similarity reflects the widespread landlessness, poverty and unemployment which exists in almost all rural areas of the homelands. There is minimal employment within most relocation areas, and heavy dependence on migrant labour. In closer settlements surveyed by the SPP, an average of 70 per cent dependence on migrant labour was recorded amongst those employed (SPP 1, p. 27). Many people in such settlements, especially women, have abandoned hope of ever finding work and dropped out of the ranks of the 'economically active', thus concealing true levels of unemployment. Despite the strains on family and community life the SPP (1, p. 28) concluded that 'having migrant labourers in the household in most cases makes the difference between mere poverty and destitution'.

Perhaps even worse than material deprivation are the social and psychological effects of removal, which emphasise people's lack of control over their lives (especially for those moved more than once) and often induce passivity and helplessness. Anger and frustration when they do surface are often turned inwards on neighbours and other newcomers with whom there is competition for scarce resources. Only rarely does community organisation in such circumstances allow people to fight effectively for improved resources, as at Ezakheni (KwaZulu) where it took a major bus boycott to get the access road tarred (SPP 4, 334). In other areas help has come from adverse publicity which has induced government action, as at Dimbaza which is now a relatively successful industrial growth point. For every such case, however, many others such as Bothashoek (Lebowa) remain unnoticed and unaided (Rogerson and Letsoalo 1981).

Resettlement in the homelands, migrant labour and frontier commuting all contribute to the apartheid aim of minimising black population in 'white' areas, albeit at great cost to those involved. The industrial decentralisation strategy examined in Chapter 8 is similarly motivated. The demographic reality, however, is one of increasing black urbanisation in 'white' areas despite all attempts to control it. It is to these urban areas that we now turn.

10
The towns: segregation and black urbanisation

Origins and development of urban segregation and influx control
During the early years of town growth in South Africa, African settlement was not controlled. Thus in Durban the mayoral minutes of 1887 report a public meeting which discussed assaults and other crimes by Africans and asked that locations should be established at a convenient distance from the town (Kuper *et al.* 1958, 30). Most Africans at that time lived in shacks and hovels and were not residentially segregated; the only planned accommodation consisted of barracks erected for male labourers by the city council and private enterprise. The general policy in Durban, as in most towns, was initially to achieve segregation without compulsion by attracting people to segregated facilities. The Orange Free State was the most deliberately segregationalist polity: by a law of 1893, only whites could own or lease fixed property in Free State towns.

Regulations for the control of urban blacks, coloureds and Indians were gradually introduced for a number of reasons; because of the obvious social, cultural and economic differences between whites and other races in the early twentieth century; to cushion the unfamiliarity of other races with white urban culture; to control and channel labour; to deal with misfits and contain crime; and to prevent the spread of contagious diseases – the establishment of locations in Cape Town, Port Elizabeth and Johannesburg was precipitated by a frantic effort to limit bubonic plague (Davenport 1971, 6). Following the Native Beer Act of 1908, enabling towns to establish a municipal beer monopoly, Durban led the way in making beer revenues the key financial support of a more intensive programme of administration than hitherto, tending with relative efficiency to restrain Africans to barracks and locations (Swanson 1976, 174). By the time of Union most blacks, coloureds and Indians lived in special areas allocated to them, but the locations themselves quickly became a problem. Thus the Tuberculosis Commission reported in 1914 that the conditions in which tuberculosis flourished were the rule rather than the exception in locations throughout South Africa. A bad influenza epidemic in 1918 revealed the distressing conditions in which blacks lived and the health threat which they posed. In Johannesburg this aroused the civic conscience and led to the first black housing schemes, but it is indicative of contemporary attitudes that 'native locations' were the responsibility of the city's Parks Department in the 1920s (Lewis 1966, 46).

As the need for a long-term black presence both on the mines and in the towns became clear, white demands for segregation and control became stronger. Official attitudes to urban blacks were expressed in the oft-quoted dictum of the Stallard (Transvaal Local Government) Commission of 1922 that

> the native should only be allowed to enter urban areas, which are essentially the White man's creation, when he is willing to enter and minister to the needs of the White man, and should depart therefrom when he ceases so to minister. (Transvaal 1922, para. 42)

Traditionally represented by liberals as an irrational ideology resting on white radical prejudice (Welsh 1971, 242; Davenport 1971, 14), 'Stallardism' is seen by Rich (1978, 190-1) as a 'rational ideological response by certain groups within the White polity, namely White labour and urban commercial capital, to what was perceived as an economic threat to their livelihood'. Whatever its roots, the doctrine strongly influenced legislation from 1923 onwards, and provided 'a ready-made basis for the development in the 1940s of the apartheid ideology' in urban policies (Rich 1978, 190). The principle of impermanence is by no means wholly absent from official attitudes to urban blacks even today, although government views appear to be changing significantly in the mid-1980s The doctrine has had far-reaching implications for the provision of services, property ownership, participation in administration, and the morphology of black townships (Smit and Booysen 1977, 5).

The 1923 Natives (Urban Areas) Act embodied Stallardist principles Africans were denied freehold rights in the face of widespread fears especially amongst Orange Free State parliamentarians, that this might ultimately undermine white security. The Act empowered urban authorities to set aside land for black occupation in locations, and to house blacks living in the town or require their employers to do so. I stopped whites from owning or occupying premises in locations, and prevented unexempted blacks from living outside them, though their right to buy property outside locations remained until 1937. Restrictions were imposed on African residence in peri-urban areas, but these were difficult to implement. Municipalities were required to keep separate native revenue accounts, and the revenue accruing from rents, fines and beer hall profits had to be spent on the welfare of the location. The Act also provided for an embryonic form of consultation through advisory boards, and sought to control location brewing and trading.

Adoption of the Act was optional. Some municipalities, especially the larger ones such as Bloemfontein and Johannesburg, adopted it without delay. Many smaller towns feared that adoption might involve them in excessive financial responsibilities, but by 1937 most urban locations had been registered. Few local authorities however, were prepared to subsidise black housing from general revenue in the inter-war years; by 1942, only 41 out of 472 urban councils had secured loans for housing (Meer 1976, 20).

Machinery providing for systematic control over the black urban influx was introduced only in the Native Laws Amendment Act of 1937. The urban black population had risen from 587,000 in 1921 to 1,150,000 in 1936, and was increasing steadily in response to the demands of expanding industry. Under the new Act, the implementation of which was at the discretion of local authorities, Africans coming to the towns were allowed 14 days to find work (reduced to 3 days in 1945), and individual Africans might be 'rusticated' if municipal returns showed a labour surplus. Influx controls were also applied to black women from 1930, but the pace of industrial development attracted increasing numbers to the towns. Controls were reinforced in 1937, but the government shrank from making women carry passes, without which the legislation was probably unenforceable, on account of the unrest which had developed in the Free State over this issue in 1913 (Davenport 1969, 102). When passes for black women were introduced in the late 1950s serious unrest broke out again. Between 1923 and 1937 housing was provided exclusively for migrant labourers, but thereafter attempts were made to provide for black families legally in urban areas.

Whilst segregation was accepted by both main parliamentary parties, the Nationalist Opposition continually criticised the United Party government after 1933 for failing to implement the policy with sufficient rigour. Between 1942 and 1948, when industrialists began to stress the value of semi-skilled blacks in manufacturing employment, the government appeared slowly to be recognising the need for reform. Wartime industrial expansion increased labour demands, whilst several official voices urged reform. The Van Eck Commission considered further black urbanisation essential if rural black incomes were to rise to a level comparable with urban ones (South Africa 1941, 248). Both the Smit Committee (South Africa 1942, para. 8) and the Social and Economic Planning Committee (South Africa 1946, para. 11) condemned the migrant labour system. The latter emphasised the need for the development of a permanent urban labour force, and would have rejected the continuation of migrant labour on the gold mines 'were it not convinced that the mines are a disappearing asset'. Smuts himself viewed black urbanisation realistically, observing that 'You might as well try to sweep the ocean back with a broom' (1942, 10). His government was none the less responsible for the Natives (Urban Areas) Consolidation Act 1945, which further restricted African rights in urban areas. Under section 10, which remains in force (as amended) in 1985, an African may claim permanent residence in an urban area only if he has resided there continuously since birth, has lawfully resided there continuously for 15 years, or has worked there for the same employer for ten years. Section 10 was, however, only applicable in areas specifically proclaimed at the request of a local authority until 1952 when it became automatically applicable in all urban areas unless specifically excluded. Dependants of those qualifying under section 10 were originally entitled to permanent residence in the same area, but since 1964 women have been refused entry unless they qualify independently of their husbands.

During the Second World War, manpower and materials were concentrated on wartime needs and housing lagged badly behind. The situation worsened in the early post-war years of further rapid industrial growth as squatter settlements mushroomed around South African cities. Most cities made some attempt to catch up on the housing backlog, but several factors combined to prevent major efforts in this direction, including the sheer immensity of the task, reluctance to increase the rates unduly, and doubts about the permanency of the urban black population. Meanwhile growth of squatter settlements produced fresh outbursts of bitterness and a more radical cadre of black, coloured and Indian leaders. Under such conditions, further strong criticism of the migrant labour system and the inhumanity of the pass laws by the Fagan Commission (South Africa 1948) went unheeded, whereas the usual *swart gevaar* (black danger) element was strengthened and contributed to the Nationalist victory in 1948.

214

The new government soon tightened up the 1945 legislation, partly in response to the increasing concern voiced by white farmers about the loss of black labour to the mines in the 1930s and early 1940s, and increasingly to the towns later in the 1940s (Morris 1977, 5). Brief reference was made in Chapter 3 to the battery of urban legislation in the 1950s, and only two Acts will be mentioned here. The Illegal Squatting Act 1951 was aimed at peri-urban squatting by Africans seeking or already in employment in adjacent towns. Previously, if a black farmworker squatted immediately outside urban limits he was legally outside the jurisdiction of the local authority and not subject to influx control. The Native Laws Amendment Act 1952 is described by Morris (1977, 36) as 'the most important piece of legislation in the postwar era'. It laid the basis for all state intervention to control the distribution of labour between town and country, and between towns, from 1952 onwards. Section 10 became mandatory and was extended to cover mineworkers who had been exempted in 1945. The Act also introduced the principle of efflux control and the practice of canalising labour through labour bureaux in rural areas, from which permission to go to 'prescribed' (mainly urban) areas had to be obtained. Similar controls were also applied to movement between prescribed areas in relation to labour demand.

Race zoning in urban areas

The Group Areas Act 1950, as amended and consolidated in 1957 and 1966, has had more far-reaching effects than any previous legislation on racial segregation. It has produced distinctive 'apartheid cities' which are systematically planned and recognisably different from the 'segregation cities' which preceded them (R.J. Davies 1981), despite clear elements of continuity which may be traced back to the origins of British colonial policy (Christopher 1983b). The Group Areas Act remains a cornerstone of apartheid, exemplifying the fundamental tenet of apartheid ideology that incompatibility between ethnic groups is such that contact between them leads to friction, and harmonious relations can be secured only by minimising points of contact. Not only does race zoning inhibit even the limited inter-group social contact which might naturally occur (within churches and sports clubs, for example, and aided by the occupational mobility of significant numbers of coloureds, Indians and blacks), but it is the basis of segregated education and health facilities and social services, and as such a highly sensitive issue in white politics (Chapter 5). Group areas have, moreover, assumed a new importance with the introduction of the 1983 constitution (Chapter 13): the coloured and Indian Chambers of Parliament cannot operate without a territorial base, and that base is effectively their respective Group Areas.

The legislation provides for the extension throughout South Africa, and to all races, of the land apportionment principle long existing in the reserves, and since 1923 for urban blacks. The operation of Group Areas legislation is essentially urban, as many of its provisions applied elsewhere already. The 1950 Act imposes control of inter-racial property transactions and inter-racial changes in occupation of property, which are subject to permit. No less than ten kinds of area are defined, but the ultimate goal – now largely achieved – is the establishment of areas for the exclusive occupation of each racial group. Group Areas may be proclaimed in respect of either ownership (with controlled occupation) or occupation (with controlled ownership), but the proclamation applies to both ownership and occupation in the final form, the full Group Area. 'Border strips' may be designated to act as barriers between different Group Areas to ensure that no 'undesirable contiguity' occurs. 'Future Group Areas' may be proclaimed if an area is considered suitable for proclamation but not immediately required: a certain amount of control is then exercised over the use and development of the area, which is intended to facilitate its eventual proclamation as a Group Area. 'Future border strips' may likewise be set aside with future needs in mind. Control over occupation may be temporarily withdrawn at any time by special proclamation; the possibility of establishing such 'open' areas, as they have come to be known, caused much controversy between several local authorities and the Group Areas Board, especially where it was decided to retain a non-white (usually Indian) commercial district in what had been proclaimed a white Group Area (Chapter 11).

Implementation is the responsibility of the Group Areas Board and, subsequently, the Community Development Board. The former, in order to provide effective recommendations, needs the assistance of experienced surveyors, engineers and planners. Such assistance can only be provided by the local authorities, whose cooperation is therefore necessary. Should a local authority refuse to cooperate, however, it risks the imposition of a completely arbitrary and probably unsuitable zoning plan. When, after opportunity for objection and inquiry, the government finally approves any recommendations, their implementation is a matter for the Community Development Board, which has to deal with housing, the development of group areas, the resettlement of dislocated persons, slum clearance and urban renewal.

The 1950 Act radically extends control over private property. The Group Areas Development Act 1955 provides machinery for compensation, but makes further inroads into ownership rights by procedures for regulating the sale price of property in the open market, and by expropriation of properties under a system of public acquisition for Group Area development. White acceptance of such revolutionary changes in traditionally sacred rights would have been most unlikely, had whites themselves not been convinced that they would benefit at the expense of other groups (Kuper *et al.* 1958, 160). That they have indeed done so is hardly surprising given that whites alone were represented on local councils and were in other ways far better able to defend their interests than other groups. Thus the vast majority of those moved have been coloureds and Indians (Table 10.1; Chapters 11 and 12). An unknown number of blacks, possibly a million or more, have also been victims of Group Areas planning; they are excluded from official statistics of Group Areas removals, because they are moved in terms of earlier legislation (without even the semblance of consultation embodied in the Group Areas Act).

Table 10.1 Removals under Group Areas legislation

(a) *Families moved, 1950–31 December 1983*

	Coloured	Indian	White
Cape	65,169	3,004	826
Natal	3,743	25,160	817
O.F.S.	2,300	–	–
Transvaal	11,647	11,728	688
Total	82,859	39,892	2,331

(b) *Families still to be moved as of 31 December 1983* (revised statement in the House of Assembly by the Minister of Community Development)

	Coloured	Indian
Cape Town	186	27
Port Elizabeth		63
Durban	67	89
Others	1,219	505
Total	1,372	684

Source: SAIRR, 1984 *Survey*, pp. 468–9.

The availability of other accommodation must be taken into consideration when Group Areas are proclaimed, and W.J. Davies (1971, 27) notes that the shortage of funds from the National Housing Commission had seriously retarded the progress of the Community Development Board's activities. Undeniably, however, far greater financial resources have been allocated to non-white housing since the implementation of the Group Areas Act than hitherto. What is so tragic is that they have been primarily directed to the fulfilment of an ideological commitment, at no small cost to what might have been achieved by devoting the same resources to the solving of housing problems *per se*, and at immeasurable cost in terms of social deprivation for individuals and communities. In many cases people may be physically better housed, but emotionally impoverished by destruction of their community and remoteness from the environment in which they have grown up: thus Hart and Pirie (1984) describe the paradox of 'emotional plenty among the material shortage' of Sophiatown, Johannesburg, before its black residents were removed. In some cases, moreover, race zoning has actually exacerbated overcrowding and squalor; it has also cultivated and even initiated the racial antipathy it was intended to circumvent (Pirie 1984).

Implementation of the Act has achieved indices of segregation approaching 100 per cent; domestic servants living with their employers are the major exception. This must be viewed in relation to the substantial degree of segregation which existed prior to implementation. In Durban, indices of segregation for 1951 include the following: Indian/white 0.91, Indian/black 0.81, coloured/white 0.84, black/white 0.81 (Kuper *et al.* 1958, 154, 156-7). In Port Elizabeth, also in 1951, the segregation index was 0.89 between whites and others, and 0.80 between coloureds and blacks (W.J. Davies 1971, 148). In both cities black/white segregation would have been almost total if domestic servants had been excluded, whilst the Group Areas Act could increase segregation substantially only in the case of Indians and coloureds, yet it has entailed extensive rezoning and wholesale movement. This implies that something more than mere segregation was intended.

This is indeed the case. Residential segregation is intended to be sufficiently effective not only to avoid contact between races within each zone, but also to discourage movement of people of one group into the zone of another, which implies a far larger scale of segregation than hitherto. Thus the Group Areas Board rejected coloured 'islands' at Fairview and South End in Port Elizabeth (W.J. Davies 1971, 233).

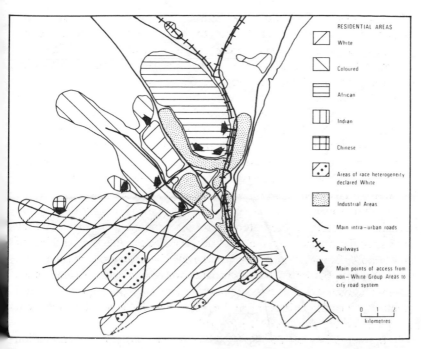

Fig. 10.1 Residential and industrial areas in Port Elizabeth, 1970

Source: W.J. Davies (1971), *Patterns of Non-White Population Distribution in Port Elizabeth with special reference to the application of the Group Areas Act.*

'Natural' borders such as rivers, steep valleys and escarpments are preferred; as these are not common in urban areas, industrial or commercial belts may be used instead, but vacant land is avoided where possible for fear of its being used by both groups for recreation. The requirement that one group should not be routed through the zone of another to reach its workplace also profoundly affects the town plan. In Durban, for instance, this is achieved by means of a long north-south industrial and commercial area from which racial zones radiate, whilst in Port Elizabeth (Figure 10.1) the industrial areas are centrally placed in relation to all Group Areas.

The implicit intention to provide for further expansion of Group Areas while preserving the above conditions has further contributed to the need for fundamental re-arrangement of pre-existing urban patterns. Security considerations have also played a part in urban planning

219

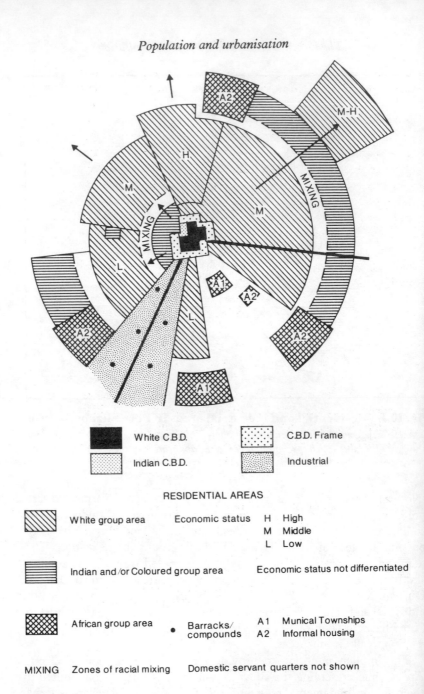

Fig. 10.2 The 'segregation city' (after R.J. Davies 1981)

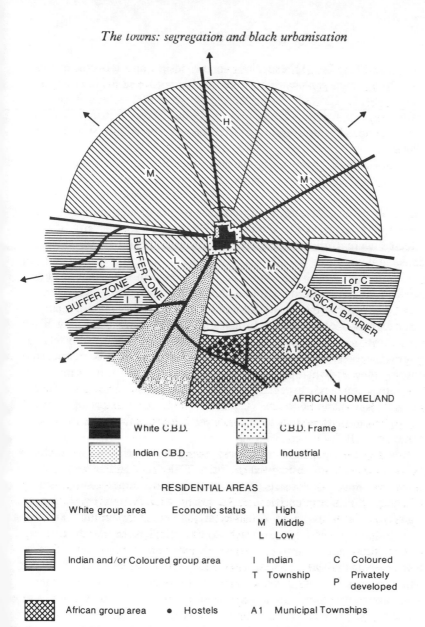

Fig. 10.3   The 'apartheid city' (after R.J. Davies 1981)

(Western 1981, 74–81), especially in the design and location of black townships which permits them to be quickly cordoned off in emergency (Adam 1971, 123). It is unlikely however, that strategic motives influenced the framing of the original Group Areas Act in 1950; such considerations became important after the widespread unrest of the early 1960s.

The effects of group areas legislation are illustrated in the contrast between 'segregation' and 'apartheid' cities as modelled by R.J. Davies (1981; Figures 10.2, 10.3). The latter characteristically focus on an originally white CBD, from which traders of other race groups have been removed in terms of the Group Areas Act; the vast majority of those affected were Indians (Chapter 11). Around the CBD, an extensive consolidated white residential core has freedom to expand in environmentally desirable and accessible sectors in suburban localities. Socio-economic patterns within white residential areas, which resemble those of American cities (R.J. Davies 1964; Hart 1975), remain relatively undisturbed. Coloured and Indian group areas, and especially black townships, are located peripherally within given sectors; hostels for migrant workers no longer adjoin the workplace but have been relocated within these townships. In some cases this has much increased commuter journeys, especially where black townships are constructed beyond homeland borders (Chapter 9), but the development of peripheral industrial areas have ameliorated journey to work problems in some cities (R.J. Davies 1981, 70).

Space in the apartheid city is very unequally distributed with whites enjoying the lowest residential densities. Coloured, Indian and African township housing consists of mass low-cost, largely single-storey housing. Building densities are not necessarily high by European standards but population densities are, given large families and the extent of illegal lodging in black homes which together produce an average occupancy of ten or more people per four-roomed house in some townships. Small areas within black townships are reserved for those who can afford to build their own homes. Areas available for coloured and Indian owner-occupation are small relative to demand, which results in high land prices and a distinctive high-density development of large, individually designed houses as in the Indian suburbs of Mountain Rise (Pietermaritzburg) and Malabar (Port Elizabeth) and parts of the coloured suburb of Eldorado Park (Johannesburg).

Despite the transparent inequity of race zoning in South African towns and cities, the government has so far given little indication of contemplating fundamental changes in group areas legislation, at least as it affects residential areas. The proposed opening of CBDs to traders of all races is potentially of most significance for Indians, at least in the short term (Chapter 11). In 1985 Mr Botha asked the President's Council (Chapter 13) to investigate ways of making the Group Areas Act more acceptable and easier to apply, but shortly afterwards he insised that the principle of separate residential areas would remain. More fundamental reform would imply a wider dismantling of the apartheid edifice, including reforms of the tricameral parliament. Meanwhile, the *de facto* relaxation of race zoning which has already occurred in some areas (for example in high-rise flats in central Johannesburg) may become more widespread in areas where it will do least political damage to the government amongst its own supporters. The President's Council may recommend that municipalities be allowed to decide which suburbs should be open to all races; its report is expected in mid-1986.

Urban blacks
Black urbanisation has for some time occupied centre stage in white political debate. The government views urban blacks in 'white' areas as a 'problem' to be 'accommodated' in terms of as yet unspecified legal and constitutional changes. The widespread unrest of 1985 indicates that they are much more than this, and that 'accommodation' will not satisfy African aspirations (Chapter 17). The numerical dimensions of black urbanisation are remarkably difficult to measure, both overall and in terms of the major categories into which apartheid policies classify urban blacks. This relates partly to the exclusion of 'independent' homelands from recent censuses (although Transkei, Bophuthatswana and Venda had separate censuses in 1980), partly to the absence of data on the proportion of migrant workers which is urban, and partly to the growing but unrecorded number of 'illegal' blacks who defy the pass laws. Official figures underestimate the urban black population, often substantially, and the acknowledged deficiencies of the 1980 census were partly responsible for the decision to undertake a further census in 1985; only preliminary results of the latter are available at the time of writing, but these appear no more convincing than those of 1980.

Official figures suggest that 38 per cent (6.5 million) of blacks lived in urban areas in 1980, and if Transkei, Bophuthatswana and Venda are included this percentage is reduced to 33. However, this not only underestimates the number of blacks in urban areas, but also excludes those living in informal settlements around Durban, East London, Port

Elizabeth, Newcastle, Pretoria and elsewhere, who are urban-oriented and earn their living in urban areas. Simkins (1983) estimates that homeland fringe urban areas such as the Winterveld north of Pretoria housed 1.45 million people in 1980, with a further 1.49 million living in 'interior urban areas' of the homelands. Together with 3.96 million blacks in metropolitan areas and 1.71 million in other 'white' urban areas, this suggests a total of 8.61 million urban blacks, or 41.5 per cent of South Africa's black population. Even this figure fails to allow for the substantial number, probably well over a million, living in metropolitan areas in defiance of the pass laws (Kane-Berman 1984, 80). Overall black urbanisation was therefore probably not far short of 50 per cent in 1980, with nearly 7 million non-homeland urban blacks compared with 4 million urban whites.

Preliminary 1985 census figures indicate a total of 8.34 million non-homeland blacks, compared with 9.47 million in 1980. Whilst this no doubt reflects continuing reductions of black farm labour and rehousing of blacks across homeland borders, it probably underestimates the number of urban blacks in 'white' areas to a greater extent than the 1980 census. At the beginning of 1985 some 3.9 million blacks qualified as permanent residents of 'white' urban areas with 'section 10' rights, whilst a further 1.7 million qualified as dependants of those who qualified in their own right. To these must be added those defying the pass laws and several hundred thousand migrant workers. In total, therefore, the urban black population of 'white' South Africa was probably not far short of 8 million in 1985.

The effect of the migrant labour system is reflected in high masculinity ratios: 1.28:1 in metropolitan areas and 1.39:1 in other non-homeland towns in 1980 according to Simkins (1984, 8). The metropolitan ratio has, however, declined from 1.66:1 in 1950 and 1.39:1 in 1960, which underlines the inability of controls to stem black urbanisation. In smaller towns, however, influx controls have resulted in an increasing masculinity ratio since 1960, when it was only 1.04:1.

With the exception of the PWV area, the urban black population has settled mainly on an ethnic basis (Smit and Booysen 1977, 1981). Thus 95 per cent of urban blacks in the south-west Cape and 98 per cent of those in Port Elizabeth/Uitenhage were Xhosa, whilst 96 per cent of blacks in Durban-Pinetown were Zulu (Smit *et al.* 1983a and b). In PWV the largest single group, Zulus, account for only 20 per cent of the total, and all major black South African linguistic groups are well represented. In such situations official policy has sought to segregate blacks in terms of language groups, but this has been largely frustrated by inadequate control over lodging, allocation of houses to linguistically mixed households, informal and irregular arrangements in acquiring housing, and new and vacated housing allocations in 'rightful' language reserves within townships (Mashile and Pirie 1977). Many urban blacks have retained few if any ties with their supposed homelands, and must have adapted themselves to urban environments. Degrees of acculturation vary, and Mayer (1971) shows that attitudes formed in rural areas significantly affect urban behaviour. Tribal tradition, heritage and customs are often retained in modified form. Thus Holzner (1970, 85) notes that of twelve significant customs practised among black tribes of southern Africa, only four seem to disappear completely in urban society: prescribed marriage, polygamy, initiation rites and consulting witch doctors before medical doctors.

Rapid black urbanisation has posed severe problems of *housing and service provision*. The latter are accentuated by the Reservation of Separate Amenities Act 1953 under which facilities may be reserved for other races, whether equal or otherwise. 'Stallardism' has discouraged provision of services for blacks, whilst group area and other removals have meant that service provision must begin anew for those displaced. Given existing residential segregation, even the opening-up of existing facilities to all races would still leave blacks at a severe disadvantage in terms of access to urban facilities. Thus Pirie (1976) found that 64 per cent of all health and social services in Greater Johannesburg were located in white areas, whereas whites constituted only 31 per cent of the area's population in 1980.

Particularly serious problems are suffered by blacks living in white residential areas who 'constitute a largely ignored category of "non-people" whose presence is tolerated because of the services they offer to whites but socially ignored both in planning and the day-to-day community life of "white" areas' (Preston-Whyte 1982, 164). Such blacks numbered 66,577 in Durban in 1980 (ibid.). The black population of Johannesburg–Randburg (which includes the black township of Alexandra but excludes Soweto) reached 1,140,000 in 1983, nearly 60 per cent of the total.[1] Blacks in white areas include those living in hostels and compounds still permitted in white areas, and larger numbers of domestic servants living on their employers' premises, where they cannot legally be joined by other family members unless they share the same employer. Facilities for these people have decreased as most churches, halls and social centres which once existed to serve blacks in such areas have been closed or moved to the townships, where all new recreational facilities are established. Thus blacks in white areas must either travel considerable distances to use these facilities, or be restricted to gathering in the street or in their *khayas* (servants' rooms, usually in the garden or adjoining the garage) when not on duty. Servants living out, on the other hand, face long and difficult journeys from townships to white suburbs, necessitating an extremely early departure in the morning and leaving little leisure time.

The black housing shortage in 'white' South Africa was officially estimated at 168,000 units at the end of 1983, although other sources put it considerably higher.[2] In addition, there was an estimated shortage of 142,000 units in the six self-governing homelands, more than half of which was in KwaZulu. Shortages in 'white' areas have been exacerbated by the virtual halt placed on the building of family housing for blacks after 1968. This policy was partially revised in 1976, but the rate of construction since then has failed significantly to reduce the shortage, let alone to meet the increased need arising from population growth and rural-urban migration. The Viljoen Committee, charged with investigating private sector involvement in the housing backlog, estimated in 1982 that R1.7 billion was needed, whereas only R280 million had been spent in the past seven years on providing 62,000 units in black urban areas (South Africa 1982c, 1–2). Following the Viljoen recommendations on ways of dealing with the shortage the government revised its housing strategy in 1983. Its own role is now limited to providing housing only for lower income groups (those earning below R150 per month), and infrastructure and services for other blacks, who are increasingly expected to pay for the provision of housing both with cash and what Viljoen termed 'sweat equity'. The government has also revised its housing standards, belatedly accepting the principles of core and shell housing and of site-and-service schemes. In 1985 the government planned to spend R225 million on the provision of sites and infrastructure for black housing,[3] but later in the year, in apparent response to widespread unrest, it made a further R100 million available for the development of black townships. These are not inconsiderable sums, especially at a time of economic recession, but the magnitude of the task is emphasised by the Venter Commission of Inquiry into Township Establishment (South Africa 1984a) which estimated that 1,940,000 new houses would be needed for Africans between 1980 and 2000.

Housing policy changes reflect increasing official acceptance of the permanence of at least limited numbers of urban blacks in 'white' areas. The same is true of both the 30-year 'home ownership' leasehold programme begun in 1976 and especially the 99-year leasehold scheme introduced in 1978. The latter has the advantage of providing for registered rights which may be used as collateral for a mortgage, but until recently only a small proportion of township houses were available for purchase under the 99-year scheme, owing partly to delays in surveying properties for sale, and take-up was very slow. By March 1982 only 1727 leases had been registered under the scheme, more than 1400 of them in Soweto and mostly for houses in the R20,000+ range (Wilkinson 1983, 272). One reason for such a limited response is that subsidised rented housing remained appreciably cheaper than the costs incurred under both the 99-year and 30-year schemes. In addition, despite official denials, continuing speculation that black freehold tenure might soon be introduced in 'white' areas probably encouraged many blacks to wait and see rather than commit themselves to the 99-year leasehold scheme. Official policy did indeed change during 1985, and legislation extending freehold rights to urban blacks was due to come before Parliament in 1986; those with 99-year leaseholds will thenceforth be able to switch to a freehold. Meanwhile the 30-year home ownership scheme is to be phased out, and houses registered under this scheme will be converted to the 99-year leasehold scheme; plans to extend the latter to the western Cape were announced in September 1984.

Government responses to the slow take-up of 99-year leaseholds amount to a 'carrot-and-stick' strategy (Wilkinson 1983, 275). The 'stick' appears to be a policy of encouraging rent increases. This has considerable dangers, for if the state overestimates the ability of blacks to pay, they are likely to respond as in the past with rent strikes and organised squatting movements. The major 'carrot' was the launching in 1983, initially for one year but subsequently twice extended and scheduled to end in June 1986, of a 'grand sale' of housing, offering 350,000 units for sale countrywide at discounts of up to 40 per cent. This included 49,000 houses in Soweto alone, most of them selling at around R1300 before discount, although the cost of registering the leasehold added an estimated R245.[4] To facilitate these sales, some building societies lowered the standards of property required for the provision of mortgage loans. By June 1984, 27,510 homes had been sold under the scheme, 18,876 of them to Africans.[5] The building and purchase of new homes by blacks should be encouraged by the less stringent building standards proposed in 1983 by the National Building Research Institute.

There are also indications that adverse conditions in the white housing market have persuaded some building firms to turn their attention to the potential demand in the black townships (Wilkinson 1983, 274).

Whatever the long-term effects of the new housing strategy, the present reality is one of overcrowded township housing and a rapidly growing *squatter population*:[6] 'the formal system of planned residence and controlled movement has been breached for all to see' (Schlemmer 1985, 168). This informally settled population is by no means wholly made up of migrants to the city; much of it reflects the natural increase of urban black population. Such developments are viewed officially as a serious problem for the orderly administration of blacks, and in some areas such as the Western Cape and the Witwatersrand repeated attempts have been made to remove squatter settlements. Squatters are, however, destined to be an enduring feature of the South African urban scene, and they may even become the dominant form of urban black community. This reality has been accorded *de facto* recognition in some areas, where the authorities are merely attempting to impose a degree of formal planning on the settlements, as in those parts of KwaZulu which are adjacent to Durban and other Natal towns. In other areas a strenuous effort to provide alternative housing has begun. But in the meantime no attempt is made to demolish shacks and rudimentary services are provided. In detail the geography of squatting is extremely complex, but brief mention will be made here of the situation in five major squatter areas.

The *Winterveld* is an area of largely freehold land in eastern Bophuthatswana within commuting distance of Pretoria. It has a population of at least 600,000, a large proportion of whom are non-Tswana. The most densely populated part, Stakaneng (shanty town) is the area closest to the official Bophuthatswana town of Mabopane. Within this area landowners, many of whom are themselves non-Tswana, have facilitated spontaneous settlement by renting plots to squatters at considerable profit to themselves (Smith 1982b, 41). People have moved to the area as a result of the rationalisation and mechanisation of white farming (Chapter 6), evictions from group areas and 'black spots' around Pretoria, and as a result of influx control. People from other homelands, finding that the labour bureaux had few jobs to offer, moved to the Winterveld as an area where they could settle within reach of major employment centres. The resultant high proportion of non-Tswana became an embarrassment to the Bophuthatswana government, which has pressured them to move in various ways since the early 1970s. Non-Tswana may obtain citizenship of Bophuthatswana only if they can prove five years of residence, which for some is difficult. Without citizenship, they must return to their ethnic homeland for work permits. A further pressure arises from the refusal of the authorities to provide non-Tswana schools, and the overcrowding of private schools which attempt to fill this need. Private schools and unregistered stores are also harassed by the authorities, as are the squatters themselves on the grounds that the plot-holders' title deeds state that the land is to be used only for agricultural purposes. The Bophuthatswana government also uses its control over pensions, health and unemployment benefits as a means of pressuring non-Tswanas to move. These pressures have largely failed: people return to their homelands long enough to renew work permits, but conditions there are such that most return to the Winterveld, notwithstanding the insecurity they face there.

In 1980 an 'Intergovernmental Management Committee' was formed by South Africa and Bophuthatswana to plan a development strategy and upgrade the Winterveld. It seems clear that Pretoria must either excise the area from Bophuthatswana or force the latter to accept non-Tswanas. The new Rosslyn II industrial site near the Winterveld is a tacit acknowledgement that the people themselves are there to stay (SPP 5, p.321).

The Bophuthatswana government's desire for 'ethnic purity' is one element in the establishment of a second major squatter settlement, Onverwacht or Botshabelo ('place of refuge'). It is administered by the Black Affairs Commissioner, Bloemfontein on behalf of the South African Black Trust (a government body which administers land intended for incorporation in a homeland: in this case QwaQwa, the South Sotho homeland whose existing territory is both distant and inaccessible from Botshabelo). The area has been transformed from barren veld in 1979 to a sprawling slum with over 300,000 people but minimal infrastructure in 1985. Some 64,000 are South Sotho people from the Bophuthatswana district of Thaba 'Nchu, unwanted by President Mangope. Many others represent the overflow from the black townships of Bloemfontein, 50 kilometres away, where no further black housing is being built; to induce these people to move to Botshabelo and face long commuter journeys relatively sound housing with water and electricity has been provided. Much larger numbers of people have come to Botshabelo under their own steam, many of them displaced from white farms. The limited employment available in Bloemfontein forces many of them to migrate in search of work on the mines and elsewhere.

Probably the largest concentrations of squatters in South Africa at present are found in the Durban metropolitan area, the outer areas of which are controlled by the KwaZulu authorities. The number of informal housing units was estimated in mid-1983 at 130,000, with an estimated occupancy ratio of eleven persons per unit giving a squatter population of 1.4 million (Schlemmer 1985, 169). The settlements are densest just beyond the boundaries of formally constituted local authorities, as close as possible to urban infrastructure and transport routes; thus the largest squatter areas, Inanda and Malukazi, are located beyond the formal Durban townships – both themselves now part of KwaZulu – of KwaMashu and Umlazi respectively. Most of the squatter settlements are under the ultimate control of chiefs and headmen whose role is limited largely to allocation of sites and collection of tribal dues. A significant minority of shacks are located on privately-owned land loosely controlled by landlords. In the absence of formal urban administration, infrastructure and services are almost wholly lacking. Schlemmer (1985, 187–8) concludes from field surveys that most people in these settlements are 'urbanised but distinctive' (from township-dwellers); some 65 per cent of the main earners work in industry and commerce in the metropolitan economy, and the main concern of the shack-dwellers is their integration into the urban system. Schlemmer argues for the planning of these settlements as 'a specific type of urban ecology suited to a marginal class with problems of adaptation to the formal system' (p. 189), but official plans to develop Inanda into a satellite city with housing for 450,000 people seemingly reflect a more conventional (and arguably inappropriate) response.

Two other major squatter areas are located in the eastern and western Cape respectively, in 'white' areas too far removed from homeland territory for 'frontier commuting' to be feasible. Port Elizabeth's squatter population was estimated in 1984 at 120,000, more than a quarter of the city's total African population.[7] Most squatters live in what is confusingly known as 'Soweto' or Soweto-on-the-Sea, a township of some 9500 plots with an average occupancy of nine per plot. Its growth reflects both the eviction of labour from white farms and the lack of employment opportunities in Ciskei. Although many squatters are illegally resident in a 'white' area, no attempt has been made to demolish Soweto, which has instead been accorded township status and receives rudimentary services. It is planned to move its residents to a new formal township, Motherwell, which should eventually provide

17,000 homes; construction began in 1984.

Influx control has been particularly harsh in the 'coloured labour preference area' of the western Cape, where the government has, since the late 1950s, used the full range of available control measures: influx control, coloured labour preference in employment, a virtual freeze on new housing for blacks, neglect of school provision and infrastructure, refusal to grant 99-year leases as in other areas, and repeated attempts to move large numbers of 'illegals' to Transkei and Ciskei (Howe 1982; Thomas 1985). These policies have failed to curtail black urbanisation, but in so far as they have limited it they may have dampened the economic development of the region, where the artificial scarcity of unskilled labour is regarded as a major factor causing the shift of labour-intensive industries from Cape Town to other parts of the country (Thomas 1985, 61). Squatting has steadily increased in the past decade, both because of chronic overcrowding in existing black townships and the persistent flow of 'illegal' migrants; the latter increased significantly in the mid-1970s as Transkei prepared for 'independence' and many blacks were uncertain as to their status thereafter. Attempts to 'repatriate' squatters failed, not least due to the resistance of the Ciskei and Transkei governments. Forced evictions of all squatters at Modderdam and Unibell, a few kilometres from Crossroads, led to the concentration of virtually all black squatters within 5 kilometres of Nyanga and Crossroads. By 1985 Cape Town's black population of 250,000 included some 100,000 'illegals'.

In April 1983 plans were announced to establish a new black township, Khayelitsha ('new home'), 35 kilometres from central Cape Town, to which residents of the existing black townships of Langa, Nyanga and Guguletu as well as 'legals' in the Crossroads and KTC squatter camps would be moved; 'illegals' would be allowed to build their own structures at Khayelitsha, but with no guarantee of long-term rights to remain in the area (Ellis 1984, 10). The proposed uprooting of relatively stable black communities caused a storm of protest. This, together with squatter residence and adverse international publicity (especially after the riots at Crossroads early in 1985 which led to 17 deaths), led to a rapid sequence of policy changes which promise to reduce or eliminate differences between Cape Town and other urban areas in terms of black urbanisation. Residents of the older townships are no longer to be resettled and the infrastructure of Langa and Nyanga is to be upgraded, whilst Crossroads itself is to be 'redeveloped' as an upgraded squatter settlement. Khayelitsha is under construction, with

5000 units built in mid-1985 and a site-and-service crash programme initiated as well. Its planned capacity is 250,000 people, which, given the above policy changes, clearly reflects official acceptance of the inevitability of continued black urbanisation in the western Cape. This was confirmed by the phasing-out of coloured labour preference in the region and the introduction of 99-year leasehold in some townships, including Khayelitsha, changes announced at the end of 1984 but slow to take effect on the ground. Forty years after Smuts recognised the futility of influx control the government appears to be reaching the same conclusion and seeking instead to formulate a black urbanisation policy in Cape Town and elsewhere.

Black urbanisation: the search for new policies
In attempting to project the course of black urbanisation, Simkins (1983) distinguishes four categories of urban blacks: those in metropolitan areas, other 'white' urban areas, the 'border' urban fringe within the homelands (including squatter areas), and interior homeland towns including capitals and growth points (Table 10.2). Envisaging scenarios of low, moderate and rapid urbanisation, it is in the 'white' or 'common' areas that black urbanisation would be significantly greater under conditions of rapid urbanisation. Even with relatively stringent influx control policies, however, the metropolitan areas are likely to double the 1980 black population to 8 million in 2000, whereas with rapid urbanisation (i.e. the phasing out of influx control) metropolitan blacks would increase to 9.52 million out of an overall urban black population of 21.3 million, or 61.2 per cent of all blacks. Simkins' low urbanisation scenario envisages a black urbanisation rate of 52.9 per cent by 2000. Such projections suggest that rigorous influx control policies, although socio-economically painful and politically costly, can only marginally change South Africa's urban pattern up to the end of this century.

The economic inevitability of black urbanisation has gradually become apparent to the government, which has begun to think in terms of a policy of 'orderly urbanisation' to replace influx control. It is not yet clear whether this represents fundamental change leading to the dismantling of influx control or merely incremental reform and adaptation of past policies (Chapter 17); there is a wide gap between current administrative practice and the apparent meaning of some proclaimed intentions of reform, which have yet to be translated into legislation. Several attempts to do so have foundered (see below), which in itself reflects the uncertain direction of official policy in reforming so

232

central a pillar of the apartheid edifice.

The report of the Riekert Commission on legislation affecting manpower utilisation (South Africa 1979b) recommended major changes in influx control policies. Its basic strategy was to differentiate between permanent urban and temporary migrant black populations. The position of the former would be improved, with the freedom to change jobs within the Administration Board area in which their rights were granted without recourse to labour bureaux, and the ability to transfer 'section 10' rights to other areas, taking their families with them. Such changes would have been subject to the availability of jobs and housing (as judged by officials), a major proviso given housing shortages, and would not have applied in the western Cape where the coloured labour preference policy still applied. The intention of such proposals was to enable labour demands of the urban industrial economy to be met more efficiently by allowing a free job market for permanent urban residents of all races. In addition rights to trade in urban areas, which for blacks had been severely restricted hitherto by central government, would henceforth be decided by local authorities. Those without permanent residence rights would, however, have been made worse-off by a new condition for migrants seeking to work in 'white' areas: to the offer of employment and the availability of housing was to be added 'the non-availability of local workseekers'. Rural blacks would thus come at the end of the queue for access to jobs (Lemon 1984b, 202). Such a widening of the gap between 'insiders' and 'outsiders' (Wilson 1975, 182–3) would be consistent with the government's proclaimed intention of creating a black middle class, whose members would experience improved opportunities for employment and advancement, better training facilities, and more effective trade union rights. The opportunities open to this class would gradually come to accord more with merit and experience than hitherto. Such benefits would derive at least in part, however, from stricter controls over the in-migration of rural blacks, thus giving insiders a vested interest in the status quo.

Viewed thus, the Riekert proposals amounted to incremental reform designed to optimise labour flows within a modified apartheid framework. As such, many of them were accepted by the government in a White Paper. Forces outside the state apparatus were driving towards changes well beyond the Riekert proposals (Hindson and Lacey 1983, 104), but so large was the gap between black aspirations and bureaucratic conservatism that two attempts to translate the Riekert proposals into legislation failed. Both the Laws on Cooperation and Development Bill

Table 10.2: Alternative projections of black urban/rural population growth, 1980–2000

| | Common area | | | | Homelands | | | | | |
| | 1 | 2 | 3 | 4 | 5 | 6 | 7 | 8 | 9 | 10 |
	Metropolitan areas[a]	Other urban areas	Rural areas	Sub-total	'Border' urban fringe	Interior urban areas	Rural areas	Sub-total	Total	Rural (3 + 7)
1980										
Population (m.)	3.96	1.71	4.35	10.02	1.45	1.49	7.78	10.72	20.74	12.13
Percentage	19.1	8.2	21.0	48.3	7.0	7.2	37.5	51.7	100.0	58.5
2000										
A. Low urbanisation										
Population (m.)	7.76	2.86	5.72	16.34	3.83	3.94	10.66	18.43	34.77	16.38
Percentage	22.3	8.2	16.5	47.0	11.0	11.3	30.7	53.0	100.0	47.1
Growth rate % p.a.	3.4	2.6	1.4	2.5	5.0	5.0	1.6	2.7	2.6	1.5

B. Moderate urbanisation

Population (m.)	8.90	2.86	5.72	17.48	3.92	4.03	9.34	17.29	34.77	15.06
Percentage	25.6	8.2	16.5	50.3	11.3	11.6	26.9	49.7	100.0	43.3
Growth rate % p.a.	4.1	2.6	1.4	2.8	5.1	5.1	0.9	2.4	2.6	1.1

C. Rapid urbanisation

Population (m.)	9.52	3.24	5.72	18.48	4.20	4.31	7.78	16.29	34.77	13.50
Percentage	27.4	9.3	16.5	53.1	12.1	12.4	22.4	46.9	100.0	38.8
Growth rate % p.a.	4.5	3.2	1.4	3.1	5.5	5.5	0.0	2.1	2.6	0.5

Note: a. PWV, Durban-Pinetown, Greater Cape Town, Port Elizabeth-Uitenhage, Pietermaritzburg, East London, Kimberley, Bloemfontein.

Source: Simkins 1983, and update 1984.

1980 and the Orderly Movement and Settlement of Black Persons Bill 1982 amended existing urban legislation in such a way as to give effect to the intensified controls advocated by Riekert, but failed to entrench, let alone extend, urban residence rights in the spirit of Riekert. Both Bills were rejected by Parliament and referred to select committees, the government announcing in 1982 that a revised Bill would be tabled in Parliament during 1984. That this did not take place apparently reflected the fact that official attitudes to black urbanisation were in a state of flux, and gave rise to hopes that when legislative change did come it would be considerably more fundamental than that proposed by the Riekert Commission.

Meanwhile, however, there has been a tightening of controls both legally and at the level of administrative structure and practice. Legally, the base of those who could hope to acquire section 10 rights has been narrowed by the 'independence' of Transkei, Bophuthatswana, Venda and Ciskei; those who had section 10 rights, and were formerly South African citizens, are unaffected, but children born after 'independence' of the homeland to which they are officially assigned can never acquire these rights, regardless of where they were born or have lived; instead they are subject at any time to deportation under the Aliens Act or the Admission of Persons to the Republic Regulation Act (Budlender 1984b, 2). For political and administrative reasons this has not yet been enforced, and in the light of impending changes in citizenship rules and even the possible reincorporation of TVBC into South Africa it seems unlikely that it will be (Chapter 17).

The number of section 10 qualifiers has been further reduced by changes in homeland boundaries, notably in Natal, where after the incorporation of Edendale (Pietermaritzburg) and KwaMashu (Durban) into KwaZulu, few people remained qualified (Bekker and Humphries 1985, 53). Their numbers will be still further reduced with the proposed incorporation of Durban's Lamontville township into KwaZulu, despite the fierce opposition of its inhabitants. Given that the coloured labour preference policy has allowed few Africans to acquire section 10 rights in the western Cape, those who do qualify are found largely in PWV, Port Elizabeth, Bloemfontein and Kimberley (Table 10.3).

In PWV and Bloemfontein their numbers are being steadily reduced by the use of housing as a control. Although the clampdown on the building of family accommodation in prescribed areas was lifted in 1978, what new housing is built tends to be designed for the better-off; available sites are seldom used for self-help housing schemes, and new land

Table 10.3. Distribution of section 10 qualifiers, 1982 (%)

Cape and southern O.F.S.	30
Western Cape	3
Eastern Cape	15
Other	12
Transvaal and northern O.F.S.	68
P.W.V.[a]	57
Other	11

Note: a. PWV is defined to include the areas of jurisdiction of four Administration Boards: Orange-Vaal, West Rand, East Rand and Central Transvaal.

Source: Bekker and Humphries 1985, 53.

to increase the area of existing townships is not being acquired. Thus many section 10 qualifiers in Bloemfontein and Pretoria are forced to accept offers of housing in new townships outside the prescribed urban areas, at Botshabelo and Soshanguve respectively, thus forfeiting their section 10 rights. Those on the East Rand are similarly moving to the new township of Ekangala, much of which is likely to be incorporated into KwaNdebele, despite fierce opposition. It is also rumoured that the population growth of Soweto is to be accommodated at Ekangala, 120 kilometres from Johannesburg (Dungan 1985, 249), which would mean a further substantial reduction in the number of section 10 qualifers.

A widening of the group potentially able to acquire section 10 rights seemed possible after two significant court victories, the Komani and Rikhoto judgements, in 1980 and 1983 respectively. The former established the rights of wives and children of those with section 10(1)(a) and (b) rights to remain with them, whilst the Rikhoto case established the right of migrant workers to qualify in terms of section 10(1)(b) after ten years' continuous employment with one employer. This would have meant a once-for-all increase in the urban African population of some 145,000, and thereafter an annual increase of around 29,000 dependants of breadwinners already in the towns (Kane-Berman 1983, 34). Had the government left the provisions of section 10 alone following these judgements, it would have been an indication of new thinking, however tentative. Instead it amended section 10 with effect from August 1983 such that the family of a secton 10(1)(b) person may join him in town only if he has a house of his own, rented or bought, or married quarters provided by his employers. Given the length of housing waiting lists this effectively means that most women and children who had not joined their section 10(1)(b) husbands and fathers before August 1983 have little chance of establishing a right to remain with them. The Rikhoto judgment stands, although officials on the ground frequently withhold section 10(1)(b) rights from those who are now legally entitled to them (Hindson and Lacey 1983, 110). The judgement anyway means little if families are barred from joining the new section 10(1)(b) qualifiers, who will inevitably return to rural areas when not at work, and retire there with their families, as they have previously. The 1983 amendment has thus effectively closed the door on any continuing legal urbanisation process (Duncan 1985, 248).

The actual machinery of influx control and labour allocation has changed considerably since 1980. The establishment of 'employment and guidance' centres within or near black townships in larger cities is intended to dissociate the economic placement of local workers from influx control. It gives effect to a major Riekert recommendation by increasing the mobility of urban Africans and giving preference to local workseekers. Since the onset of recession early in 1982, stricter controls have been exercised over the entry of workers without section 10 qualifications into prescribed areas, and workers with temporary contracts have found it increasingly difficult to have them renewed (Hindson and Lacey 1983, 109). Pass control has been focused increasingly on the workplace and residential areas rather than on the streets; the threat of large fines has probably induced many employers to fill vacancies with local workseekers where possible and to retrench illegal workers first.

In the homelands, Greenberg and Giliomee (1985) document the breakdown of tribal labour bureaux and the recruitment system of TEBA (the Chamber of Mines' recruiting organisation) as the labour market has contracted and the labour surplus grown. Instead the Administration Boards (renamed Development Boards in 1985) are becoming increasingly involved in regulating black labour mobility. They have established facilities in parts of the homelands close to white towns to 'process' black labour. At Durban, the Development Board treats Umlazi and KwaMashu residents as 'administrative section 10s', giving them preferred access to housing and employment. A form of 'local' status has similarly been conferred on the townships around Empangeni and Richard's Bay in Natal and on fixed areas around Pietersburg and Tzaneen, taking in Seshego in Lebowa and Nkowakowa in Gazankulu (Greenberg and Giliomee 1985, 79). In remoter areas, African workseekers must find their way to the much more distant magistrates offices and be present in person to stand any chance of employment when a 'requisition' arrives. Vast areas and populations are in practice virtually outside the legal labour market.

Thus by 1985 little had been done to implement the proposals of the Riekert Commission and the two parliamentary select committees to which subsequent Bills were referred. Even section 10 rights have been eroded by the 'independence' of the 'TBVC countries', changes in homeland boundaries, the use of housing as a control, and the actions of the middle and lower level bureaucracy. The position of rural workseekers has deteriorated still further in the face of a contracting labour market, centralisation of the recruitment process, and *de facto* preference being given to those living in certain areas of homelands close to white towns. None of this will halt the process of black urbanisation: the desperation of many homeland blacks will push them to swell the illegal population of the cities, where employment is increasingly hard to find and where they must survive constant arrests, convictions and punishment for being in prescribed areas without permission.

The withdrawal in 1984 of the Orderly Movement and Settlement of Black Persons Bill was accompanied by the promise of a new Urbanisation Bill. This duly appeared in March 1985 as the Laws on Cooperation and Development Amendment Bill. In terms of the Bill, blacks who qualify in terms of section 10(1)(a) or (b) will be able to retain these rights when they live or work in prescribed areas other than that in which they obtained the qualifications. This will encourage the freer flow of labour *within* urban areas which Riekert was concerned to secure. The Bill also allows section 10(1)(b) rights to be accumulated during ten years of living or working in different prescribed areas which will help people such as construction workers who are constantly moved from one area to another in the course of employment. Finally, the Bill allows blacks who settle in the self-governing or 'independent' homelands, or on South African Black Trust land, or whose home becomes part of any of these areas, to retain any section 10 rights they already have; this does not appear to help children unless they were born in a prescribed area and had lived there until their parents ceased to do so.

The 1985 Bill falls far short of any expectation of fundamental reform, leaving influx controls *per se* untouched and the situation of rural blacks unchanged. This appeared to indicate that the government has no intention of lifting influx control in the near future: changing the details

239

of legislation is an expensive process and would presumably not be undertaken if the whole law was to be scrapped and a new policy adopted. Expectations of further change were nontheless encouraged by Mr P.W. Botha's description of influx control policies as 'costly and impractical' in his speech to the Natal National Party in August 1985, and shortly afterwards by a recommendation for their abolition from the President's Council (Chapter 17).

Black local government
Prior to 1977 the only official representation permitted to urban blacks was through Advisory Boards and Urban Bantu Councils (UBCs) neither of which had any real powers to influence decisions of either the white municipalities or the Administration Boards which controlled black townships after their establishment in 1972–73. Despite this powerlessness, official attitudes in the late 1960s and early 1970s favoured the abolition of Advisory Boards and UBCs, and their replacement with a system of homeland government representatives in urban areas. The creation in 1977 of Community Councils with limited executive powers thus represented a major change of course. Despite official denials, this was undoubtedly related to widespread black township unrest in 1976, the year of the Soweto riots. The Community Councils Act enabled the Minister of Cooperation and Development, after consultation with the relevant Administration Board, to decide what powers to vest in individual councils; the most important were the capacity to allocate and administer accommodation for migrant labourers, and family accommodation for section 10 qualifiers; to approve building plans for private dwellings, and prevent illegal occupation and building of dwellings; and to allocate trading sites and maintain essential services. The greatest transfer of functions from Boards to Councils generally occurred in the larger urban areas, where Dr Koornhof envisaged a few wealthier black areas attaining 'full autonomy' within a 'reasonably' short period over the functions specified in the Act (Bekker and Humphries 1985, 100,101).

By early 1980, the process of establishing Community Councils in black urban areas had been virtually completed with 224 councils in operation. Only just over one-third of the wards were contested in elections, however, and polls were generally low, particularly in major urban areas. In Soweto especially the steady decline in the percentage poll in UBC and Community Council elections from 32 per cent in 1968 to 14 per cent in 1974 and only 6 per cent in 1978 clearly indicated rejection of officially sanctioned structures (Bekker and Humphries 1985, 105). The image of the Community Councils was not improved by their ambiguous relationship with Administration Boards; in particular their control of housing allocation necessarily involved the Community Councils in influx control.

The Riekert Report recommended new legislation to formalise the relationship between the Boards and the Councils. The draft legislation which followed suffered the same fate as that dealing with influx control, for similar reasons, but after two referrals to Select Committees and amendments introduced by the PFP in Parliament, the Black Local Authorities Act was passed in 1982. The Act created two new structures, Town and Village Councils, and also provided for Advisory Committees in smaller urban areas; these authorities are responsible to a Director of Local Government within the Department of Cooperation and Development (the administration of black urban areas has since been transferred to the Department of Constitutional Development and Planning, and the Department of Cooperation and Development renamed the Department of Development Aid, with responsibilities for the six self-governing homelands). The new Town Councils enjoy far wider powers than those listed in the Community Councils Act, and no longer at the discretion of the Minister, whereas the latter continues to decide what powers to vest in Village Councils. In areas administered by Town Councils, Administration Boards are restricted to assisting in administration and execution of council policy in so far as such help is requested. Financial viability and administrative expertise are in practice the criteria which the Minister uses in deciding whether to establish a Town or Village Council. In smaller urban areas Community Councils may continue to operate, or the Minister may appoint Advisory Committees.

Town Councils, although officially regarded as independent local authorities, remain subject to wide-ranging powers of ministerial intervention which far exceed those of the Provincial Administrations to which white local authorities are responsible. In particular, the failure of a Town or Village Council to agree to 'adequate charges' for municipal services is a ground for intervention. Given the politicisation of service charges during the last decade, this had inevitably been a sensitive issue now that the Councils are (unlike Community Councils) financially responsible, and given that their income depends upon service charges in the absence of direct Treasury subsidy. The Black Local Authorities Act again involves Councils in the administration of influx control, this time more explicitly in the exercise of their scheduled powers; these include the approval of building plans, the removal or demolition of unauthorised structures and the prevention of unlawful occupation of housing which entails checking residential qualifications of prospective tenants (Bekker and Humphries 1985, 115).

In practice the new Councils are perceived as little different from Community Councils, given continuing close links with Administration Boards and the continuing responsibility of the Councils to the Ministry of Constitutional Development and Planning. Above all, the over-whelming reliance of these local authorities on income from services such as water, electricity and refuse removal does not provide a sufficient base from which to upgrade infrastructure and social facilities. The latter can only be achieved by ending the principle of financial self-sufficiency in black urban areas and introducing a redistributive mechanism in the allocation of finances raised within the wider urban community (Bekker and Humphries 1985, 163). The need for this basic reform was stressed as long ago as 1945 by the Social and Economic Planning Council (South Africa 1945); it appears to have received belated and tentative official acceptance in legislation establishing new Regional Services Councils (Chapter 14).

Part 5
INDIANS AND COLOUREDS

11
The Indian community

An uncertain position: Indians in a 'European' society

Indian immigration to South Africa has been limited to the dependants of existing residents since 1913, when the importation of indentured labour ceased. By 1960, only 5.5 per cent of Indians had been born outside South Africa (Sadie 1970, 7). Of 890,000 South African Indians in 1984, over 70 per cent were descendants of indentured immigrants and the remainder largely descendants of the small number of 'passenger' immigrants who entered the country independently in the 1880s and early 1890s. The latter opened shops, not only on the sugar plantations where their fellow countrymen worked but also in African areas and European towns. Many Indians were offered land as an inducement to reindenture, but as their numbers increased an earlier promise of citizenship was not fulfilled, and the offer of land was subsequently withdrawn. Nearly all of them nevertheless remained in South Africa, turning mostly to market gardening and trading in peri-urban and urban areas (Lemon 1980, 109).

European attitudes to Indians have been characteristically ambivalent; employers found their labour useful, but traders and businessmen feared competition. Between 1891 and 1985 Indians were excluded altogether from the Orange Free State. In the Transvaal they were hedged in by restrictions on employment and property-owning, but many of these were either never fully enforced or successfully circumvented. The Cape was more permissive, but owing to its distance from Natal attracted relatively few Indians. Continued restriction of inter-provincial movement after 1910 maintained concentration of Indians in Natal, excluding certain northern areas where exclusion of those not already resident was imposed in 1927. Inter-provincial movement has been unrestricted since 1975, but 82 per cent of Indians remained in Natal in 1980. Had it not been for past restrictions, many more Indian

245

businessmen and traders would almost certainly be found in Transvaal and Free State towns today. As it is 73 per cent of all South African Indians lived in the Durban-Pinetown metropolitan area, where they constituted 37.5 per cent of the total population, in 1980; strong community institutions and family ties tend to discourage out-movement. Other major concentrations of Indians are found in the PWV area (99,000 – 12 per cent in 1980) and Pietermaritzburg (51,000 – 6.2 per cent).

Europeans found a new cause for grievance in the late 1930s as Indians began to 'infiltrate' predominantly white residential areas, especially in Durban, and trading areas in Transvaal towns. The white reaction was wholly disproportionate to the scale and nature of penetration, but led to restrictions on Indian occupation and ownership of property in 1943 and 1946. Indians further increased their unpopularity with Europeans by bringing their lack of citizenship rights to the United Nations in 1946, through the agency of the Indian government, an action which first drew international attention to South Africa's racial policies (Palmer 1957, Chapter 7). Voluntary 'repatriation' schemes continued until 1975, although immigration has exceeded emigration since 1933; this, together with South Africa's extraordinarily belated recognition of Indians as a permanent part of her population in 1961, underlines the continuing ambivalence of European attitudes. These reflected the underlying conviction that Indians were 'alien' and 'unassimilable', a view based largely on visible symbols of cultural pluralism such as religion, food and dress. In practice, cultural differences cut across such categories, and Natal Indians, although certainly distinctive, have long been more westernised than any other overseas Indian community (Brookfield and Tatham 1957, 50). European dress predominates, wage labour has done much to break down the joint family system, and almost all Indians speak English (Chapter 4).

Whites seldom recognise that Indians are themselves culturally diverse, especially in terms of religion. Hinduism is dominant in Natal, whilst Moslems (20 per cent of all South African Indians) are more numerous in the Transvaal and the Cape, but these are umbrella terms which conceal great complexity. Only 16 per cent of Indians are Christians, although there are notable Roman Catholic minorities in Kimberley and Port Elizabeth. But religion is not necessarily so significant a barrier to assimiliation as it seems. Hinduism is singularly eclectic (Kuper 1971, 250), and western influences are particularly noticeable in the Arya Samaj (reform movement). Religion is in any case a personal, private affair for both Hindus and Moslems, and as such it need impinge relatively little on everyday social relations with people of other races.

Despite the effects of residential resettlement under the Group Areas Act, the extended family or *kutum* remains important for most Indians. It consists of all those with whom consanguinity can be traced through a common paternal grandfather or grandfather's brother, and it is 'the primary community which insulates Indians in South Africa from the rigours of the larger society' (Meer 1979, 136, 141). As such it lays the base for group solidarity. *Kutum* bonds have come to extend across barriers of religion, language, economics and caste, resulting in a relatively close-knit Indian community. Whilst wishing to retain this composite identity, however, Indians do desire integration into the wider South African social system. Instead, their place in South African society as traditionally viewed by whites exemplifies Furnivall's characterisation of a plural society as a 'business partnership rather than a family concern' in which 'the social will linking the sections does not extend beyond the common business interests' (1948, 308). But for Indians the spontaneous expression of that social will is difficult if not impossible to measure, restricted as it is by both white laws and white attitudes.

The Indian occupational role

The agricultural sector remained the largest single source of Indian employment in 1936, when it employed 37.8 per cent of Indian workers. It subsequently decreased as a source of employment in favour of manufacturing, commerce and services (Maasdorp and Pillay 1975a), and employs less than 5 per cent of Indian workers today. Indian smallholders and market gardeners remain in the Durban-Pinetown area, but their numbers have declined due to urban growth, rising costs, insufficient capital and the inadequacy of their land; smallholders have been displaced from areas such as the Bayhead, Springfield Flats and Chatsworth, without the provision of any alternative agricultural land. In the coastal districts north and south of Durban most Indian farmers grow sugar cane. They suffer from steeply sloping land (much of which would be rejected by white farmers), lack of expertise and capital, and the small size of individual holdings which precludes scale economies; many rely on supplementary income from non-farm activities. These problems have been accentuated by widespread fragmentation, as no additional land has been made available for Indian agriculture; some former cane growers now work in sugar mills. Indian agricultural potential remains an under-utilised resource; production could have been greatly increased given training facilities, easier capital availability, and more land.

Indian employment in manufacturing rose sharply in the 1940s, when large numbers of whites were in the armed forces. In the ensuing decades many Indians displaced from commerce were forced to take manufacturing jobs. Indians are strongly represented in those sectors where Indian industrialists are most involved: clothing is the largest of these, with textiles, footwear, food and drink, furniture, paper and printing industries also important. However, Indians are now employed in almost all manufacturing sectors (Table 11.1). The number of Indian artisans and apprentices has risen from 4100 in 1969 to 13,200 in 1983, which as a proportion of the Indian labour force remains lower than the corresponding figures for coloureds (60,000) and whites (218,600).[1] Average wages of Indian workers are less than half those of whites in most manufacturing sectors, and fall to below a quarter in the largest sector, clothing, which employs many Indian women at low rates (Table 11.1). In most sectors, however, Indians earn more than coloureds, often substantially so, whilst blacks trail far behind.[2]

Economic circumstances in the 1950s and 1960s virtually forced the Indian community to accept female employment, despite cultural constraints. With high unemployment and low wages, most Indians were living close to or below the poverty datum line (PDL). The rapid economic growth of Natal since the mid-1960s enabled increasing numbers of Indian women to enter the labour force as secretaries, typists, receptionists and sales assistants in both white and Indian firms. Others took operative jobs in clothing and other industries. Some became teachers, nurses and social workers, and smaller numbers qualified as doctors and lawyers. By 1983 the Indian activity rate of 32.9 per cent was not far behind that of coloureds (35.5 per cent), though still significantly below that of whites (42.2 per cent).

The creation of the Department of Indian Affairs in 1961, the government takeover of Indian education from the provinces, and the extension of Indian local government created wider job opportunities for Indians, although they would undoubtedly have entered administrative employment much earlier if competition had been unrestricted. The 1983 constitution will result in increasing Indian recruitment to jobs in national government where, in contrast to local authorities, their average earnings are close to those of whites (Table 11.1).

Table 11.1: Indian wages and employment, June 1984

Sector	Numbers employed	Average wages (R month)	% of average wage of:		
			Whites	Coloureds	Blacks
Insurance	1,007	1,463	68.8	154.7	177.6
Transport	1,990	1,265	97.4	340.1	354.3
National government	16,654	1,073	85.8	159.2	250.1
Provincial administration	4,654	1,035	85.0	216.1	295.7
Chemicals	3,200	969	60.8	164.0	200.6
Construction	8,400	944	57.9	193.4	303.5
Posts and tele-communications	1,997	934	78.9	195.4	261.6
Mines	910	916	58.8	169.0	314.8
Wholesale trade	12,600	880	59.1	183.0	283.0
Beverages	700	876	63.8	198.2	202.8
Basic metals	1,300	843	55.1	109.5	186.9
Banks	3,271	827	71.8	118.3	160.9
Building societies	750	767	75.2	125.3	187.5
Electrical machinery	3,000	748	48.5	144.4	161.6
Machinery	3,200	707	44.8	97.4	150.4
Rubber products	900	698	45.8	98.0	139.9
Motor trade	5,300	696	56.4	152.0	224.5
Metal products	3,200	655	43.4	118.4	154.1
Printing/newspapers	2,900	647	53.2	112.7	151.2
Paper	4,000	631	41.3	122.0	139.6
Wood and cork	700	613	45.1	235.8	395.5
Local authorities	6,400	602	39.1	130.9	192.3
Food industries	9,700	584	43.8	176.4	200.0
Plastic products	1,500	504	31.7	109.3	133.0
Textiles	8,400	502	34.4	151.7	178.6
Furniture	3,600	454	35.3	113.8	137.6
Retail trade	20,100	430	55.3	136.1	163.5
Hotels	3,500	429	63.0	173.0	222.3
Footwear	7,100	386	28.1	110.9	124.9
Clothing	26,200	326	24.4	114.0	184.2
Leather	1,200	321	24.9	100.0	124.4

Source: SAIRR, 1984 *Survey*, 265–98.

Indians have enjoyed a degree of access to higher education since 1938. Almost all professions are now open to them, including some such as engineering, architecture and accountancy where lack of training facilities was previously a constraint. In 1984 over 15,000 Indians were enrolled at South African universities, including 6200 at their 'own' university of Durban–Westville and a further 6173 registered for correspondence degree courses with the University of South Africa (UNISA). Proportionately, this represents more than twice the number of coloureds in universities, although the latter are fast catching up as the Indian proportion was five times higher a decade earlier. White university enrolment remained 50 per cent higher, proportionately, than that of Indians in 1984.

Indian industrialists
With a few exceptions the emergence of Indian industrialists was delayed until the 1950s, when several of the wealthier Indian trading families acquired manufacturing interests. This trend was encouraged by the Department of Indian Affairs after 1961 in the hope that industrial opportunities might compensate for the negative effects of the Group Areas Act. The latter certainly encouraged those few Indians with capital and know-how to diversify into manufacturing, as did the tendency for Indian wholesalers to suffer from changing trade patterns whereby department stores and supermarkets dealt directly with manufacturers. Most Indian concerns remain small, with repair and service establishments (including laundry and dry-cleaning businesses) important in addition to the manufacturing sectors mentioned above; the number of large enterprises has, however, increased considerably. Indians also figure prominently in the building industry where they compete for government contracts.

Indian industrial development areas were designated in 1965 at Stanger, Tongaat and Verulam on the north coast of Natal, and in Pietermaritzburg. Several industrial sites were also designated for Indians in and around Durban. The Industrial Development Corporation began to assist small numbers of Indian firms in the 1960s, and in the mid-1970s began to develop selected industrial sites for Indians. However the relatively small areas of land allocated specifically for Indian use meant that prices were higher than for 'white' land in similar locations, which resulted in 'flatted' factories for Indian tenants in heavy demand areas. Some Indian industrialists found themselves in areas proclaimed white, or non-Indian, which restricted their expansion and prompted them to search for new sites where practicable: others suffered from uncertainty in areas such as Clairwood at the head of Durban Bay and Durban's Grey Street complex (see below).

Indian industrialists were the major beneficiaries of the Group Areas Amendment Act 1977 which eliminated the operation of the Act's restrictions on ownership, occupation, purchase and use of land and property by unqualified persons in areas zoned for industrial purposes. Although this did not apply to industrial areas situated in proclaimed group areas, many such areas were subsequently deproclaimed, enabling Indians to compete on more equal terms with white industrialists.

Indian traders and the Group Areas Act

Owing to the extent of their commercial involvement, Indians suffered disproportionately from the implementation of the Group Areas Act. Afrikaners have tended to regard Indians as non-productive and parasitical due to their association with commerce, and a prominent South African Indian, Fatima Meer, probably voiced the feelings of many in her community in asserting that 'one of the prime purposes of the Group Areas Act is to eliminate, or at least to reduce to a minimum, Indian commerce' (1971, 23). Whether or not the intentions behind the Act were so blatantly anti-Indian, the effects are undeniable: of 2765 traders removed between the commencement of the Group Areas Act and the end of 1983, 91.3 per cent (2524) were Indians; of these, 1545 were in the Transvaal, 576 in Natal and 403 in the Cape.[3] From these figures it is evident that dislocation has been particularly great in the Transvaal and the Cape, where absolute numbers of Indians are relatively small but the proportion dependent on commerce was very high – as many as 87.6 per cent of Transvaal Indians in 1963 (ibid.). By 1966, only 7.5 per cent of Transvaal Indians remained unaffected by proclamation of group areas. Even in Pretoria where the proclamation left nearly one-third of Indian traders unaffected, the removal of black and coloured populations living in close proximity to the Asiatic bazaar made loss of business inevitable.

Pageview, near the centre of Johannesburg, was part of an old Malay location allocated to coloureds and Asians by the Transvaal Republican government in 1887. In terms of the Group Areas proclamation of 1956 it was allocated to whites, although it was then about 95 per cent Indian-owned and was occupied by a mixed population of coloured, Indian and African families. Pageview's Indian traders used every device including Supreme Court action to deflect the government from its purpose in

251

moving them to Lenasia, 35 kilometres away. Eventually the government assisted the city authorities in building a R16 million Oriental Plaza, only a stone's throw from their old shops, but with rents too high for many small traders who were unable to re-establish their businesses. Had there been consultation, the Indians might well have agreed to live in Lenasia while continuing to run their original businesses, with the money spent on the plaza instead going towards Indian housing improvement (Poovalingam 1979, 79).

In the small towns of Natal and the Transvaal, many Indian traders lost their livelihood when they removed to Indian group areas. Towns such as Piet Retief and Bethal offer no scope for suburban shopping centres, thus removal of Indian traders to group areas 2 or 3 kilometres from the centre of town effectively kills their businesses, which depended largely on white and African custom (Maasdorp and Pillay 1975b). The trading potential of all but a few Indian group areas in other towns is similarly insufficient to enable more than a handful of traders to make a living.

The most important Indian trading area in South Africa is in the Grey Street complex of Durban, an area of mixed residential, office, industrial and retailing functions, 95 per cent of it Indian-owned. Over half Durban's Indian traders operated there, as well as some 200 industrialists, in 1970 (Watts *et al.* 1971). The complex had an invaluable function in generating profits for Indian industrial investment, which accorded with official policy. It was a major centre of Indian employment, and had important cultural and residential functions, although these would probably have declined in the face of commercial pressures. There was little evidence that the Grey Street complex was retarding or limiting expansion of the white CBD, whilst important activities in the latter, such as banking and wholesale trade, would probably have suffered if Indian rights in the Grey Street area were curtailed. As a central area accessible to all parts of the widely dispersed Indian residential areas, it was the only area in which higher order services and shopping facilities for Indians could be suitably located: to proclaim the area white would have been tantamount to demanding that the Indian urban economy become completely decentralised.

Despite these arguments, a decision on the future of the area was made only in 1973. Meanwhile development was discouraged by difficulties in obtaining planning permission and the restrictions accompanying such permission when granted. Conflicting impressions of official intentions created a climate of insecurity which made loans difficult to raise and deterred many owners from properly maintaining their premises. Grey Street was eventually proclaimed an Indian Group Area for trading and light industrial, but not residential, purposes. This meant that some 13,000 people were required to move, despite the existing shortage of Indian housing in Durban; in practice only half had done so by 1981. In addition, the proclaimed area excluded an important educational and cultural complex representing a large investment by the Indian community. In 1983 Indians were once again allowed to live legally in the Grey Street area, but by this time the damage to family and community had been done; new developments of flats are likely to attract a very different population from that which has been lost.

Indian CBDs have also survived in Newcastle (Schulze 1974) and Pietermaritzburg (Wills and Schulze 1976). Indian traders in the latter are fortunate in that their CBD forms the apex of a 'wedge' of the city set aside by Group Area proclamations for coloured and Indian residential use. Distinctive features of Indian CBDs include the absence of hotels and government buildings, and a very low proportion of both offices and vacant building space. Retailing occupies a correspondingly higher proportion of floorspace, but the more specialised shops are lacking. Many of these features are not directly attributable to apartheid legislation, and the present degree of development may well be a stage in the evolution towards a fully-fledged CBD (Davies and Rajah 1965).

The opening of CBDs to all races

A limited step towards non-racial trading areas was taken in the 1966 Group Areas Act, section 19 of which allowed the proclamation of Group Areas for a specific purpose or use, such as trading, instead of for ownership or occupation by a specific group. Initially limited use was made of this provision, and only eight such trading areas had been identified by 1979, including districts of Port Elizabeth, East London, Pretoria and Newcastle. By May 1983, however, there were 26 such areas; most were small in size and three cities – Durban, Port Elizabeth and Kimberley – actually had two separate 'section 19' areas. The cumbersome nature of the procedure is reflected in the fact that it took five years of negotiations between the Pietermaritzburg City Council and the Department of Community Relations to establish a free trade area in upper Church Street, an area once owned and occupied by Indians, many of whom continued to own properties and trade there using the unofficial 'nominee' system. The widespread use of the latter practice, whereby businesses were nominally registered under white ownership, was one of the factors encouraging the legalisation of open trading areas.

In January 1984 the Strydom Committee report on the Group Areas Act and related legislation (South Africa 1984b) recommended that provision be made for the desegregation of CBDs on application by local authorities and after ministerial approval. The Committee's terms of reference excluded Africans, but in February the government announced that they too would be allowed to participate in the plan for open trading, subject to certain regulations yet to be formulated. A month later the Economic Committee of the President's Council made a similar recommendation, urging that the opening of CBDs be accelerated in larger towns and cities; it recommended that black businessmen be given the same trading rights in CBDs as those envisaged for coloureds and Indians, but not to own property.

In terms of the Group Areas Amendment Act 1984, local authorities, other organised bodies or the Minister may submit requests to have areas investigated for the purpose of declaring them free trade areas. The procedure is again cumbersome: the proposals would be advertised in advance to allow written representations, a public enquiry would follow, and the Group Areas Board would then report to the Minister. By October 1985 a total of 46 municipalities had applied for open trading areas; the first ones likely to be declared early in 1986 included those applied for by Johannesburg, Cape Town and Durban.[4]

The new system will partially restore to Indians the freedom to trade which they enjoyed before 1950, although it cannot of course undo the immense damage inflicted upon the Indian community by the Group Areas Acts over the past 35 years, nor restore businesses to many who lost their livelihood as traders. The new policy is, moreover, a characteristically incremental reform (Chapter 17), highly bureaucratic in its mode of operation and very much an apartheid measure in the race-conscious manner of its framing; as such it is a measure which seems anachronistic even before it has begun to operate. When it does, the experience of open trading areas will undoubtedly add to already growing pressures for the total removal of ethnic considerations from the statute book on urban trading.

12
The coloured people

The question of identity

The very existence of a separate and identifiable coloured population in South Africa is questionable. The definition of coloureds in the Group Areas Act is purely residual: 'any person who is not a member of the white group or the native group', hence the Coloured People's Convention in 1961 declared that 'a Coloured person is one who is discriminated against in a particular sort of way' (Whisson 1971, 64). Many coloured intellectuals refer to themselves as 'so-called coloureds', and the black consciousness movement regards all coloureds as blacks. In terms of skin colour miscegenation has produced a continuum, and definition of coloureds at the lighter and darker ends of their section of the spectrum is arbitrary; even members of the same family have sometimes been classified in different categories.

There is, however, a coloured awareness, partly perhaps because 'persons of colour' have been considered as different by whites almost since the first settlers arrived in 1652 (Western 1981, 9), although economically there was no discrimination between coloureds and whites until the urban influx of the latter from the *platteland* produced competition for jobs (Chapter 2). Nearly four decades of apartheid, with its enforcement of group areas and discrimination in many spheres of life, have magnified whatever collective awareness already existed. On any criteria other than those of descent and physical characteristics of race, coloureds belong to the white population from whom they are partly descended, and whose language and culture they share (Chapter 4). Thus Hellmann (1972, 19) says of the coloured reaction to apartheid that

> the Coloured people ... whose lives and destinies have always been inextricably linked with the White group, and whose loyalties to South Africa

have been unshakeable, are being spiritually lacerated by the rejection they are now experiencing.

It is hardly surprising that the government's belated attempt to bring back the coloureds into the *laager*, even then as separate and conspicuously junior partners, was widely rejected by coloureds, whose experience of discrimination had led them to identify increasingly with blacks in the political arena despite their cultural affinity with whites (Chapter 13).

By its very nature the coloured population embraces immense variation in background, experience, class and current social situation. Several components contribute to class differentiation, although poverty alone is an insuperable handicap to upward social mobility for many. There is a definite advantage in being light-skinned, or straight- or light-haired, particularly if one can occasionally pass as white. Fluency in English is a second index of social class (Chapter 4). In the rural areas, where relatively little English is spoken, the distinction between urban and rural is itself a status indicator. Rural coloureds are generally poorer, less well educated, more conservative and fatalistic in their outlook.

None of these social indicators is absolute: the main determinants of coloured status and class are education, wealth and occupation. Higher-status coloureds have traditionally made great efforts to prove to others, including whites, that they are 'respectable'; their attitudes to whites have been ambivalent, a desire to identify conflicting with revulsion against discrimination and paternalism. The latter emotion has predominated in recent years, with the result that the coloured middle class overwhelmingly rejected cooptation in the 1984 elections (Chapter 13).

The mass of less well-educated and articulate urban coloureds face frustration in their attempts to attain the goals of economic and social self-respect which their society idealises. This has traditionally led many to feel a sense of impotence and racial inferiority, and to internalise the white stereotype of themselves. The latter has been well summarised by Western (1981, 15-27), who distinguishes eight elements in the white image of coloureds:

1. *White 'possession'* of coloureds, as exemplified in master–servant relationships and the names given to coloureds by slaveowners which survive today as family names.
2. *Bastardy*: the juxtaposition of coloureds' classification as mixed race and the prohibition until 1985 of mixed marriages implies that coloureds are impure, immoral creations.

3. *Drunkenness*, which undoubtedly relates to the 'tot system' whereby coloured farm labourers have been traditionally part paid in wine (on fruit and grain farms as well as vineyards); the system still survives on some farms. The fact that licensed premises are not easily accessible to coloured farm workers also encourages a buying pattern of weekly acquisitioning with heavy consumption at weekends, when for most there is no alternative recreation. Both alcoholism and the smoking of *dagga* (cannabis) reflect the search for immediate gratification in the face of underlying frustrations. Retreat is also found in religion, with many coloureds attracted to emotional worship in small churches, with a strong emphasis on individual salvation. These evangelical churches, by tending to regard segregation as almost irrelevant to personal salvation, appeal to many coloureds in much the same way that they once attracted poverty-stricken white American farmers in the Appalachian mountains.

4. A *musical image* related to troupe-style entertainment, together with the image of coloureds as happy jesters, both of which are deeply resented by politically aware coloureds.

5. Coloureds are regarded as *powerless and discountable*, people who can be ignored with impunity.

6. They are assumed to be *ignorant*, fecklessly irresponsible and vulnerable.

7. Involvement in *crime and violence*. Crime statistics have long borne out the truth of this stereotype, and in the year 1982–83 the number of prisoners, including those awaiting trial, was 3527 per 100,000 population in the case of coloureds, 2475 for Africans (many of them involved in pass law offences not relevant to other groups), but only 476 for Indians and 392 for whites.[1] Drunkenness is by far the most frequent cause of convictions, followed by assault (both serious and common) and various forms of theft. Such crimes are indicative of a low level of sensitivity to feelings of human worth and dignity, which are clearly related to the marginal position of coloureds in the wider society (Cilliers 1979, 266). In addition, the prevalence of crime in the coloured community cannot be divorced from the large proportion of coloureds who either live in overpopulated slums or who have been recently moved into low-cost housing schemes where the physical setting is conducive to crime given the absence of effective policing, the inadequacy of street lighting, social services, transport, public amenities and educational facilities (ibid.).

8. *Sexual profligacy*: this stereotype Western (1981, 25–6) relates partly to the tradition of whites seeking illicit pleasures in coloured areas of Cape Town (District 6, Mowbray), and even to a secret envy on the part of middle-and upper-class whites of what they suppose to be the 'earthy, or even sensuous qualities of *real* life enjoyed by working-class coloureds'.

Those officially classified as coloured include two sub-cultural groups, the Griquas and the Cape Malays. The Griquas, to whom reference was made in Chapter 2, are gradually being absorbed into the wider coloured population. They live in the north-western and north-eastern parts of the Cape Province, and speak a broken form of Dutch-Afrikaans. The

Cape Malays number nearly 150,000, the vast majority of whom live in the Cape Peninsula, particularly in the Malay Quarter of Cape Town. They are descendants of Muslim slaves imported by the Dutch East India Company, and remain faithful to Islam. Cape Malays are well known for their distinctive food, including dishes such as *bredie* and *babotie* which have become popular with white South Africans. Originally the Cape Malays were highly valued as craftsmen and artisans, but their economic position (and to some extent that of coloureds generally) was weakened by the 'civilised labour' legislation of the 1920s, which caused them to lose ground in some traditional fields of employment such as woodworking and building. Changing industrial patterns have also reduced the demand for craft skills, forcing many coloureds to take factory jobs instead.

Rural Coloureds

The coloureds' first title to agricultural land came when legal recognition of ten scattered rural areas developed as mission stations and communal reserves for coloureds was consolidated in the Cape Act 1909. A further series of enactments made provision for the inclusion of other areas and for changes in the control, administration and development of these areas. They are 24 in number, covering 2 million hectares with a population of 70,000; except for two areas in the Orange Free State, all are situated in the Cape. They are mostly either small mission stations such as Suurbrak and Mamre which are little more than villages, or vast expanses of sparsely populated semi-desert areas such as Richtersveld and Steinkopf in the north-west Cape. In the latter areas the population consists overwhelmingly of children under 18 and people over 50 (Whisson 1971, 64). The older people tend to be conservative and fatalistic in their outlook, having lived through drought and, at Port Nolloth on the Namaqualand coast, the decline of the fishing industry. For some who have lived their whole lives in rural poverty the aspirations of the mass of urban coloureds have little meaning. One of the few commercial activities in the Namaqualand reserves is the mining of both base minerals and precious stones in the areas of Concordia, Steinkopf, Kamaggas and Richtersveld; the rentals of the mining leases provide some income for the local management boards. The Rural Coloured Areas Amendment Act 1983 empowered the government to subsidise essential services in rural centres, several poor areas not having been able to collect sufficient funds to maintain such services themselves. The Act also made provision for the purchase of land in coloured rural areas by individual farmers, who had been able only to lease land hitherto.

Despite the relative lack of land, 23 per cent of all coloureds lived in rural areas in 1980. 16.1 per cent of economically active coloureds were employed in the primary sector in 1980, virtually the same proportion as in 1970 and an increase in absolute terms. This reflects the labour-intensive nature of European fruit and vegetable growing, wine production and mixed farming in the south-west Cape. Mechanisation has reduced labour needs in wheat-growing areas such as the Malmesbury district, but much of this decrease occurred before 1970 (Cilliers 1963, 18–19). Agricultural production in the winter rainfall area of the Cape also demands much seasonal labour; wage-earners in rural areas often seek employment in urban areas in the off-season, especially if they live within commuting distance, yet statistically they remain rural. Coloured urbanisation has also been discouraged by housing shortages, with resultant squatting and urbanisation, as well as by African migration to urban areas of the Cape.

African migration has also been the cause of some insecurity for coloured farm workers, as Africans have been willing to work for even lower wages. Most farmers prefer coloured workers, however, except in dairying and cattle-rearing where the services of Africans are more valued. Wage levels tend to decrease with increasing remoteness from Cape Town, reaching minimal levels in the north-west Cape where the expected standard of living is very low.

Urban employment and coloured labour preference

New opportunities for coloureds are largely confined to urban areas. Coloured workers have long been important in manufacturing industry and constitute over 90 per cent of the manufacturing labour force in the western Cape, where their position in many industries has been protected by the coloured labour preference policy. Most important numerically are clothing (46,700 coloured employees nationwide in 1983), textiles (21,900) and food industries (26,700), whilst coloureds formed the largest group of workers in the footwear industry (10,900). The number of coloured employees in central and local government has increased sharply since the 1960s, reaching nearly half the number of whites in these sectors by 1984 when there were 71,500 coloureds working for the central government and 28,800 in local authorities, with a further 28,000 in provincial employ. Coloureds are proportionately the best represented group in the construction industry (62,000 workers in

1984), and are proportionately almost as numerous as Indians in retail trade (50,100), where coloured women have tended to replace whites who have taken advantage of more attractive opportunities in other sectors. Opportunities for coloured women in manufacturing have also risen rapidly since 1950, but domestic service continues to be a major source of female employment, especially in the Cape.

Most coloureds continue to be employed in unskilled or semi-skilled jobs and in very few sectors do their average earnings reach even half the white figures (Table 11.1). Some of the industries where coloureds are best represented are low-wage sectors where average coloured earnings are closer to those of blacks than whites, often substantially so; this is true of clothing, footwear and textiles as well as retail trade and local authority employment. Where coloureds enjoy higher absolute and/or relative earnings, as in banks, building societies and insurance, their numbers generally remain small, with the important exception of central government.

Coloured advancement since 1970 has nevertheless been substantial, whereas that of blacks in the western Cape has been minimal, many of them occupying low-skilled positions for which they are overqualified. Bekker and Coetzee (1980) found that employers in Greater Cape Town, the area most affected, were explicit in their desire for black advancement and black permanence, but their demands for skilled black workers could not be met because of the coloured labour preference policy. The repressive nature of the policy, which has exacerbated black housing shortages as well as restricting occupational mobility, has not surprisingly contributed to the politicisation of black youth. Even coloureds themselves do not see influx control, the coloured labour preference policy and the razing of squatter camps in the Cape metropolitan area as actions on their behalf: they have come to identify with the victims rather than the authorities (Lemon 1984c, 103). The announcement in 1985 that coloured labour preference was to be ended was therefore widely welcomed, but officialdom on the ground has been slow to implement the change and blacks in Greater Cape Town are unlikely to experience a sudden upsurge in either job opportunities or occupational mobility.

Coloured entrepreneurship
Apart from the Cape Malay people, coloureds have, like Afrikaners, almost no business tradition: both communities were tied to the land, poorly educated and remote from a business environment. Most of the

coloured enterprises which were established were small and risk-prone, many of them one-man ventures, with limited liquid capital and an intimate dependence on a small group of customers. They included shops and cafés, hawkers, service establishments, small clothing, furniture and other factories, and independent artisans owning small enterprises such as engineering and maintenance workshops and construction firms. Such enterprises found it virtually impossible to move when group areas were proclaimed, whilst long periods of uncertainty about relocation and the freezing of expansion years before eviction discouraged growth. Thus most coloured businesses affected in this way failed to consolidate and rationalise, whilst many enterprises in predominantly coloured business areas near the town centre, such as District 6 and the Malay Quarter in Cape Town and Korsten in Port Elizabeth, were forced out of existence.

Coloured enterprises have nevertheless expanded considerably since the mid-1960s, with individual enterprises increasing in size, and with enterprises as a whole diversifying both horizontally and vertically. Expansion has occurred especially in those enterprises where success is dependent on local demand in coloured group areas and in the categories where coloured artisans already had a strong interest. Access to the capital market has been a problem for coloured entrepreneurs, but limited assistance has been given by the Coloured Development Corporation which was established by the government for this purpose in 1962. The Corporation has also established or acquired a number of businesses which it uses for coloured management training.

The greatest obstacle to wider coloured entrepreneurial expansion is the restriction of coloured businesses to coloured group areas which are residential and have provision only for small shops and other enterprises; they offer no economies of scale and put coloured businessmen at a disadvantage *vis-à-vis* the central business districts. Competition for the few business premises available pushes prices to unrealistic levels, whilst high crime rates and insecurity increase insurance costs. Coloured purchasing power is in any case spent very largely outside the group areas, and the expansion of white-controlled downtown and suburban shopping complexes in Cape Town, Port Elizabeth and elsewhere is partly dependent on the coloured market; sometimes such developments are deliberately planned on the edges of coloured group areas (Meulen 1969). Coloured participation in such developments is, however, only permissible in the form of mixed enterprises with up to 49 per cent coloured shareholding.

Planning issues in the Cape metropolitan region

Poor housing conditions have existed at the Cape virtually since the founding of the settlement in 1652. Rapid growth of the coloured population in the Cape metropolitan area accentuated housing shortages in the 1950s and 1960s, with the result that in the early 1970s between 150,000 and 200,000 coloureds were living under squatter conditions at Vrygrond ('free ground'), Werkgenot, Mitchell's Plain, Lourdes Farm and other sites. Inadequate housing has been a major source of coloured insecurity, and the single most important factor hindering social and economic advance. It contributed to the instability of coloured labour, lowering the physical and psychological abilities of workers, and largely negated the potential benefits to be derived from social, cultural, economic and educational measures aimed at uplifting and advancing the population.

The Group Areas Act contributed substantially to the size of the coloured housing crisis in the 1970s. By the end of 1974, 53,203 families had been resettled in South Africa as a whole; this increased to 82,859 families, 78 per cent of them in the Cape, by the end of 1983.[2] Not only has this broken the spirit of many once thriving coloured communities such as that of District 6, but it has diverted resources away from the alleviation of the coloured housing shortage. The Theron Commission recognised this, recommending in its report that in the allocation of houses, squatters should be given priority over people to be moved under group areas proclamations (van der Horst 1976), and this has to some extent been the case since. By 1984 there were only about 2500 coloured squatter families in the Cape Peninsula, and there were official plans to house them all within three or four years.[3] Newer, planned areas of coloured housing such as Bonteheuwel and Hanover Park have, however, been unfavourably compared with older, unplanned areas such as Woodstock–Salt River which evolved spontaneously (Dewar, Uytenbogaardt *et al.* 1977).

Few government actions have caused as much misery, resentment and frustration among coloureds as the proclamation of *District 6* as a white group area, which was opposed by the Cape Town City Council and by almost every authority on town planning, architecture and property development. The white group area proclaimed in 1966 housed 33,446 people, 93 per cent of them coloured; 90 per cent of its 8500 workers were employed in and around the Cape Town CBD (Centre for Intergroup Studies 1980, 2). Most of those subsequently moved were rehoused in bleak townships on the Cape Flats, greatly increasing their journeys to work. Some went to Mitchell's Plain (see below), whilst a few more fortunate people managed to find accommodation closer to their workplace in the existing coloured areas of Walmer Estate (part of District 6 which was declared coloured in 1975) and Woodstock.

Within the framework of apartheid planning, District 6 offered the best possibility in South Africa of developing a coloured CBD comparable with the Indian commerical area of Grey Street in Durban. This was ignored in favour of a government plan to redevelop it as a white business and residential area, but the plan finally unveiled in 1971 was considered excessive even for that time of economic boom (ibid., 3). A later proposal to site a technikon (technical college) in the heart of District 6 was strongly opposed by a combination of local authorities, private enterprise and city planners. Private enterprise has largely declined to purchase land and so become associated with what has come to be regarded as 'tainted land'. District 6 has therefore remained an empty shell since the removal of its coloured population, and has become a symbol of the hurt and distress which has resulted from group area removals. The President's Council recommended in 1981 that the whole area be returned to the coloured people and that plans for the technikon should be abandoned, but the government rejected these recommendations. It did, however, reproclaim one-fifth of District 6 coloured in January 1983.

A major attempt to solve the coloured housing shortage and provide a better environment for more affluent coloureds was the building of a new city at *Mitchell's Plain* on False Bay, some 27 kilometres south-east of central Cape Town. Construction began in 1974 with the object of accommodating 250,000 people by 1984. A railway link was completed in 1980, reducing commuting time if not cost. It was intended to shed the image of low-cost housing and instead plan Mitchell's Plain as a town for owner-occupiers 'which could materially promote social stability, security, privacy and personal satisfaction by creating an environment which would encourage upward social mobility and assist in the formation of social groups and community interests' (Brand 1979, 3). It was anticipated that relatively affluent families would move to Mitchell's Plain, creating vacancies in established townships for families on the waiting-list who could not afford Mitchell's Plain houses. This did not occur at the desired rate, partly because relatively few coloureds on existing schemes could afford Mitchell's Plain houses, and partly because those who could were deterred by distance from Cape Town. Some new homes therefore remained empty for substantial periods, but by 1984 more than 30,000 housing units were occupied, representing a substantial contribution to the coloured housing problem. Although Mitchell's Plain compares not unfavourably with new towns in Europe, it remains an expression of apartheid planning. Environmental design does little to assuage deeply felt resentment and rejection, and Mitchell's Plain did not escape the unrest and violence which affected most coloured areas of the Cape Peninsula in 1985.

Another element of the official plan for accommodating coloured population growth in the Cape metropolitan area is the building of *Atlantis* some 45 kilometres north-west of central Cape Town. In the late 1970s Atlantis was put forward as the only area where further industrial and coloured residential expansion would take place for greater Cape Town. With the aid of decentralisation incentives and direct government decisions such as the location of Atlantis Diesel, the new growth point was given all possible encouragement, despite strong criticism from local authorities and organised business (Thomas 1985, 64). At that stage a future town of 300,000–500,000 people was postulated for the Atlantis–Saldanha axis. In the event, the anticipated development of both Atlantis and Saldanha has failed to materialise. No steel plant has been built at Saldanha, which remains a highly automated ore-exporting port employing few people; few linkage effects have developed and there has been a minimal multiplier effect (a problem experienced by other new raw material handling ports such as Fos in southern France). In 1985, after nine years of development, Atlantis had a population of only 40,000, many of whom have to seek employment in Cape Town. Rising building costs have resulted in rents and house prices which are beyond reach of many coloureds. Prospects for industrial expansion at Atlantis are limited, partly because of the national economic situation, but also because the planning focus for further expansion of Cape Town has shifted from Atlantis to the south-east where the new towns of Mitchell's Plain, Khayelitsha (Chapter 10), Macassar and Belhar are situated.

Attempts to shift coloured population growth away from the Cape Town area have thus largely failed. Some 40 per cent of all South Africa's coloured people live in the Cape Peninsula, and it is here in the coloured heartland that the most radical political leadership has developed, rejecting all participation in apartheid structures and identifying strongly with blacks through participation in the United Democratic Front and its affiliated organisations.

We now turn to government attempts to develop such political structures for coloureds and Indians and the reaction of these communities to them.

13
Political structures for Indians and coloureds

'No constitution can succeed unless
the people whom it serves wish it to
succeed.' (P.W. Botha, on his inaugura-
tion as State President)

The dynamics of 'parallelism'

The government has long accepted that what is regarded as the 'coloured
problem' was incapable of a geographical solution on homeland lines.
This led to the quest for a coloured policy which was both workable and,
at least in official eyes, morally defensible. The answer was found in the
early 1970s in the concept of parallel development which was intended to
meet the government's basic demands of non-integration and non-
domination. This involved progressive elimination of the more odious
forms of discrimination and the creation of coloured political institutions
which would be responsible for running the purely domestic affairs of
coloureds within the spatial and institutional framework of separate
development. The constitutional development of Indians, a small and
even weaker minority, lagged behind that of coloureds, although the
impossibility of an Indian homeland and official rejection of integration
again implied parallelism.

At a national level the Coloured Representative Council (CRC) was
established in 1964 and the South African Indian Council (SAIC) in
1968. The CRC was given legislative as well as consultative functions in
1968, although legislation was subject to official scrutiny and approval
before it was introduced and after it was passed. One-third of its
members were still nominated by the government when its abolition was
announced in 1979. It was only in 1974 that half the members of the
SAIC were elected for the first time, and then by Indians already
occupying elected positions in local government; the SAIC did not

become a fully elective body until 1981. It remained purely advisory until 1976, when it acquired executive functions in respect of Indian education and social welfare, but no legislative powers.

Coloureds and Indians were also denied real power at local level. In 1975 there were 97 coloured management committees, of which 81 had elected as well as nominated members, and four coloured local affairs committees in Natal, of which two were fully elective. Most Indian townships had only nominated local officers, management or consultative committees in the mid-1970s; the Indian local authority of Isipingo, near Durban, became a fully-fledged borough council in 1975, and town boards functioned at Verulam and Umzinto. By 1980 there was some increase in democracy if not in power: all 171 Indian and coloured management committees and six local affairs committees in Natal were fully elective, but they remained advisory. Consultation by (white) local authorities was frequently inadequate, and there was growing dissatisfaction and frustration with the system on the part of its coloured and Indian members. They increasingly demanded the abolition of management and local affairs committees and the establishment of direct representation on a non-racial basis on city and town councils. One city council, Cape Town, expressed its wish for such representation by all ratepayers in 1985, but this will not be permitted under the Regional Services Council Act of 1985 (Chapter 14).

In both its national and local structures parallelism thus constituted a very unequal form of partnership, with Indians and coloureds as minor partners whose status was determined by their weak bargaining power. With regard to coloureds, however, Rhoodie (1973, 49) argues that 'the obvious historical, economic and even socio-cultural enmeshment of the two groups within a common motherland will, in the long run, be more conducive to closer association than to increasing disassociation.' He foresaw that increasing sophistication at all levels of human endeavour would progressively enhance the bargaining power of coloureds: 'brown power' was a function of white rejection (ibid., 50), and thus in sociological terms a self-fulfilling prophecy. Given the impossibility of a coloured 'homeland', such power would ultimately have to be met with closer coloured–white association. Even the government appeared to see parallelism as an interim policy, whilst publicly resisting any suggestion of socio-political integration, and firmly rejecting the recommendations of the Theron Commission for direct coloured representation in existing parliamentary, provincial and local government bodies. In 1979 the government decided to abolish the CRC in the face of non-cooperation by the Labour Party which controlled the majority of seats, and to replace it with a nominated council. Such a retrogressive step was doomed to failure, and merely underlined the urgency of developing new political structures for coloureds at national level.

Steps towards a new constitution

In August 1977 a new constitutional plan was unveiled. Africans were totally excluded, but the plan contained limited elements of consociational democracy (Chapter 16) for other groups (Vosloo 1979). It provided for parallel coloured, Indian and white Parliaments which would legislate on matters pertaining exclusively to the group concerned. Each Parliament would have its own budget, the total amount being decided upon by an umbrella financial committee. Matters of mutual concern would be dealt with by a multi-racial Council of Cabinets, legislation being adopted by consensus wherever possible. Ultimate power would be with an executive State President. The latter would be elected for five years by an electoral college consisting of 50 white, 25 coloured and 13 Indian members, elected by majority vote of the various Parliaments (thus giving the majority party in the white Parliament the ability to secure an overall majority in the electoral college). The same white: coloured: Indian ratio of 4:2:1 would be applied in respect of membership of all the new bodies, roughly in accord with population numbers, although the plan suggested that there should be 17 white Cabinet ministers, five coloureds and three Indians. A President's Council would be constituted as an advisory, non-parliamentary body consisting of 55 members, of whom 35 would be elected by the three Parliaments according to the 4:2:1 ratio and the remainder appointed by the State President. The existing Senate and the Departments of Coloured Relations and Indian Affairs would be abolished. White provincial councils were likely to be phased out and replaced by separate white, coloured and Indian regional councils, whilst each area or town qualifying for municipal status would have separate municipalities for the three race groups.

The plan was subsequently endorsed by the four NP provincial congresses. Elsewhere, it was attacked above all for its exclusion of the African majority. Criticism was also levelled at the exclusion of opposition parties from the Council of Cabinets, where the National Party would have complete control over the most important national affairs: South Africa would, it was argued, become a *de facto* one-party state. The CRC rejected the proposals and called for a national convention to negotiate a new constitutional dispensation, albeit by a majority of only one vote, whilst the SAIC unanimously rejected the plan.

In 1979, after widespread opposition criticism of the government for undue haste in imposing a constitution about which there was no agreement, and representations by coloured and Indian leaders with whom no consensus had been reached, the proposals were referred in the form of draft legislation to a joint Select Committee of both Houses of Parliament, which was subsequently converted to an all-party commission of inquiry (the Schlebusch Commission). The draft legislation shifted some power away from the white Chamber to the State President and Council of Cabinets, but was otherwise similar to the 1977 plan. In its report in May 1980, the Schlebusch Commission effectively delayed implementation of the new constitution by making only interim recommendations. In particular it recommended the appointment of a new President's Council with at least four committees – constitutional, economic, planning and community relations – to consider draft legislation. It would include white, coloured, Indian and Chinese members, and would consult with a separately constituted council of blacks. When the new President's Council was duly created later in 1980, its prime task was a constitutional investigation designed to give Indians and coloureds some form of political representation in a common state with whites. The PFP and several Indian and coloured leaders refused to serve on the President's Council given its exclusion of Africans, but the government reiterated that the constitutional future of Africans lay within other institutions.

Table 13.1: Composition of the Tricameral Parliament

	House of Assembly	House of Representatives	House of Delegates
Directly elected	166	80	40
Nominated by the President	4	2	2
Elected by directly elected members, by proportional representation	8	3	3
Total	178	85	45

The constitutional committee of the President's Council presented two reports in 1982. The first formulated several political choices for South Africa and favoured a combination of existing (confederal) policies regarding Africans, combined with a consociational or power-sharing system for whites, coloureds and Indians. Both urban and rural blacks would have to exercise political rights through homelands, as hitherto. More detailed proposals for other groups were spelt out in the second report, which provided the basis for the Constitution Bill presented to Parliament in May 1983. On 22 September 1983 the Republic of South Africa Constitution Act received the assent of the State President, five weeks before whites were due to vote on the new constitution in a referendum.

Provisions of the 1983 constitution
The new constitution retains many features of the 1977 proposals. The greatest difference is the creation of a single, tricameral Parliament consisting of the House of Assembly (white), House of Representatives (coloured) and House of Delegates (Indian). Representation is broadly proportionate to population using the 4:2:1 ratio (Table 13.1). The legislation embodies a provincial allocation of directly elected seats for each House. That for the House of Assembly perpetuates the favourable treatment accorded to the Cape Province under existing arrangements (Chapter 5), whilst minorities of coloureds and Indians outside the Cape and Natal respectively also receive relatively large numbers of seats.

The electoral college that elects the State President consists of 50 members of the House of Assembly, 25 from the House of Representatives, and 13 from the House of Delegates. In each case these members are designated by resolution, which effectively means that all will be members of the majority party in the House concerned. The majority party in the House of Assembly thus controls the election of the President and P.W. Botha, the National Party candidate, was duly elected as the first executive State President and installed on 14 September 1984.

The constitution makes a crucial distinction between the 'own affairs' of each population group and 'general affairs'. The former include, with qualifications, social welfare, education, art, culture, recreation, health, housing, community development, local government, agriculture and water affairs. Each House controls these matters for its own people, with the major constraint that budgetary allocations fall outside its sphere of responsibility, since finance is classified as a 'general affair'. Questions of interpretation over what constitutes 'own affairs' will be decided by the State President, whose decision is final. Joint sittings of the three Houses may be called by the State President, but no resolutions may be passed on such occasions, which are likely to be largely ceremonial. The constitution also makes provision for the absence of members of a given House, or failure to perform the functions of their office. In this eventuality, Parliament would simply consist of the remaining House or Houses.

There is a Ministers' Council for each population group and a Cabinet consisting of the State President and Ministers appointed by him to administer departments of state, or otherwise designated by him. The spirit of the constitution arguably demands a multi-racial Cabinet drawn from all three Houses, but no quotas are specified. Executive authority for 'own affairs' is vested in the State President acting on the advice of the Ministers' Council in question. For 'general affairs', executive authority is vested in the State President acting in consultation with the Cabinet.

The constitution also provides for a President's Council of 60 members. The Houses of Assembly, Representatives and Delegates designate 20, 10 and 5 members, respectively. The State President nominates the remainder, including 10 persons designated by the three Houses (6, 3 and 1, respectively) who are supporters of opposition parties in each House. In the event of unresolved disagreement between the Houses over a Bill concerning 'general affairs', the State President may refer the Bill (or different versions of it that have been passed) to the President's Council for decision. It approved by the latter, the Bill will be deemed to have been passed by Parliament.

To aid the three Houses in reaching consensus, joint standing committees will meet to discuss 'general affairs' prior to the second reading debates in the respective Houses. Joint rules and orders for these committees, which are vital to the functioning of the new system, are not laid down in the Constitution Act, but were approved by the white Parliament in the final hours of its existence (Lemon 1984c, 86). Opposition parties in each House may be represented in joint standing committees, but resolutions of such committees require majority support from standing committee members of the majority party in each House.

The constitution has many implications, of which two are perhaps most fundamental. The first is of course the exclusion of blacks: the extension of voting and other rights to blacks was not precluded by the old constitution *per se*. Second, the Population Registration Act now

270

enjoys constitutional entrenchment for the first time, whilst the practicality of the 'own affairs' concept rests on the Group Areas Act, a second keystone of apartheid. In these respects the constitution has been attacked as a major reinforcement of apartheid, and those urging a 'no' vote in the referendum and a boycott of the Indian and coloured elections were at pains to dismiss the view that it was 'a step forward'.

The tricameral arrangement and the preclusion of voting at joint sittings are clearly designed to prevent a liberally inclined white minority such as the PFP combining with Indian and coloured MPs to outvote a National Party government. The voting conditions to be applied to the joint standing committees will have the same effect. In this sense 'the constitution is apparently designed to *avoid consensus* of a kind deemed undesirable by its architects' (Lemon 1984c, 86). Austin (1985, 190) describes it as 'incorporation at arm's length'.

Although ostensibly giving equal representation to individuals of the three recognised population groups, the constitution is so structured that the State President will inevitably be the nominee of the majority party in the House of Assembly. His power to decide what constitute 'own' and 'general' affairs, and which measures should be passed to the President's Council in the event of disagreement between the Houses, gives the President a degree of power that is incompatible with a truly consociational democratic system (Chapter 16). He is chairman not only of the Cabinet and the President's Council, but also of the Committee of Priorities in respect of new legislation, and of the National Intelligence Service, which includes the State Security Council. Measures concerning 'general affairs' could become law with the assent of one House, the President's Council and the President himself: thus the Houses of Representatives and Delegates could be overruled. Parliament could also continue to operate in the event of a boycott of both these Houses. The functions of the latter do include a substantial measure of autonomy over 'own affairs', but within critical financial constraints and a framework of group differentiation imposed by whites (Lemon 1984c, 87).

The white referendum on the constitution

Normal party affiliations were blurred in the referendum debate. Officially the NP and NRP recommended a 'yes' vote whilst the constitution was opposed by the PFP, CP and HNP, strange bedfellows who produced embarrassingly similar slogans (Lemon 1984a, 32). But for many NP and PFP supporters in particular the situation was confusing and the right decision far from obvious.

271

Divisions in Afrikanerdom were evident in the universities, churches and cultural institutions. They were underlined by well-publicised struggles within the Broederbond, whose chairman Dr Carl Boshoff resigned in protest against a decision by the executive committee to support the constitution. Dr Boshoff supported a report on the constitution by the South African Bureau of Racial Affairs (SABRA). SABRA had traditionally provided intellectual support for apartheid, but its report described the new constitution as 'farcical', predicting that it would stimulate conflict. Both the CP and HNP argued that the constitution would lead to racial integration; HNP posters pointing out simply that 'Rhodesia said yes' were clearly intended to suggest that the new constitution was a step in the direction of black rule.

The PFP campaigned strongly against the constitution, on the grounds that it was imposed not negotiated, it entrenched many aspects of apartheid, it gave the President unacceptably wide powers, and above all because it excluded the black majority. To do this in a new constitution would, it was argued, dangerously alienate moderate and radical blacks alike. Moderate black opposition was underlined by a statement condemning the constitution signed by Chief Buthelezi and five other homeland leaders, and by organisations representing African business, clergy and councillors. Black alienation was also stressed by Mr Harry Oppenheimer, ex-Chairman of the Anglo-American Corporation, but divisions within the business community were evidenced by the support for the constitution given by his successor, Mr Gavin Relly. The English-language press was also divided, with some PFP-inclined papers recommending a 'yes' vote, on the grounds that a 'no' vote would stifle all hope of reform. Progressively-inclined voters were thus faced with a dilemma: would their 'no' votes merely strengthen the forces of reaction represented by the CP and HNP? Fearing this, many supported the constitution in the hope that it would lead to further reform.

The overall 'yes' vote of 66.3 per cent was higher than generally expected, and viewed as a resounding success for Mr Botha. Votes were counted in 15 regional centres and no breakdown is available for parliamentary constituencies, but the decisive character of the results allow clear conclusions to be drawn even from crude regional data (Lemon 1984a, 34–6). The only region voting 'no' was the rural northern Transvaal, and even here the majority was small. Elsewhere Pretoria and the south-west Transvaal were least enthusiastic; the large 'no' vote in Pretoria (42.9 per cent) may have indicated strong right-wing opposition within the Afrikaans bureaucracy, although the region also included large rural areas of the eastern Transvaal. The Orange Free State, East Rand and the northern Cape, all regions thought likely to harbour strong CP and HNP support, produced 'yes' votes of between 60 and 70 per cent. Even higher 'yes' votes were registered in regions centred on the PFP strongholds of Johannesburg and Cape Town. Other cities with some PFP representation in Parliament – Durban, Pietermaritzburg and Port Elizabeth – were the foci of regions which recorded 'yes' votes of similar proportions. The threats made by Chief Buthelezi appeared to have little effect on Natal's voters, who were presumably influenced by the positive recommendations of the NRP.

The referendum represented the largest degree of English-speaking support ever given for a Nationalist policy. The PFP had failed to mobilise much (perhaps half) the support it had received in 1981, a setback from which it had not fully recovered in 1985. The CP had failed its first nationwide test, and appeared to be relegated to the status of a rural party, threatening the NP only in the deep Transvaal *platteland*. Whites had given their verdict, but what of those whom the new constitution was intended to incorporate?

The Indian and coloured elections of 1984.
The first elections under the new constitution took place on 22 August for the House of Representatives and on 28 August for the House of Delegates. The life of the existing House of Assembly, elected in 1981, was extended to eight years instead of five so that all three Houses could be elected simultaneously at the next general election.

Of the nine political parties contesting the elections (five Indian and four coloured) only the Labour Party of the Revd Allan Hendrickse had substantial electoral experience. Labour had won convincing majorities of elected seats in the CRC in both 1969 and 1975, and had several veteran politicians. Without Labour participation the new constitution would have lacked all credibility. This being so, the party could arguably have demanded concessions as a condition for its participation, but it failed to do so. Its decision to participate was consistent with Allan Hendrickse's long-held stance of using any structure created by the government to dismantle apartheid. Hendrickse declared that he would give the constitution five years to produce real progress to this end, failing which Labour would withdraw. Its participation led, however, to suspension and subsequent resignation from the South African Black Alliance, of which the other major members were Chief Buthelezi's Inkatha movement (Chapter 17) and the Indian Reform Party, which boycotted the election. Labour's decision was also strongly opposed by the Cape Housing Action Committee, representing 22 civic associations in the western Cape, and by trade unions who saw it as undermining the unity built up between workers of different races.

The main opposition to Labour came from the People's Congress Party of Mr Peter Marais, which had grown out of the Congress of the People formed in 1980 by Labour politicians dissatisfied with the confrontationist stance of the party leadership. Marais stressed bread-and-butter issues and sought to unleash the forces of coloured nationalism. The party suffered from a shortage of prominent, experienced politicians and from limited organisation. Two other coloured parties, the Freedom Party and the Reformed Freedom Party, were also weak in organisation and resources, and conducted a low-profile campaign.

The Indian election was largely a battle between the National People's Party (NPP), seasoned by its control of the SAIC since 1981, and Solidarity, which contested all 40 seats despite its formation only a few months before the election. The SAIC became an elective body only in 1981, thus party politics were relatively unfamiliar to the Indian community: even the NPP was formed only *after* the election by a group of those elected, led by Mr Amichand Rajbansi. This inexperience was reflected in the ease with which candidates defected to other parties after the promise of a seemingly more hopeful seat. Such defections might be seen as typical of the 'village politics' mentality pervasive in the Indian community, or they could be viewed as evidence that attractive parliamentary salaries were the prime motivation. The large number of Independents could be interpreted in similar terms.

The NPP's experience was a double-edged sword. The SAIC lacked legitimacy after a 10.5 per cent poll in the 1981 election which included many spoiled papers. The NPP's record on the SAIC was far more ambivalent than that of Labour on the CRC, and the party had been strongly criticised for its handling of Indian education and social welfare. Rajbansi was personally distrusted by many for his handling of education in particular. His stance, and that of the SAIC, on the need for an Indian referendum on the constitution had been unclear and inconsistent. Despite these shortcomings, the NPP entered the election campaign as the established Indian party with superior grass roots organisation, and soon demonstrated its effectiveness in gaining special (postal) votes.

Unlike the NPP, Solidarity attracted a small group of the Indian intelligentsia, which was otherwise more associated with the anti-election Natal Indian Congress. Its finances were aided by the affluence of some of its supporters. Solidarity's organisation was strongest in Natal, where it was helped by control of one of the three weekly Indian newspapers, *The Graphic*, by its chairman, Pat Poovalingam. Solidarity's credibility was boosted by its leader, Dr J.N. Reddy, whose stature and financial abilities were admitted in private even by his opponents. He relinquished many of his business interests to lead Solidarity, and his speeches were such as to establish him as a potential national leader, beyond the confines of 'own affairs'.

Both the NPP and Solidarity produced manifestos which, given the known needs of the Indian community, were similar in their material aspirations. Solidarity's manifesto had a more economic emphasis, reflecting Dr Reddy's concerns. Both parties advocated safeguards for minorities, a point of obvious significance coming from a 2.8 per cent minority group in the population.

In the absence of referenda amongst Indians and coloureds, the elections inevitably became a test of the acceptability of the new dispensation. The debate between boycotters and participants tended to eclipse all other campaign issues. The strength of the boycott movement was evidenced by large attendances at anti-election meetings in most parts of the country, at which people were urged to boycott 'apartheid elections' under a constitution based on ethnicity, which entrenched white dominance and excluded the African majority. The movement was spearheaded by the United Democratic Front (UDF), a non-racial body launched in July 1983 in response to a call from Dr Allan Boesak. By late 1983 it had some 100 affiliated bodies, most of them in coloured areas, but it grew dramatically during 1984 and claimed 600 affiliates during the election campaign. As a front rather than a formal organisation, it does not make policy for its affiliates, which take up UDF campaigns in ways suited to their own activities and constituencies. Affiliates which played a leading role in the boycott campaign included the Natal and Transvaal Indian Congresses, the Cape Action League, and to a lesser extent the United Committee of Concern, based in Natal, and the Johannesburg Democratic Action Committee. The UDF was also supported by APDUSA (the African People's Democratic Union of South Africa), many religious bodies including the Islamic Council, student organisations and youth movements, and sporting bodies. Support of the younger age groups was crucial given the youthful age structure of both the Indian and coloured populations. The boycott movement encompassed many leading coloured and Indian figures, and a high proportion of the professional group from whom candidates might otherwise have been drawn. This left the participating parties bereft of suitable candidates, and many of those chosen were tarnished in the eyes of electors by their membership of official bodies whose past record had been poor. This undoubtedly deterred many from voting, especially Indians who tended to vote on personal rather than party lines, and to emphasise candidates' records of community service.

The outcome of the coloured election was an overwhelming victory for Labour, which won 76 of the 80 elected seats and 73.2 per cent of the total poll. The Indian elections were less decisive, with the NPP gaining 18 seats and 36.5 per cent of votes cast, and Solidarity winning 17 seats and 36.6 per cent. After some unseemly 'wheeling and dealing' on both sides, the NPP managed to win the support of three Independent MPs, giving it an overall majority of the 40 elected members of the House of Delegates.

These results were overshadowed by low percentage polls of 30.9 per cent for coloureds and 20.3 per cent for Indians. Whilst the explanation of low polls involves more than the strength of the boycott movement, the level of participation inevitably raises questions of legitimacy and credibility. This is particularly so when participation is measured in relation to all eligible voters rather than those who actually registered, which reduces the overall percentage polls to 17.8 per cent for the House of Representatives[2] and 14.25 per cent for the House of Delegates. Comparisons may be made with previous elections for the CRC and SAIC. In the former, 48.7 per cent of registered electors voted in 1969, and 47.3 per cent in 1975; allowing for eligible but unregistered electors, these represented approximately 38.7 per cent and 27.4 per cent polls, respectively (Lemon 1984c, 98). Thus it appears that the trend of declining acceptance of the CRC between these elections has continued to produce the low 1984 turnout, notwithstanding the offer on this occasion of parliamentary representation. Amongst Indians, however, even the 1984 poll is an improvement on the 10.5 per cent of registered electors who voted for the SAIC in 1981.

Nationwide figures disguise significant regional variations. Coloureds polled relatively well in constituencies comprising rural areas and small towns (38.9 per cent overall). There was a relatively high urban turnout in the four constituencies of Allan Hendrickse's home area, Port Elizabeth–Uitenhage (36.1 per cent), where his party won overwhelmingly. The poll exceeded 50 per cent only in the Orange Free

State, Pretoria and the northern Transvaal where the electorates are very small and have voted conservatively in CRC elections (Whisson 1971). Even the seven constituencies of the Witwatersrand and environs produced an above average poll of 37.1 per cent. Natal coloureds registered the lowest provincial turnout (25.5 per cent), which may reflect some diffusion of opinion from their more numerous Indian neighbours, as well as the success of the campaign waged by the United Committee of Concern. The anti-election stance of Archbishop Denis Hurley and the Roman Catholic Church, to which many Natal coloureds belong, may also have been a factor.

By far the lowest turnout, however, was in the 20 Cape Peninsula seats (11.1 per cent), the urbanised heartland of the coloured community (Chapter 12). Political awareness and the tradition of boycott have always been strong here, but whereas 44,270 people voted in the 1975 CRC elections, a mere 25,154 – 5 per cent of those eligible – voted in 1984. Such figures bode ill for the government's strategy of political incorporation of urban 'insiders', beginning with the highly urbanised Indians and coloureds and proceeding to some form of 'accommodation' of urban blacks. The strategy depends on those concerned identifying their interests with those of the government, but middle-class coloureds have refused to be coopted. In the Peninsula constituency of Liesbeek, for instance, where the electorate consists largely of owner-occupiers, most of whom have at least two years of high school education and are either qualified artisans or professional people, the official poll of 5.24 per cent was the second lowest in the country.

Indian voters also turned out in greater numbers in areas where they were more dispersed or isolated. Their lowest percentage polls were recorded in Lenasia, Johannesburg (10.8 per cent), the scene of election day violence, and Pietermaritzburg (9.7 per cent), where the SAIC turnout was only 6 per cent in 1981. The overall poll in the 16 constituencies of Durban, the Indian heartland, was 17.8 per cent. In urban Natal, Indian fears of Zulu reaction, accentuated by Chief Buthelezi's threat of a consumer boycott of Indian traders and his reminder of the 1949 Zulu–Indian riots, probably deterred many Indians from voting.

Many reasons may be adduced for the low overall polls. A degree of apathy (20–30 per cent?) must be allowed for in any election. The voters' rolls reached the parties only a month before polling day, and proved highly inaccurate in many cases. The human and financial resources of most of the participating parties were limited. Coloured and Indian workers tend to get home later in the evening than whites, leaving less time for canvassing, and the number of volunteers available to most parties was small. Beyond these explanations, however, is the fact that the turnout was lowest in urban areas where voters were more easily reached, transport to the polling booths posed fewer problems, the proportions of middle-class voters were highest, and political awareness is generally accepted to be greatest. This clearly points to the success of the boycott movement.

Whatever its purpose, the detention of prominent UDF and Indian Congress leaders on the eve of the elections undoubtedly lowered the percentage poll. Police actions during the campaign may also have antagonised people. Intimidation of voters by UDF supporters and others also occurred, but so did intimidation of voters by candidates. In addition there appears to have been considerable abuse of the special vote procedure, intended for those genuinely unable to vote on polling day: such votes accounted for 30 per cent of all Indian votes, out-numbering ordinary votes in many constituencies.

The elections left bitter divisions within the Indian and coloured communities. Paradoxically, the success of the boycotters increased pressure on the government to make concessions, both economic and political, to those elected, in order to demonstrate the effectiveness of the new dispensation. Its ability to do so is constrained both by political pressures from the right and by an economy which is in recession and increasingly under siege. It is in any case clear that the majority of Indians and coloureds do not wish the new constitution to succeed, whilst its exclusion of the African majority must ensure that it cannot be more than an interim measure. The long-term importance of the constitution rests in its recognition that the government of South Africa cannot remain in white hands alone, a principle which can hardly be reversed. In the words of van der Ross (1983): 'In this failure lies our hope'.

Part 6
CONSTITUTIONAL
ALTERNATIVES

14
Modifying the status quo

Homeland consolidation and enlargement

Homeland consolidation proposals have a long history. The government rejected the relatively ambitious proposals of the Tomlinson Commission (Chapter 3), arguing that successful implementation of separate development depended on national, not geographical, units. Thus the consolidation proposals approved by Parliament in 1973 and 1975 were based on the amount of land promised in the 1936 Native Trust and Land Act. They left 37 pieces of land divided amongst ten homelands, of which the most fragmented were KwaZulu (10), Bophuthatswana (7) and Lebowa (7). Land transfers both to and from African occupation have continued on the basis of these proposals, and by the end of 1983 only a further 80,000 hectares had still to be purchased, most of it in Natal.[1]

The 1975 consolidation proposals are subject to major criticisms, even within the framework of separate development. First, the official claim that the homelands correspond to the 'traditional' homelands of the Bantu peoples is not substantiated by the history of contact between white and black in South Africa (Chapter 2), from which it is clear that Africans are entitled to far more than 13.8 per cent of the land. Secondly, the reserves envisaged in the 1936 Act were not expected to provide a territorial base for independent states, but merely a home for rural blacks, including migrant workers residing there between periods of paid employment; land reserved for such purposes would by its very nature tend to be peripheral to the space economy. Thirdly, these reserves were similar in extent to those regarded by the Beaumont Commission in 1916 as necessary for an African population of just over 4 million, whereas the homeland population alone exceeded 13 million by 1984. Fourthly, given that the basic premise of the policy is ethnic and recalling the principles on which nation states were delimited after the First World War, it might be expected that areas in which more than half the total population belonged to a given ethnic group might be allocated to the appropriate homeland. Instead, as Christopher (1972) has shown in a series of maps based on the 1970 census, the area in which more than half the population belongs to each ethnic group greatly exceeds the area of its proposed homeland in all cases except Venda and Gazankulu.

In 1979 Mr Botha announced the establishment of a commission of enquiry into consolidation under the chairmanship of Mr H. van der Walt, and intimated that the government was prepared to go beyond the settlement envisaged in the 1936 legislation. There followed unconfirmed reports of recommendations for the consolidation of Bophuthatswana into a single block of land, the establishment of two 'joint-venture' areas at East London (South Africa–Transkei–Ciskei) and Richard's Bay (South Africa–Swaziland–KwaZulu), and the transfer of an enlarged QwaQwa to Lesotho. During 1980, however, official policy on consolidation began to change fundamentally, the emphasis moving away from incorporation of pieces of land and towards regional economic cooperation. The Minister of Cooperation and Development, Dr Koornhof, spelt out new Cabinet guidelines concerning consolidation. In future, land transfers would take place only if the land would be used productively, and would satisfy major development needs of the homelands concerned; where boundary adjustments were deemed beneficial, existing white landowners should be allowed to remain on the land.[2] Reflecting the new approach, Mr van der Walt himself said in 1981 that geographical consolidation was no longer possible, because it would require the addition of 3 million hectares of land to the homelands at an estimated cost of R6000 million over ten years; economic development was the answer, and not necessarily within the framework of separate development, because 'there cannot be nine or ten economies in Southern Africa'.[3]

The van der Walt Commission presented final proposals to the Cabinet in July 1982. These were not published, but the main features of the report were outlined at a press conference. It recommended that implementation of the 1975 proposals be accelerated and made proposals for the time-scale and financing of further land purchases. Henceforth, however, geographical consolidation should be seen in the context of proposals for regional economic development and a confederation of states in Southern Africa. The report encouraged what it termed 'consolidation of peoples', such as the incorporation of KaNgwane into Swaziland (see below). These recommendations were broadly accepted by the government, which proceeded to consider a series of specific consolidation proposals submitted by the Commission during 1983. These usually remained confidential until the Cabinet had approved them as a basis for further negotiations, after which proposals were submitted to Parliament. Only in September 1985, with the announcement of consolidation plans for KwaZulu, Lebowa, Gazankulu and KwaNdebele (Chapter 9), were all the van der Walt proposals known to the public.

Whilst the Commission recommended the transfer of more land than was promised in 1936, the proposed additions will increase the total area of the homelands by less than 1 per cent of South Africa's surface area. The shift in emphasis of official policy from geographical consolidation to regional economic development and confederation has allowed the government to retreat from the costly logic of separate development as it did 30 years earlier. The additional land will do little to reduce the fragmentation of the homelands, and indeed the proposals for KwaZulu actually increase its fragmentation from the 10 blocks of land envisaged in 1975 to fifteen. The government's rejection of the Commission's proposals to incorporate King William's Town in Ciskei in 1981 appeared to mark the end of major changes (Christopher 1982c), the concept of cross-border regional economic cooperation being used to justify the argument that land itself was no longer of primary importance. But such cooperation does nothing to reduce homeland dependence on South Africa, whilst the denial of more land merely increases this dependence by denying geographical consolidation and restricting the fiscal base of the black states, whose political compliance with the policy of regional economic development is thus ensured.

More fundamental consolidation and enlargement of the homelands has been advocated from many quarters, not least the homeland governments themselves. Several homeland leaders made it clear in the 1970s that enlargement need not mean the dispossession of whites already settled in the areas concerned: the boundary would simply be moved to include them and their farms, but they could remain South African citizens if they wished. Chief Mangope of Bophuthatswana emphasised in 1974 that 'we would heartily welcome Whites as citizens in our midst. And not only for the sake of their know-how and their capital, but as people.'[4] Many ambitious territorial claims by homeland governments have been based on this premise, which would necessarily underlie any major enlargement of the homelands.

Meaningful homeland consolidation and enlargement was viewed by

283

Cilliers (1971) as part of a wider constitutional solution for South Africa which would involve the simultaneous evolution of both ethnically-based societies within the homelands and a common society outside them. He suggested the accommodation of the *de facto* and possibly part of the *de jure* homeland population within enlarged homelands. In the rest of the country he believed that whites had sufficient in common with coloureds, Indians and permanently urbanised blacks to form the basis of a shared society in which those who shared 'what is commonly called Western civilisation and culture' would be a comfortable majority. Although going far beyond what the government or most whites were prepared to contemplate when he wrote, and helpful in its emphasis on shared values, Cilliers' proposal nevertheless implies a white-imposed division of blacks into urban and rural which few if any black leaders would support today.

P. Roelf Botha (1978) is both more specific and more conservative than Cilliers in his plan for enlarged homelands. He distinguishes three forms of pluralism: open, institutional and territorial. Open pluralism assumes spontaneous, unconstrained formation of ethnic and group associations, but does not seek to give pluralism an institutional or territorial expression. Institutional pluralism accepts the geographical mixing of groups and does not emphasise territorial links, but tries to create institutional structures for participation in group and common matters. Territorial pluralism emphasises the link between people and territory, regarding this connection as fundamental to the maintenance and strengthening of group identity as well as for the creation of constitutional structures. Botha argues that territorial pluralism has the best chance of preventing a power struggle at national level, and satisfies the deep urge of groups for their own territories. Using physiographic, functional and ethnic criteria he redraws the internal boundaries of South Africa to create six provinces and seven considerably enlarged black states of Venda, Lebowa, Gazankulu, Bophuthatswana, Ciskei, Transkei and KwaZulu (Figure 14.1). The latter are fully consolidated apart from KwaZulu, which consists of two blocks north and south of the Durban–Pietermaritzburg corridor. KaNgwane and QwaQwa are eventually to be incorporated in Swaziland and Lesotho, respectively, whilst KwaNdebele, the last homeland to be officially created and the least ethnically homogeneous, disappears. Four of the six provinces are white-ruled and the other two, Boland and Natal, are areas of open pluralism where whites would share power with coloureds and Indians respectively. All coloureds in South Africa would acquire 'full

284

Fig. 14.1 P. Roelf Botha's 'Plan for the Future'

285

participation at national level' via Boland, and all Indians via Natal. Blacks living in the six provinces would exercise their political rights at national level as citizens of the various black states, but major black urban concentrations, as in PWV, would have city authorities which might be expanded to a black metropolitan authority and ultimately a city state.

The fundamental conservatism of Botha's approach is that he sees coloureds, Indians and urban blacks as 'problems' to be 'accommodated' by a white minority which must (implicitly) retain political dominance. It is therefore hardly surprising that his scheme bears strong resemblance to the status quo, both in its geographical outlines and its institutional framework. Thus both the East London–Queenstown and Durban–Pietermaritzburg corridors are excluded from the black states, whilst the southern block of KwaZulu carefully avoids the 'white' south coast of Natal and includes no significant towns. Johannesburg, the Witwatersrand and all the country's major mineral resources apart from those already in Bophuthatswana remain in white hands. For coloureds in Boland and Indians in Natal the scheme offers genuine power-sharing, but for those living elsewhere it imposes an artificial geographical channelling of their rights which is absent from the 1983 constitution.

SABRA's model, Oranje and the Boerestaat
The South African Bureau of Racial Affairs (SABRA) continues to regard the homelands policy as the only practical one for South Africa, but believes that each homeland must be consolidated to form a single geographical entity and that a new demarcation of homelands must enable the resettlement of all blacks within them. SABRA proposes four blocs of homeland territory, as follows (Geldenhuys 1981, 199):

1. A southern bloc, consolidating the Xhosa and South Sotho areas, together with Lesotho, into one.
2. An eastern bloc, including the Zulu and Swazi areas, together with Swaziland.
3. A western bloc, with Bophuthatswana and Botswana in one area.
4. A northern bloc for the North Sotho, Shangaan-Tsonga and Venda.

The inclusion of Botswana, Lesotho and Swaziland, although not affecting their independence, would bring the ratio between 'white' and 'black' land 'more in line with history' according to Professor Carel

Boshoff, the Chairman of SABRA,[5] giving blacks over 40 per cent of the combined land area (much of it, however, in the Kalahari Desert).

SABRA has also proposed a small white 'homeland' within the larger South Africa, an essentially Afrikaner heartland within which blacks would not be allowed to live or work. This enclave, provisionally called Oranje, would initially consist of a town and surrounding farms in the vicinity of the Hendrik Verwoerd Dam, but would expand through purchase of more land to embrace parts of the southern Orange Free State and northern Cape (Geldenhuys 1981, 199–200).

The extreme right-wing *Afrikaner Weerstandsbeweging* (Afrikaner Resistance Movement) advocates a more ambitious white national state – the 'Volkstaat' or 'Boerestaat' – which would restore the 'sullied liberty' of the South African (Transvaal) and Orange Free State Republics (Figure 14.2). Whites in northern Natal and part of the northern Cape could decide whether they wished to be part of this state or to form part of a 'non-racial cosmopolitan unit' (Terre Blanche 1985). Within the Conservative Party support was reportedly growing in 1985 for a faction calling itself Wit Tuisland-aksie (Action for a White Fatherland), although the leaders of both the CP and HNP reject the idea as impracticable.[6] Both parties do, however, support the idea of homelands for coloureds and Indians.

A 'constellation' or confederation of states

In November 1979 Mr P.W. Botha proposed a constellation of southern African states which would not be a formal organisation but a grouping of states with common interests, between which a desire existed to extend areas of cooperation. This represented an attempt by South Africa to use the level of economic dependence to enforce such cooperation, and as originally conceived the constellation would have linked South Africa with other southern African states including preferably Botswana, Lesotho, Swaziland and Zimbabwe, in a close functional and security relationship. The response of the southern African states was to form the Southern African Development Coordination Conference (SADCC) with the objective of reducing economic dependence on South Africa (Chapter 18). With the subsequent failure of Bishop Muzorewa's 'moderate' United African National Council in the Zimbabwe independence elections in 1980, the relevance of the constellation was effectively reduced to South Africa and the 'independent' homelands.

The form of association envisaged is a confederation of independent states which would cooperate closely in terms of inter-state political

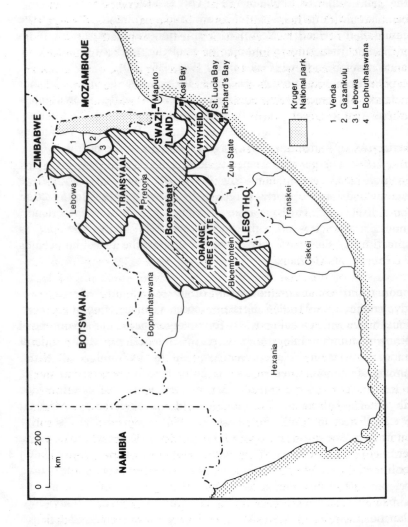

Fig. 14.2   The proposed *Boerestaat*

relations, economics, social affairs and security. The six self-governing homelands or 'national states' would be drawn into the constellation in two ways: economically, they would participate in and thus benefit from various development programmes, and politically they would participate in the deliberation of a 'council of states' as observers and advisers. Urban blacks with no homeland links could also participate through the representation of their local authorities on the proposed council. It is clear that such structures would operate wholly within the framework of separate development, with continuing exclusion of the black majority from political decision-making at national level outside the 'independent' homelands. To date the only significant result of these proposals is the Southern African Development Bank (Chapter 8).

Restructuring regional and local government

During 1984 the government proposed a major reorganisation of regional and local government – 'the third tier' – involving greater local autonomy consistent with the principles of the 1983 constitution. The proposals followed investigation by several bodies including the Browne Committee, the Croeser working group (renamed the Permanent Finance Liaison Committee in 1983), and the constitutional committee of the President's Council which reported in 1982. Their reports noted the necessity of financial viability for the effective exercise of local autonomy, and pointed to the need for some redistribution of resources to give coloured and Indian authorities such viability; they suggested various means of achieving this. The Croeser group proposed that recommendations applying to white, coloured and Indian communities should also apply to African communities. In addition to all these committees, a new statutory forum for liaison between whites, coloureds and Indians regarding regional, metropolitan and local government affairs, the Council for the Coordination of Local Government Affairs, was established in 1983. In January 1984 it appointed six sub-committees to investigate a proposed constitutional dispensation for local government in South Africa. They did so with unusual speed, producing a confidential six-volume report for the Minister of Constitutional Development and Planning in May 1984.

A spate of local government legislation quickly followed. The Local Authorities Loan Fund Act 1984 arose mainly out of recommendations of the Croeser working group on the role that the existing local loans fund could play in assisting local authorities which would otherwise experience difficulty in obtaining loans on the capital market. Its provisions involve some centralisation, in that the Minister has power to withhold or grant funds, and thus to ensure the implementation of government policies. Another centralising measure is the Promotion of Local Government Affairs Amendment Act 1984, which is designed to ensure a uniform system of local government for whites, coloureds and Indians throughout the country. It enables the Minister of Constitutional Development and Planning to set the criteria and conditions for local authorities and the extent of their power. The Act is likely to be used to accelerate the replacement of management and local affairs committees with fully-fledged coloured and Indian local authorities. The Local Government Franchise Act 1984 provides for a uniform franchise qualification for whites, Indians and coloureds in the election of local authorities, which has hitherto been a matter for provincial councils. The three groups will, however, continue to be registered on separate voters' rolls and to vote for separate institutions. The Act also gives the franchise to owners of immovable rateable property, including 'juristic persons' such as businesses, in the area of a local government body. A person is entitled to one such 'property vote' per ward, and to multiple votes if property is owned in more than one ward. This bias in favour of property owners will clearly militate against working class control (Todes and Watson 1985, 207).

The most far-reaching local government reform is contained in the Regional Services Council Act 1985, which attempts to reconcile official insistence on the maintenance of an apartheid framework in local government with the need to provide many services at regional or metropolitan level. The complex fragmentation of existing local government militates against efficient planning and service provisions, as the example of Pietermaritzburg (Figure 14.3) illustrates. The white city council controls the central business district, major industrial areas and white residential areas. Coloured and Indian Group Areas are also ultimately controlled by the city council, advised by coloured and Indian local affairs committees. The black township of Sobantu, within the city boundaries, is the responsibility of the Natalia Development Board, whilst the black townships of Ashdown and Imbali, outside the city boundaries, are administered by the South African Black Trust (a body which controls land destined for incorporation within the homelands). Finally, the black urban and peri-urban areas of Edendale, Mfumuza and Georgetown fall under the jurisdiction of KwaZulu.

The Regional Services Council Act will at least mitigate the problems caused by such complexity. It establishes two-tier structure of service

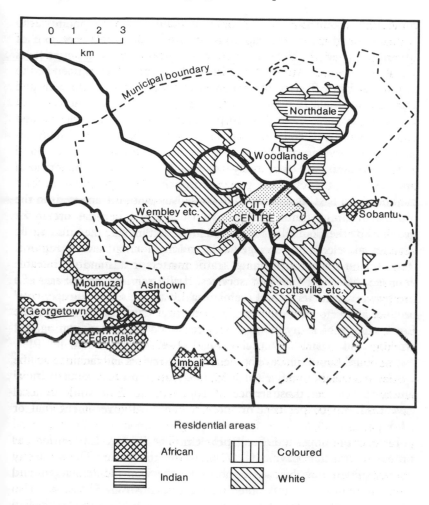

Fig. 14.3 Local government responsibilities in Pietermaritzburg

provision in urban areas consisting of lower-level primary local authorities (PLAs) established on a group area basis to operate local services, and regional service councils (RSCs) to provide services over a whole urban region. Each RSC will be managed by representatives from PLAs, remaining management and local affairs committees, and (black)

291

community councils. The provincial administrator appoints the chairman, and may also appoint representatives of other bodies administering areas which use RSC services. Representation on the RSC is biased in favour of richer PLAs, since its strength is determined by the amount which a PLA or other body pays for RSC services, with one councillor for each 10 per cent of the voting power or part thereof.[7] No member may have more than 50 per cent of the voting power, whilst decisions will be taken by consensus or a two-thirds majority. Thus no single authority can dominate decision-making, although two or more white members will frequently command a two-thirds majority in practice, given the relationship between wealth and representation. The members of a RSC decide through consensus (with the approval of the provincial administrator and the Minister) which services are to be provided by the Council. Those listed in the Act include the bulk supply of water and electricity, sewage works and main outfall sewers, regional land use and transport planning, traffic matters, roads and stormwater drainage, passenger transport services, health services, ambulance and fire services, cemeteries and crematoria, abattoirs, refuse dumps, fresh produce markets and 'other regional services' such as regional parks. Local aspects of many of these services, such as the reticulation and provision of water, electricity and sewerage, will remain PLA responsibilities, but the development of new services and facilities will be a RSC responsibility. Even if a RSC chooses to exercise all possible functions, however, those services still operated by PLAs would hitherto have made up 60 per cent or more of the local government budget (Humphries 1985, 86).

Finance presented a difficult problem. The Browne Committee had proposed transfer payments from white to coloured and Indian municipalities, but this was opposed by the white United Municipal Executive and would undoubtedly have aroused strong opposition from white ratepayers. Instead the government has opted for two new taxes: a regional service levy based on employment or (in sole trader firms or partnerships) profit, and a regional establishment levy based on general sales tax (GST) or on a basis determined by the Minister of Finance for firms not paying GST. These will be collected by the RSCs and used to operate the new structures, to carry out functions 'devolved' from national, provincial and other levels, and to upgrade and overcome backlogs in coloured, Indian and black areas. These taxes too have been criticised, *inter alia* as a tax on employment when jobs are vitally needed, as placing undue burdens on business and industry (burdens which will inevitably increase given the extent of the backlog in non-white areas), and as potentially giving rise to regional tax differentials which could cause industry to move away from high-tax RSCs.

By October 1985 draft proposals had already been drawn up for PWV, the Cape Peninsula, Port Elizabeth–Uitenhage, Durban–Pinetown and greater Bloemfontein. The Minister of Constitutional Development and Planning, Mr Chris Heunis, asked provincial administrators to prepare plans for introducing the first RSCs from the beginning of 1986, and established a Demarcation Board to determine the boundaries of the proposed RSCs.

These reforms of third-tier government are not without positive features. Coloureds, Indians and blacks will all benefit from the redistribution of wealth which is an explicit function of the RSCs, and a marked departure from previous local government practice in South Africa. Their representatives, albeit indirectly chosen, will sit and vote jointly with whites for the first time in the RSCs.[8] The rapid transformation of management and local affairs committees to PLAs will bring a degree of real control over their own local affairs to many Indian and coloured communities. Even for whites there will be a greater sense of participation. Since 1948 local government bodies had increasingly become agents of central governments infused with apartheid ideology and 'inward-oriented' in that they were often more responsive to pressures from Pretoria than those from their local electorate (Todes and Watson 1985, 206). The new PLAs will be small in size with a high councillor/vote ratio, and subject to fewer overt administrative controls than under the previous system.

The new structures are clearly intended to defuse conflict. The devolution of certain functions from central and provincial level to local government counters a steady centralising trend under successive Nationalist governments. As Mr Botha himself has noted, 'The conflict potential at the central level will be greatly alleviated by devolving more functions and powers to local authorities.'[9] At the same time many white local authorities will be less powerful than hitherto, and will no longer be able to obstruct government policy at local level; this applies equally to right-wing authorities which have obstructed power-sharing and the redistribution of resources, and relatively liberal authorities such as the Cape Town and Pietermaritzburg city councils which in 1981 demanded that all ratepayers be directly represented on local government bodies. Some of the more sensitive functions are PLA responsibilities under the new system, thus removing a source of dissension from RSCs, whilst the increasing involvement of the private sector in some of these functions, such as housing, will make opposition more difficult to target (Todes and Watson 1985, 208). Coloured and Indian PLAs are arguably more likely than white city councils to feel threatened by popular local organisations and thus to restrict their activities and deny them use of facilities, as many black councils have already done (ibid.); this defuses conflict at higher levels, if at considerable local cost.

Despite the substantial changes embodied in the new system of third-tier government, its most fundamental characteristic remains the ethnic basis of its structuring. Group areas remain the base of PLAs and therefore of indirect representation on RSCs. Although the introduction of a dual voting system based on property qualifications and of consumer power as a basis for representation on RSCs may appear to emphasise class rather than race as a structuring element in society, the effect is to minimise the voting power of Indians, coloureds and blacks on RSCs and to maximise voter support for more conservative elements on the PLAs. The indirect system of representation, the provincially appointed chairman and the right of the provincial authority to intervene in the event of a dispute all point to reduced local democratic control over the strategic services for which RSCs have responsibility. Blacks in particular will be in a small minority on RSCs, despite forming a majority of the populations they serve. This limited representation of black councils on RSCs is, moreover, being introduced after a year of unrest in which black rejection of these apartheid institutions has been made manifest.

The end of provincial councils

The planned replacement of provincial councils by appointed second-tier authorities with much reduced functions was announced in May 1985. With the devolution of some provincial responsibilities to RSCs and the removal of others, especially hospitals and white education,[10] to the administration of 'own affairs' at national level, the need for elected provincial councils was arguably much reduced. Their abolition does, however, remove an opportunity for creating genuinely multi-racial democratic institutions. For this reason it has attracted particularly strong criticism from supporters of the 'Natal–KwaZulu option' (Chapter 16), who see it as a severe setback to hopes for a representative joint government for the combined region. Thus Dr Oscar Dhlomo (1985, 40), Secretary-General of Inkatha, accuses the government of 'a remarkable insensitivity and callous disregard for a growing momentum of opinion in making their decision on second-tier government applicable to Natal'.

15
Radical partition

Conflict regulation in plural societies

South Africa's uniqueness rests not in her problems, difficult as these undoubtedly are, but in the response of the white minority in legalising enforced segregation. It has done so in a society which was already deeply divided between whites, blacks and, in a few urban areas, Indians before 1948, and indeed before the Act of Union in 1910. As such South Africa was bound eventually to face the constitutional problems confronting any deeply divided, or 'plural' society which seeks to become, or to remain, democratic.

In the postwar period of decolonisation there was much optimism on the part of the European colonial powers about the prospects for 'nation-building' in ethnically diverse societies. This rested in turn on an optimism about the plasticity of human society, which is present in both liberalism and Marxism (Slabbert and Welsh 1979, 33). Such optimism has not been justified by events; the 'modernisation' process has seldom reduced ethnic attachments in favour of identification of the individual with the nation-state in decolonised societies, nor has ethnic solidarity been superseded by inter-ethnic class solidarity. Rather, ethnicity has proved remarkably enduring as a divisive force in human society.

In the face of this empirical reality, students of comparative politics have focused considerable attention in recent years on means of regulating conflict in divided plural societies. Simple majority rule, as in the Westminster model of democracy, depends for its success on the possibility of changing the government through the electoral process. To the extent that this happens, the system provides an alternating monopoly of power. But in a plural society it produces a continuing 'dictatorship of the majority' as in Northern Ireland during the years of Protestant ascendancy at Stormont. This will be unacceptable to sizeable minority groups in a divided society (unless the ruling group shows exceptional enlightenment) and makes conflict probable. Arend Lijphart (1977), in a major contribution to the search for alternative constitutional models, identified three means of dealing with the tensions of a plural society which are compatible with the maintenance or establishment of democracy. One is the elimination of the plural character of the society through assimilation. In most cases, and certainly in South Africa, this is an option only in theory, and it has accordingly received scant attention in the literature. The second is some form of consociational democracy or institutionalised power-sharing between population groups in a society: this is considered in the following chapter. Lijphart's third alternative is that of partitioning the state into two or more relatively homogeneous states, which is the subject of the present chapter.

Partition in the twentieth century

Stultz (1979) distinguishes various kinds of partition. In some cases it has represented a compromise between great power rivalries (Germany, Korea) or a division by victor nations of the spoils of war (Togoland, Cameroons). There are also many instances of secession, which is the breaking away from a state of part of its territory with some previously established identity (Norway from Sweden in 1905, Bangladesh from Pakistan in 1971): here a nation is 'liberated' rather than founded. Stultz finds only three examples of partition in the sense of creating entirely new national entities: Ireland (1921), British India (1947) and Palestine (1948). He examines these cases, plus that of Cyprus which has been subjected to *de facto* but unrecognised partition since 1974, to identify common elements in the circumstances of partition. These Stultz reduces to six 'favourable conditions' for partition, noting however that they are unlikely to be *sufficient*, and may not even be *necessary* conditions for partition to occur.

Stultz's six conditions, and their significance in the case of South Africa, are as follows:

1. *Minority encapsulation*: the existence of a minority which is relatively isolated in terms of the voluntary affiliations of its members. If such a group is also territorially isolated, this improves the practical prospects of partition. After three centuries of segregation white South Africans are certainly an encapsulated minority, many of whom would prefer to see their group as a separate nation. Their territorial isolation is primarily at local (group area) level, which is crucial in forming and preserving social

297

attitudes but falls short of the regional isolation which would favour partition.

2. *Imbalance of communities*: the motive tending towards partition is fundamentally communal insecurity. This is very much a characteristic of white South Africans, most of whom doubt that their group distinctiveness or material privileges could survive long under black or majority rule.

3. *Bipolarity*: since social conflict tends to moderate as the number of parties to a conflict increases, a bipolar conflict is the most difficult to bridge. In South Africa the 1983 constitution and subsequent Indian and coloured elections (Chapter 13) have demonstrated the bipolar nature of confrontation in South Africa, with most coloureds and Indians as minority partners in the black camp.

4. *Political stalemate*, tending towards higher levels of violence: as with marital divorce, irretrievable breakdown makes partition more acceptable. The events of 1985 in South Africa certainly point to a long-lasting and (given the force available to the state) inconclusive escalation of violence, although the situation was far from irretrievable breakdown, however that is identified, in early 1986.

5. *Isolation from world politics*: it is important to avoid the intervention of major international forces committed to defeating partition. This is possible, according to Stultz (p. 10), if 'the primary issues of the dispute are inherently parochial and do not impinge upon broader international sentiments'. If they do so impinge, partition may still be favoured if world sentiment is sympathetic to the aspirations of the minority community, and if the area and its resources are not strategically significant in terms of great power rivalries. South Africa represents the obverse of these conditions: her location and resources have well-recognised strategic significance (Chapter 7), whilst her political problems are seen as epitomising the north–south, First World–Third World dimension of world politics as well as the major international issue of racial discrimination.

6. *External linkage*: the practicability of partition is increased if there is a third party which perceives itself to have a special obligation and/or interest in the country concerned, and if the right of this third party to intervene is acknowledged by at least the minority population. Given international perception of the South African situation, no western power seems likely to intervene to protect

whites from the consequences of black rule; their motivation is seen to rest not on the self-determination which was sought by Irish Protestants, Indian Muslims, Palestine Jews and Turkish Cypriots, but on the preservation of material and political privilege. The prevalence of this perspective is probably the most significant factor militating against partition, as Stultz found third party involvement crucial in all the four cases he examined.

South African conditions are thus favourable to partition in several respects, but it is the international dimensions – the centrality of the issues involved in world politics, the strategic significance of South Africa, and international perception of white motivations – which minimise the chances of partition taking place.

Preconditions for partition

With or without third-party intervention, partition would have to be the result of negotiation between the conflicting parties: it could not be imposed by whites or other groups, as successive variations of apartheid have been hitherto. It seems likely that the white position in such negotiations would be weak, since partition is regarded as a last resort by most writers on the subject. Blenck and von der Ropp (1976) see partition as viable only if it appeared to represent the sole alternative to years of bloodshed, whilst Schlemmer (1978b) sees it as a last resort policy adaptation by a government which has failed to make internal concessions in time. The government might well respond in this way, but as Maasdorp (1980, 113) argues, it is difficult to see why resolute African Nationalists should not hold out for total victory, given sufficiently broad-based external support to prevent the conflict escalating into an east-west confrontation in southern Africa.

At the very least, blacks could be expected to hold out for control of the crucial southern Transvaal industrial region: Mander (1964, 18) suggests that they would be prepared to concede only the western half of the Cape and the Orange Free State. Partition would clearly depend on fundamental redrawing of boundaries (against the spirit of Organisation for African Unity policy)[1] sufficient to provide each state with a share of resources proportionate to its population, and so avoid undue dependence by one state on the other. Africans (and international opinion) would almost certainly insist that any population transfers were voluntary, as in the four cases considered by Stultz. The alternative – a total racial partition – would raise a host of logistical and economic problems, including the liquidation and redistribution of assets between population groups and shortages of labour in certain categories of employment in both states.

Some Afrikaners undoubtedly do see partition as offering the last chance of continued domination of at least a part of South Africa: the Boerestaat concept (Chapter 14) is evidence of such thinking. As their situation deteriorates the number who think in this way is likely to increase. Yet it is unlikely in practice that a radical partition would leave whites in a majority in either state; they would probably be outnumbered by coloureds in any 'white' state centred on the western Cape, and a large black population would also be likely to remain there. Thus partition would offer neither continued domination nor an escape from integration. Its attraction, presumably, is that it would leave whites in the western state predominantly in the company of those who share 'what is commonly called western civilisation and culture' to repeat Cilliers' (1971) words. Even this assumes that coloureds would see their future as lying with whites rather than blacks. The alienation and radicalism among younger coloureds in particular (Chapter 13) render such an assumption far more questionable than it might have been in the 1950s.

Specific partition proposals
Several schemes of partition have been suggested mostly by non-South African writers. All centre the 'white' state on the western half of the Cape province. Mander, writing in 1964, felt able to propose a partition which he himself recognised as unlikely to prove acceptable to African nationalists. Whites would retain both the Orange Free State and the Transvaal highveld, including the Witwatersrand, leaving predominantly English-speaking whites in Natal and the eastern Cape in the black state. The latter would at least include Durban and Richard's Bay as ports on which the Witwatersrand is heavily dependent.

Rather similar in some respects is the proposal of a group of Afrikaner intellectuals sponsored by the South African Bureau of Racial Affairs (St Jorre 1977). They propose a black state including both East London and Port Elizabeth but divided into two parts, separated by a white corridor from Johannsburg to Durban, with self-governing enclaves for coloureds in the western Cape, Port Elizabeth and the Witwatersrand, and for Asians in Durban. This would leave three of the four metropolitan areas and 60 per cent of South Africa under white control. As such it bears too

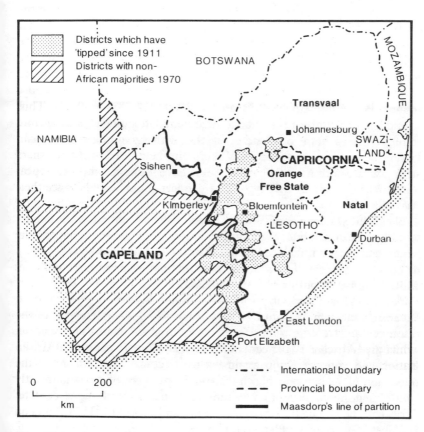

Fig. 15.1   A possible partition of South Africa (Maasdorp 1980)

close a resemblance to the status quo to rank as a serious contribution to any future negotiations on partition.

Tiryakian (1967) proposed that whites should retain the Orange Free State and southern Transvaal but not Johannesburg. He also envisaged Lesotho and Swaziland (which became independent in 1966 and 1968 respectively) joining the black state. Showing a rare external sympathy for whites he argued that the case for a white homeland in South Africa was as legitimate as that for a Jewish homeland in Israel; he also predicted that it would occupy a similarly precarious position within its region.

Later suggestions centred around the Sishen/Kimberley/Bloemfontein/Port Elizabeth line (Maasdorp 1980, 120; Figure 15.1). This would leave the bulk of the Orange Free State, including its mining and industrial areas, in the black state, together with the southern Transvaal. Given the importance of the PWV region in the political and economic structure of South Africa, however, some have suggested the creation of a multi-racial state in this region;[2] a condominium would be another possibility.

Blenck and von der Ropp (1976) opt for the Sishen/Kimberley/Bloemfontein/Port Elizabeth line, arguing that this would include primarily land which had been uninhabited rather than land which had been taken by dispossessing blacks. The white area would then have minerals (unlike a white state based purely on the late eighteenth-century borders of the Cape), industrial potential, ports, a tourist base and access to the Orange River scheme which would be necessary to augment meagre water resources and resettle white farmers on irrigated land. The scheme would give Africans 50 per cent of the total area but 75 per cent of GDP. Blenck and von der Ropp assume a total radical partition involving relocation of 72 per cent of whites and 97 per cent of Indians (to the 'white' state), but only 15 per cent of coloureds and 7 per cent of Africans. They argue that the growth poles and axes of the 1975 National Physical Development Plan could be further developed in such a way that both their proposed states have closed systems to ensure independent economic development.

Like Blenck and von der Ropp, Maasdorp (1980) draws the boundary between his two proposed states of 'Capeland' and 'Capricornia' (Figure 15.1) on the basis of both historical factors and the need for economic viability. He takes account of racial shifts of population as revealed by census data at magisterial district level between 1911 and 1970, and in economic regions used by the Department of Statistics. His economic data refer to the homelands (all of which would become part of Capricornia) and to the 42 planning regions demarcated in the National Physical Development Plan. These data include their gross geographical products, broken down by magisterial districts.

Maasdorp includes in Capeland some districts in which Africans have become a majority since 1911, defending this on historical grounds, and others which have never had a non-African majority but to which, after the establishment of the eastern frontier at the Fish river in 1980, Africans only returned in large numbers after the cattle-killing of 1857 (Chapter 2). Two magisterial districts in the Orange Free State are included in Capeland despite their having African majorities; in one, Philippolis, this is justified by the migratory character of the black population; whilst the other, Fauresmith, is an old Khoisan area where coloureds are the largest single group and the African population is ethnically diverse (ibid., 125). In the north-west Cape the districts of Postmasburg and Kuruman are included despite their African majorities in order to afford Capeland a mining base.

Capeland would not be a white state: 48.5 per cent of its population would be coloured and only 27.4 per cent white, prior to any (voluntary) relocation, and there would actually be more whites in Capricornia at the time of partition. The per capita GDP of Capeland would be 50 per cent higher than that of Capricornia, but Maasdorp suggests, reasonably, that this difference might be reduced by net emigration to Capeland for work by blacks and by relocation of whites. Both states could develop closed transport systems, although Maasdorp assumes that a negotiated partition would be compatible with continuing close economic relationships. Capeland would have three ports, the Cape Town and Port Elizabeth metropolitan areas, the Kimberley diamond mines and the newer mines at Sishen and Prieska. Its agricultural base would be substantially weaker than that of Capricornia and water would be a problem, despite the inclusion of both the Orange river scheme dams.

Conclusion

If circumstances do make partition politically feasible in South Africa, despite the unfavourable external factors identified by Stultz and the likely weakness of whites attempting to negotiate it as a last resort, it would be difficult to improve upon Maasdorp's scheme. It rests upon a careful analysis of demographic and economic data, and would produce both a fair division of resources and a reasonable economic base for the smaller coloured and white state. Capeland itself would be an unavoidably plural society, but one whose greater cultural homogeneity would reduce white fears of domination. The greatest challenge to the new order would be the inevitable inclusion in Capricornia of precisely those areas where CP and HNP support is strongest. Employment problems would probably deter too many whites from relocating to Capeland; some would no doubt leave South Africa altogether, but many would adjust – from choice or necessity – to live in an essentially black state.

Unlike others whose designs for partition have been described here, Maasdorp does not actually advocate partition as a solution, although he accepts that it is administratively and economically feasible and believes it to be historically justifiable. Von der Ropp (1979), in a later paper, also has second thoughts, offering consociational democracy and 'plural integration' – a confederal model stemming from an evolutionary development of separate development policies – as possible alternatives to partition. Maasdorp's preferred solution is geographical (non-ethnic) federation, which he sees as offering the best basis for constitution-making in a plural society, perhaps in combination with a consociational framework. It is to these less dislocating alternatives that we now turn.

16
Federal and consociational models

Federalism as a political concept in South Africa
Federalism has a long tradition in South African political history (du Toit 1974). In the 1850s Sir George Grey attempted unsuccessfully to federate the four territories, and in the 1870s Lord Carnarvon's federal policy led to the annexation of the Transvaal but foundered on the Transvaal war of independence in 1880–81 (Chapter 2). When the movement towards closer union got under way after the Anglo-Boer war of 1899–1902, it was at first widely assumed that it would take the form of a federation. But in the debates which preceded unification in 1910, only the Natal delegates argued for federation. The solution to what was then referred to as the 'race problem' (the Anglo-Boer division) was seen by most delegates to lay in an amalgamation of the races which would be best promoted by a unitary government. In relation to the so-called 'Native question', it was similarly assumed (with remarkably little rational basis) that the creation of constitutional unity would lead to a gradual reduction of prejudice. After Union there were sporadic revivals of federalist proposals and policies as a means of accommodating different white interests, mainly from Natal, but in practice South Africa became an increasingly centralised state (Duminy 1977).

In 1960 federalism became an important plank in the then Progressive Party's policy, which may be seen as the beginning of a wider concept of federation. It was only in the 1970s, however, that federation as a means of accommodating the interests of all race groups gained prominence. Leo Marquard (1971) envisaged a federation of Southern Africa which would include Botswana, Lesotho, Swaziland and Namibia, although this larger political unit is not essential for the application of his ideas. He proposed eleven regions which would not be ethnically defined, although some would in practice be relatively homogeneous in terms of ethnic composition and others far less so. Marquard's requirement of a reasonable degree of economic balance between the regions would require a radical redrawing of internal political boundaries.

The Progressive Federal Party is the only South African political party which stands for a non-racial or geographical federation embracing not only the common area but also the homelands, including those 'independent' homelands which are willing to join. Many if not most of the present homeland boundaries could be expected to disappear in the redrawing of the map. In this respect PFP ideas have much in common with those of Marquard, but they also include consociational elements based on a combination of proportional representation and a minority veto.

The leader of the PFP until February 1986, Dr F. van Zyl Slabbert, is co-author of an important study of South Africa's constitutional options (Slabbert and Welsh 1979). It gives detailed attention to the experience of other pluralist states, including attempts by many of them to operate consociational and federal systems. Whilst recognising the many problems inherent in a federal solution (ibid., 134–44), the authors none the less propose that 'the map be redrawn to carve out perhaps ten regions that constitute reasonably coherent entities, none of which has overwhelming influence or leverage within the system' (p. 140). As in the proposals of Marquard or the PFP itself, such regions would not be ethnically determined.

Amongst black politicians, explicit support for federation comes only from homeland leaders, subject to considerable but unspecified redrawing of the political map. The persistent efforts of Dr Cedric Phatudi of Lebowa have succeeded in shaping a general preference for federation amongst most homeland leaders apart from President Mangope of Bophuthatswana (Magyar 1983, 18). President Matanzima of Transkei announced in 1983 his willingness to rejoin South Africa via a new federal arrangement,[1] whilst President Sebe of Ciskei was in 1985 reportedly anxious, in the face of domestic difficulties, for some form of reincorporation.[2] More radical black leaders within and outside South Africa would clearly reject any federal model based on the homelands, but a non-racial federation could reasonably be a subject of negotiation by all parties.

Federalism and geographical diversity
Federalism is usually regarded as implying a spatial or territorial division of power in which the component units are geographically defined. In the past it was seen as dualistic, with federal and state governments

pursuing virtually independent courses of action, but the functions of the modern state are such as to necessitate cooperation and coordination of functions, whatever the ultimate responsibilities of each tier of government (Dikshit 1971, 102). In addition to this primary federal principle of a central-regional division of power, Lijphart (1979, 507–8) identifies five secondary characteristics: a written constitution, bicameralism, equal or disproportionately strong representation of the smaller components in the Federal Chamber, decentralised government, and the right of the component units to be involved in the process of amending the federal constitution but to change their own constitutions unilaterally.

Several authors have proposed sets of conditions as desirable or necessary for the creation and successful operation of a federation. Earlier analyses such as those by Wheare (1946) and Deutsch (1957) emphasise the expectation of economic advantage and the existence of social and cultural bonds which generate a feeling of community. They are of limited relevance to South Africa, as they are based on the merging of previously autonomous territories. More recent federations have been formed mainly as a result of decolonisation, and often virtually imposed by the outgoing colonial power. In such cases the presence of a 'state-idea' or a will to make federation succeed is perhaps the major prerequisite. In the words of Franck (1968), both leaders and their followers must 'feel federal' if federation is to succeed. The vast majority of South Africa's people of all groups do indeed have a sense of common destiny as South Africans, and most of their leaders wish South Africa to remain a single political entity, be it unitary, federal or confederal. There is unquestionably a strong state-idea, but does federation provide the most appropriate means of expressing it?

Political scientists have tended to regard federation as the most suitable form of government where a state is geographically or territorially diverse. Thus Carnell (1961, 23) argues that 'If the major diversities have no inclusive territorial base but traverse the whole society in the form of radical or communal conflict between intermingled communities, it is extremely doubtful if federation can serve any useful purpose.' In this view federation clearly does not fit the facts of South African geography. The geographical mixing of all population groups has been an inevitable accompaniment of economic development, industrialisation and urbanisation (Chapters 9 and 10). At least since the discovery of diamonds at Kimberley and gold on the Witwatersrand, the growing mutual dependence of all races has been an irreversible process which is necessarily expressed geographically. This is the fundamental contradiction of apartheid, which must make any attempt to base a South African federation upon territorial diversity unacceptable to most South Africans for much the same reasons that apartheid itself is rejected.

There is however an alternative, less 'orthodox' view of federation which is arguably more relevant for South Africa, not least because it lends itself more easily to the possibility of a unitary state adopting a federal constitution (as distinct from previously autonomous states coming together). Tarlton (1965) sees federations as displaying varying degrees of 'symmetry'. In a completely symmetrical federation, the regions would be microcosms of the whole in terms of physical environment, economy, culture, population and political institutions. There would be no significant social, economic or other peculiarities which might demand special forms of representation or protection, and no dominant state or region in terms of population or resources. Federation would simply be a response to a feeling that some problems were most appropriately handled at regional level. An asymmetrical federation, where political units are based on community of interest, corresponds more closely to the orthodox view of federation as a means for the expression of diversity. But Tarlton argues that both unilateral federal-state conflict and conflict between member states are more likely to occur in asymmetrical federations, given the diverse interests of the various states. He concludes that a federal constitution can only sustain unity if the degree of diversity is relatively small and the degree of symmetry high, allowing centripetal tendencies to overwhelm separatist tendencies.

Marquard (1971) and Slabbert and Welsh (1979) also implicitly reject the orthodox view of federation as far as South Africa is concerned (Lemon 1980, 11). In advocating a non-racial federation they imply that regional boundaries be drawn so as to produce heterogeneous units, not in most cases microcosms of the whole as in Tarlton's idealised symmetrical model, but implicitly corresponding as far as geography permits to that model. Regional boundaries would cut across the major recognised cleavages of the society. In so doing they would, it is hoped, serve to minimise inter-group conflict, whilst the very division of power inherent in federation would help to defuse potential conflict (as in the current devolution of power to the third tier of government: see Chapter 15). Any such non-racial federation in South Africa would fall far short of the ideal symmetrical model. The continuing concentration of particular groups and sub-groups in given parts of South Africa precludes the creation of regions that are microcosms of the whole. The spatial concentration of the modern economy (Chapter 7) likewise prevents the creation of regions with approximately equal resources and economic importance. To avoid a single region dominating the rest, at least eight or ten regions would be needed, whilst the division of the PWV economic core, although a functional whole, might be necessary. Although many regions would not include metropolitan areas, it would be essential to draw their boundaries to include what Friedman (1966, 39–44) has called 'upward transitional areas': no region could be confined to the periphery of the space economy, as are most of the present homelands. Provision for the distribution of federal revenue would certainly need to encompass more than the principle of derivation: considerable transfer of wealth between the regions would be essential.

Given such provisions, there do appear to be definite advantages in a consciously non-racial division of South Africa into regions with a degree of autonomy. The various regions would no doubt reach differing accommodations according to their population composition and the prevelant traditions of their component groups (see discussion of Natal-KwaZulu, below). Such diversity could be instructive, with the experience of one region benefiting another with a different approach. A political party which lost in one region might win elsewhere, thus helping to avoid its alienation from the wider political system. Most important, the fragmentation of power could help to defuse conflict from a single, all-powerful government in a unitary state.

Whilst geographical, non-racial federation does therefore appear capable of contributing to the solution of South Africa's constitutional problems, it seems doubtful that it can be the whole solution, or even the primary component of a solution (Lemon 1980b, 20). The fundamental cleavages in South Africa are ethnic, and the peaceful negotiation and operation of a new constitution in South Africa seems unlikely unless both sides can agree on a constitution which accommodates the reality of these divisions. This implies consciously consociational arrangements of a non-spatial kind, to which we now turn.

Consociational democracy

In an exploration of legitimacy in plural societies van Dyke (1983, 23) concluded that 'the more deeply divided the society, the stronger becomes the case for full-fledged communalism'. The theory of consociational democracy was developed with particular reference to such divided societies from 1960 onwards. It is particularly associated with the writings of Arend Lijphart (1968a, 1977), who defines it in terms of four principles, all of which deviate from the Westminster model of majority rule. 'Grand coalition' entails the sharing of power by leaders of all segments of the plural society. The 'mutual or minority veto' provides a guarantee that minorities will not be outvoted when their vital interests are at stake. 'Proportionality' is not only applied to political representation but also to civil service appointments and the allocation of public funds. 'Segmental autonomy' means that decision-making is delegated to the separate segments so far as possible. If such autonomy can be territorially based, the result is likely to be some form of federation. Lijphart argues that federal theory embodies all the basic consociational principles, at least in rudimentary form (Lijphart 1979, 506). However, a federally organised state is only consociational when it is democratic, when it operates in a plural society, and when it is asymmetrical and based on the territorial expression of pluralism (ibid., 509–10).

The theoretical literature on consociationalism is extensive and much of it critical of Lijphart's theory from various standpoints (van Schendelen 1983). In part, criticism revolves around the very concept of pluralism and the definition of a plural society. Consociational theory is also attacked for its reliance on the election of élites, which has undemocratic implications. It also presupposes the absence of competition at élite level, assuming that élite accommodation is a necessary and sufficient condition for stability; this conclusion is not reached after extensive empirical research in plural societies, but is apparently formulated on the basis of normative thinking.

These and many other criticisms are, however, directed primarily to Lijphart's theory as an analysis of the functioning of plural societies, and especially of Dutch politics in the period 1917–67 which Lijphart (1968b) himself studied. Our concern here is with consociationalism as an approach to conflict resolution in the specific circumstances of South Africa. It may be viewed as a transitional stage between conflict pluralism and open pluralism (Degenaar 1982). The conflict model stresses ethnic divisions as divisive forces in society, with political power usually centred in one group which dominates others. Consociational pluralism also recognises cultural diversity as divisive but points to instances in which group conflicts are handled by élite negotiation. Open pluralism 'also recognises cultural diversity, assumes the effectiveness of consociationalism and hopes to overcome group conflict by means of cross-cutting group affiliations and to create mutual trust in order to build an integrated society' (ibid., 8–9). In short, 'Conflict pluralism partly describes the factual situation, open pluralism projects the ideal while consociational pluralism represents the strategy for getting there' (ibid., 15). The situation is one of conflict pluralism with the possibility of development towards consociational pluralism. The latter is, however, at best a distant goal, thus consociational pluralism is arguably the most practical intermediate goal *en route* to an open society.

Several practical problems are raised by this approach in the South African context. The strategy is a gradualist one involving a transition stage to a future ideal. Does this imply continuing *de facto* minority control during the intermediate stage? This seems to underlie Degenaar's advocacy of a 'statement of intent ... in order to create hope in the lives of the suppressed groups whose co-operation is essential' (p. 9). Alternatively it may imply élite agreement on consociationalism as an interim stage to open pluralism, which raises obvious questions about the time-scale envisaged or the criteria by which the society is deemed 'ready' for further constitutional change.

There is also an inherent contradiction in the concept of con-sociationalism as transitional, since the very use of such a system would be likely to perpetuate ethnic awareness. This would certainly be the case if the operation of the system depended on continued legal classification of South Africans into ethnic groups, as Lijphart's principles of proportionality and segmental autonomy demand. More acceptable as a transitional model, perhaps, would be a modified consociationalism which included some form of minority veto and other measures to force consensual decision-making, but allowed political groupings to define themselves at the ballot box. Segmented autonomy, which Lijphart himself recognises to be more difficult to achieve where diversities are not territorially expressed, would have to be sacrificed at the national level, where it would anyway be uncomfortably close to the 1983 constitution. At the local level, however, the likely persistence of a high degree of residential segregation (as in present-day Harare) would enable considerable *de facto* control by ethnic communities of local social, education and welfare facilities.

In several respects South African circumstances are not propitious for giving effect to Lijphart's consociational principles (Hugo and Kotzé [undated]; Venter 1981; Boulle 1984). Black numerical preponderance means that South Africa lacks a multiple balance of power between the various groups or segments; official insistence on ethnic divisions between blacks has not only failed to gain wide acceptance among blacks but may actually have promoted black unity (Geldenhuys 1981, 177). South Africa has no common history of consociational experience among the various segments of society; the shared experience is one of segregation and white supremacy. Consociationalism also demands an overriding national solidarity which is more than the 'state-idea' found to be a prerequisite of successful federation. Such loyalties are lacking in South Africa, largely because of the divisive and polarising impact of past policies. According to Venter (1981), the evidence also suggests that consociationalism is more likely to be successful in societies divided along lines other than race and colour which constitute the primary divisions in South Africa.

Finally some mention must be made of the crucial economic issue. Alexander (1979) criticises Slabbert and Welsh for operating as though a dichotomy existed between economics and politics, a criticism which could be addressed with some validity to much theorising on constitutional change in South Africa. Degenaar (1982) adds to his discussion of pluralism the vital qualification that consociational democracy, and even the ideal of open pluralism, are meaningless unless accompanied by a 'social democracy' in which economic exploitation and domination have been identified as such, and a programme devised to counter economic injustices. Archer (1980) considers ways in which redistribution might take place but acknowledges that the precedents are unpromising. The difficulty is summed up by Edelman (1977, 2) who identifies the ideological basis of a productive system emphasising individual maximisation which takes inequality for granted and regards mass challenges to it as a 'phenomenon' calling for inquiry. Such attitudes would have to change, for a consociational democracy which permitted whites to employ their minority veto to preserve privilege in its totality would be unlikely to enjoy either popular acceptance or lasting stability.

Compromise, negotiation and minority interests
Commenting on the quest for constitutional alternatives in South Africa, Gibson Thula of Inkatha observed that 'in the quiet surroundings of the campus, the constitutional lawyer and the social scientist have busied themselves in grappling with various (often aesthetic) alternatives' (Thula 1980, 144). This recalls Edgar Brookes' rejection of the complex two-stage model for transition to an open plural society proposed by the SPROCAS Political Commission (1973) as 'yet one more example of

South Africans evading the real issue of human equality, and going along flowery garden paths' (Brookes 1973, 244). His comment highlights the weakness of all such designs which inevitably reflect the preoccupations of white élites with the protection of minority interests in a new constitutional dispensation.

Neither federalism nor consociationalism is likely to arouse much popular enthusiasm, even among whites. The oft-quoted comment of Sir Ivor Jennings (1953, 55) that 'Nobody would have a federal constitution if he could possibly avoid it' applies equally to consociational democracy. Both are complex systems requiring considerable maturity of statesmanship to ensure their successful operation, which is an important reason for what Slabbert and Welsh (1979, 135) refer to as the 'wreckage of failed federation in the modern world, not least in Africa'. The carefully constructed Nigerian constitution of 1979, which embodied both federal and consociational elements, is a sad case in point: it failed to bring democracy or stability to Nigeria despite its undoubted merits.

Federation and consociational democracy, or some combination of the two, nevertheless represent the major available compromise options between majoritarian Westminster democracy and radical territorial partition. Mr Botha's emphatic rejection in 1980[3] of both federation 'in whatever form' and 'models which are based on the idea of consociation' was therefore unwise, sacrificing as it did his party's political manoeuvrability. Even the 1983 constitution has consociational elements, and as Boulle (1980, 27) observes, the longer accommodation is delayed the more difficult it will be to achieve. If violent revolution is to be avoided in South Africa, the National Party will almost certainly need to use some combination of federal and consociational approaches in negotiating a future constitutional dispensation.

A major lesson of the 1983 constitution has been the inevitability of failure when a constitution is imposed upon the people whom it is intended to coopt. It is crucial that any future constitution arises not from imposition or even consultation, but from genuine negotiation between representative leaders of all groups involved. This in itself poses formidable difficulties in the South African context, and as Fisher (1981, 1) observes, 'The problem in a conflict is not what is the answer but how best do we develop a collective process for developing an answer.' In the absence of such a process South African society will remain at the conflict stage of pluralism, and the longer it does so the more dangerous it will become.

Power-sharing in Natal-KwaZulu

One region of South Africa where there are distinct signs of movement away from the conflict model is Natal–KwaZulu. It is appropriate that such change should begin in Natal, given its federal preferences in 1910 and recurrent secessionist murmurings thereafter. Malherbe (1974) suggested that Natal was the most suitable region to pioneer his concept of 'multistan' – the setting aside of a portion of South Africa in which apartheid would be dismantled and a genuinely multi-racial society would be allowed considerable political autonomy. If the experiment succeeded, Malherbe argued, it could point the way to a wider solution of South Africa's constitutional dilemma.

Malherbe's work remained of purely academic interest until the prospect of substantial consolidation of KwaZulu alarmed Natal business and agricultural interests, especially the South African Sugar Association which commissioned a study of the interlocking nature of the Natal/KwaZulu economy and of alternatives to the consolidation of KwaZulu (Lombard 1980). The resulting 'Natal plan' recommended that KwaZulu, metropolitan Durban and the white areas along the main transport corridors could serve as three building blocks for a new 'Natal dispensation'. Each would have its own legislative and executive structure, and there would be a joint assembly elected by the three sub-provincial authorities with executive power over affairs common to the three regions.

Chief Buthelezi, the Chief Minister of KwaZulu, dismissed the Lombard Report as too hypothetical and impracticable, but appointed his own commission which started work in October 1980 and reported in 1982. The commission's political and constitutional sub-committee, whilst regarding Natal–KwaZulu as a microcosm of South Africa, noted four unique attributes which made the region susceptible to constitutional experimentation (Buthelezi Commission 1982, 2, 21–2):

1. The relative size of the white minority is smaller than elsewhere (less than 10 per cent).
2. Existing homeland territory constitutes a far larger proportion of the region (38 per cent) than in South Africa as a whole.
3. The National Party does not enjoy majority support among Natal's white voters, and a relatively large proportion of white opinion leaders and prominent citizens in the region recognise the need for a political solution other than that proposed by the government.
4. The black areas of Natal–KwaZulu are the 'centrepoint' of the

314

largest black ethnic group, the Zulus, whose leadership has consistently rejected independence for KwaZulu.

One negative consideration is also significant: KwaZulu is the most fragmented of the homelands, and would remain so under the van der Walt proposals which envisage it consisting of 15 blocks of territory. The resultant interdigitation of black and 'white' areas leads to many practical problems of planning and service provision.

The commission examined a wide range of constitutional options. It rejected 'continuous cooption' (the gradual extension of the franchise to subordinate groups) on the grounds that no black spokesman could be seen to support this strategy and retain his leadership position. Non-ethnic or geographical federation was regarded as a serious possibility, but would require a satisfactory method of defending minority interests to gain white acceptance. Consociationalism was preferred as it acknowledged the right of all groups to be involved in government and ensured the protection of minority rights and representation in the executive.

The commission recommended a regional structure with lower-tier areas based on community interests but delineated so as to encompass cross-cutting cleavages between groups. The wider region would be governed by a legislative assembly elected by universal suffrage from recognised groups in each 'community of interest' area by proportional representation, subject to guaranteed miniumum representation. The Assembly would elect a Chief Minister who would choose a consociational executive consisting 'for historical reasons only' of equal numbers of whites and blacks, together with Indian and coloured representatives, until such time as group associations had moved away from a racial towards a political and economic basis. The Assembly would be constrained by a Bill of Rights, a right of veto over fundamental matters by minority groups, and an independent judiciary which could test legislation. The report also recommended, *inter alia*, the removal of racial controls on labour and property markets, the ending of influx control and the abolition of the Group Areas Act.

The KwaZulu government accepted the Buthelezi Commission report as a basis for negotiation with the central government, whilst emphasising that its goal was still universal suffrage in a unitary state; this remains its position. The report was also supported by two Indian parties, the National People's Party and the Reform Party (the latter a partner of Inkatha in the South African Black Alliance), but rejected by the Natal Indian Congress which remained committed to full rights in a unitary state. The South African government, which had rejected an invitation to serve on the commission stating that it was entitled to enquire into the future of KwaZulu but not of Natal, rejected the report's advocacy of a single political unit for Natal–KwaZulu. The governing party on the Natal Provincial Council, the New Republic Party, also rejected the commission's proposals on the ground that a minority veto could not work in a legislature where one group, Africans, had 80 per cent of the representation.

The NRP criticism is echoed by Southall (1983) in a penetrating radical critique of the Buthelezi Commission proposals. The minority veto would, he argues, immobilise the legislature if it tried to enact measures deemed to undermine the basic structures of privilege, prosperity and power, whilst the Bill of Rights would entrench private property, medicine and education. Southall sees the Commission's economic proposals as 'manifestly congruent with the requirements of large-scale capital in South Africa' (p. 99). Lack of proportionality in the civil service would leave whites to administer even those black-oriented policies 'which had successfully run the gamut of the legislative and executive process' (p. 98). Southall also questions the freedom of radical groups to operate freely in the proposed dispensation, and attacks the idea that the ANC be tolerated only if it renounced commitment to the armed struggle. He also regards the proposed community-of-interest areas as seeking 'to de-emphasise, if not obscure, the objective basis of racial inequality as rooted in the economy' (p. 96).

More fundamentally, Southall questions why those seeking to challenge white power should 'patiently await the outcome of the consociational experiment' (p. 103), rather than increase the costs of white domination as a means of achieving more fundamental change. He does not oppose consociationalism *per se*, but fears that 'its too precipitate use in schemes which would conserve rather than undermine the essence of white power might work to discredit rather than promote its potential utility' (p. 104). In essence, Southall regards the Buthelezi Commission proposals as part of a wider counter-revolutionary strategy aimed to underpin existing structures of power and wealth.

There is undoubtedly much substance in Southall's critique, but the fact that the Buthelezi Commission proposals emanate from a black initiative and have the qualified support of Inkatha does give them major significance, notwithstanding other influences which operated on and within the commission. The proposals are indeed counter-revolutionary, but this is likely to be true of any peacefully negotiated political change in South Africa. Much would depend on the spirit with which whites participated in the new dispensation. At best, their strong desire to make it work, given the implication of failure, could prove a critical restraint on abuse of the minority veto and other aspects of the system to preserve existing economic and social structures.

Within Natal itself there has been growing white recognition of the need to follow a unified approach to the development of Natal–KwaZulu, and continued discussion of the form this might take (Boulle and Baxter 1981; Coetzee and van der Kooy 1985). The Natal Provincial Administration and KwaZulu government have operated joint consultative groups for some years, and in 1985 a Joint Planning Committee was established. The weight of economic and demographic evidence in the Lombard Report, the KwaZulu Development Plan (KwaZulu 1978) and numerous other documents points clearly to the fact that Natal and KwaZulu are inextricably interwoven. White attitudes towards power-sharing in Natal, although not manifestly different from those of whites elsewhere in the country, appear more flexible in certain key respects (Schlemmer 1981, 203), and surveys done in 1981 for the Buthelezi Commission indicate wide support amongst whites, Indians and coloureds for its proposals. There is clear evidence of growing leadership opinions in favour of inter-regional accommodation between Natal and KwaZulu in companies and other sectors, and not only among English speakers: the Afrikaanse Handelsinstituut (Chamber of Commerce) opposes independence for KwaZulu and supports closer cooperation between the Natal and KwaZulu administrations.[4]

But what of the South African government? Perhaps the greatest obstacle to progress on the Natal–KwaZulu option is that it would provide for increased credibility and an established power-base for the PFP and NRP, both of which support a degree of power-sharing (ibid, 204). However, other pressures on the government may yet persuade it to look favourably on a new dispensation for the region. In its acknowledged concern for reform, it is easier for the government to introduce *regional* than national initiatives. To do this in Natal, where it has limited white support to lose, would be easier than elsewhere. Secondly, the government must be aware of Chief Buthelezi's ability to hold the allegiance of large numbers of Zulus and maintain discipline within Inkatha, which was clearly manifested in 1985 when Natal's black townships were relatively unaffected by the violence occurring elsewhere. What can be controlled can also be unleashed, a fact which the

317

government ignores at its peril. It is also arguable, quite simply, that Mr Botha and Chief Buthelezi need each other. Chief Buthelezi has lost support among politically-aware blacks (Chapter 17), and needs something to show for his moderation, whilst Mr Botha needs a credible black leader prepared to settle for something less than undiluted black majority rule to give substance to his promise of reform and negotiation.

There were signs during 1985 of official reconsideration of the 'Natal option' including an official admission that the government was looking at certain aspects of the Buthelezi Commission report. The Minister of Constitution Development and Planning, Mr Chris Heunis, was quoted as saying: 'The solution may not be the same in all provinces. We must be flexible and take local and regional conditions into consideration.'[5] Several proposals have been unofficially aired, including the possibility that the seven or so regional services councils envisaged for Natal could form the basis of a new executive authority for Natal–KwaZulu. What is certain, however, is that anything less than the Buthelezi Commission proposals would offer too little to blacks to be workable. If the government is serious about reform these proposals offer an opportunity which it would be foolish to ignore.

Part 7
FORCES OF CHANGE

17
Change from within

Incremental reform in the 1980s

Before attempting to signpost the major forces of change at work in South Africa, it is perhaps useful to take stock of what has already been achieved by summarising the reforms which have already occurred or which the government has actually set in motion, in order to facilitate evaluation of their collective significance.

The central reform of political structures is the introduction of the Tricameral Parliament under the 1983 constitution in the face of low Indian and coloured polls and fierce opposition of blacks which has contributed to widespread unrest in black areas during 1985–86. Two reforms subsequent to the introduction of the new constitution are in keeping with its intended spirit. With the abolition of the Prohibition of Political Interference Act racially mixed parties are now allowed, and the PFP formally reopened membership to all races in June 1985. In September 1985 the government accepted a recommendation from the Orange Free State National Party Congress to repeal the law prohibiting Indians from living in the Free State.

Changes at the second and third tiers of government include the abolition of white provincial councils and the introduction, initially in urban areas, of multi-racial, indirectly elected regional service councils on which representation will be proportionate to consumption of the services provided. Indian and coloured management and local affairs committees will be more speedily transformed into fully-fledged local authorities. These new local government structures imply a reversal of the centralising tendencies which have prevailed since 1948 in favour of more devolved political decision-making. The financing and operation of regional services councils involves a new element of resource distribution in favour of coloured, Indian and black areas. New black town councils in many urban areas have wider powers than the community councils

321

which they have replaced from 1982 onwards, but they lack a sufficient revenue base from which to upgrade infrastructure and social facilities, and a major question-mark hangs over all black local government structures in view of the violence aimed at them during 1985–86. Similar factors suggest that Mr Botha's proposed inclusion of blacks on the President's Council may be unworkable without a clear statement of the direction of change.

The government has accepted that the homelands policy as originally envisaged has failed, and has indicated that homeland blacks, including those in the 'TVBC countries' are no longer to be excluded from South African citizenship. Power-sharing in a unitary state continues to be ruled out, but the government does not regard the 1983 constitution as immutable, and has recognised the need for a new form of representation for blacks outside the homelands. It appears to intend accommodating the homelands themselves in an as yet unspecified regional structure which may well, contrary to previous policy, include federal elements. In January 1985 the establishment of an informal, non-statutory negotiating forum for black and white leaders to discuss the constitutional status of blacks was announced. Later the same year President Botha announced a proposal to include blacks on the President's Council, and in February 1986 he proposed a National Statutory Council with black representation. Black leaders have so far declined to participate in any of these bodies, which most see as likely to lack real power. Chief Buthelezi did not immediately rule out participation on the statutory council, which would certainly lack credibility without him, but the Lebowa Chief Minister, Dr Cedric Phatudi, said that blacks did not want to be mere advisers but to share power,[1] whilst Bishop Tutu described the proposed council as 'a body with no clout'.[2] The willingness of black leaders to participate in such bodies will depend on the limits within which the government declares itself willing to negotiate; the indications in early 1986 were unpromising.

Urban settlement issues have been the subject of important changes. The announcement in February 1985 that all forced removals of blacks were to be provisionally suspended pending a policy review was an apparent response to the major international as well as domestic repercussions of forced removals. The suspicion remains, however, that the government uses the assent of appointed chiefs or faction leaders to move people against their wishes, and uncertainty continues to exist with regard to certain threatened communities.

Within the towns a number of central business districts in

metropolitan areas are being opened to traders of all races. Full landownership rights as an alternative to the 99-year leasehold are being made available to urban blacks who qualify for section 10 rights (5.6 million in 1985). This final demonstration that urban populations in 'white' areas are regarded as permanent is a fundamental reversal of the homelands policy.

The removal of the coloured labour preference policy was announced in September 1984. This step, which was advocated by the coloured Labour Party, will enable the inhabitants of black townships in Cape Town to obtain permanent residence rights (although grassroots implementation of this change has been slow to take effect) and will also encourage the development of housing and infrastructure which has long been frozen. In the country as a whole blacks with permanent residence rights will have the freedom to live and work in urban areas other than those where they currently reside and where they obtained their residence qualifications.

The government now appears to accept the inevitability of continuing black urbanisation. This is already reflected in changes in housing policy which provided for 'controlled unconventional housing'[3] with an emphasis on self-help housing projects such as site-and-service schemes. Urgent priority is being given in 1986 to a new Bill to provide a positive strategy of 'orderly urbanisation' in line with the recommendations of the constitutional affairs committee of the President's Council (South Africa 1985a). This will eliminate discriminatory aspects of influx control and shift the emphasis from limiting urban growth to the accommodation of and planning for growth, emphasising the development role of the urbanisation process (ibid., 198). 'Orderly urbanisation' means the ordering and directing of urbanisation mainly by indirect incentives and disincentives but also by '*direct control measures*, mainly through existing legislation' (ibid.), including that concerning Group Areas, squatting and slums, health, immigration and security. It seems probable that control of housing availability will become an increasingly important tool in distributing labour and population, so that a form of influx control will continue to exist. Nevertheless the expected changes do amount to a very significant reversal of traditional policy which is associated with some of the most widely criticised and strongly resisted aspects of apartheid including the pass laws, the insecurity of impermanence within the cities, migrant labour and the splitting of families. None of these will disappear, but controls will be reduced and more attention will be focused on the provision of housing, infrastructure and social services. Attempts to divert black urbanisation towards industrial growth points under the decentralisation strategy are likely, but the realism of this approach given the size of the economy and large number of growth points is highly questionable.

Equally significant have been reforms in labour legislation following publication of the Wiehahn Report in 1979. The last statutory job reservation determinations were removed in 1983, and the government has made clear its intention of removing residual job discrimination in the mining industry with or without the support of white mineworkers. Most important has been the official recognition of trade union rights for Africans who may now join and form both registered and unregistered trade unions and participate in the same conciliation machinery as other workers; the wider significance of these reforms is considered separately below. In addition, the government is slowly working towards the removal of racially discriminatory wage structures for those in its own employ.

Reforms in the social sphere include the abolition of the Mixed Marriages Act and section 16 of the Immorality Act despite strong opposition from conservative whites. These measures are of little practical effect but considerable symbolic importance. The dismantling of micro-scale or petty apartheid continues, with most city hotels and restaurants obtaining permits to overcome segregation laws but much slower progress in the rural *platteland*. Most theatres are now multi-racial and cinemas in specified areas became so in 1985. South African Railways displayed characteristic conservatism by desegregating only a small proportion of coaches on its trains during 1985.

Less publicised overseas but of vital importance in the medium term is the government's commitment to create equal educational standards and opportunities for all races. In pursuance of this objective the government is implementing space and cost norms for physical facilities which will apply equally to all schools together with equal conditions of service for teachers of all race groups. Private schools are to receive greater government subsidies which will give more parents the choice of racially integrated education for their children, but will by the same token increase the removal of black middle-class children from the state system. Educational expenditure has increased from 2.9 per cent of GNP in 1979 to 4.6 per cent in 1984, when it reached R4695 million or 16 per cent of the national budget (South African Foundation 1985, 9–10). Expenditure on non-formal education, including adult education and training by the private and public sectors, has increased fivefold to more than R4000 million in the same period (ibid., 9). Given the resources required and the shortage of qualified teachers it is clear that equality must be a long-term objective in the absence of racial integration of schools and a downgrading of white educational standards. To narrow the racial gap in per capita educational expenditure, whites will increasingly have to pay for schooling and related activities; school fees became compulsory in 1986. At university level the racial quota system was ended early in 1986.

Despite these changes boycotts of schools and universities have been widespread in the mid-1980s, and it is clear that the educational system will remain a focus of dissatisfaction and unrest among blacks and coloureds until education is administered through a single system as recommended by the De Lange Commission. The government has at least agreed that a single department be responsible for macro-policy and a multi-racial educational Council has been appointed to advise this department; committees of Education Ministers and Heads of Education Departments also meet to coordinate policy. However positive the intentions behind them, these characteristically bureaucratic measures will do little to appease black dissatisfaction.

The National Party as an instrument of change

By the late 1970s it was clear to most members of the South African government that existing policies, because of the resentment and resistance they caused, had become a source of political instability. It was apparent that Verwoerdian apartheid ideals were increasingly at odds with demographic and economic realities. The rapid economic growth of the 1960s and 1970s had demanded increasing black urbanisation and occupational mobility which were at odds with the perpetuation of job reservation and a rigid influx control system, and which accentuated the unreality of channelling all black political expression through the homelands. Black consumer power also grew substantially as the African share of national wealth rose from 26 per cent in 1970 to 40 per cent in 1980.

Faced with these realities, Mr Botha's government has unquestionably taken the reform processes much further than any of its predecessors. Nevertheless the reforms are collectively incremental rather than fundamental. Many of them are arguably intended to protect white hegemony (Schlemmer 1983, 287), including policies aimed to incorporate or coopt coloureds, Indians and middle-class blacks into positions of privilege closer to that of whites. This was clearly the intention of the new constitution and it underlies many actual and projected changes in urban policies. The latter also serve the interests of capital, as does the ending of job reservation and the gradual equalisation of educational opportunities. Other reforms such as the dismantling of 'petty' apartheid are essentially cosmetic, having only superficial effects on the lives of blacks, whilst the forms they take often serve to underline just how much of the apartheid structure remains intact. Foremost in this category is the Group Areas Act, of which Mr Botha has emerged as an uncompromising defender, to the dismay of more reformist members of the Nationalist parliamentary caucus.

Even the legalisation of the independent black trade union movement was undoubtedly intended to impose a degree of control on a process which the government was unable to prevent altogether, although legalisation has facilitated the mobilisation of the black working class and increased its bargaining power. With the potential exception of trade unions, however, none of the reforms noted above has significantly increased black political power, which leaves the central contradiction between economic participation and political exclusion unresolved. This issue is at the heart of black political protest and it became unmistakably clear during 1985 that no amount of incremental reform would satisfy black aspirations even in the short term.

Such reform is, indeed, one of the causes of black unrest. The implementation of piecemeal reforms, many of them reversing previously applied policies, opens a Pandora's box of other possibilities and actually serves to increase black awareness of injustice and inequality. Lacking the clear sense of direction evinced by its predecessors in the Verwoerdian era, the government is perceived to be vaccillating and vulnerable. In this sense Mr Botha is regarded by some as getting the worst of all worlds, reforming faster and more significantly than his predecessors yet increasing black dissatisfaction and resistance in the process. It is now widely believed by those close to government thinking that Mr Botha and his colleagues are influenced by a Harvard professor's model of 'Reform and stability in a modernizing, multi-ethnic society' (Huntington 1981).

Huntington recognises that the days of minority-dominated hierarchical multi-ethnic societies are numbered. He sees a political solution based on the existing racial structure of South Africa, allowing all four racial communities to play 'appropriate roles', as the least difficult of the possible alternatives, involving fundamental but not revolutionary change. Such a policy would necessarily have to function largely through the institutional devices of consociational democracy or, as Huntington prefers to call it, 'consociational oligarchy'. For such institutions to take root in a hierarchical multi-ethnic system will, however, 'necessarily involve a unique and extraordinarily difficult effort at reform' (p. 14). Highly talented political leadership is needed to fight simultaneously against conservatives and revolutionaries. This demands 'a combination of Fabian strategy and blitzkrieg tactics' (p. 17), similar to that employed by Mustafa Kemal in converting the Ottoman Empire to the Turkish Republic, and more recently by President Geisel of Brazil. Reforms are disaggregated and individually proposed over a sustained period of time, the government minimising the significance of each reform and implying that it is the last. The success of each reform is also ensured by drafting it in relative secrecy, revealing it to a small group of political leaders whose support is essential, dramatically unveiling it at the appropriate moment, and enacting it before its opponents can mobilise effectively against it. Reforms must, Huntington argues, be granted from a position of strength; if they appear to result from the pressure of events and the demands of radical groups, as in the case of the Shah's reforms in Iran in the 1960s, they can only further weaken the regime. Some centralisation of power may be necessary for the government to maintain the control over violence that is essential to carry through major reforms. Within limits, reform and repression may proceed together: 'Effective repression may enhance the appeal of reform to radicals by increasing the costs and risks of revolution and to stand-patters [conservatives] by reassuring them of the government's ability to maintain order' (p. 20).

The actual process of reform, according to Huntington, is usually 'tedious, inconsistent, and most unsatisfactory for almost everyone involved' (p. 21). New institutions must be legitimated in terms of old values, and progress will often consist of 'sliding two steps forward and dodging one step backward' (p. 24). The reform process may also demand 'substantial elements of duplicity, deceit, faulty assumptions, and purposeful blindness' (p. 21). Its ultimate success will depend upon the ability of the leadership to create one or more coalitions with sufficient political strength to ensure the enactment and implementation of reform.

Huntington's model certainly bears striking resemblance to the behaviour of the Botha government, with the exception of the years 1978–79 when the necessity of reform was more openly proclaimed in 'adapt or die' terms which led to a serious erosion of Afrikaner support in the 1981 General Election (Chapter 5). Since then the government has pursued precisely the combination of Fabian strategy and blitzkrieg tactics described by Huntington, leading to predictable dissatisfaction and frustration on all sides. Increased centralisation is reflected in the increased role of the State Security Council and, since Huntington wrote, in the concentration of power in the hands of an executive President and certain aspects of local government reform including the abolition of elected provincial councils (Chapter 14). The government has long shown awareness of the dangers of giving ground when under pressure, and its refusal to change either the pace or the course of reform in the face of unprecedented internal unrest and international pressure in the mid-1980s is consistent with this approach.

At the same time the government clearly recognises the need to mould a coalition or coalitions in support of reform, and it has sought to persuade or coopt all the groups suggested by Huntington (p. 23) as potential elements of such coalitions: key sections of the National Party hierarchy, the Afrikaner bourgeoisie, the English-speaking business and professional establishment, some elements in the civil service, the military establishment, leaders of the coloured and Asian communities, urban middle-class blacks, traditional black leaders, and, externally, the governments of the United States and the United Kingdom.

The government's success to date is mixed. The opposition of the Reagan and Thatcher governments to comprehensive mandatory sanctions may indicate a degree of understanding and acceptance on their part of Pretoria's strategy, although other motives are present and both governments desire an acceleration of the reform process (Chapter 18). Within South Africa, most of the white groups mentioned above are broadly behind the reform process, but some are publicly urging a faster, more open approach. Thus Denis Venter (1985), of the African Institute in Pretoria, urges the government to make a declaration of intent defining the goals and ideals that are foreseen, and containing as many elements as possible of the policy programmes of black political movements. Venter sees such a declaration as an essential prerequisite for the legitimation of a negotiating forum or national convention, arguing that the longer genuine negotiation is delayed 'the more it will appear that the government is not initiating a defined reform strategy but responding with *ad hoc* concessions to the violence itself' (ibid., p. 5). Venter's fears are confirmed by media interpretation of reforms announced during the mid-1980s unrest; although most if not all were planned prior to the escalation of violence, they have been widely perceived overseas as a response to it.

Much of the business community also wants accelerated reform and negotiation. It was thoroughly alarmed by the decline in the value of the rand which followed Mr Botha's anti-climactic speech to the National Party congress in Durban in August 1985, and even more so by the subsequent refusal of American banks to reschedule South Africa's short-term loans and Pretoria's suspension of repayments of principal which followed, further damaging the rand. The following weeks witnessed a meeting of South African business leaders with ANC officials in Lusaka which was condemned by Mr Botha. In September 1985 92 executives of major South African corporations called for the negotiation of power-sharing with 'acknowledged' black leaders.[4] The following month, the Congress of the Associated Chambers of Commerce (ASSOCOM) called for the 'urgent' repeal of all discriminatory legislation and asked Mr Botha to drop all preconditions to negotiation, including the demand that black leaders or organisations should renounce violence before he will speak to them.[5] During this period meetings with the ANC became almost fashionable. PFP leaders as well as businessmen held talks in Lusaka, and in October student leaders at the Afrikaans university of Stellenbosch announced their intention of meeting the ANC Youth League. They were prevented from doing so by the withdrawal of their passports, which was criticised even in the Afrikaans press. In the same month a group of ministers from the NGK and its sister churches withdrew their plans to meet the ANC after discussion with government officials.

Given such problems with its natural supporters, it is hardly surprising that the government has enjoyed little success in coopting non-white groups. Analysis of the 1984 elections (Chapter 13) has already shown the refusal of most coloureds and Indians to be coopted, whilst continued unrest in black townships and widespread rejection by blacks of local government structures offers little sign of middle-class black cooperation. Even moderate black leaders, led by Chief Buthelezi, demand a clear statement of intended progress towards minimally acceptable goals before agreeing to participate in the government's proposed national forum. In Huntington's terms, such setbacks need not be regarded as fatal to the official strategy, since he emphasises the long-drawn-out nature of the reform process. Others will, inevitably, question whether the government has such time available, especially given the speed with which events on both the domestic and international fronts began to move from 1984 onwards. The outside world has always tended to underestimate the time available to Pretoria; the clock has long been 'stuck at five minutes to midnight' (Johnson 1977, 288), but is the minute hand finally moving?

The politics of compromise: Chief Buthelezi and Inkatha

Inkatha yeNkululeko yeSiswe – the 'National Cultural Liberation Movement' – was originally formed by the Zulu king, Dinizulu in 1928. Chief Mangosuthu Gatsha Buthelezi revived the movement and in 1975 reshaped its goals so that it became a far more politically-oriented mobilisation organisation. Its colours, songs and slogans are those of the ANC, in whose ideals Inkatha is rooted, according to Chief Buthelezi who is a former member of the ANC himself. As the governing party of KwaZulu, Inkatha has had to contend with minimal open opposition, despite the rejection in 1974 by the South African government of a request from the KwaZulu Legislative Assembly for powers to control opposition parties. Inkatha's aims include the promotion of cultural liberation, self-reliant community development and black educational advance, the abolition of racial discrimination, and above all the full incorporation of blacks in political decision-making (Schlemmer 1980, 111). Majority rule is the clear goal, preferably in a unitary state, but neither federation nor some form of consociationalism have been ruled out: Inkatha's acceptance of the Buthelezi Commission proposals for Natal-KwaZulu has already been noted (Chapter 16).

With over a million members, mainly but not exclusively Zulus, Inkatha is the largest black political organisation in South African history. By 1982 it had 1200 branches, the majority in rural KwaZulu but many also in urban areas, those outside Natal being found especially in areas with a strong Zulu presence such as Soweto which alone had 30 branches (Kane-Berman 1982, 155). Inkatha is compromised as a national political force by its role as the governing party of KwaZulu which forces it to manipulate a Zulu ethnic base (Brewer 1985, 131). Radicals see it as an ethnically divisive and collaborationist organisation: Southall (1981, 457; 1983, 112) regards it as a petty bourgeois organisation whose populist membership transcends class divisions in order to cloak its petty bourgeois nature, which is revealed by its support of private enterprise and inter-ethnic power-sharing. In contrast, Schlemmer (1980) concludes that Inkatha members are not primarily ethnocentric in their attitudes, and that the wide range of occupational groups from which they are drawn ensures that Inkatha is not narrowly class-based but has a broad socio-political platform. Brewer (1985), in a survey of urban Inkatha members in KwaMashu (Durban), found Schlemmer's view to be more in accord with the empirical evidence. Inkatha was quite successful in mobilising all socio-economic classes in KwaMashu, and particularly among non-migrant workers. Its members shared a high degree of political sophistication and were motivated by policy considerations rather than traditional support for Chief Buthelezi. They rejected Zulu ethnicity as having a political role, favoured power-sharing between blacks and other ethnic groups, and were over-whelmingly opposed to political violence. Different results might have been obtained in a survey of rural members, and Brewer stresses that Inkatha is a coalition of members with diverse social backgrounds, interests, attitudes and aspirations (and thus potential for internal policy conflicts). This is undoubtedly true, but in the broader political context Schlemmer (1980, 121) is probably correct in suggesting that a strong Zulu pride does not so much clash with as add fuel to a wider African nationalism.

Chief Buthelezi himself is remarkable as a Zulu aristocrat with traditional legitimacy who acts through government institutions and has yet won strong populist support. He has done so with a skilful blend of principle and pragmatism which enables him to make clear his total rejection of apartheid and insistence on majority rule, yet to leave open the door to negotiated solutions which could find sufficient acceptance among whites. His total rejection of independence for KwaZulu has been a major stumbling-block to Pretoria's implementation of the apartheid grand design, but he is prepared to countenance power-sharing in Natal–KwaZulu, given a government declaration of intent on the broader political front. He has consistently opposed both violence and economic sanctions as means of resolving South Africa's problems.

A 1977 survey of black opinion in Soweto, Pretoria and Durban revealed that Chief Buthelezi had more support than any other black political leader including Nelson Mandela, with some 44 per cent naming him as the political figure they most admired (Hanf *et al.* 1981, 352–61). His support did not fall below 20 per cent in any black ethnic group, and was only slightly below average among middle-class blacks (ibid., 355–7). However, Southall (1981) chronicles the waning of Chief Buthelezi's popularity, beginning with his ambivalent role at the time of the 1976 Soweto riots. After being forced by an angry crowd to leave the funeral of Robert Sobukwe in 1977, Buthelezi sought to counter the claims of the black consciousness movement, which had become very influential among educated urban blacks by the time of its banning in

October 1977. He created the South African Black Alliance (SABA) between Inkatha, the (coloured) Labour Party and (Indian) Reform Party. It was subsequently joined by the Chief Ministers of QwaQwa and KaNgwane, but with the departure of the Labour Party following its decision to participate in the new constitution (Chapter 13), SABA lost any claim to be a major political force. With the announcement in October 1985 of talks between Mr Enos Mabuza, Chief Minister of KaNgwane, and the ANC, Chief Buthelezi appeared increasingly isolated.

In the late 1970s, however, he tried increasingly to identify Inkatha with the ANC, recognising the likely revival of the latter's active support within South Africa. In November 1979 he actually had talks with the ANC leadership in London, but antagonised the latter by subsequent attempts to make capital out of what the ANC had viewed as a private dialogue. A year later it repudiated Chief Buthelezi in uncompromising terms. Surveys conducted in Soweto during 1980 showed far higher support for Dr Ntatho Motlana and his Soweto Committee of Ten, an unofficial body formed to run urban affairs after the collapse of the Soweto Urban Bantu Council in 1977, than for Buthelezi; even a slight majority of Zulus preferred Motlana. Southall (1981) saw Buthelezi as increasingly alienated from the country's black youth and predicted that Inkatha's power-base had begun to crumble as Buthelezi moved towards more open negotiation and collaboration with the government.

In the 1980s Buthelezi has diminished his stature by his authoritarian behaviour in KwaZulu itself, where political opposition is ruthlessly treated and coercion is used on some, such as teachers, to join Inkatha. There have been violent clashes between Inkatha and United Democratic Front (UDF) supporters, especially in Durban, and the battle of words between Chief Buthelezi on the one hand, and the UDF and ANC on the other, has intensified. Buthelezi's stature among whites, increasing numbers of whom see him as the best hope of peaceful change, has led to an analogy with Bishop Muzorewa, the Zimbabwe/ Rhodesian leader who lost the pre-independence election of February 1980 because he had become too closely identified with white power. It is indeed difficult to see Chief Buthelezi ever becoming the accepted leader of all black South Africans, but unlike Bishop Muzorewa he does have a genuine power-base in Natal where Inkatha's membership continues to grow. His position as the one moderate black leader with a major, identifiable support base makes him indispensable to the government's reform strategy. Given the regional nature of his power-base, this implies eventual government acceptance of the Natal–KwaZulu option, seen by Southall (1983) as divisive but conceivably the first block in a wider federal–consociational structure.

The political significance of trade unions

The legalisation of black trade unions which formed part of the restructuring of labour relations in the wake of the 1979 Wiehahn Report is regarded by many as the most significant reform to date. The Industrial Conciliation Amendment Act (1979) established a National Manpower Commission (NMC) to make investigations into and recommendations to the Minister concerning all labour matters, and an Industrial Court to hear disputes arising out of labour laws, or disputes between two parties regarding their interests or rights. The Act established a system of prior regulation for newly constituted unions. Statutory union rights were extended to Africans living in the Republic excluding the self-governing and 'independent' homelands, but shortly afterwards the same rights were extended to homeland residents: this concession, a response to widespread criticism, widened the spectrum of unions prepared to register. The Act specifically prohibits the existence of racially mixed trade unions, but allows ministerial exception in certain circumstances.

An important purpose of this legislation was undoubtedly the extension of control over a growing black union movement which had already achieved substantial *de facto* recognition by employers. This object is reflected, *inter alia*, in the system of provisional registration and the requirements for it, and in both NMC surveillance of the election of office bearers and inspection of union financial affairs. None the less the reform has established the first legal channel for democratically elected black leaders to negotiate directly with the white economic power structure. Since 1979 overall registered union membership has risen from 808,000 to 1,400,000, or some 13 per cent of the economically active population. Membership of unregistered unions is more difficult to quantify, but was estimated at 400,000 in 1983.[6] An emergent trade union movement organising mainly for African workers has presented a major challenge to the established unions which have traditionally sought to consolidate the position of their white, coloured and Indian workers at the expense of blacks (Cooper, c.1983).

Membership of the conservative, all-white South African Confederation of Labour (SACLA) declined from 240,000 in 1980 to 124,000 in 1984, mainly as a result of the disaffiliation of several unions in 1981.[7] Of those which remain, the two major ones, South African Iron and Steel and the Mine Workers Union, have responded differently to the new dispensation, the former proving more pragmatic. Most traditional unions belong to the Trade Union Council of South Africa (TUCSA), and welcomed the Wiehahn reforms. Many applied for an extension of their scope of registration to include Africans or set up parallel unions, and by September 1983 some 29 per cent of their members (139, 567) were black (Webster 1984, 84). As a result the number of all-white unions decreased from 71 in 1982 to 54 in 1983. Most TUCSA affiliates see the emerging unions as rivals who are 'poaching' their members; their defence of the closed shop is central to their struggle with the emerging unions. Most of the latter belong to either the Council of Unions in South Africa (CUSA) or the Federation of South African Trade Unions (FOSATU). The former claimed 249,000 signed-up members in October 1984, and the latter 106,000 in 1983.[8] CUSA is more black consciousness-oriented and reserves leadership posts for blacks, whereas FOSATU is non-racial. Both have taken up clear political positions, however, opposing the new constitution and supporting the November 1984 'stay-away' in the southern Transvaal (see below). A third group of black 'emergent' unions is the Azanian Confederation of Trade Unions (AZACTU), which is a recently formed federation of six unions committed to the black consciousness philosophy, with a combined membership of 75,000 in 1984.

There are several obstacles to greater unity amongst the emerging trade unions. Issues of principle often appear to reflect leadership conflict rather than the genuine expression of members' feelings (Hindson 1984, 97). At a series of unity meetings extending over four years, the only principle accepted by all unions was worker control, and even this was defined by CUSA as black worker control (ibid., 99). A major line of division emerged, largely in terms of different methods of organising workers, between unions organising in specific industries and general unions. The latter are regionally based which aids organisation and makes their offices more accessible, but they have found it more difficult than industrial unions to develop strong shop-floor structures and branch executives (ibid., 99–100).

Many of the general unions, including the South African Allied Workers Union and the General and Allied Workers Union, finally joined FOSATU in a new federation, the Congress of South African Trade Unions (COSATU), in December 1985. This brought together 34 unions with 450,000 paid-up members, with the aim of providing a new focus for the wider political aspirations of black workers. It aims to reorganise its workers on a one-union, one-industry basis. Given its overtly political ambitions, the formation of COSATU is arguably the most significant event in black politics since the formation of the UDF in August 1983. COSATU's choice of Durban for its headquarters is a deliberate challenge to the power of Chief Buthelezi. The COSATU President has called for the nationalisation of mines and major industries, declared COSATU's support for the foreign disinvestment movement, and promised to lead a new pass-burning campaign if the government did not abolish the pass laws within six months.[9] Despite this militant stance, however, CUSA and AZACTU remain outside COSATU because of its commitment to non-racialism; the black union movement thus remains split along lines which mirror the division between the ANC and the Pan African Congress (PAC). COSATU nevertheless includes workers in all key areas of the economy and wields considerable industrial muscle.

By January 1985 18 black unions had affiliated to the UDF. Others have not done so because they see the task of creating an independent workers movement as ruling out affiliation to a single political organisation, and because they do not wish to create division among their members, some of whom support AZAPO or Inkatha rather than the UDF. However, this does not prevent cooperation between the UDF and non-affiliated unions, which took place during the Indian and coloured elections in 1984, and later the same year in the staging of a two-day work stay-away in the southern Transvaal in protest against military and police raids on Sebokeng and other Vaal Triangle townships. On this occasion several hundred thousand black workers stayed at home in support of demands which included the release of all detainees and the abandonment of increases in rents, service charges and bus fares.

Despite such an impressive display of unity and discipline, the general secretary of CUSA, Mr Phiroshaw Camay, is probably correct in saying that 'too much has been made of the political implications of union power'.[10] He went on to say that power comes from the membership, not the leadership, and that before unions could wield real political power they had to show the ability to 'deliver on economic issues'. Unions are not themselves vehicles for revolution, but they can play an important role in destabilising the current order and preparing the stage for fundamental change, whether revolutionary or otherwise.

Black consciousness, AZAPO and the National Forum

Black consciousness has been described as an attempt by black people to create something positive out of a negative situation.[11] It aims to create a sense of pride instead of passivity which results from the sense of psychological inferiority induced by apartheid, so that blacks will affirm themselves. Of the organisations adopting this philosophy, the most important were the South African Students Organisation (SASO), formed in 1969, and the Black People's Convention (BPC), established in 1972. In October 1977, a month after the death of Mr Steve Biko, the BPC President, most black consciousness organisations including the BPC and SASO were banned. The gap was filled by the Azanian People's Organisation (AZAPO) which was formed in April 1978 and placed itself unequivocally in the black consciousness camp with its motto 'One people, one Azania'. Despite the detention of most of its national and local leadership shortly afterwards, AZAPO resurfaced in 1979, electing a new executive dominated by Sowetans (Lodge 1983, 344). Within South Africa AZAPO is the major upholder of the political tradition represented externally by the PAC.

AZAPO conceives its role as more than generating black awareness: it seeks the political involvement of black workers in a class struggle. White workers were seen as having defected to the capitalists, whilst the black petty bourgeoisie was seen as providing leadership from its ranks for the liberation struggle. Despite its stated strategy, AZAPO's activities have not involved the mobilisation of workers as such, partly because its officials tend to be contemptuous of negotiated reforms involving bread-and-butter issues which no trade union, however politically radical, can afford to dismiss (ibid., p. 346).

AZAPO was strengthened in December 1982 when several black consciousness leaders were released from prison on Robben Island (Barrell 1984, 11). Prominent among them was Mr Saths Cooper, who was elected AZAPO Vice-President soon after his release and subsequently convened the National Forum. The latter is not a formal organisation but a mechanism for consultation between existing organisations. AZAPO is its driving force and the intention of the first National Forum in June 1983 was to broaden AZAPO's base as the vanguard of the 200 organisations attending. In this it was not wholly successful; representatives of many organisations present disassociated themselves from the manifesto presented to the forum which demanded the 'establishment of a democratic, anti-racist workers' Republic in Azania'.

AZAPO is highly critical of the UDF, alleging that it has revived ethnically-based structures (such as the Transvaal Indian Congress), has no long-term programme, and is essentially reactive to events. Hostility between the two organisations has fuelled township unrest since mid-1985, particularly in the eastern Cape where it has been responsible for a number of black deaths. In most areas, however, the popular following of AZAPO is limited. Although influential within the black intelligentsia, it does not present a formidable political challenge to the state.

The United Democratic Front
The UDF is a non-racial body launched in July 1983 in response to a call from Dr Allan Boesak, President of the World Alliance of Reformed Churches, when addressing the Transvaal Anti-South African Indian Council Committee six months earlier. By late 1983 the UDF had some 100 affiliated bodies, mostly in coloured areas, but it grew rapidly in 1984 and claimed some 650 affiliates with a combined membership of over 2 million at the time of the Indian and coloured elections. The UDF adopts a broad, inclusive approach, albeit tempered by a declared commitment to the primacy of the working class in the national democratic struggle (Barrell, 1984, 13). Despite the latter, overtures by UDF activists failed to attract AZAPO. In contrast Chief Buthelezi initially welcomed plans for the UDF but Inkatha was excluded from affiliation and by the end of 1983 the two organisations were bitterly hostile to one another, with Buthelezi even claiming that the UDF planned to have him killed.

The UDF campaign against the constitution (opposition to which was its initial *raison d'être*) was a major factor in the low coloured and Indian polls recorded in August 1984 (Chapter 13). Much less impressive was a million-signature campaign to demonstrate opposition to apartheid which was launched by the UDF in January 1983, but had reached only 400,000 signatures by October; the UDF blamed police harassment of its supporters for the shortfall. Intimidation of the UDF reached new levels on the eve of the Indian elections in August 1984, with the arrest of 14 UDF leaders, including one of the organisation's presidents, Mr Archie Gumede, and its publicity secretary, Mr Patrick Lekota. Since then some have been released and others arrested; a treason trial of 16 UDF leaders began in Pietermaritzburg in May 1985.

The government regards the UDF and some of its affiliates as being directly or indirectly responsible for the persistent unrest in black urban areas which began in the Vaal Triangle at the end of August 1984, and of preparing for a revolutionary climate. These accusations were first voiced in October 1984 by the Minister of Law and Order, Mr Louis le Grange, who subsequently described the UDF as a 'revolutionary organisation involved in the same revolutionary work' as the banned ANC and South African Communist Party.[12] The UDF denied any links with the ANC and disclaimed responsibility for violence and unrest in the black townships: it could hardly afford to do otherwise. During 1985, however, it became increasingly apparent that the UDF had indeed developed close links with the ANC, and was assisting the latter's stated objective of making the townships ungovernable. It is also clear that a crucial role was played by the Congress of South African Students (COSAS), a UDF affiliate which was later banned, in terms of both formulation of ideology and nationwide organisation. In the eastern Cape, for instance, groups of black school children and students moved from one area to another helping the UDF to organise support among youth, women's organisations, and within township communities generally.

Black township violence and the state of emergency
Violence in black townships continues and a state of emergency remained in operation in 30 magisterial districts at the beginning of 1986. The unrest was widespread and the immediate catalysts many and varied, albeit with recurring themes. Only some of the major incidents and most troubled areas can be mentioned in the brief account which follows.

In early September 1984, immediately after the coloured and Indian elections which were themselves marked by considerable violence, unrest broke out in several black townships in the Transvaal, especially those of the Vaal Triangle, an industrial area south of Johannesburg which included the townships of Sebokeng, Sharpeville, Evaton and Bophelong. The immediate causes were recently announced rent increases (which were subsequently withdrawn) and higher transport costs. In addition a boycott of schools by black pupils was under way to protest at the inferior quality of black education. Black town councillors elected in the face of a popular boycott of the polls in December 1983 were blamed for the proposed rent increases and became the target of violence. This was a pattern to be repeated in many places; the number of councillors actually killed has been small but many have had their homes destroyed; by July 1985 at least 250 councillors across the country were known to have resigned and there was a widespread breakdown of black local government.

The authorities imposed a weekend ban on meetings in the Johannesburg area on 8–9 September 1984, the seventh anniversary of Steve Biko's death. This was widely ignored, and the funerals of several people killed in riots in the Vaal Triangle townships became expressions of protest, which was to be another recurring theme in the unrest. School boycotts continued despite the announcement of reforms in black education, including the election of class leaders and student representative councils. In the face of continuing unrest the deployment of the South African Defence Force (SADF) in a supportive role to the police began in October. Some 7000 troops surrounded Sebokeng and conducted house-to-house searches. Eventually the atmosphere in the Vaal Triangle simmered down, but unrest spread to the East Rand, parts of the Orange Free State and the eastern Cape.

In the early months of 1985 the eastern Cape was the region most affected by violence. Here school children staged a prolonged boycott of classes in protest against the detention of COSAS leaders, whilst the effects of economic recession were causing increased hardship amongst black workers, especially in the motor industry. In the eastern Cape the violence was not confined to major urban areas; tiny *platteland dorps* such as Graaff-Reinet, Colesberg, Cradock, Balfour, Jansenville, Hankey and Albany all became flashpoints. On 21 March, the 25th anniversary of the Sharpeville massacre, police opened fire killing 20 people in a procession of mourners on their way from Langa township to the funerals of six unrest victims in Kwanobuhle township near Uitenhage. This incident provoked widespread outrage both domestically and internationally, and a subsequent official report, whilst not actually blaming the police, was highly embarrassing to them. Continuing violence in other areas included eight deaths from a series of hand-grenade explosions in the East Rand townships of Tsakane, Duduza and Kwathema on 26 June 1985; more deaths followed in subsequent funerals and a police raid on Duduza in early July. Victims ranged from those killed by the police to local authority officials, black policemen, informers (suspected or actual) and 'sell-outs'. In mid-July an upsurge of violence occurred in Soweto, hitherto relatively quiet although the location of a virtually total school boycott. Also in mid-July a boycott of all non-black shops was organised by the UDF and black civic organisations in the eastern Cape in protest at the disappearance of community leaders and at the failure of the authorities to arrest anyone for the death of four Cradock community representatives in early July. This lasted until at least November in most areas and was resumed in several places after a brief suspension; it occasioned further violence against blacks discovered shopping in white areas where goods are cheaper and shops stock many items unavailable in small township stores.

For reasons already mentioned, Natal's black townships experienced relatively little violence (Chapter 16). On 7 August 1985, however, violence spilled over from black areas near Durban to neighbouring Indian residential areas of Inanda and lasted several days, causing over 50 deaths and hundreds of injuries. It appeared, however, that this incident was largely divorced from violence elsewhere in the country in terms of its causes. The same is true of violence between Zulus and Pondos near Durban in 1985 and early 1986 which caused many deaths.

On 21 July 1985 a state of emergency came into operation in 36 magisterial districts in the East Rand and the eastern Cape (Figure 17.1). This gave the police even more sweeping powers of arrest and detention than they have under permanent security legislation, and also gave both police and army immunity against prosecution for any action taken 'in good faith'. They took full advantage of these powers, arresting 1399 people in the first two weeks of the emergency; by the end of October emergency arrests had reached 5119, of whom 3063 had been released. The state of emergency was lifted in eight districts on 25 October, but a new one imposed in eight districts of the western Cape, the latest major trouble spot, the following day. In Cape Town and environs unrest affected black and coloured areas alike, and violence even spread to the fringes of neighbouring white suburbs for the first time; for a brief period the main road from central Cape Town to the city's D.F. Malan Airport became potentially unsafe.

The state of emergency was lifted in eight more districts of the East Rand and eastern Cape in early December, but continued into 1986 in eight eastern Cape districts, fourteen in the East Rand, and all eight in the western Cape (Figure 17.1). The necessity for the state of emergency was questioned from its initial imposition, given the extensive powers already enjoyed by the police; a major motive may well have been to reassure whites of the government's determination to restore order on its own terms. In the country as a whole the daily death toll increased from an average of 1.4 in 1985 prior to the imposition of the state of emergency to an average of 3.4 between 21 July and 5 November, by which time 834 people had died since the unrest began on 3 September 1984.[13] Although the state of emergency may have helped to restore uneasy calm in certain areas, the underlying national trend remained

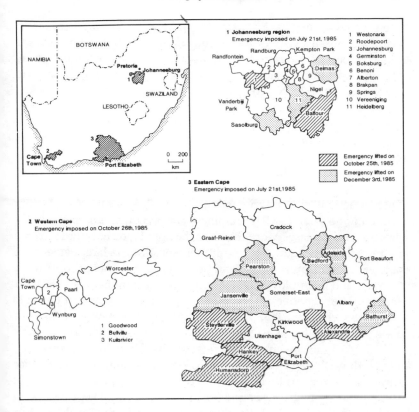

Fig. 17.1   The State of Emergency, 1985

one of increasing unrest in early 1986. The final lifting of the State of Emergency in March 1986 appeared to be more closely related to concern about South Africa's external image, as attempts were made to reschedule short-term loans (Chapter 18), than to a changed internal situation.

Much has been said and written about the underlying causes of unrest. Some, including the government, blame the UDF and its affiliates. They see violence as following 'the established pattern of provocation of the authority of the police and of the state in the knowledge that order will have to be preserved at all costs. The police are therefore manoeuvred into a position of either over-reacting or under-reacting. Either response suits the aims of the agitators'.[14] There is some truth in such analyses,

341

but to succeed as they have agitators must be operating in a very fertile climate. The insensitivity of a new constitution which totally excluded blacks was an important catalyst, adding to the frustration of all politically aware urban blacks. Incremental reforms probably do more to raise expectations than to satisfy aspirations. Blacks suffer from a lack of real political representation at all levels; even at the local level, where many who serve on community and town councils are serious, even courageous in battling to produce results, they are nevertheless seen as 'collaborators' who work within an ethnically structured system with little or no redistribution of resources, and who are to blame for unpopular measures such as evictions and rent increases.

Dissatisfaction with inferior education facilities, an unsatisfactory curriculum and poor teacher training make the organisation of school boycotts relatively easy. More than half the population of South Africa's black townships is under 18 years old; this constitutes a large category of people with few responsibilities and little to lose. School boycotts, work stay-aways and unemployment together put large numbers of people on the streets. The economic recession caused black unemployment to rise to 25–30 per cent by late 1985, by which time total unemployment (most of it black) was rising by an estimated 100,000 per month. Unemployment for urban blacks means more than financial hardship; in the words of a *Sowetan* editorial: 'Very soon the unemployed have to face those regular pass raids, and woe betide the man who is not employed for some time.'[15]

Even for many blacks in employment wages have not kept pace with the high inflation South Africa has experienced in the 1980s, and in times of economic depression the stings of petty apartheid are felt even more keenly. As both economic and political expectations have risen, there is a growing sense of relative deprivation. As Nthato Motlana asks, having described living conditions in Duduza on the East Rand, 'How can white South Africans hope to live in peace in the midst of such deprivation, living as they do in prosperity to which blacks have contributed?'[16]

The long-term significance of previous unrest in South Africa has often been exaggerated. That of the mid-1980s is, however, of a different order from Sharpeville or Soweto. It is widespread, deep-seated and gives every sign of continuing indefinitely. It is unlikely to be continuous in any one area, given the strains and costs to the protestors themselves of continuous unrest; rather it is likely to wax and wane, but on a gradually rising plane. In itself such unrest does not pose a major threat to the state. It has induced the government to announce in October 1985 an increase in the size of the police force from 45,000 to 56,000, but it will remain small by European standards. The scale of violence has also led to the use of the SADF to back up the police. Yet the state has, as Mr Botha has not hesitated to remark, much power in reserve. It is in the wider repercussions of unrest that its significance lies. First, it has greatly increased political awareness of blacks throughout the country, even in rural areas, and aroused their expectations of reform as never before. Secondly, the standing of the ANC has grown considerably. Thirdly, the unrest has influenced the business community and white élites generally (see above) resulting in pressure for change from some unexpected quarters. At a regional level consumer boycotts have not achieved most of their stated aims but they have, especially in the eastern Cape, made business interests anxious for change. Finally, the unrest has greatly intensified international concern over South Africa, leading to increased pressures from both governments and private capital (Chapter 18). Inside the country there is an unprecedented climate of expectation, shared to some degree by all races, that change must now come. Young blacks may be unrealistic in expecting it to be both fundamental and imminent, but many whites too have dramatically compressed their time-scales of reform.

18
External factors

The geography of dependence in southern Africa

When the Portuguese revolution of 1974 led rapidly to the independence of Angola and Mozambique, a major portion of South Africa's *cordon sanitaire* was replaced by hostile governments which rapidly developed close links with the Eastern bloc and Cuba. The victory of Robert Mugabe's ZANU (PF) in the Zimbabwe independence elections of 1980 was a shock to Pretoria and brought South Africa another Marxist neighbour, at least in terms of rhetoric, albeit one less friendly towards the Soviet Union. But these dramatic changes, whilst heightening super-power interest in southern Africa, have done little to change the basic geography of dependence in the region.

South Africa may be described as a 'semi-peripheral' state or developing secondary core in the world economy, in terms of which she has a subordinate relationship with the major industrial countries but a superordinate relationship with her peripheral Third World neighbours. In Marxian terms, South Africa belongs to the group of 'sub-imperial' states 'which simultaneously are exploited by the core and exploit the periphery' (Samoff 1978, 496). The world economic system offers peripheral Third World countries only limited opportunities to advance (Wallerstein 1974); ultimately they must choose between strategies of 'dependent development' and 'revolutionary transformation' (Rogerson 1979). In southern Africa dependent development is the path chosen by Botswana, Lesotho and Swaziland (BLS), which belong to a customs union with South Africa, and by Malawi, whilst the 'TVBC countries' have little option but to pursue this strategy. Revolutionary transformation is the choice of Angola and Mozambique, although neither has yet managed significantly to reduce its dependence on the world economic system (and in the case of Mozambique, on South Africa). A SWAPO government in Namibia would probably opt for revolutionary transformation too, although it would face major problems in realising such a strategy given the extent and nature of its dependence on South Africa and the character of its economy (Thomas 1981b). Zambia and Zimbabwe fall somewhere between the two strategies, constrained to a greater extent than Angola and Mozambique by inherited structures from following a truly radical path.

Present patterns of dependence in southern Africa revolve around four major elements: migrant labour, communications, food and industrialisation (Lemon 1986). In 1984 some 350,000 foreign migrants worked legally in South Africa, including 139,000 from Lesotho and 60,000 from Mozambique. In addition, South Africa estimates that there are 1.2 million foreign blacks working illegally in South Africa, many of whom remit funds and support families in their countries of origin (South Africa 1985b, 4). Dependency arising from such labour migration is essentially one-way. Where migration has declined, as in Mozambique, there is little evidence that the supplier states are responsible. It arises rather from the Chamber of Mines policy of reducing the foreign component of its labour force (Chapter 7), together with growing black unemployment in South Africa, whose government recently threatened 'to give preference to the needs of its own citizens' if employment opportunities were to be further reduced by international sanctions (ibid., 5). This would not be without difficulties for South Africa herself, but it would be disastrous for Lesotho, 50 per cent of whose GNP consists of remittances from migrant workers, for whom no alternative employment is available in Lesotho. For Mozambique a further loss of jobs in South Africa would worsen an already desperate economic situation. Even small numbers of migrants can be of crucial significance to the sending states: thus Botswana's 26,000 migrant workers were equivalent to nearly one-third of all the wage-earners in Botswana herself in 1983, and the possibility of a limited spell of employment in South Africa is important to a large part of Botswana's population.

Communications are the most damaging element of dependence for South Africa's neighbours, and one which South Africa has sought to accentuate in the 1980s by her support for guerrilla movements seeking to disrupt alternative routes in Angola and Mozambique. Reitsma's description (1980, 139) of Third World landlocked states as 'a periphery within a periphery' applies not only to BLS, which are often described as 'South Africa's hostages', but also to Zimbabwe, Zambia and Malawi which inherited trade links largely dependent on Portuguese Mozambique (Figure 18.1). All these countries depend heavily on South African

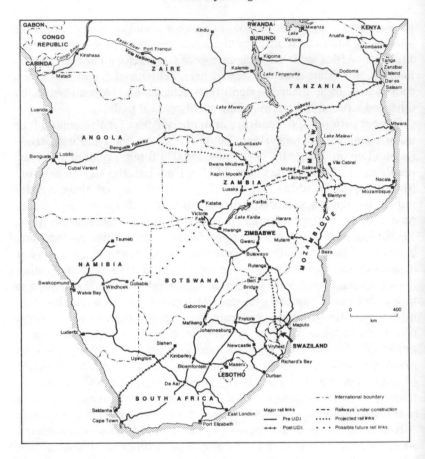

Fig. 18.1 The southern African rail network

Transport Services (SATS); several thousand South African freight cars are in use in their territories at any given time, and they also hire SATS locomotives (35 in July 1985).

South Africa has often pointed out the damaging effects of sanctions against herself on BLS in particular. In January 1986 she imposed a virtual blockade on Lesotho, which is surrounded by South Africa, with the apparent aim of forcing Lesotho into signing a security pact forbidding ANC activities within her territory; a military *coup* deposed the Lesotho government of Chief Jonathan while the blockade was still

346

in operation, and ANC members were expelled to Lusaka soon afterwards. Swaziland is more fortunate in that she has a rail link to Maputo, but the latter's port is dependent on South African assistance for its efficient operation (Azevedo 1980). The construction in the late 1970s of a southern link from Swaziland to Richard's Bay in Natal is attributed by Crush (1979, 62) to 'unease at the proximity of a radical ideology' on the part of Swaziland's conservative government and the multinational corporations operating within her borders. Botswana could theoretically trade via Zimbabwe and Mozambique, but in practice rail links to Beira and Maputo are functioning imperfectly and Zimbabwe herself is currently forced to rely on her two South African rail outlets, one of them hastily constructed after the closure of the Mozambique border in 1976 (Table 18.1). A new rail link between Zimbabwe and Swaziland will add to the capacity of trade routes to Zimbabwe and Zambia, but given its passage through the eastern Transvaal and Natal to Richard's Bay will do nothing to reduce dependence on South Africa. Zambia has faced a transport crisis since at least 1973 (Lemon 1986) and continues to do so in the face of continuing disruption of the Benguela railway by UNITA guerrillas in Angola, similar problems caused by Renamo guerrillas attacking communication links between Mutare (Zimbabwe) and Beira, and the limited functioning of the Tanzam railway to Dar es Salaam owing to administrative inefficiency and chronic shortage of motive power. Malawi's rail link to Nacala in Mozambique is also regularly put out of commission by Renamo.

Neighbouring states also depend in varying degrees on South African Airways maintenance and repair facilities and spare parts stocks, as well

Table 18.1   Trade of southern Africa countries routed via South Africa, October 1983

	Imports (% of total)	Exports (% of total)
Malawi	60	50
Zaire	57	45 (copper), 60 (lead and zinc), 40 (cobalt)
Zambia	70	40
Zimbabwe	68	65

Source: Leistner 1985, 50.

as Safair cargo planes which ferry urgently needed supplies throughout the region. Johannesburg's Jan Smuts Airport remains the major international passenger link for BLS, although all three have developed alternatives. There are also major telecommunications links between South Africa and BLS. South Africa's Electricity Supply Commission (ESCOM) supplies 100 per cent of the electricity used in Lesotho, 79 per cent in Swaziland and 52 per cent in Botswana, as well as 60 per cent of that used in Maputo (South Africa 1985b, 6). ESCOM also has an agreement to buy power from the Cahora Bassa hydro-electric power plant on the Zambezi river in Mozambique; the frequent sabotage of transmission lines by Renamo is a relatively minor inconvenience to South Africa, but results in substantial lost revenue for Mozambique.

Food is a third area of dependence. In the 1970s South Africa's production of maize, the staple food of rural populations in most of southern Africa, varied from only 4.2 million tons (1972) to 11 million tons (1974). The 1981 harvest was a record 14.2 million tons, leaving an export surplus equivalent to the total cereal needs (as estimated by the United Nations Food and Agriculture Organisation) of 28 deficit countries in Africa, including Angola, Mozambique, Zambia, Malawi and Lesotho. Exceptional droughts in 1982–84 necessitated large-scale imports to meet domestic requirements of around 7 million tons. The general trend of maize production is nevertheless upward (Chapter 6). Zimbabwe is the only other country in the region currently able, in good years, to achieve a grain surplus, thanks partly to a major increase in the marketed production of the peasant agricultural sector since 1980. With rapid population growth and ever-increasing pressure on the communal lands[1] (Kay 1980), however, Zimbabwe's surpluses are unlikely to make much impact on the regional food deficit.

Thus it seems likely that South Africa will become the 'bread basket' of the region in all but exceptional drought years, when South Africa will import on commercial terms and her neighbours will appeal for emergency aid, most of which must still pass through South African harbours and along South African railways. South Africa is unlikely to make direct use of the food weapon, which 'is an imprecise economic instrument which takes time to have an impact and which is seen by the international community as an anti-humanitarian instrument' (Henderson 1983, 47), but she is likely to use it indirectly to maintain the political status quo in terms of inter-state relations in southern Africa.

South Africa's industrial dominance in Africa is in many respects continental as well as regional: she produces 40 per cent of all Africa's manufactured goods. Although some goods remain relatively expensive because of the small market for which they are produced, there are many industrial goods which South Africa could or does supply to her neighbours more cheaply than other, more distant producers. Her exports to African states increased by 15 per cent p.a. in the 1970s, but declined from R1035 million in 1981 to R891 million in 1984, or about 8 per cent of total non-gold exports. An apparent increase in 1985 largely reflected the depreciation of the rand. This trade would undoubtedly be far greater were it not for political factors, although South Africa's very limited imports from other African states has led the central banks of several countries to issue warnings that South Africa must find ways of evening out the imbalance (Gallagher 1985, 7). Much of the existing trade is clandestine and South Africa refrains from breaking down her exports by country, but customers include BLS, Mozambique, Zimbabwe and Malawi. In addition to the customs union with BLS, South Africa retains a preferential trade agreement with Zimbabwe; she provided 24 per cent of the latter's imports and purchased 18 per cent of her exports in 1982.[2] Zambia and Malawi are similarly dependent on South Africa in trade terms: ironically the 'Botzam' road, designed to facilitate Botswana's northbound trade with Zambia, has simply become an extra conduit for South African goods conveyed more easily by road to Zambia and Malawi.

Responses to dependence

South Africa has repeatedly stressed the mutual benefits of regional economic integration, which were intended to induce her neighbours to join the 'constellation' of southern African states proposed by Mr Botha. For South Africa herself such integration would expand her markets, which some argue to be not only logical but essential: thus Amin (1977, 362) comments bluntly that 'South African capital accumulation needs an expanding space'. More important, however, is the politically stabilising effect of such enhanced integration: thus Kgarebe (1981, 12) described constellation as 'simply apartheid as foreign policy'. Other southern African states share his view, believing that they would be tied into an even more irreversible dependence on South Africa. Instead they formed the Southern African Development Coordination Conference (SADCC) in 1980 with the effect of promoting economic cooperation amongst themselves in the interests of accelerated social and economic development, greater self-reliance and reduced economic development. The nine member states – Angola, Botswana, Lesotho, Mozambique,

Swaziland, Malawi, Zambia, Zimbabwe and Tanzania – have agreed on a programme of action and allocated different responsibilities to each government concerning the formulation of regional approaches to transport and communications, foot and mouth disease, crop research, food security, training facilities, industrial development, energy policies and a development fund.

The SADCC has had some success in attracting international aid to further these aims (Lemon 1986), especially with regard to transport and communications. The major political theme of the SADCC's annual summit meetings has been South Africa's policy of destabilisation in the region in the early and mid-1980s. This is believed to include not only support for UNITA in Angola and Renamo in Mozambique, but also for the Lesotho Liberation Army (the military wing of the exiled Basutoland Congress Party). Zimbabwe has also accused South Africa of several clandestine actions aimed at destabilising its government, including the infiltration of military and civil structures and the training of dissident elements in the northern Transvaal, Botswana and the Caprivi strip (see Patel 1985, 236–8). The SADCC is apparently correct in believing that South Africa, having failed to secure regional economic integration and so strengthen her dominance by peaceful means, is attempting to do so instead through policies of both economic and political destabilisation, especially of Mozambique, Angola and Zimbabwe whose regimes she finds ideologically least acceptable.

The SADCC has brought together states with diverse ideologies which are pursuing opposing development strategies. Its members have shown a level of political and organisational coherence which is unexpected in a group so recently formed, and presentation of projects has been impressively detailed. Yet economic progress is inevitably slow given that SADCC objectives effectively constitute an attempt to counter the world economic system as it operates in southern Africa. To do so in anything approaching a fundamental and lasting fashion would require massive and sustained external aid on a scale which the SADCC has not even dared to request.

Meanwhile South African dominance is unchallenged, and forces most SADCC states to deal with Pretoria in economic matters and to restrict to a symbolic level the support they give to the ANC. South Africa's most spectacular achievement to date in this respect was the Nkomati Accord of March 1984. This ten-year non-aggression pact with Mozambique has denied the ANC its most important base; it also includes plans for greater economic cooperation which fly directly in the face of SADCC's objectives. Given Mozambique's ideological stance, Nkomati is a dramatic demonstration that destabilisation can produce compliance. During 1985, however, Renamo's activities actually increased, and South Africa was forced to admit 'technical' violations of the Accord in the face of Mozambiquan evidence, claiming that these were designed to bring Renamo to the conference table with the Mozambique government. The latter's decision not to cancel the Accord reflected its economic weakness.

The failure of Nkomati to secure the intended benefits for Mozambique has increased distrust of South Africa by SADCC countries. South Africa's May 1985 raid on Angola's northern enclave of Cabinda, apparently aimed at oil installations with the intention of reducing the flow of American dollars which Angola uses to pay for Cuban troops, reinforced SADCC feelings. They were further compounded by South Africa's June 1985 raid on supposed ANC targets in Gaborone, Botswana and the January 1986 blockade of Lesotho.

Whilst South African destabilisation is clearly achieving its short-term objectives, it carries serious dangers (Geldenhuys 1982). It increases the hostility of the target states, possibly to the point of 'irrationality' (from South Africa's viewpoint): Zimbabwe's strong support for mandatory comprehensive sanctions is a case in point. Destabilisation also damages South Africa's international standing still further, and offers the international community ample justification for punitive action. There is also the danger that instability in neighbouring states could spill over into South Africa. The victims of destabilisation might well call on outside military support, thus widening the conflict and perhaps posing a greater threat to South African security than the target state itself or guerrilla operations based on its territory. Alternatively, if South African actions resulted in a change of government in the target state, there is the danger that the new government would need South African assistance to safeguard its position, thus further widening the fronts on which South Africa is involved. Finally, a wider regional conflict would be economically disastrous for southern Africa, not least in its effect on foreign investment. Despite these risks, 'it would none the less be naive to expect South Africa to renounce the destabilisation option for at least as long as the black states remain committed to destabilise the Republic' (Geldenhuys 1982, 31).

The African National Congress
The ANC was founded in 1912 out of several different groups. At first it

was a nationally-based organisation with a conservative constitution. Even with the rise of more radical black leaders in the 1930s and 1940s, and the imposition of apartheid after 1948, the emphasis remained overwhelmingly in favour of peaceful persuasion, with some use of traditional passive resistance methods. It was the violence of the state, the declaration of a state of emergency in March 1960 after Sharpeville, and the subsequent banning of both the ANC and PAC which forced the ANC underground. Between 1961 and 1964 it attempted, together with the South African Communist Party (SACP), to create a violent insurgent movement, Umkhonto we Sizwe ('spear of the nation'), based and led from within the country and aimed at infrastructure and symbolically important buildings. The ANC still tried to avoid bloodshed; for some of its leaders this was a question of principle, whilst both ANC and SACP leaders wished to avoid alienating potentially sympathetic whites and to precipitate external intervention by placing the moral responsibility for growing instability on the authorities. At this stage the methods employed by Umkhonto were crude and the damage inflicted superficial. In late 1963 most members of the high command were arrested, and subsequently the underground organisations of the ANC, SACP and Umkhonto were located and destroyed by the police.

In the following years the ANC reconstituted itself in exile, but between 1965 and 1976 there was little evidence of its activity within South Africa. Until 1975 the possibility of establishing secure lines of communication between its base camps in East Africa and the main concentrations of population in South Africa was inhibited by the *cordon sanitaire* of hostile colonial and settler regimes. Attempts to promote a rural-based insurgency in these years came to nothing. More important was the alliance between the ANC and the Conferencia des Organizacaos Nacionalistas das Colonias Portuguesas (CONCP); through CONCP, the ANC consulted regularly with Frelimo in Mozambique and the MPLA in Angola after 1963. When these movements became the governments of their respective territories, their support for the ANC transformed its situation. Meanwhile an increasingly intimate relationship developed between overlapping ANC and SACP leaderships in exile, leading to financial and military support from the Soviet Union and Eastern Europe. This support helped the ANC to absorb many new recruits from the exodus of refugees in the wake of the Soweto and related riots of 1976.

The ANC policy document 'Strategy and tactics of the South African revolution' which emerged from its first consultative conference at

Morogoro, Tanzania in 1969 emphasised the need for extensive preparations to ensure political mobilisation prior to the transition to guerrilla warfare in the countryside (Lodge 1985a, 3–4). Such thinking was perhaps influenced by the rural struggles of Frelimo and the MPLA, but these occurred in circumstances very different from those in South Africa. In the event the second Umkhonto campaign which began in 1977 was largely urban, and sabotage attacks have sought to promote the conditions for political mobilisation to take place rather than vice versa. Once again Umkhonto tried to avoid civilian casualties. Its targets, which included administrative buildings, commuter rail links to black townships, and police stations in black residential areas, were apparently chosen for their impact on urban blacks and their association with the state (ibid., 5). The object seemed more to build a local political following than to present a serious challenge to the state.

The Nkomati Accord was widely perceived as a setback for the ANC, given its presumed dependence on external lines of communication. In practice the armed struggle has intensified since Nkomati. Continuing Umkhonto activity has depended partly on the transit of guerrillas through Botswana, and 1985 saw several clashes between Umkhonto bands and police in Bophuthatswana and the western Transvaal. Police discovery of several recently formed arms dumps also reflects continuing outside support. But the ANC has clearly succeeded in significantly internalising its operations since 1984. Recruitment and simple training is now going on within South Africa, and externally trained men are functioning inside the country for longer periods. Rapid reaction to internal political events, as in the bombing of two gold-mining headquarters in Johannesburg within a day of the sacking of 17,000 striking workers, demonstrates the extent to which guerrillas within the country are operating on their own initiative (Lodge 1985a, 6). Even before Nkomati, ANC strategists had talked of the need to transfer the 'armed propaganda' campaign into a 'people's war'. Subsequent attacks on private companies in central business districts are consistent with this, as are ANC pamphlets urging that the black townships be rendered ungovernable (an objective already accomplished in some areas). In April 1985 the ANC issued a statement calling for the coordination of strike activity, the replacement of community councils with popular bodies, the formation of crime-prevention units made up by youths to stop anti-social elements, the registration of participants in government structures and refusal of orders by those serving in the army and police (Phillips 1985, 13). The second consultative conference of the ANC in

Kabwe, Zambia in June 1985 went further, rescinding the embargo on 'soft' targets. It argued that the line between hard and soft targets is often blurred in South Africa where farmers, for example, often belong to a rural defence system and are sometimes enrolled in a system of military radio communications (Lodge 1985b, 87). Later the same year a series of landmines near the Zimbabwe and Botswana borders killed white civilians, heralding a new phase in ANC tactics.

The ideological position of the ANC is contained in the Freedom Charter which it adopted in 1956. Economically, this implies nationalisation of land, the mining industry, banks and monopoly industry. ANC leaders have however made it clear that they are not opposed in principle to foreign capital involvement in the South African economy, albeit under different rules and conditions from those now prevailing. The ANC leadership remains ideologically eclectic; about half the enlarged National Executive elected at Kabwe are members of the SACP, but the significance of this is easily exaggerated. The ANC and SACP have long retained separate identities, and scholars who have made close analyses reject the charge that the ANC is communist-dominated. The shared experiences of three generations on the executive cut across ideological divisions. The SACP has a long tradition of tempering its socialist principles with non-working-class considerations of national unity (Lodge 1985b, 95). Moreover South African blacks have increasingly come to understand oppression in terms of class as well as race, given their treatment in a capitalist society and the apparent intertwining of the interests of capital and state. Lodge therefore argues that the main source of radical pressure on the ANC leadership comes not from its Eastern bloc allies, nor from its communist leaders, but from the mood of black South Africans.

The political resolutions adopted at Kabwe make no radical departure from the Freedom Charter, although the decision to admit whites, coloureds and Indians to the 'internal' ANC and positions on the executive was a break with tradition. The working class was formally recognised as the leading social element in the liberation struggle and the importance of trade unions was stressed, but these resolutions appear to be more significant strategically than ideologically (ibid., 82–3). The concept of a political settlement either through negotiation or a national convention was rejected in favour of the necessity of the 'seizure' of power. The ANC is, however, prepared to talk with organisations within South Africa, both those it regards as allies such as 'progressive' trade unions, students, women's and religious organisations, and non-government elements of the white power bloc, such as big business and the PFP. Talks with the latter groups are part of the ANC's strategy of isolating the Botha government politically (Barrell 1985, 5). It will talk with the National Party only on the central precondition that the objective is the total dismantling of apartheid and the means of transferring power to the people. Although the ANC has not spelt out exactly what it means by these terms, the total rejection of negotiated power-sharing (and of any talks involving Chief Buthelezi) make talks with Pretoria unlikely in the short term. Increasing attacks by the ANC on 'soft' targets since late 1985 are likely to harden white opinion and reduce the persuasive power of leadership groups favouring negotiation. This situation might change if Pretoria were to declare its intention of dismantling apartheid, release detainees, allow an unconditional return of exiles and permit an open political process within the country; in such circumstances, the ANC might be pressed by both African and western governments to come to the negotiating table, as the Zimbabwean liberation movements were pressed to attend the Lancaster House conference. Unless this happens in South Africa, continuation and probably intensification of the armed struggle seems inevitable.

Support for the ANC has increased dramatically in recent years, especially among young blacks. If it were to be legalised and allowed to campaign freely, there is little doubt that its support would prove as great or greater than survey data suggest. The ANC believes with some justification that it is winning the war politically and psychologically. The fact remains, however, that South Africa's power is virtually invulnerable to revolutionary overthrow: as Welsh (1984, 61) observes, 'there is no single case of a developed state, whose army and other coercive agencies remained loyal, succumbing to revolution.' Through internalisation and intensification of the armed struggle and increasing unrest the economic and psychological costs of retaining white dominance can be greatly magnified, but it is neither certain nor even likely that Pretoria will bow to such pressures in the foreseeable future, unless by doing so it can at least negotiate some continuing share of power for white South Africans.

Economic sanctions

All realistic indicators suggest that mandatory economic sanctions against South Africa could seriously impinge on the growth of the South African economy (Cooper J. 1983). South Africa's proportion of foreign trade to GDP fluctuates considerably, primarily because of variations in the domestic economy caused by changes in the gold price, but has remained consistently high and was 71.3 per cent in 1980. South African economc growth also relies heavily on direct foreign investment, which is dominated by multinational corporations whose investment is largely undertaken through reinvestment of their South African earnings, and foreign direct lending, on which the public sector has had to rely significantly to finance its expansion.

Whilst it may be true that South Africa is technically able to produce almost anything she requires, the associated costs and misallocation of resources would be substantial. The Reynders Commission (South Africa 1972, 23) found that, 'At the present stage of South Africa's development the main potential of a programme of import replacement has been realised.' Imports of machinery, vehicles and transport equipment, chemicals and chemical products, base metals and metal products would be difficult to replace from within; these capital and intermediate goods account for nearly half South Africa's imports. Agriculture is also vulnerable to sanctions on imported inputs including oil-based fuels, over 75 per cent of agricultural machinery, and certain fertilisers and pesticides.

Sanctions on South Africa's major exports would impose considerable costs on those applying them. The replacement of South African strategic minerals may not be impossible in the long run (Chapter 7), but would give rise to major short-term problems, especially for Western European industrial economies which have inadequate stockpiles. South Africa's position as the world's leading gold producer would also render sanctions difficult to implement (Cooper J. 1983, 32–3); pro-sanctions commentators propose the gradual substitution of special drawing rights for gold reserves, but the demand for gold rests upon broader considerations, as the general upward trend of the gold price since the official demonetisation of gold suggests. Sanctions could do considerable damage to South Africa's commercial agriculture, but at great cost to employment, given that those agricultural sectors which are the most labour-intensive are also among the most export-oriented.

Since the mid-1985 South Africa has already begun to suffer from declining foreign investment, not as a result of government sanctions but because multinational corporations have begun to reduce their involvement in South Africa and American banks asked at short notice for large-scale repayments of their short-term loans, forcing South Africa temporarily to suspend repayments. A brief consideration of the effects of these essentially commercial, and therefore possibly short-term, actions will give some indication of the more deep-seated implications of mandatory withdrawal of investment and prohibition of lending. The withdrawal of foreign direct investment by multinationals may have the positive short-term effect of allowing domestic capital to purchase foreign assets cheaply, but it could threaten future South African access to modern technology and sophisticated managerial skills. More immediately, it has a negative effect on employment. The action of the American banks is potentially very serious. They acted under pressure from the US anti-apartheid movement, demonstrated in the withdrawal of deposits by local authorities including New York City, and growing support within the US Congress for sanctions. Other banks, notably the Swiss, emphasised that they were not willing to fill the gap left by withdrawal of American credit. Until agreement is reached on the restructuring of this short-term debt, no fresh medium- or long-term credit will be available to South Africa.[3] Were this situation to be prolonged its effects on the South African economy would be highly adverse. Due to its high import propensity, economic growth represents a constant potential strain on the balance of payments, which needs to be offset by foreign loans. The expansion of public corporations such as ARMSCOR and SASOL (Chapter 7), which has underpinned the growth of the South African economy since the late 1960s, creates enormous investment demands which cannot easily be met by the domestic capital market.

During 1985 international pressures for comprehensive mandatory sanctions increased considerably, with the Reagan and Thatcher governments becoming increasingly isolated in their refusal to impose meaningful sanctions. Mr Reagan was finally forced by domestic political pressures to introduce a nominal sanctions package, whilst Commonwealth pressures at the Nassau conference induced Britain to do the same, but the Commonwealth achieved unity only by accepting for the time being Britain's rejection of serious sanctions. Much of the international community believes that no radical change will come from a white community which is prepared to defend with total violence a system which gives its members power and privilege. Revolutionary armed struggle is therefore seen as unavoidable; the role of sanctions would be to weaken Pretoria's ability and will to resist, and so shorten the struggle. The Anti-Apartheid Movement sees all western connections with South Africa as supporting white power, making the struggle more violent and prolonged than it need be. Legassick and Hemson (1976) go further; using a Marxian interpretation of South

African history, they argue that disengagement of foreign capital must be accompanied by international working-class mobilisation to combat the attempts of domestic capital in South Africa to transform the country into a normal capitalist state.

Most of those who oppose mandatory sanctions see more hope of peaceful evolutionary change. Whilst accepting the need for a much accelerated pace of change, they see comprehensive mandatory sanctions as a blunt instrument which is most unlikely to achieve the desired objectives. Their doubts about the ability of the international community to make sanctions watertight and effective are amply supported by all previous evidence. But even if sanctions were universally applied, there could be no guarantee of their success in securing fundamental change. The year 1985 witnessed unprecedented pressures on South Africa both from within and without; ironically perhaps, the American banks damaged the country's economy far more severely than any previous international action. The results are instructive; business and other élites have certainly sought to accelerate the reform process and initiate negotiations with the ANC, but the government has been totally unresponsive. Reform continued, but along lines already mapped out in, for instance, Mr Botha's inaugural speech as State President. His much heralded 'Rubicon' speech to the National Party in Durban in August 1985 was entirely characteristic in its refusal to change in the face of pressure, despite expectations generated in part by elements within the government itself. This situation could change with new leadership, which may not be far off given Mr Botha's age and reported health problems. Were his successor to be more convinced of the inevitability of fundamental change, however, the application of comprehensive sanctions would hardly assist him. In part this is for reasons already given, and in part because the more damaging sanctions are to the South African economy, the less able the state will be to make the economic changes needed. Redistribution of a shrinking cake would be dangerous politically (in terms of white support) and of limited benefit to blacks. To redistribute effectively, any South African government needs substantial economic growth and continued overseas credit and investment. If it is objected that the purpose of sanctions is not accelerated reform by the present government but the latter's rapid and effective surrender, the answer must be that sanctions cannot possibly achieve this result.

Economic growth is important for another reason. It is the rapid growth of the 1960s and 1970s which has resulted in black urbanisation and an increasing degree of black occupational mobility. Without such changes, the government would not have been faced with the necessity of the incremental reform process pursued since the late 1970s. Supporters of sanctions are correct in arguing that previous expansion has not always resulted in social and political reform: rapid economic growth in the 1960s was actually accompanied by declining real wages for blacks, although the opposite has been true since. There is, however, an inevitable time-lag during which the government is forced to respond to growing contradictions between apartheid ideology and economic reality. Ultimately, it can be argued, stagnation is the only economic situation compatible with apartheid, which it reinforces by perpetuating the dual nature of the economy. Such an argument actually implies that foreign pressures should seek to achieve intensified economic development in South Africa in order to achieve political change. In practice, however, the results of such a strategy would be no more certain than those of sanctions, whilst the wider international repercussions will certainly deter western governments from adopting it, whatever their private inclinations. It is none the less true that sanctions, by slowing down South Africa's economic growth, will create more unemployment and so weaken the trade union movement, will reduce the scope for and impact of consumer boycotts, and will generally slow down the very processes which have heightened the contradictions of apartheid and made change inevitable.

Whilst there are thus many reasons to doubt the efficacy of sanctions, there can be no question of the suffering they would cause. When foreign investments dropped after the Soweto protests of 1976, Pretoria decided to reduce imports, maximise exports and limit growth. This was done with very limited harm to whites, while 1 million Africans lost their jobs (van der Merwe 1984, 15). With black unemployment levels of 25–30 per cent in 1986, further job losses would leave many urban families without any wage-earner at all, and would drastically reduce the possibility of extended or family community support for those who were desperate. It may well be true that black support for sanctions increased considerably during 1985; both sides of the sanctions debate attempt to make capital from surveys of black opinion, but such data present serious problems of interpretation. One may question, however, whether this would remain so for long once the real effects of sanctions had become apparent, and once people realised that no quick success was in prospect but instead a prolonged struggle with no assured result.

The consequence of comprehensive mandatory sanctions for South

Africa's neighbours have frequently been elaborated, most recently by Leistner (1985) and, with obvious self-interest, by the South African Department of Foreign Affairs (South Africa 1985b). It is true that most southern African countries formally support sanctions (some, including Zimbabwe, vehemently so), despite the devastating effect on their own economies; but will the brave words of their political leaders ('We can go back to the bush and live on sadza')[4] be echoed by their people, especially when it becomes clear that for any hope of success, sanctions must be maintained over a long period? In the words of Botswana's Foreign Minister, 'Why should Botswana be made to suffer for something that will never work?'[5]

The western dilemma in South Africa

Sanctions against South Africa would be meaningless without the participation of western countries. Foreign investment in South Africa comes overwhelmingly from the EEC (R22.9 billion in 1983) and the USA (R26.5 billion).[6] In recent years South Africa has become more reliant on four countries – the USA, Japan, West Germany and the UK – for her imports (Table 18.2); her exports are more widely distributed but the pattern is again dominated by western countries. There are arguably many worse tyrannies than South Africa, including many states pressing for sanctions, against which the West is not expected to act, but South Africa is the only *western* state which openly denies the intellectual basis of western social and political thought (Mayall 1979, 371). The western powers are committed to securing international recognition not only of the rights of sovereign states but of individuals, as for example under the provision of the European Convention on Human Rights. This conception of international order is seriously compromised by what African states perceive to be continued western support for South Africa. This offers a major propaganda weapon to the Soviet Union in her relations with Africa and the Third World, to which her material aid is negligible beside that of western governments. The latter are painfully aware of this, but they none the less remain unwilling to impose the blunt instrument of sanctions; they seek rather a form of intervention which sets precise objectives which stand a reasonable chance of being achieved, and one which will allow western governments to extricate themselves if necessary, rather than sucking them irretrievably into an escalating situation with an uncertain outcome.

Barber and Spicer (1979) suggest three centrist options between comprehensive mandatory sanctions on the one hand, and intensified

Table 18.2:   South Africa's major trading partners in 1984

| | Import source | | Export destination | |
	Rm	*% share*	*Rm*	*% share*
USA	3,402.9	15.69	2,106.7	8.30
Japan	2,800.5	12.91	1,957.2	7.71
West Germany	3,425.8	15.80	977.7	3.85
UK	2,416.0	11.14	1,060.9	4.18
Switzerland	388.1	1.79	1,679.3	6.62
Italy	761.1	3.51	648.0	2.55
France	820.0	3.78	561.7	2.21
Netherlands	393.5	1.81	612.7	2.41

Source: South African Foundation (1986), *Information Digest*, p. 9.

economic development on the other. The first, *communication*, rests on the belief that the West is in a position to influence change in South Africa through contact and communication. To achieve this selective sanctions could be employed, but they would be positive (offering rewards) as well as negative, and they would be most effective in those matters where whites were already considering reform. Under this option the West would emphasise that the problem is one for South Africans to solve: western governments would therefore seek to influence but not dictate both the pace and direction of change, encouraging both incremental reform and the exploration of constitutional arrangements for sharing power. It is implicit in this approach that much of the western pressure would be quietly, even privately, applied, so that the South African government would not be embarrassed at home by too open a response to external pressures.

A second option for the West is *disengagement*, or 'keeping at a distance' (ibid., 393). This involves a general downgrading of western involvement in South Africa's affairs, with the ending of diplomatic, cultural and sporting ties. Whilst recognising that certain economic ties must be retained, and that some countries, notably Britain, could not afford to break all their links, a sustained effort to develop alternative trading relationships is implied. In this view so much uncertainty surrounds the future of South Africa that it is wise for the West to minimise its involvement, whilst clearly condemning apartheid. This is consistent with the view of Henry Kissinger, when he was US Secretary of State, that the major powers should avoid involvement in Third World conflicts: they should try to mediate where possible, but otherwise remain aloof, leaving the peoples and states concerned to sort out their own problems.

The third centrist option is one of *graduated pressure*. This approach assumes that black rule is inevitable, whatever the precise constitutional arrangement, and that the West, which is too involved to distance itself from the problem, should attempt to accelerate peaceful evolutionary change. To do so would involve active pressure, including a wide range of sanctions. This might stimulate further internal violence but, it is argued, reforms can be achieved without a breakdown of society. Such pressure would serve western interests, including trade with black Africa, countering communist influence, and retaining influence and trust in the Third World. Advocates of this approach vary in their emphasis from the limited but concrete gains of pragmatic incrementalism (as with the application by American and EEC firms in South Africa of the Sullivan and EEC codes towards their labour forces) to pressures which would graduate from diplomatic sanctions through non-military support of liberation movements and 'front-line' states to economic sanctions of increasing severity.

In practice western governments will probably continue to seek change in South Africa within the framework of all three of these approaches. They are not always compatible, and western policies will probably shift between them over time. Changes of emphasis will depend not only on the course of events in South Africa and southern Africa, but on the values of particular western governments, and the pressures to which they are subjected at home and abroad, the state of their own and the international economy, and the international political situation.

Conclusion

The title of this book implies a question, which can only be half answered. Apartheid is in transition, but the future course and end-product of the transition is far from clear. Verwoerdian apartheid is being dismantled, however tortuously. Whatever intermediate attempts there may be to 'modernise' and adapt apartheid, the only logical end to the process which has started is, as Dr Verwoerd himself would have seen so clearly, a South Africa in which whites have at best a minority share of political power.

The role of external pressures in this transition is easily exaggerated. If carefully and skilfully used, often in private, such pressures can speed the process of change and minimise bloodshed and suffering. If bluntly used they can accelerate collapse into revolutionary chaos which few in the West regard as likely to enhance the long-term economic prosperity, social well-being or political freedom of more than a handful of South Africans. South Africa may be a microcosm of the developed and developing worlds but ultimately her problems, like those of other African countries, must be understood in their own terms and solved if possible by her own people. An awesome responsibility rests on all South Africa's political leaders within and outside her borders, and especially on the whites who wield power. Were they to succeed South Africa could take her place as a respected member of the international community and make a unique contribution to the southern Africa region, the African continent, and to North–South relations in the world as a whole. But first she must emerge from the isolationism of the third Great Trek which began in 1948.

Notes

References to the annual *Survey of Race Relations in South Africa*, published by the South African Institute of Race Relations, Johannesburg, are referred to as SAIRR, *Survey*.

Chapter 3

1. The Representation of Natives Act 1936 for the first time provided for the representation of the African population of the whole of South Africa in the Union Parliament. It established four new seats in the Senate for elected representatives of the following constituencies: Transkei, the rest of the Cape Province, Natal (including Zululand) and the Transvaal and Orange Free State. Three new seats in the House of Assembly were to be filled by representatives of Africans in the Cape Province only, and two new seats in the Cape Provincial Council were to be filled by representatives of Africans. In all cases only British subjects of European descent were eligible for election. For a detailed account of the experiences of one elected representative of Africans during this period, see Ballinger, (1969).
2. See *Hansard* 31 May 1950, cols. 7722–30 (Dr Malan) and 29 May 1950, col. 7434 (Dr Dönges). Both statements are cited by de Villiers (1971), p. 410.

Chapter 4

1. The *laager* was a circular arrangement of oxwagons to protect trekking Boers from wild animals and attacks by Africans. The use of the term to symbolise the modern Afrikaner's isolation of himself from the world outside has become widespread.
2. See *Hansard* 21 March 1945, cols. 3878–87.
3. This point emerged from personal communication with Professor Bernard Lategan of Stellenbosch University, himself one of the signatories of the letter in *Die Kerkbode*.
4. 'For the foundation, nobody can lay any other than the one that has already been laid, that is Jesus Christ'.
5. These figures are based on census data for 'home languages'. They do not

364

mean that English has displaced Indian languages altogether in 85.1 per cent of homes in 1980, but that it was stated to be the primary language used in these homes.

6. See, for instance: 'Catholic Church in South Africa', *Africa South* 2 (2), 1958; Meyer, P.M. (1979), *The Roman Catholic Church in South Africa: a select bibliography*, University of Cape Town; Roman Catholic Bishops, 'Declaration of Commitment', *South African Outlook* 107 (1271), 1977, pp. 50–2.

7. National Initiative for Reconciliation, *Statement of Affirmation*, 12 September 1985.

Chapter 5

1. Electoral quotas varied slightly between provinces until 1965. Between 1965 and 1973 a single quota was calculated for the Republic as a whole. In 1973 the Electoral Amendment Act froze the number of seats allocated to each province for ten years. The resulting electoral quota was significantly larger in the Transvaal than in other provinces initially, and more rapid population growth in the Transvaal has substantially widened the gap, resulting in under-representation of the Transvaal by between 14 and 18 per cent against other provinces by 1980 (Lemon 1984a, 11–12).

2. The categories of *verligte* and *verkrampte* were first distinguished by Professor W.J. de Klerk in October 1966 (Heard 1974, 183). He characterised *verligte* Afrikaners as promoting dangerous 'liberalist' tendencies in Afrikanerdom and *verkramptes* as ultra-conservative Afrikaners opposed to all change. Subsequently *verligte* has come to mean 'reformist', 'positive' or 'enlightened', and *verkrampte* to mean 'hard-line' or 'reactionary'.

3. Mr B.J. Vorster in a speech reported in the *Eastern Province Herald*, 5 April 1974.

4. Dr C.P. Mulder in a speech reported in the *Rand Daily Mail*, 24 April 1974.

5. Leader in the *Eastern Province Herald* (Port Elizabeth) 26 April 1974.

6. As reported in the *Rand Daily Mail*, 21 September 1977.

7. The scandal arose when a spot-check on the Department of Information by the Auditor-General revealed that funds were being used for propaganda purposes without parliamentary approval. Initially only R400,000 was thought to be involved, but further disclosures by the press and official enquiries put the figure nearer R70 million.

8. Leader on 29 November 1977.

9. The then President's Council was a body consisting of white, coloured and Indian appointees whose task was to advise the government on constitutional change.

10. *Die Afrikaner* (HNP newspaper), 27 March 1981, p. 10.

11. Reported in the *Daily Dispatch* (East London) on 19 March 1981.

12. Reported in the *Daily Dispatch* on 20 March 1981.

13. The term 'informal sector' refers to spontaneous, self-help housing (as in 'squatter' settlements) and to employment which is not formally registered

but helps to support large sections of the population of most Third World cities. It is largely of a 'service' character, but may include crafts and small-scale manufacturing. See Rogerson and Beavon (1980) for a discussion of the informal sector in southern Africa.

14. Reported in the *Eastern Province Herald* on 24 April 1981.
15. Personal communication.
16. The Liberal Party disbanded rather than shed its multi-racial character with the passing of the Prohibition of Political Interference Act 1968. The Progressive Party reluctantly confined its membership to whites to conform to the new law.
17. The PFP gained 38.1 per cent of the votes in a three-cornered contest with the NP (53.4 per cent) and NRP (9.6 per cent).
18. Reported in *Keesings Contemporary Archives* (1982), p. 31653.
19. English-speaking support for the NP rose again in 1983, reaching 28 per cent in July according to a poll by Market and Opinion Surveys.

Chapter 6

1. A dramatic fall in the value of the rand during 1985 has in any case made all imported goods far more expensive than hitherto.
2. Based on a report in the Johannesburg *Star*, 3 August 1984.
3. *Hansard* 6 Q col. 328, 8 September 1981 (quoted in SAIRR 1981 *Survey*, p. 157).
4. A university research team found that wages for unskilled African men in the Transvaal and Orange Free State were about R25–30 per month at the beginning of 1980 (*Star*, 9 September 1981).
5. *Hansard* 16 Q col. 7980 (quoted in SAIRR 1983 *Survey*, p. 158).
6. 'A new era of reclamation': policy statement by D.L. Smit, Secretary for Native Affairs, at a special session of the Ciskeian General Council at King William's Town on 8 January 1945. In Native Affairs Department report 1945–47.
7. See, for example, Wolpe 1972; Legassick 1974 and 1977; Palmer and Parsons 1977; Magubane 1975 and 1979. A useful summary of the extensive literature expounding this viewpoint is provided by Rogerson and Letsoalo 1981.

Chapter 7

1. Leading article in *The Times*, 15 November 1984.
2. According to the California-based company NUEXCO, at a price of $25 per lb of uranium oxide in 1981 South Africa had approximately a quarter of the non-communist world's uranium reserves (quoted in the *Financial Times* South Africa Survey, 26 May 1981, p. x). This proportion would decrease with higher world prices.
3. An estimate made by Alan Hill, a leading Johannesburg energy analyst, and quoted in the *Financial Times* South Africa Survey, 10 May 1985, p. xl.
4. *Star*, Johannesburg, 3 August 1984.
5. Car sales reached 301,000 in 1981 but are expected to be only 210,000 in

1985, representing a return to 1976 levels (*Financial Times*, 13 June 1985).
6.   Innes (1983, 183) identifies the main features of a 'monopoly capitalist' society as:
      (a) concentration of production and capital giving rise to monopolies which play a *decisive* role in economic life;
      (b) the emergence of finance capital (and a financial oligarchy) out of the merging of bank and industrial capital.
7.   Quoted by Chisholm and Christie (1983), p. 260.

Chapter 8

1.   Estimated by BENSO (Buro vir Ekonomiese Navorsing Saamwerking en Ontwikkeling).
2.   Mafeking has since been incorporated into Bophuthatswana and renamed Mafikeng. It forms part of the larger municipality of Mmabatho which includes the new capital city of that name.
3.   *Business Day*, 4 October 1984.
4.   *Financial Mail*, 15 March 1985.
5.   *Rand Daily Mail*, 14 November 1981, quoted by Zille (1983), p. 60.
6.   Speech to Afrikaanse Sakekamer at Worcester, 27 August 1981, p. 31, cited by Zille (1983), p. 63.
7.   Speech to the Natal Congress of the National Party in Durban, 15 August 1985.

Chapter 9

1.   This and subsequent estimates for the years 1980–83 have been made by the Bureau of Market Research at UNISA (the University of South Africa).
2.   SAIRR, 1982 *Survey*, p. 43.
3.   SAIRR, 1983 *Survey*, pp. 99–100.
4.   SAIRR, 1981 *Survey*, p. 52.
5.   SAIRR, 1983 *Survey*, p.102.
6.   Report compiled by the Human Awareness Programme, reported in the 1982 SAIRR *Survey*, p. 304.
7.   Later in 1985 it was announced that Lamontville was to be incorporated in KwaZulu, against the wishes of its inhabitants, many of whom support the United Democratic Front and oppose Chief Buthelezi's Inkatha movement.

Chapter 10

1.   *South Africa Foundation News*, March 1985, p. 2.
2.   SAIRR, 1984 *Survey*, pp. 374–5.
3.   Speech by Mr S. de Beer, Deputy Minister of Education and Development Aid, reported in *Pretoria News*, 31 August 1985.
4.   Information from the West Rand Administration Board, quoted in SAIRR, 1983 *Survey*, p. 271.
5.   SAIRR, 1984 *Survey*, p. 378.
6.   The term 'squatters' is used here to include all those living in informal or

shack settlements. Only a small proportion of these may be there without permission (perhaps one-tenth in the Durban region), whilst the rest occupy their sites under a complex variety of tenurial arrangments. In South Africa the term 'squatter' is increasingly used only of illegal residents, the remainder being described as 'informal settlers'.

.7. Institute for Planning Research, University of Port Elizabeth, cited in SAIRR, 1984 *Survey*, p. 384.

Chapter 11

1. SAIRR, 1984 *Survey*, p. 252.
2. Such figures are necessarily crude: they conceal the occupational levels at which people of different race groups are employed, the qualifications held, and the existence or otherwise of differential remuneration for the same job according to the ethnic classification of the worker. The latter is, however, increasingly unusual.
3. SAIRR, 1984 *Survey*, p. 470.
4. *Business Day*, 29 October 1985.

Chapter 12

1. Calculated from data in the annual report of the Department of Justice, Police and Prisons for the period 1 July 1982 to 30 June 1983, cited in the SAIRR 1984 *Survey*, pp. 794–6, and the 1983 official mid-year population estimates.
2. SAIRR, 1975 *Survey*, p. 69 and 1984 *Survey*, p. 468.
3. *Hansaard* 15 Q cols. 1287–88, cited in SAIRR, 1984 *Survey*, p. 400.

Chapter 13

1. For a fuller account of these elections, see Lemon (1984c), on which this section is largely based.
2. Based on a calculation of the number of coloureds eligible to vote (1,578,771) by the Unit for Futures Research at Stellenbosch University.

Chapter 14

1. Dr George Morrison, Deputy Minister of Cooperation and Development (*Hansard* 19, col. 8563, cited in SAIRR, 1984 *Survey*, p. 502).
2. SAIRR, 1980 *Survey*, p. 392.
3. Reported in the *Rand Daily Mail*, 2 February 1981, and much cited in subsequent political debate as evidence of the failure of apartheid. Mr van der Walt's estimate of R.6000 million compares with a total of R804 million spent on land purchases for homeland consolidation by the end of January 1984 (*Hansard* 2 Q col. 251, cited in 1984 *Survey*, p. 502).
4. At the annual Council Meeting of the SAIRR (cited in 1974 *Survey*, p. 183).
5. Address to the *Afrikaanse Studentebond* in 1977, cited by Geldenhuys (1981), pp. 161–2.
6. 'Volkstaat nou 'n tameletjie', *Die Volksblad* 15 August 1985.

7. This calculation excludes the contribution made by CBDs open to all races.
8. Coloureds in the Cape were, however, able to elect their own people to the Cape Provincial Council and the Cape Town City Council until such representation was ended by a Nationalist government.
9. Opening address to the 80th Congress of the Municipal Association of Transvaal, *Local Government in Southern Africa*, February 1984, p. 3 (cited by Todes and Watson (1985)).
10. Indian and coloured education became 'own affairs' in the 1983 constitution, having been transferred much earlier from provincial to central government control. Black education also remained in the hands of central government in 1983, but as a 'general affair'.

Chapter 15

1. At its second summit conference in 1964 the OAU approved a resolution declaring that 'all member states pledge themselves to respect the borders existing on the achievement of national independence' (Prescott 1979, p. 5).
2. Such suggestions are made by M.E. Leistner in a paper delivered to a conference of the Foreign Affairs Association at Umtata in 1976, and by Lawrence Schlemmer (1970), pp. 44–5. Both are cited by Maasdorp (1980), p. 120.

Chapter 16

1. Natal *Mercury*, 3 March 1983.
2. President Sebe was expecting President Botha to include mention of reincorporation of the 'TVBC countries' in his 'Rubicon' speech at Durban in August 1985. His failure to do so appeared to result from President Mangope's refusal to contemplate reincorporation.
3. *Hansard* 6 February 1980, col. 247, cited by Rhoodie (1980), p. 105.
4. *Financial Mail*, 9 August 1985, p. 33.
5. Ibid., p. 32.

Chapter 17

1. *Sunday Times*, 2 February 1986.
2. *The Times*, 1 February 1986.
3. Minister of Cooperation and Development 29 January 1985, cited by South Africa Foundation (1985), p. 6.
4. *Pretoria News*, 28 September 1985.
5. *The Citizen*, 18 October 1985.
6. SAIRR, 1984 *Survey*, p. 308.
7. Ibid., p. 311.
8. Ibid., p. 309.
9. *Financial Times*, 5 December 1985.
10. Cited in SAIRR, 1984 *Survey*, p. 337.
11. SAIRR, 1976 *Survey*, p. 22.
12. *Sunday Times*, 7 October 1984.

13. SAIRR statistics cited in the *Weekly Mail*, 8–14 November 1985. The total number of deaths reached 1028 by the end of 1985.
14. *Beeld*, 5 September 1984.
15. *Sowetan*, 4 September 1984.
16. *South Africa Foundation News*, July 1985, p. 1.

Chapter 18

1. Zimbabwe's 'communal lands', formerly known as tribal trust lands, are those reserved for communal occupation on traditional lines.
2. *Economist* survey of Zimbabwe, 21 April 1984, p. 14.
3. An interim agreement was reached in February 1986, whereby 5 per cent of South Africa's short-term debt would be repaid by 31 March 1987, with the rest rolled over for another year.
4. This paraphrases the statements of several Zimbabwean political leaders during 1985 (sadza is the maize porridge eaten regularly by most ordinary Zimbabweans).
5. Quoted by van der Merwe (1984), p. 15.
6. SAIRR, 1984 *Survey*, p. 199.

References

Adam, H. (1971), *Modernizing Racial Domination*, University of California Press, Berkeley.

Adam, H. and Giliomee, H. (1979), *Ethnic Power Mobilized: Can South Africa Change?*, Yale University Press, New Haven.

Addleson, M.S., Pretorius, F. and Tomlinson, R. (1985), 'The impact of industrial decentralisation policy: the businessman's view', *South African Geographical Journal* 67 (2), 179–200.

Alexander, N. (1979), 'Examining South Africa's options' (review of Slabbert and Welsh, *op.cit.*), *Social Dynamics* 5 (2), 56–9.

Amin, S. (1977), 'The future of South Africa', *Journal of South African Affairs* 2 (2), 355–70.

Archer, S.F. (1980), 'Redistribution issues and policies in the South African economy', in F. van Zyl Slabbert and J. Opland (eds.), *op cit.*, 121–48.

Atmore, A. and Marks, S. (1974), 'The imperial factor in South Africa in the nineteenth century: towards a reassessment'. *Journal of Imperial and Commonwealth History* 3 (1), 105–39.

Austin, D. (1985), 'The Trinitarians: the 1983 South African Constitution', *Government and Opposition* 20 (2), 185–95.

Azevedo, M.J. (1980), 'A sober commitment to liberation'? Mozambique and South Africa, 1974–1979', *African Affairs* 79 (317), 567–84.

Baldwin, A. (1974), *Uprooting a Nation: The study of three million evictions in South Africa*, Africa Publications Trust, London.

Baldwin, A. (1975), 'Mass removals and separate development', *Journal of Southern African Studies* 1 (2), 215–27.

Ballinger, M. (1969), *From Union to Apartheid: a trek to isolation*, Juta, Cape Town.

Barber, J. and Spicer, M. (1979), 'Sanctions against South Africa: options for the West', *International Affairs* 55 (3), 385–401.

References

Barrell, H. (1984), 'The United Democratic Front and National Forum: their emergence, composition and trends', in SARS, *op.cit.*, 6–20.

Barrell, H. (1985), 'The tactics of talks', *Work in Progress*, 39, 4–8.

Beavon, K.S.O. and Rogerson, C.M. (1981), 'Trekking on: recent trends in the human geography of South Africa', *Progress in Human Geography* 5 (2), 159–89.

Bekker, S.B. and Coetzee, J.H. (1980), *Black Urban Employment and Coloured Labour Preference*, Institute of Social and Economic Research, Rhodes University, Grahamstown, working paper 1.

Bekker, S. and Humphries, R. (1985), *From Control to Confusion: the changing role of Administration Boards in South Africa*, Shuter and Shooter, Pietermaritzburg in association with the Institute of Social and Economic Research, Rhodes University, Grahamstown.

Bell, R.T. (1973a), 'Some aspects of industrial decentralisation in South Africa', *South African Journal of Economics* 41 (4), 401–31.

Bell, R.T. (1973b), *Industrial Decentralisation in South Africa*, Oxford University Press, Cape Town.

Bell, R.T. (1973c), 'Bantustan economic development', *Third World* 2 (6).

BENSO (Bureau for Economic Research, Cooperation and Development) (1982), 'Black development in the independent national states: tables', *Development Studies Southern Africa* 5 (1), 95–137.

BENSO (1983), 'Statistical supplement: Black development in South Africa', *Development Studies in Southern Africa* 6 (1), 76–108.

Best, A.C.G. (1971), 'South Africa's border industries: the Tswana example', *Annals of the Association of American Geographers* 61 (2), 329–43.

Bisschop, J.H.R. (1979), '"South Africa: two agricultures?"', *Social Dynamics* 5 (2), 29–31.

Bisschop, J.H.R. (1980), '"South Africa: two agricultures?": a reply to Merle Lipton', *Social Dynamics* 6 (1), 49.

Black, P.A. (1980), 'Consumer potential in Mdantsane', in Cook and Opland (eds.), *op.cit.*, 65–72.

Black, P. *et al.* (1985), 'The potential impact of abolishing company tax in Ciskei', *Development Southern Africa* 2 (2), 165–73.

Blenck, J., and von der Ropp, K.B. (1976), 'Republik Südafrika Teilung oder Ausweg?', *Aussen Politik* 27 (3), 308–24.

Bloch, Graeme (1981), '"Room at the top?" The development of South Africa's manufacturing industry 1939–1969"', *Social Dynamics* 7 (2), 47–57.

References

Blumenfeld, J.A. (1980), 'The South African economy: potential and pitfalls', *The World Today* 36 (9), 334–42.

Board, C. (1964), 'The rehabilitation programme in the Bantu areas and its effect on the agricultural life of the Bantu in the eastern Cape', *South African Journal of Economics* 32 (1), 36–52.

Bosch, D. (1985), 'The fragmentation of Afrikanerdom and the Afrikaner churches' in Villa-Vicencio and de Gruchy (eds.), *op. cit.*, 61–73.

Boserup, E. (1965), *The Conditions of Agricultural Growth*, George Allen and Unwin, London.

Botha, C.G. (1923), 'The dispersion of the stock farmer in Cape Colony in the eighteenth century', *South African Journal of Science* 20, 574–80.

Botha, P. Roelf (1978), *South Africa Plan for the Future: a basis for dialogue*, Perskor, Johannesburg.

Boulle, L.J. (1980), 'The new constitutional proposals and the possible transition to consociational democracy', in Slabbert and Opland (eds.), *op. cit.*, 14–35.

Boulle, L.J. (1984), *South Africa and the Consociational Option: a constitutional analysis*, Juta, Cape Town.

Boulle, L.J. and Baxter, L.G. (1981), *Natal and KwaZulu: Constitution and Political Options*, Juta, Cape Town.

Bowman, L.W. (1982), 'The strategic importance of South Africa to the United States', *African Affairs* 81 (323), 159–91.

Brand, J.G. (1979), *Building a New Town: City of Cape Town Mitchell's Plain*, Cape Town.

Brewer, J.D. (1985), 'The membership of Inkatha in KwaMashu', *African Affairs* 84 (334), 111–35.

Brookes, E. (1968), *Apartheid: a documentary study of modern South Africa*, Routledge and Kegan Paul, London.

Brookes, E. (1973), Minority Report following the Majority Report of the SPRO-CAS Political Commission, *op. cit.*

Brookes, E.H. and Webb, C. de B. (1965), *A History of Natal*, Natal University Press, Pietermaritzburg.

Brookfield, H.C. (1957), 'Some geographical implications of the apartheid and partnership policies in South Africa', *Transactions of the Institute of British Geographers* 23, 225–47.

Brookfield, H.C. and Tatham, M.A. (1957), 'The distribution of racial groups in Durban: the background of apartheid in a South African city', *Geographical Review* 47 (1), 44–65.

Brotz, H. (1977), *The Politics of South Africa: Democracy and racial diversity*, Oxford University Press, London.

Browett, J.G. (1976), 'The application of a spatial model to South Africa's development regions', *South African Geographical Journal* 58 (2), 118–29.

Browett, J.G. and Fair, T.J.D. (1974), 'South Africa 1870–1970: a view of the spatial system', *South African Geographical Journal* 56 (2), 111–20.

Budlender, D. (1984a), 'Technological change and labour on "white" farms', in SARS, *op.cit.*, 300–7.

Budlender, D. (1984b), *Incorporation and Exclusion: Recent developments in labour law and influx control*, SAIRR, Johannesburg.

Bundy, C. (1972), 'The emergence and decline of a South African peasantry', *African Affairs* 71 (285), 369–88.

Bundy, C. (1979), *The Rise and Fall of the South African Peasantry*, Heinemann, London.

Bunting, B. (1969), *The Rise of the South African Reich*, Penguin, Harmondsworth.

Burger, J.J. (1970), 'Transport systems as a basis for the application of separate development', paper delivered to the South African Bureau of Racial Affairs Congress on 'Homeland development', Port Elizabeth, 6 August.

Buthelezi Commission (1982), *The Requirements for Stability and Development in KwaZulu and Natal* (2 vols.), H & H Publications, Durban.

Butler, F.G. (1976), 'The nature and purpose of the conference', in de Villiers (ed.), *op.cit.*, 7–16.

Butler, J. *et al.* (1978), *The Black Homelands of South Africa: the political and economic development of Bophuthatswana and KwaZulu*, University of California Press, Berkeley.

Carnegie Commission (1932), *The Poor White Problem in South Africa*, 5 vols, Pro-ecclesia Drukkery, Stellenbosch.

Carnell, F.G. (1961), 'Political implications of federalism in new states', in U.K. Hicks *et al.*, *Federalism and Economic Growth in Underdeveloped Countries*, Allen and Unwin, London.

Carter, G.M. (1958), *The Politics of Inequality: South Africa since 1948*, 2nd edn, Praeger, New York.

Centre for Intergroup Studies (1980), *District Six*, Occasional Paper 2, Centre for Intergroup Studies, University of Cape Town.

Charney, C. (1982), 'Towards rupture or stasis? an analysis of the 1981 South African General Election', *African Affairs* 81 (325), 527–45.

Charton, N. (ed.) (1980), *Ciskei: a South African Homeland*, Croom Helm, London.

Chisholm, L. and Christie, P. (1983), 'Restructuring in education', in SARS, *op.cit.*, 254–63.

Christopher, A.J. (1972), 'South Africa and the nation state', *Zambezia* 2 (2), 23–37.

Christopher, A.J. (1973), 'Environmental perception in southern Africa', *South African Geographical Journal* 55 (1), 14–22.

Christopher, A.J. (1976a), *Southern Africa*, Dawson, Folkestone.

Christopher, A.J. (1976b), 'The variability of the southern African standard farm', *South African Geographical Journal* 64 (2), 97–113.

Christopher, A.J. (1982a), 'Towards a definition of the nineteenth-century South African frontier', *South African Geographical Journal* 64 (2), 97–113.

Christopher, A.J. (1982b), *South Africa*, Longman, London.

Christopher, A.J. (1982c), 'Partition and population in South Africa', *Geographical Review* 72 (2), 127–38.

Christopher, A.J. (1983a), 'Official land disposal policies and European settlement in southern Africa 1860–1960', *Journal of Historical Geography* 9 (4), 369–83.

Christopher, A.J. (1983b), 'From Flint to Soweto: reflections on the colonial origins of the apartheid city', *Area* 15 (2), 145–9.

Christopher, A.J. (1984a), *The Crown Lands of British South Africa 1853–1914*, The Limestone Press, Kingston, Ontario.

Christopher, A.J. (1984b), *South Africa: the impact of past geographies*, Juta, Cape Town.

Christopher, A.J. (1984c), *Colonial Africa*, Croom Helm, London.

Cilliers, C.P. (1963), *The Coloureds of South Africa: a factual survey*, Banier Publications, Cape Town.

Cilliers, S.P. (1971), *Appeal to Reason*, University Publishers and Booksellers, Stellenbosch.

Cilliers, S.P. (1979), 'Crime in the coloured community' in Hare, Wiendieck and von Broembsen (eds.), *op. cit.*, 261–7.

Ciskei (1983), *Report of the Commission of Inquiry into the Economic Development of the Republic of Ciskei*.

Coetzee, S.F. and van der Kooy, R.J.W. (eds.) (1985), *The Development of Natal/KwaZulu*, Development Society of Southern Africa, Sandton.

Coker, C. (1983), 'Bophuthatswana and the South African homelands', *The World Today* 39 (6), 231–40.

Cole, M.M. (1956), 'Vegetation studies in South Africa', *Geography* 41 (2), 114–22.

Cole, M.M. (1961), *South Africa*, Methuen, London.

Cook, G.P. (1980a), 'Scattered towns or an urban system?' in Charton (1980), *op. cit.*, 30–47.

Cook, G.P. (1980b), 'Position in an urban hierarchy', in Cook and Opland (eds.), *op. cit.*, 73–88.

Cook, G.P. and Opland, J. (eds.), (1980), *Mdantsane: Transitional City*, Institute of Social and Economic Research, Rhodes University, Grahamstown, Occasional Paper 25.

Cooper, C. (1983), 'The established trade union membership', in SARS, *op. cit.*, 204–17.

Cooper, J.H. (1983), 'Economic sanctions and the South African economy', *International Affairs Bulletin* 7 (2), 25–47.

Cornevin, M. (1980), *Apartheid Power and Historical Falsification*, UNESCO, Paris.

Cowley, J. and Lemon, A. (1986), 'Bophuthatswana: dependent development in a black "homeland"', *Geography* 71 (3), 252–5.

Cox, B.A. and Rogerson, C.M. (1984), 'The structure and geography of interlocking corporate directorates in South Africa', *Die Suid-Afrikaanse Geograaf* 12 (2), 133–48.

Crush, J.S. (1979), 'The parameters of dependence in Southern Africa: a case study of Swaziland', *Journal of Southern African Affairs* 4 (1), 55–66.

Daniel, J.B. McI. (1970), 'Rural settlement schemes in African areas', *Journal for Geography* (South Africa), 3 (6), 639–51.

Daniel, J.B. McI. (1981), 'Agricultural development in the Ciskei: review and assessment', *South African Geographical Journal* 63 (1), 3–23.

Davenport, R. (1969), 'African townsmen? South African Natives (Urban Areas) legislation through the years', *African Affairs* 68 (271), 95–109.

Davenport, T.R.H. (1966), *The Afrikaner Bond (1880–1911)*, Oxford University Press, Cape Town.

Davenport, T.R.H. (1971), *The Beginnings of Urban Segregation in South Africa: the Natives (Urban Areas) Act of 1923 and its background*, Institute of Social and Economic Research, Rhodes University, Grahamstown, Occasional Paper 15.

Davies, R.J. (1964), 'Social distance and the distribution of occupational categories in Johannesburg and Pretoria', *South African Geographical*

Journal 46, 24–39.

Davies, R.J. (1981), 'The spatial formation of the South African city', *GeoJournal*, supplementary issue 2 (1981), 59–72.

Davies, W.J. (1971), *Patterns of Non-White Population Distribution in Port Elizabeth with Special Reference to the Application of the Group Areas Act*, Series B, Special Publication 1, Institute of Planning Research, University of Port Elizabeth.

Davies, W.J. (1985), 'Regional development cooperation in the SATVBC context and the Ciskei tax reform issue', *Development Southern Africa* 2 (2), 187–94.

Degenaar, J. (1982), 'Reform quo vadis?', *Politikon* 9 (1), 4–18.

de Gruchy, J.W. (1979), *The Church Struggle in South Africa*, David Philip, Cape Town.

de Kiewiet, C.W. (1957), *A History of South Africa: social and economic*, Oxford University Press, London.

de Klerk, M. (1984), 'Technological change and farm labour: a case study of maize farming in the western Transvaal', in SARS, *op.cit.*, 308–17.

de Klerk, W.A. (1975), *The Puritans in Africa: a story of Afrikanerdom*, Rex Collings, London.

Desmond, C. (1971), *The Discarded People*, Penguin, Harmondsworth.

Deutsch, K.W., *et al.* (1957), *Political Community in the North Atlantic Area*, Princeton University Press, Princeton, New Jersey.

de Villiers, A. (ed.) (1976), *English Speaking South Africa Today: proceedings of the national conference*, July 1974, Oxford University Press, Cape Town.

de Villiers, F. (ed.) (1983), *Bridge or Barricade?*, Jonathan Ball, Johannesburg.

de Villiers, R. (1971), 'Afrikaner nationalism', in Wilson and Thompson (eds.), *op.cit.*, 365–423.

Dewar, D., Uytenbogaardt, R.S. *et al.* (1977), *Housing, a Comparative Evaluation of Urbanism in Cape Town*, Transvaal Printers, Johannesburg.

de Wet, C.J. (1980), 'Betterment and trust in a rural Ciskeian village', *Social Dynamics* 6 (1), 24–35.

Dhlomo, O.D. (1985), 'Inkatha's views on development and cooperation in KwaZulu/Natal' in Coetzee and van der Kooy (eds.), *op.cit.*, 37–49.

Dikshit, R.D. (1971), 'Geography and federalism', *Annals of the Association of American Geographers* 61 (1), 97–115.

References

Duminy, A.H. (1977), 'Federation – the lost cause', Paper given at a symposium entitled 'Natal – a case for devolution', at the University of Natal, Durban.

Duncan, S. (1985), 'Social and practical problems resulting from the law relating to urban Africans', *Acta Juridica 1984*, Juta for the Faculty of Law, University of Cape Town 247–54.

Dutch Reformed Church (1966), *Human Relations in South Africa*, report adopted by the General Synod of the NGK, English translation published by the DRC Information Bureau.

Dutch Reformed Church (1975), *Human Relations and the South African Scene in the Light of Scripture*, Report of the General Synod of the NGK, 1974, English translation published by DRC Publishers, Cape Town.

du Toit, A. (1974), *Federalism and Political Change in South Africa*, Maurice Webb Memorial Lectures, University of Natal, Durban.

du Toit, A. (1980), 'Nat. split: why it's unlikely', *Rand Daily Mail*, 23 June (the first of four articles appearing on successive days).

du Toit, P.J.D. (1982), 'Southern Africa's regional industrial development policy for the 1980s: its possible role in regional development', *Development Studies Southern Africa* 4 (3), 249–67.

Edelman, M. (1977), *Political Language: Words that Succeed and Policies that Fail*, Academic Press, New York.

Edwards, I.E. (1934), *The 1820 Settlers in South Africa: a study in British colonial policy*, Longman, London.

Ellis, G. (1984), *Khayelitsha: the present situation*, Regional Topic Paper 84/1, SAIRR (Cape Western Region), Mowbray.

Elphick, R. (1985), *Khoikhoi and the Founding of White South Africa*, Ravan Press, Johannesburg.

Fair, T.J.D. (1982), *South Africa: Spatial frameworks for development* Juta, Cape Town.

Fisher, J. (1969), *The Afrikaners*, Cassell, London.

Fisher, R. (1981), 'South Africa: problems and choices', *Politikon* 7 (1), 1–13.

Franck, T.M. (ed.) (1968), *Why Federations Fail: an inquiry into the requisites for successful federalism*, New York University Press, New York.

Fredrickson, G.M. (1981), *White Supremacy: a comparative study in American and South African history*, Oxford University Press, New York.

Friedman, J.R. (1966), *Regional Development Policy: a case study of*

Venezuela, MIT Press, Cambridge, Massachusetts.

Furnivall, J.S. (1948), *Colonial Policy and Practice*, Cambridge University Press, London.

Gallagher, S. (1985), *Nkomati: One year later (with a note on South Africa's trade with Africa)*, SAIRR, Johannesburg.

Geldenhuys, D. (1981), 'South Africa's constitutional alternatives', *South Africa International* 11 (4), 190–227.

Geldenhuys, D. (1982), 'The destabilisation controversy: an analysis of high-risk foreign policy option for South Africa', *Politikon* 9 (2), 16–31.

Giliomee, H. and Schlemmer, L. (eds.) (1985), *Up Against the Fences: Passes and Privilege in South Africa*, David Philip, Cape Town.

Greenberg, S. and Giliomee, H. (1985), 'Managing influx control from the rural end: the black homelands and the underbelly of privilege', in Giliomee and Schlemmer, *op.cit.*, 68–84.

Grobler, J.H. (1972), 'The agricultural potential of the Bantu homelands', *Journal of Racial Affairs* (SABRA) 23 (1), 37–43.

Gutteridge, W. (1984), *Mineral Resources and National Security*, Conflict Studies no. 162, Institute for the Study of Conflict, London.

Hackland, B. (1980), 'The economic and political context of the growth of the Progressive Federal Party in South Africa, 1959–1978', *Journal of Southern African Studies* 7 (1), 1–16.

Hailey, Lord (1957), *An African Survey*, Oxford University Press, London.

Hanf, T. *et al.* (1981), *South Africa: the prospects of peaceful change*, Rex Collings, London, David Philip, Cape Town/Indiana University Press, Bloomington.

Hare, A.P., Wiendieck, G. and von Broembsen, M.H. (eds.) (1979), *South Africa: Sociological Analyses*, Oxford University Press, Cape Town.

Harrison, D. (1981), *The White Tribe of Africa: South Africa in Perspective*, British Broadcasting Corporation, London.

Hart, T. (1975), *The Factorial Ecology of Johannesburg*, Urban and Regional Research Unit, University of the Witwatersrand, Johannesburg, Occasional Paper 5.

Hart, T. (1976), 'Patterns of black residence in the white residential areas of Johannesburg', *South African Geographical Journal* 58 (2), 141–50.

Hart, D.M. and Pirie, G.H. (1984), 'The sight and soul of Sophiatown', *Geographical Review* 74 (1), 38–47.

Heard, K.A. (1974), *General Elections in South Africa 1943–1970*, Oxford

University Press, London.

Hellmann, E. (1972), 'The crux of the race problem in South Africa', in Rhoodie (ed.), *op.cit.*, 14–33.

Henderson, R.D'A (1983), 'The food weapon in Southern Africa', *International Affairs Bulletin* 7 (3), 38–52.

Hendrie, D. and Kooy, A. (1976), 'Some employment patterns in South African agriculture', Paper presented for a conference on farm labour in South Africa, convened by the Southern Africa Labour and Development Research Unit, University of Cape Town, September.

Hexham, I. (1974), 'Dutch Calvinism and the development of Afrikaner Calvinism', in C.R. Hill and P. Warwick (eds.), *Southern Africa Research in Progress, Collected Papers vol. 1*, Centre for Southern African Studies, University of York.

Hindson, D. (1984), 'Union unity', in SARS, *op.cit.*, 90–107.

Hindson, D. and Lacey, M. (1983), Influx control and labour allocation: policy and practice since the Riekert Commission', in SARS, *op.cit.*, 97–113.

Hockley, H.E. (1949), *The Story of the British Settlers of 1820 in South Africa*, Juta, Cape Town.

Holzner, L. (1970), 'Urbanism in Southern Africa', *Geoforum* 1 (4), 75–90.

Horner, D. and Kooy, A. (1976), *Conflict on South African Mines 1972–1976*, South African Labour and Development Research Unit, University of Cape Town, working paper 5.

Houghton, D.H. (1971), 'Economic development 1865–1965', in Wilson and Thompson (eds.), *op.cit.*, 1–48.

Houghton, D.H. (1973), *The South African Economy*, 3rd edn, Oxford University Press, Cape Town.

Howe, G. (1982), *Squatter Crisis*, Occasional Paper 3, Centre for Intergroup Studies, University of Cape Town.

Hugo, P. and Kotzé, H.J. (n.d.), *Suid-Afrika: oorlewing in politieke perspektief*, Jonathan Ball, Johannesburg.

Humphries, R. (1985), 'The evolution of black urban politics', in *Energos* 11, 'The urbanisation challenge', 87–91.

Huntington, S.P. (1981), 'Reform and stability in a modernizing, multi-ethnic society', *Politikon 8 (2)*, 8–26.

Innes, D. (1983), 'Monopoly capitalism in South Africa', in SARS, *op.cit.*, 171–83.

Inskeep, R.R. (1969), 'The archaeological background', in Wilson and Thompson (eds.), *op.cit.*, 1–39.

References

Jackson, M.K.C. (1981), 'Development of industry in Transkei – strategic considerations', *Transkei Development Review* 1 (2), 48–54.

Jennings, Sir I. (1953), *Some Characteristics of the Indian Constitution*, Oxford University Press, Madras.

Johnson, R.W. (1977), *How Long will South Africa Survive?*, Macmillan, London.

Kane-Berman, J., (1982), 'Inkatha: the paradox of South African politics', *Optima* 30 (3), 142–77.

Kane-Berman, J. (1983), 'The irrestistible tide', *Leadership South Africa* 2 (4), 27–34.

Kane-Berman, J. (1984), 'City blacks', *Leadership South Africa* 3 (4), 78–80.

Kaplan, D. (1974), *Capitalist Development in South Africa*: Class conflict and state, Institute of Development Studies, University of Sussex, Brighton, working paper 20.

Kaplan, D. (1983a), 'The internationalisation of South African capital: South African direct foreign investment in the contemporary period', *African Affairs* 82 (329), 465–94.

Kaplan, D. (1983b), 'Monopoly capitalism in South Africa', in SARS, *op.cit.*, 158–70.

Katzen, L. (1984), 'Economy', in *Africa South of the Sahara*, 14th edn, Europa Publications, London, 786–92.

Katzen, M.F. (1969), 'White settlers and the origin of a new society 1652–1778', in Wilson and Thompson (eds.), *op.cit.*, 187–232.

Kay, G. (1980), 'Towards a population policy for Zimbabwe-Rhodesia', *African Affairs* 79 (314), 95–114.

Keatley, P. (1963), *The Politics of Partnership*, Penguin, Harmondsworth.

Keenan, J. (1984), Agribusiness and the Bantustans', in SARS, *op. cit.*, 318–26.

Kgarebe, A. (1981), 'SADCC 2: a perspective', in Kgarabe, A. (ed.), *SADCC 2- Maputo*, SADCC Liaison Committee, London.

Kleynhans, W.A. and Labuschagne, G. (1970), Contributions to a discussion entitled 'The 1970 election analysed', *New Nation*, 2–8 and 20 June.

Knight, J. (1977), *Labour Supply in the South African Economy*, South African Labour and Development Research Unit, University of Cape Town, working paper 7.

Kraayenbrink, E.A. (ed.) (1984), *Studies on Urbanisation in South Africa*, SAIRR, Johannesburg.

Kuper, H. (1971), 'Strangers in plural societies: Asians in South Africa and Uganda', in L. Kuper and M.G. Smith (eds.), *Pluralism in Africa*, University of California Press, Berkeley, 248–82.

Kuper, L. (1971), 'African nationalism in South Africa 1910–1964', in Wilson and Thompson (eds.), *op.cit.*, 424–76.

Kuper, L., Watts, H., and Davies, R.J. (1958), *Durban: a Study in Racial Ecology*, Jonathan Cape, London.

KwaZulu (1978), *Towards a Plan for KwaZulu: a preliminary plan*, KwaZulu Government, Ulundi.

Lamar, H. and Thompson, L. (1981), *The Frontier in History: North America and Southern Africa compared*, Yale University Press, New Haven.

Lange, J.H. (1973), Comment following Bell (1973), *op.cit.*, 435–7.

Lanham, L.W. (1976), 'English as a second language in Southern Africa since 1820', in de Villiers (ed.), *op.cit.*, 279–96.

Legassick, M. (1974), 'South Africa: capital accumulation and violence', *Economy and Society* 3 (3), 253–91.

Legassick, M. (1977), 'Gold, agriculture and secondary industry in South Africa, 1885–1970: from periphery to sub-metropole as a forced labour system', in Palmer and Parsons (eds.), *op.cit.*, 175–200.

Legassick, M. and Hemson, D. (1976), *Foreign Investment and the Reproduction of Racial Capitalism in South Africa*, Anti-Apartheid Movement, London.

Leistner, G.M.E. (1985), 'Sanctions against South Africa in regional perspective', *Africa Institute of South Africa Bulletin* 25 (5), 49–59.

Lemon, A. (1976), *Apartheid: a Geography of Separation*, Saxon House, Farnborough.

Lemon, A. (1978), 'Electoral machinery and voting patterns in Rhodesia, 1962–1977', *African Affairs* 77 (309), 511–30.

Lemon, A. (1980a), 'Asian overseas settlement in the nineteenth and twentieth centuries', in Lemon and Pollock (eds.), *op.cit.*, 103–25.

Lemon, A. (1980b), 'Federalism and plural societies: a critique with special reference to South Africa', *Plural Societies* 11 (2), 3–24.

Lemon, A. (1981), 'The geography of voting patterns in South African General Elections, 1974–77', in A.D. Burnett and P.J. Taylor (eds.), *Political Studies from Spatial Perspectives*, John Wiley, Chichester, 419–42.

Lemon, A. (1982a), 'Issues and campaigns in the South African General Election of 1981', *African Affairs* 81 (325), 511–26.

Lemon, A. (1982b), 'Migrant labour and frontier commuters: reorganizing South Africa's Black labour supply', in Smith (ed.), *op.cit.*, 64–89.

Lemon, A. (1984a), *White Voters and Political Change in South Africa 1981-1983*, School of Geography, University of Oxford, research paper 32.

Lemon, A. (1984b), 'State control over the labor market in South Africa', *International Political Science Review* 5 (2), 189–208.

Lemon, A. (1984c), 'The Indian and coloured elections: co-option rejected?', *South Africa International* 15 (2), 84–107.

Lemon, A. (1986), 'A geo-political perspective', in C.A. Woodward (ed.), *On the Razor's Edge: prospects for political stability in Southern Africa*, Africa Institute, Pretoria, Chapter 2.

Lemon, A. and Pollock, N.C. (eds.) (1980), *Studies in Overseas Settlement and Population*, Longman, London.

Lenta, G. (1982), 'Land, labour and capital in KwaZulu: some failures in coincidence', *Journal of Contemporary African Studies* 1 (2), 307–27.

Lever, H. (1972), 'Factors underlying change in the South African General Election of 1970', *British Journal of Sociology* 23 (2), 236–43.

Lewis, J. (1984), '"The Rise and Fall of the South African Peasantry": a critique and reassessment', *Journal of Southern African Studies* 11 (1), 1–24.

Lewis, P.R.B. (1966), 'A "city" within a city – the creation of Soweto', *South African Geographical Journal* 48, 45–85.

Leys, R. (1975), 'South African gold mining in 1974: the gold of migrant labour', *African Affairs* 74 (295), 196–208.

Lichtenstein, H. (1812), *Travels in Southern Africa 1803 to 1806*, reprinted by the van Riebeeck Society, Cape Town, 1928.

Liebenberg, J. (1975), 'From the Statute of Westminster to the Republic of South Africa, 1931-1961', in C.J.F. Muller (ed.), *500 Years: a History of South Africa*, Academica, Pretoria, 408–39.

Lijphart, A. (1968a), *The Politics of Accommodation*, University of California Press, Berkeley.

Lijphart, A. (1968b), *Verzuiling, pacificatie en kentering in de Nederlandse politiek*, De Bussy, Amsterdam.

Lijphart, A. (1977), *Democracy in Plural Societies: a comparative exploration*, Yale University Press, New Haven.

Lijphart, A. (1979), 'Consociation and federation: conceptual and empirical links', *Canadian Journal of Political Science* 12 (3), 499–515.

Lipton, M. (1975), 'White farming: a case history of change in South Africa', *Journal of Commonwealth and Comparative Politics* 12 (1), 42–61.

Lipton, M. (1977), 'South Africa: two agricultures?', in Wilson *et al.*, (eds.), *op.cit.*, 72–86.

Lipton, M. (1979), 'Some realities of African agriculture: a reply to Professor Tomlinson and Professor Bisschop', *Social Dynamics* 5 (2), 31–5.

Lipton, M. (1980), 'Men of two worlds: migrant labour in South Africa', *Optima* 29 (2–3), 72–202.

Lodge, T. (1983), *Black Politics in South Africa Since 1945*, Longman, London.

Lodge, T. (1985a), *The ANC after Nkomati*, SAIRR, Johannesburg.

Lodge, T. (1985b), 'The second consultative conference of the African National Congress', *South Africa International*, 16 (2), 80–97.

Lombard, J.A. (final editor) (1980), *Alternatives to the Consolidation of KwaZulu: Progress Report*, special focus no. 2, Bureau for Economic Policy and Analysis, University of Pretoria.

Louw, L. (1965), *Dawie 1946–64*, Tafelberg-Uitgewers, Cape Town.

Maasdorp, G. (1974), *Economic Development Strategy in the African Homelands: the role of agriculture and industry*, SAIRR, Johannesburg.

Maasdorp, G. (1980), 'Forms of partition', in Rotberg and Barratt, *op.cit.*, 107–50.

Maasdorp, G. (1981), 'Investment opportunities in Transkei – problems and prospects', *Transkei Development Review* 1 (2), 8–16.

Maasdorp, G. and Pillay, N. (1975a), 'Occupational mobility among Indian people of Natal', Paper presented at the fifth workshop on Mobility and Social Change in South Africa, Centre for Intergroup Studies, University of Cape Town.

Maasdorp, G. and Pillay, N. (1975b), *Memorandum on behalf of the Indian traders of Bethel regarding their proposed removal to a shopping centre in Milan Park township* and *Memorandum on behalf of the Indian traders of Piet Retief regarding their proposed removal to a shopping centre at Kempville township*, Department of Economics, University of Natal, Durban (mimeograph).

McCarthy, J. (1982), 'Radical geography, mainstream geography and southern Africa', *Social Dynamics* 8 (1), 53–70.

McCarthy, J. and Swilling, M. (1985), 'South Africa's emerging politics of bus transportation', *Political Geography Quarterly* 4 (3), 235–49.

McCrystal, L.P. (1969), *City, Town or Country: the economics of concentration and dispersal with particular reference to South Africa*, A.A. Balkema, Cape Town.

Macmillan, W.M. (1930), *Complex South Africa*, Faber, London.

Macmillan, W.M. (1963), *Bantu, Boer and Briton*, Clarendon Press, Oxford.

Magubane, B. (1975), 'The "native reserves" (Bantustans) and the role of the migrant labour system in the political economy of South Africa', in H.I. Safa and B.M. du Toit (eds.), *Migration and Development*, Mouton, The Hague, 225–67.

Magubane, B. (1979), *The Political Economy of Race and Class in South Africa*, Monthly Review Press, New York.

Magyar, K.P. (1983), 'Federation vs. confederation in Southern Africa: the neglected economic dimension', *International Affairs Bulletin* 7 (2), 16–24.

Malherbe, P.N. (1974), *Multistan: a way out of the South African Dilemma*, David Philip, Cape Town.

Mander, J. (1964), 'South Africa: revolution or partition', *Encounter* 21 (4), 11–20.

Marais, J.S. (1939), *The Cape Coloured People 1652–1937*, Longman, London (reprinted in 1957 by Witwatersrand University Press, Johannesburg).

Maré, G. (1980), *African Population Relocation in South Africa*, SAIRR, Johannesburg.

Maree, J. (1977), 'Farm labour in the Dealesville district, O.F.S.', in Wilson *et al.*, (eds.), *op. cit.*, 131–6.

Maree, J. and de Vos, P.J. (1975), *Underemployment, Poverty and Migrant Labour in the Transkei and Ciskei*, SAIRR, Johannesburg.

Marquard, L. (1955), *The Story of South Africa*, Faber, London.

Marquard, L. (1969), *Peoples and Policies of South Africa*, 4th edn, Oxford University Press, London.

Marquard, L. (1971), *A Federation of Southern Africa*, Oxford University Press, London.

Mashile, G.G. and Pirie, G.H. (1977), 'Aspects of housing allocation in Soweto', *South African Geographical Journal* 59 (2), 139–49.

Mastoroudes, C.C. (1983), 'The transfrontier commuting system in South Africa: a comparative review', *Development Studies Southern Africa* 5 (4), 391–417.

Matravers, D.R. (1980), 'It's all in the day's work', in Cook and Opland (eds.), *op. cit.*, 27–48.

Mayall J. (1979), 'Africa in the international system: the Great Powers in search of a perspective', *Government and Opposition* 14 (3), 349–72.

Mayer, P. (1971), *Townsmen and Tribesmen*, Oxford University Press, London.

References

Meer, F. (1971), 'Indian people: current trends and policies', in *South Africa's Minorities*, SPRO-CAS Publication no. 2, 13–32.

Meer, F. (1976), 'Domination through separation: a résumé of the major laws enacting and preserving racial segregation', in Smith (ed.), (1976a), *op. cit.*, 17–24.

Meer, F. (1979), 'Portrait of Indian South Africans', in Hare, Wiendieck and von Broembsen, *op. cit.*, 134–44.

Meth, C. (1983), 'Class formation: skill shortage and black advancement', in SARS, *op. cit.*, 193–8.

Meulen, E.J. Ter (1969), 'Shoplocation Claremont: the effects of socio-economic changes as expressed in the development of a suburban shopping centre in Cape Town, Republic of South Africa', *Tijdschrift voor Economische en Sociale Geografie* 60 (4), 208–20.

Midlane, M. (1979), 'The South African General Election of 1977', *African Affairs* 78 (312), 371–87.

Milkman, R. (1979), 'Contradictions of semi-peripheral development: the South African case', in W.L. Goldfrank (ed.), *The World-System of Capitalism: Past and present*, Sage, Beverly Hills, 261–84.

Moodie, T. Dunbar (1975), *The Rise of Afrikanerdom: Power, apartheid and Afrikaner civil religion*, University of California Press, Berkeley.

Moolman, J.H. (1974), *Consolidation*, Paper read at the 44th annual council meeting of the SAIRR, Cape Town.

Morris, M. (1977), *Apartheid, Agriculture and the State: the farm labour question*, South African Labour and Development Research Unit, University of Cape Town, working paper 8.

Nathan, M. (1937), *The Voortrekkers of South Africa*, Gordon and Gotch, London.

National Party (1981), *Manifesto of the National Party*, Information Service of the Federal Council of the National Party, Cape Town.

Nattrass, J. (1976), 'Migrant labour and South African economic development', *South African Journal of Economics* 44 (1), 65–83.

Nattrass, J. (1977), 'Migration flows in and out of capitalist agriculture' in Wilson *et al.* (eds.), *op. cit.*, 51–61.

Nattrass, J. (1981), *The South African Economy: its growth and change*, Oxford University Press, Cape Town.

Niddrie, D.L. (1968), *South Africa: Nation or nations?*, Van Nostrand, Princeton.

Nolutshungu, S.C. (1972), 'Party system, cleavage structure and electoral performance: the South African General Election of 1970', *The African Review* 2 (4), 449–65.

References

Olivier, N.J.J. (1981), *The 1981 Election*, unpublished memorandum for the Progressive Federal Party.

Oosthuizen, G.C. *et al.* (1985), *Religion, Intergroup Relations and Social Change in South Africa*, Human Sciences Research Council, Pretoria.

Oppenheimer, H. (1973), 'Black labour: charting the way – (1) the Corporation's policies and objectives', *Optima* 23 (2), 68–70.

Oppenheimer, H. (1974), 'South Africa after the election', *African Affairs* 73 (293), 399–407.

Palmer, M. (1957), *The History of the Indians in Natal, Natal Regional Survey, vol. 10*, Oxford University Press, Cape Town.

Palmer, R. and Parsons, N. (eds.) (1977), *The Roots of Rural Poverty in Central and Southern Africa*, University of California Press, Berkeley.

Parsons, J.A. (1977), 'Manpower needs for the future – projections, issues, strategies', *South African Journal of African Affairs* 7 (2), 121–33.

Patel, H.H. (1985), 'No master, no mortgage, no sale: the foreign policy of Zimbabwe', in T.M. Shaw and Y. Tandon (eds.), *Regional Development at the International Level, vol. 2, African and Canadian Perspectives*, University Press of America, Lanham and New York.

Paton, Alan (1985), *Federation or Desolation*, SAIRR, Johannesburg.

Peach, G.C.K. (ed.) (1975), *Urban Social Segregation*, Longman, London.

Peel, S. and Morse, S.J. (1974), 'Ethnic voting and political change in South Africa', *American Political Science Review* 68 (4), 1520–41.

Pelzer, A.N. (ed.) (1966), *Verwoerd Speaks: Speeches 1948–1966*, APB Publishers, Johannesburg.

Phillips, I. (1985), *The African National Congress – 1985*, Senate Lecture, Rhodes University, Grahamstown, 11 September 1985.

Pirie, G.H. (1976), 'Apartheid, health and social services in Greater Johannesburg', in D.M. Smith (ed.) (1976b), *op.cit.*, 85–95.

Pirie, G.H. (1982), 'The decivilizing rails: railways and underdevelopment in Southern Africa', *Tijdschrift voor Economische en Sociale Geografie* 73 (4), 221–8.

Pirie, G.H. (1984a), 'Race zoning in South Africa: board, court, parliament, public', *Political Geography Quarterly* 3 (3), 207–21.

Pirie, G.H. (1985), 'Toward an historical geography of missions in nineteenth century southern Africa', *South African Geographical Journal* 67 (1), 14–30.

Pirie, G.H. *et al.* (1980), 'Covert power in South Africa: the geography of the Afrikaner Broederbond', *Area* 12 (2), 97–104.

Platzky, L. and Walker, C. (1985), *The Surplus People: Forced Removals in South Africa*, Raven Press, Johannesburg.

Pollock, N.C. (1980), 'The English in Natal and the Welsh in Patagonia', in Lemon and Pollock (eds.), *op.cit.*, 207–24.

Pollock, N.C. and Agnew, S. (1963), *An Historical Geography of South Africa*, Longman, London.

Poovalingam, P. (1979), 'The Indians of South Africa: a century on the defensive', *Optima* 28 (2), 66–91.

Prescott, J.R.V. (1979), 'Africa's boundary problems', *Optima* 28 (1), 2–21.

Preston-Whyte, E. (1982), 'Segregation and inter-personal relationships: a case study of domestic service in Durban' in Smith (ed.) (1982a), *op.cit.*, 164–82.

Price, R.M. and Rosberg, C.G. (eds.) (1980), *The Apartheid Régime: political power and racial domination*, David Philip, Cape Town.

Ransford, O. (1972), *The Great Trek*, John Murray, London.

Reitsma, H.J.A. (1980), 'Africa's landlocked countries: a study of dependency relations', *Tijdschrift voor Economische en Sociale Geografie* 71 (3), 130–41.

Rhoodie, N.J. (ed.) (1972), *South African Dialogue*, McGraw-Hil, Johannesburg.

Rhoodie, N.J. (1973), 'The coloured policy of South Africa: parallelism as a socio-political device to regulate white-coloured integration', *African Affairs* 72 (286), 46–56.

Rhoodie, N.J. (1980), 'Federalism/confederalism as a means of white–black conflict resolution: conceptual dissonance in white Nationalist ranks', *Politikon* 7 (2), 101–10.

Rich, P.B. (1978), 'Ministering to the white man's needs: the development of urban segregation in South Africa 1913–1923', *African Studies* 37 (2), 177–91.

Riekert, P.J. (1970), 'Die Tswana en sy tuisland', *Journal of Racial Affairs* (SABRA) 21 (4), 131–9.

Rogerson, C.M. (1974a), 'The geography of business-management in South Africa', *South African Geographical Journal* 56 (1), 87–93.

Rogerson, C.M. (1974b), 'Growth point problems – the case of Babelegi, Bophuthatswana', *Journal of Modern African Studies* 12 (1), 126–30.

Rogerson, C.M. (1975), 'Corporations in South Africa: a spatial perspective', *Die Suid-Afrikaanse Geograaf* 5 (1), 41–5.

Rogerson, C.M. (1979), 'Industrialization in the Southern African periphery: a world systems analysis', Paper presented to the IGU

Commission on Industrial Systems at the Economic Geography Institute of the Erasmus University Rotterdam, 7 June 1979.

Rogerson, C.M. (1981), 'Industrialization in the shadows of apartheid: a world-systems analysis', in F.E.I. Hamilton and G.J.R. Linge (eds.), *Spatial Analysis, Industry and the Industrial Environment: international industrial systems*, Wiley, Chichester, 395–421.

Rogerson, C.M. (1982a), 'Multinational corporations in Southern Africa a spatial perspective', in M.J. Taylor and N.J. Thrift (eds.), *The Geography of Multinationals*, Croom Helm, London, 179–220.

Rogerson, C.M. (1982b), 'Apartheid, decentralization and spatial industrial change', in D.M. Smith (1982a), *op.cit.*, 47–63.

Rogerson, C.M. and Beavon, K.S.O. (1980), 'The awakening of "Informal Sector" studies in Southern Africa', *South African Geographical Journal* 62 (2), 175–90.

Rogerson, C.M. and Letsoalo, E.M. (1981), 'Rural underdevelopment, poverty and apartheid: the closer settlements of Lebowa, South Africa', *Tijdschrift voor Economische en Sociale Geografie* 72 (6), 347–61.

Roodt, M.J. (1984), 'Capitalist agriculture and Bantustan employment patterns: case studies in Bophuthatswana', in SARS, *op.cit.*, 327–34.

Ross, R. (1976), *Adam Kok's Griquas: a study in the development of stratification in South Africa*, Cambridge University Press, Cambridge.

Rotberg, Robert I. (1981), *Towards a Certain Future: the politics and economics of southern Africa*, David Philip, Cape Town.

Rotberg, Robert I. and Barratt, J. (eds.) (1980), *Conflict and Compromise in South Africa*, David Philip, Cape Town.

Sadie, J.L. (1970), 'An evaluation of demographic data pertaining to the non-White population of South Africa', *South African Journal of Economics* 38 (1), 1–34 and (2), 171–95.

Sadie, J.L. (1972), *Projections of the South African Population 1970–2020*, Industrial Development Corporation, Johannesburg.

St Jorre, J. de (1977), *A House Divided: South Africa's Uncertain Future*, Carnegie Endowment for International Peace, New York.

SAIRR (annually), *Survey of Race Relations in South Africa*, SAIRR, Johannesburg.

Samoff, J. (1978), 'Transnationals, industrialization and black consciousness: change in South Africa', *Journal of South African Affairs* 3 (4), 489–520.

SARS (South African Research Service) (1983), *South African Review*

One, Ravan Press, Johannesburg.

SARS (1984), *South African Review Two*, Ravan Press, Johannesburg.

Schapera, I. (ed.) (1953), *Travels in the Interior of South Africa 1822 (2 vols.) by W.J. Burchell*, The Batchworth Press, London.

Schlemmer, L. (1970), *Social Change and Political Policy in South Africa*, SAIRR, Johannesburg.

Schlemmer, L. (1976), 'English-speaking South Africans today: identity and integration into the broader national community' in de Villiers (ed.), *op.cit.*, 91–135.

Schlemmer, L. (1978), 'White voters and change in South Africa: constraints and opportunities', *Optima* 27 (4), 62–83.

Schlemmer, L. (1981), 'An overview: a summary of the major points emerging from the workshop', in Boulle and Baxter (eds.), *op. cit.*, 201–11.

Schlemmer, L. (1980), 'The stirring giant: observations on the Inkatha and other black political movements in South Africa' in Price and Rosberg (eds.), *op.cit.*, 99–126.

Schlemmer, L. (1983a), 'South African politics and the English speakers', *Leadership South Africa* 2 (3), 24–9.

Schlemmer, L. (1983b), 'Social indicators for change', in van Vuuren *et al.* (eds.), *op.cit*, 267–90.

Schlemmer, L. (1985), 'Squatter communities: safety valves in the rural-urban nexus', in Giliomee and Schlemmer (eds.), *op. cit.*, 167–91.

Schreiner, O. (1883), *The Story of an African Farm*, republished 1971 by Penguin Books, Harmondsworth.

Schreuder, D.M. (1980), *The Scramble for Southern Africa 1877–1895: the politics of partition reappraised*, Cambridge University Press, Cambridge.

Schulze, R.E. (1970), 'A geographical survey as a basis for land planning in the Tugela Location' *Journal for Geography* (South Africa), 3 (6), 621–37.

Schulze, R.E. (1974), 'The business land use of central Newcastle: present and future', *South African Geographer* 4 (4), 308–19.

Schumann, C.G.W. (1938), *Structural Changes and Business Cycles in South Africa 1806–1936*, Staples Press, London.

Seidman, A. and Makgetla, N. (1980), *Outposts of Monopoly Capitalism: Southern Africa in the changing global economy*, Lawrence Hill, Westport, Connecticut.

Selby, J. (1973). *A Short History of South Africa*, George Allen and Unwin, London.

Selwyn, P. (1975), *Industries in the Southern African Periphery*, Croom Helm, London.

Serfontein, J.H.P. (1979), *Brotherhood of Power: an exposé of the secret Afrikaner Broederbond*, Rex Collings, London.

Shafer, M. (1982), 'Mineral myths', *Foreign Policy* 47, 154–71.

Simkins, C. (1980), *Agricultural Production in African Reserves 1918–1969*, Development Studies Research Group, University of Natal, Pietermaritzburg, working paper.

Simkins, C. (1981), 'Agricultural production in the African reserves of South Africa, 1918–1969', *Journal of Southern African Studies* 7 (2), 256–83.

Simkins, C. (1983), *Four Essays on the Past, Present and Possible Future of the Distribution of the Black Population of South Africa*, SALDRU, University of Cape Town.

Simkins, C. (1984), 'The distribution of the African population of South Africa by age, sex, and region-type 1950–80 and a note on projecting African population distribution and migration to the year 2000', in Kraayenbrink (ed.), *op.cit.*, 6–15.

Slabbert, F. van Zyl and Opland, J. (eds.) (1980), *South Africa: Dilemmas of Evolutionary Change*, Institute of Social and Economic Research, Rhodes University, Grahamstown.

Slabbert, F. van Zyl and Welsh, D. (1979), *South Africa's Options: Strategies for Sharing Power*, Rex Collings, London and David Philip, Cape Town.

Smit, P. (1976), 'The Black population', in D.M. Smith (ed.) (1976a), *op.cit.*, 39–62.

Smit, P. (1979), 'Urbanisation in Africa: lessons for urbanisation in the homelands', *South African Geographical Journal* 61 (1), 3–28.

Smit, P. and Booysen, J.J. (1977), *Urbanization in the Homelands – a new dimension in the urbanization process of the black population of South Africa?*, Institute for Plural Societies, University of Pretoria, Monograph Series on Inter-group Relations 3.

Smit, P. and Booysen, J.J. (1981), *Swart Verstedeliking: Proses, Patroon en Strategie*, Tafelberg, Cape Town.

Smit, P., Booysen, J.J. and Cornelius, I. (1983a), *Population Distribution in the RSA, Transkei, Bophuthatswana, Venda and Ciskei: explanatory notes accompanying the 1980 population distribution map*, HSRC, Pretoria.

Smit, P., Booysen, J.J. and Cornelius, I. (1983b), 'Die sosio-ekonomiese en politieke posisie van die stedelike swart bevolking', *South African*

Journal of Sociology 14 (1), 81–9.

Smith, D.M. (ed.) (1976a), *Separation in South Africa 1. People and Policies*, Queen Mary College London, Department of Geography, Occasional Paper 6.

Smith, D.M. (ed.) (1976b), *Separation in South Africa 2. Homelands and Cities*, Queen Mary College, London, Department of Geography, Occasional Paper 7.

Smith, D.M. (ed.) (1982a), *Living under Apartheid: Aspects of urbanization and social change in South Africa*, George Allen and Unwin, London.

Smith, D.M. (1982b), 'Urbanization and social change under apartheid: some recent developments', in D.M. Smith (ed.) (1982a), *op.cit.*, 24–46.

Smith, D.M. (1983), *Update: Apartheid in South Africa*, Queen Mary College, London, Department of Geography and Earth Sciences, Special Publication 6.

Smuts, J.C. (1942), *The Basis of Trusteeship*, New Africa Pamphlet 2, South African Institute of Race Relations, Johannesburg.

South Africa (1932), *Report of the Native Economic Commission 1930–2*, UG 22/1932, Pretoria.

South Africa (1941), *Third Interim Report of the Industrial and Agricultural Requirements Commission*, UG 40/1941, Pretoria.

South Africa (1942), *Report of the Interdepartmental Committee on the Social, Health and Economic Conditions of Urban Natives*, Annexure 47/1943, Pretoria.

South Africa (1945), *Local Government Functions and Finances*, Social and Economic Planning Council Report no. 8, UG 40/1945, Pretoria.

South Africa (1946), *The Native Reserves and their Place in the Economy of the Union of South Africa*, Social and Economic Planning Council, UG 32/1946, Pretoria.

South Africa (1948), *Report of the Native Laws Commission, 1946–1948*, UG 28/1948, Pretoria.

South Africa (1955), *The Report of the Commission for the Socio-Economic Development of the Bantu Areas within the Union of South Africa*, UG61/1955, Pretoria.

South Africa (1965), *Report of the Commission of Inquiry into Secret Organisations*, RP 20/1965, Pretoria.

South Africa (1970), *Second Report of the Commission of Enquiry into Agriculture*, RP 84/1970, Pretoria.

South Africa (1972), *Report of the Commission of Enquiry into the Export*

Trade of the Republic of South Africa, RP 69/1972, Pretoria.

South Africa (1979a), *Report of the Commission of Inquiry into Legislation affecting the Utilisation of Manpower* (excluding the legislation administered by the Departments of Labour and Mines), RP 32/1979, Pretoria.

South Africa (1979b), *Report of the Commission of Inquiry into Labour Legislation*, (Wiehahn Report), RP 97/1979, Pretoria.

South Africa (1981a), *Partners in Development: Economic Programme for the Republic of South Africa 1977-1987*, 2nd edn, Government Printer, Pretoria.

South Africa (1981b), *Investigation into Education*, report of the work committee (de Lange Report), Human Sciences Research Council, Pretoria.

South Africa (1982a), *Report of the National Manpower Commission 1 January-31 December 1981*, RP 25/1982, Pretoria.

South Africa (1982b), *The Promotion of Industrial Development: an element of a coordinated regional development strategy for Southern Africa*, Information newsletter issued as a supplement to *South African Digest*, 2 April, Department of Foreign Affairs and Information, Pretoria.

South Africa (1982c), *Report of the Committee to Investigate Private Sector Involvement in Resolving the Housing Backlog in Soweto*, RP 14/1982, Pretoria.

South Africa (1983a), *South Africa 1983* (official yearbook), van Rensburg, Johannesburg.

South Africa (1983b), *Second Interim Report of the Commission of Enquiry into Bus Passenger Transportation in the Republic of South Africa*, RP 103/1983, Pretoria.

South Africa (1983c), *Report of the Commission of Inquiry into the South African Council of Churches*, RP 74/1983, Pretoria.

South Africa (1984a), *Report of the Commission of Inquiry into Township Establishment and Related Matters*, Government Printer, Pretoria.

South Africa (1984b), *Report of the Technical Committee of Inquiry into the Group Areas Act and Related Legislation* (the Strydom Committee), Government Printer, Pretoria.

South Africa (1985a), *Report of the Committee for Constitutional Affairs of the President's Council on an Urbanisation Strategy for the Republic of South Africa*, Government Printer, Cape Town.

South Africa (1985b), *South Africa: Mainstay of Southern Africa*, Department of Foreign Affairs, Pretoria.

References

South Africa Foundation (1985), *Indicators of Change in South Africa* (mimeographed).

Southall, R. (1981), 'Buthelezi's Inkatha and the politics of compromise', *African Affairs* 80 (321), 453–81.

Southall, R. (1982), *South Africa's Transkei: the political economy of an 'independent' Bantustan*, Heinemann, London.

Southall, R. (1983), 'Consociationalism in South Africa: the Buthelezi Commission and beyond', *Journal of Modern African Studies* 21 (1), 77–112.

Spandau, A. (1980), 'A note on black employment conditions on South African mines', *South African Journal of Economics* 48 (2), 214–7.

SPRO-CAS Political Commission (1973), *South Africa's Political Alternatives*, SPRO-CAS, Johannesburg.

Stadler, A.W. (1975), 'The 1974 General Election in South Africa', *African Affairs* 74 (295), 209–18.

Stultz, N.M. (1979), 'On partition', *Social Dynamics* 5 (1), 1–13.

Suckling, J. (1975), 'The nature and role of foreign investment in South Africa', in J. Suckling et al. (1975), *Foreign Investment in South Africa – the Economic Factor*, African Publications Trust, London, 11–48.

Surplus People Project (1983), *Forced Removals in South Africa, Vols. 1–5*, Surplus People Project, Cape Town.

Swanson, M.W. (1976), '"The Durban System": roots of urban apartheid in South Africa 1913–1923', *African Studies* 35 (3–4), 159–76.

Swart Commission, members of (1984), 'Report of the Commission of Inquiry into the Economic Development of the Republic of Ciskei, 1983: rejoinder', *Development Southern Africa* 1 (3/4), 486–94.

Talbot, W.J. (1947), *Swartland and Sandveld*, Oxford University Press, Cape Town.

Tarlton, C.D. (1965), 'Symmetry and asymmetry as elements of federalism: a theoretical speculation', *Journal of Politics* 27 (4), 861–74.

Terre Blanche, E. (1985), 'Comment on current political changes', *South Africa Foundation News*, April.

Thomas, W.H. (1981a), 'Private sector involvement in Transkei's economy – obstacles and opportunities', *Transkei Development Review* 1 (2), 55–60.

Thomas, W.H. (1981b), *Independence and Beyond: Two scenarios of possible future developments in South West Africa/Namibia*, Unit for Futures Research, Stellenbosch University, Occasional Paper 81/4.

References

Thomas, W.H. (1985), 'The Western Cape: urban growth and influx', *Energos* II (the Urbanisation Challenge), 61–4.

Thompson, L. (1971), 'Great Britain and the Afrikaner Republics, 1870–1899', in Wilson and Thompson (eds.), *op. cit.*, 289–324.

Thompson, L. (1981), 'The Southern African frontier in comparative perspective', in G. Wolfskill and S. Palmer (eds.), *Essays in World History*, University of Texas Press, Austin, 86–120.

Thompson, L. and Butler, J. (eds.) (1975), *Change in Contemporary South Africa*, University of California Press, Berkeley.

Thula, G. (1980), 'A basis for the constitutional transformation of South Africa', in van der Merwe and Schrire (eds.), *op. cit.*, 144–54.

Tiryakian, E.A. (1967), 'Sociological realism: partition for South Africa', *Social Forces* 46 (2), 208–21.

Todes, A. and Watson, V. (1985), 'Local government reform in South Africa: an interpretation of aspects of the state's current proposals', *South African Geographical Journal* 67 (2), 201–11.

Tomlinson, F.R. (1979), '"South Africa: two agricultures?"', *Social Dynamics* 5 (2), 28–9.

Tomlinson, F.R. (1980), '"South Africa: two agricultures": a reply to Merle Lipton', *Social Dynamics* 6 (1), 49–52.

Transvaal (1922), *Report of the Transvaal Local Government Commission*, TP1/1922.

Turner, F.J. (1894), 'The significance of the frontier in American history', reprinted in *American Historical Association Report for 1893*, Government Printer, Washington, 199–227.

van der Horst, S.T. (1942), *Native Labour in South Africa*, Oxford University Press, London.

van der Horst, S.T. (ed.) (1976), *The Theron Commission Report: A Summary*, SAIRR, Johannesburg.

van der Kooy, R.J.W. (1982), 'A preliminary review of the new industrial development proposals', *Development Studies South Africa* 4 (2), 207–24.

van der Merwe, H.W., (1984), 'Economic boycott: a sure way to violence', *Friends Journal*, 1 February 1984, 14–15.

van der Merwe, I.J. (1983), 'Differential urbanization in South Africa', *Geography* 58 (4), 335–9.

van der Merwe, H.W. and Schrire, R. (1980), *Race and Ethnicity: South African and International Perspectives*, David Philip, Cape Town.

van der Ross, R.E. (1983), 'In this failure lies our hope', in de Villiers (ed.), 117–21.

References

van Dyke, V. (1983), 'Legitimacy in plural societies', *Politikon* 10 (2), 6–25.

van Eeeden, F.J. (1980), ''n kritiese ontleding van die vordering met ontwikkelings programme in die nasionale state', *Development Studies Southern Africa* 2 (4), 416–35.

van Jaarsveld, F.A. (1964), *The Afrikaner's Interpretation of South African History*, Simondium Publishers, Cape Town.

van Jaarsveld, F.A. (1975), *Van Riebeeck tot Verwoerd 1652–1974: 'n inleiding tot die geskiedenis van die Republik van Suid-Afrika*, Perskor, Johannesburg.

van Schendelen, M.C.P. (1983), 'Critical comments on Lijphart's theory of consociational democracy', *Politikon* 10 (1), 6–32.

van Vuuren, D.J. *et al.* (eds.) (1983), *Change in South Africa*, Butterworth, Durban.

Venter, A.J. (1981), 'Some of South Africa's political alternatives in consociational perspective', *South Africa International* 11 (3), 129–41.

Venter, D. (1985), 'Democratizing South Africa through negotiation: the need for a declaration of interest', paper presented to the seventh biennial congress of the Political Science Association of South Africa at the University of Natal, Pietermaritzburg, September 1985.

Verwoerd, H.F. (1948), Speech on the policy of apartheid in the Senate, 3 September (*The Senate of South Africa: Debates*, 1st session, 10th Parliament, 5th Senate, 2, 223–58).

Villa-Vicencio, C. (1985), 'Theology in the service of the state: the Steyn and Eloff Commissions', in Villa-Vicencio and de Gruchy (eds.), *op.cit.*, 112–25.

Villa-Vicencio, C. and de Gruchy, J. W. (eds.) (1985), *Resistance and Hope: South African Essays in honour of Beyers Naudé*, David Philip, Cape Town.

Voges, E.M. (1983), *Accessibility, Transport and the Spatial Structure of South African Cities: An Historic Perspective*, National Institute for Transport and Road Research, CSOR, Pretoria.

von der Ropp, K.B. (1979), 'Is territorial partition a strategy for peaceful change in South Africa?', *International Affairs Bulletin* 3 (1), 36–47.

Vosloo, W.B. (1970), 'The election of 1970 (or who really won?)', *New Nation*, 4–7 August.

Vosloo, W.B. (1979), 'Consociational democracy as a means to accomplish peaceful change in South Africa: an evaluation of the constitutional change proposed by the National Party in 1977', *Politikon* 6 (1), 13–28.

Walker, E.A. (1965), *The Great Trek*, 5th edn, Black, London.

Wallerstein, I. (1974), 'Dependence in an interdependent world: the limited possibilities of transformation within the capitalist world economy', *African Studies Review* 17 (1), 1–26.

Watts, H.L. (1976), 'A social and demographic portrait of English-speaking White South Africans', in de Villiers (ed.), *op. cit.*, 41–89.

Watts, H.L., *et al.* (1971), *Group Areas and the 'Grey Street' Complex, Durban*, University of Natal, Durban (mimeograph).

Webster, E. (1984), 'New force on the shop floor', in SARS, *op.cit.*, 79–89.

Welensky, Sir Roy (1964), *Welensky's 4000 Days: the life and death of the Federation of Rhodesia and Nyasaland*, Collins, London.

Wellings, P. and McCarthy, J.J. (1983), 'Whither southern African human geography?', *Area* 15 (4), 337–45.

Welsh, D. (1971), 'The growth of towns', in Wilson and Thompson (eds.), *op.cit.*, 172–243.

Welsh, D. (1984), 'South Africa: from regional to domestic détente?', *Leadership South Africa* 3 (2), 58–64.

Western, J. (1981), *Outcast Cape Town*, George Allen and Unwin, London.

Wheare, K.C. (1946), *Federal Government*, Oxford University Press, London.

Whisson, M.G. (1971), 'The coloured people', in P. Randall (ed.), *South Africa's Minorities*, SPROCAS publication no. 2, Johannesburg.

Wilkins, I. and Strydom, H. (1979), *The Broederbond*, Paddington Press, London (subsequently published as *Broederbond: the Super-Afrikaners* by Corgi, London).

Wilkinson, P. (1983), 'Housing', in SARS, *op.cit.*, 270–7.

Wills, T.M. and Schulze, R.E. (1976), 'Segregated business districts in a South African city', in D.M. Smith (ed.) (1976b), *op.cit.*, 69–84.

Wilson, F. (1972a), *Migrant Labour in the South African Gold Mines 1911–1969*, Cambridge University Press, Cambridge.

Wilson, F. (1972b), *Migrant Labour in South Africa*, South African Council of Churches and SPRO-CAS, Johannesburg.

Wilson, F. (1975), 'The political implications for Blacks of economic changes now taking place in South Africa', in Thompson and Butler (eds.), *op.cit.*, 168–200.

References

Wilson, F. (1984), 'The platteland connection', *Leadership South Africa* 3 (3), 78–86.

Wilson, F. *et al.* (eds) (1977), *Farm Labour in South Africa*, David Philip, Cape Town.

Wilson, M. (1969), 'The Nguni people', in Wilson and Thompson (eds.), *op.cit.*, 75–130.

Wilson, M. (1971), 'The growth of peasant communities', in Wilson and Thompson (eds.), *op.cit.*, 49–103.

Wilson, M. and Thompson, L. (eds.) (1969 and 1971), *The Oxford History of South Africa, vol.1, South Africa to 1870* (1969) and *vol.2, South Africa 1870–1966* (1971), Clarendon Press, Oxford.

Wolpe, H. (1972), 'Capitalism and cheap labour power in South Africa: from segregation to apartheid', *Economy and Society* 1 (4), 425–56.

Woodward, C.A. (1980), 'One party dominance in democracy: widening the perspective on the regnancy of the National Party in South Africa', *Politikon* 7 (2), 111–25.

Woodward, C.A. (1981), 'Reform or revolution in South Africa', *The Round Table* 282, 101–15.

Wright, H.M. (1977), *The Burden of the Present: Liberal–radical controversy over southern African history*, David Philip, Cape Town.

Yawitch, J. (1981), *Betterment: the myth of homeland agriculture*, SAIRR, Johannesburg.

Zille, H. (1983), 'Restructuring the industrial decentralisation strategy', in SARS, *op.cit.*, 58–71.

Index

413